HIGH PERFORMANCE FUTURES TRADING

POWER LESSONS FROM THE MASTERS

Joel Robbins, Editor

PROBUS PUBLISHING COMPANY
Chicago, Illinois

Library of Congress Cataloging-in-Publication Data
High performance futures trading : power lessons from the masters /
  Joel Robbins, editor.
    p. cm.
  Previously published in 1989 in a 3-ring binder.
  Includes bibliographical references.
  ISBN: 155738-149-6 : $35.00
  1. Futures—Handbooks, manuals, etc. I. Robbins, Joel.
  HG6024.A3H53 1990
  332.63'28—dc20
                                        90-44092
                                        CIP

Printed in the United States of America
BB

        4   5   6   7   8   9   0

■ CONTENTS ■

PREFACE   vii

CHAPTER ONE
GOING FOR THE CHECKERED FLAG   1
JOEL ROBBINS

SECTION ONE
REVIEWING THE BASICS   11

CHAPTER TWO
ON DISCIPLINE   15
JAKE BERNSTEIN

CHAPTER THREE
TWENTY-ONE TOOLS FOR SUCCESSFUL TRADING   25
JAKE BERNSTEIN

CHAPTER FOUR
ONE STEP BACK—HOW BASICS ARE IMPORTANT   33
MARK SILBER

CHAPTER FIVE
EDUCATION: THE WAY TO SUCCESS IN THE FUTURES MARKETS   47
DON SARNO

CHAPTER SIX
PRESERVE THE FREEDOM TO TRADE: CONSERVE CAPITAL   65
KENNETH UPSHAW, Ed. D.

SECTION TWO
MASTER STRATEGIES   93

WAVES AND RETRACEMENTS

CHAPTER SEVEN
CHARTING YOUR COURSE TO PROFITS   101
DAN RAHFELDT

CHAPTER EIGHT
FIBONACCI EXPANSION ANALYSIS:
A Method to Determine Logical
Profit Objectives   131
JOE DiNAPOLI

CHAPTER NINE
BASIC TENETS OF THE ELLIOTT WAVE PRINCIPLE   147
ROBERT R. PRECHTER & A. JOHN FROST

CHAPTER TEN
A LONGER-TERM APPROACH TO
COMMODITY FUTURES TRADING   165
EDWARD deLANOY

PATTERNS AND SIGNALS

CHAPTER ELEVEN
TRADING WITH SEASONAL PRICE PROBABILITIES
ON YOUR SIDE   191
JAKE BERNSTEIN

CHAPTER TWELVE
THE CAMBRIDGE HOOK   211
JAMES KNEAFSEY, Ph.D.

CHAPTER THIRTEEN
BEHAVIOR OF TECHNICAL INDICATORS IN   221
MARKET STAGES
WILLIAM F. ENG

CHAPTER FOURTEEN
TRADING LOGIC AND THE MARKET PROFILE®:
An Introduction to Technical Applications   231
JAMES F. DALTON AND ERIC T. JONES

CONTENTS   v

CHAPTER FIFTEEN
MARKET PERSONALITY PROFILE   253
BILL M. WILLIAMS, Ph.D., C.T.A.

CHAPTER SIXTEEN
HOW TO FIND TRADES WITH 10/1 ODDS   263
LARRY R. WILLIAMS

CHAPTER SEVENTEEN
A NEW LOOK AT MARKET SENTIMENT   289
MARK LIVELY

WEATHER AND TIMING

CHAPTER EIGHTEEN
**HOW TO TURN DROUGHTS, FLOODS AND HURRICANES
INTO SUCCESSFUL SPECULATIVE OPPORTUNITIES**   301
JAMES ROEMER

SECTION THREE
TRADING WITH OPTIONS   321

CHAPTER NINETEEN
**MAJOR OPTION MOVES:
A Strategy and Rules for Using Futures Options
to Profit from Major Market Moves**   325
JOE KRUTSINGER

CHAPTER TWENTY
**USING A MOVING AVERAGE SYSTEM TO TRADE
COMMODITY OPTIONS**   343
MICHAEL CHISHOLM

SECTION FOUR
PARTICIPATING IN THE MARKETS WITH THE MASTERS   359

CHAPTER TWENTY-ONE
ADVISORY SERVICES: HOW TO USE THEM,   363
HOW TO CHOOSE THEM
BRUCE BABCOCK

CHAPTER TWENTY-TWO
COMMODITY POOLS, SELF-DIRECTED ACCOUNTS   375
AND MANAGED ACCOUNTS
JAMES S. SCHLIFKE

SECTION FIVE
DEVELOPING YOUR OWN MASTER TRADING SYSTEMS   383

CHAPTER TWENTY-THREE
WHAT TO LOOK FOR IN COMPUTER HARDWARE
AND INVESTMENT SOFTWARE   387
WILLIAM T. TAYLOR

CHAPTER TWENTY-FOUR
DESIGNING AND TESTING TRADING SYSTEMS:
How to Avoid Costly Mistakes   423
LOUIS B. MENDELSOHN

SECTION SIX
CONCLUSION   435

CHAPTER TWENTY-FIVE
COMMON THREADS OF THE MASTER STRATEGIES
(AND STRATEGISTS)   437
SUSAN ABBOTT

RESOURCES   445

■ PREFACE ■

FUTURES TRADING HAS, until recent years, been relegated to a secondary or even tertiary position in the world of finance. Long regarded as a speculator's game of high risk and low probability of success, the reputation of futures trading changed dramatically with the introduction of stock index futures trading in 1982. Stock traders, mutual fund managers and pension fund managers began to see the futures markets in a new light. They could hedge their long stock positions by selling stock index futures against their holdings, thereby "protecting" their longs in the event of a decline in stock prices. The great popularity of stock index futures was, however, overshadowed by the even greater trading volume and growth of Treasury bond futures and currency futures. As world political conditions continued to destabilize, as the power of OPEC continued to wax and wane, and as international economic stability suffered one assault after another, trading volume and volatility in financial and precious metals futures continued to grow. And then came the drought of 1988 to add more fuel to the growing fires of interest in futures trading. Now, in 1989, the futures markets have become more well-known to all types of traders and, although the risks of trading are, perhaps, greater than ever, the rewards are also immense.

In spite of growing popularity and increased public and professional awareness, the systems, methods, techniques, and psychology of futures trading are still relatively unknown to many traders. Due to the inherent risks involved in this high stakes game of forecasts and leverage, many traders have risen to fame and fortune only to sink rapidly into failure and obscurity. Yet some trading advisors, speculators, and market analysts have, by virtue of their common sense, expertise, and discipline weathered the storms of adverse market conditions. Their experiences, knowledge, learning, and observations provide a solid structure to the otherwise delicate foundation of futures trading. To tap into the collective knowledge and resources of the "survivors" and veterans is to have access to a vast font of information which cannot be duplicated other than by experience itself.

We have attempted to achieve the following in editing this book:

1. To bring together some of the most well-known traders and trading advisors; individuals who have shown by their longevity and persistence that futures trading is, indeed, subject to the laws of reason, good sense, and technical analysis;

vii

2. To share with you some new concepts in the area of market analysis, timing, and forecasting; and

3. To help provide some new directions to your own trading, timing, and research.

Some books are meant to be read. This book is meant to be studied. Some books are bought and put on the shelf to gather dust. However, I am certain that this collection of works will find a permanent place on your desk.

Acknowledgments

The quality of each selection in this book reflects the commitment of its author to the twin ideals of excellence and clarity. A project of this magnitude can only be possible when each contributor unselfishly devotes a significant amount of time and effort to the task of writing, rewriting, and writing again. Thanks to each of you for your dedication to these ideals.

To support that effort, the staff of Probus Publishing Company expended extraordinary efforts in the interest of meeting deadlines and staying on schedule. Ken Upshaw, of Robbins Trading Company, spent many hours helping to coordinate the project. I am grateful to each of them for their patience and diligence.

A special note of thanks goes to Commodity Quote Graphics, 6916 Highway 82, Glenwood Springs, CO 81602, for permission to reproduce charts from their TQ 20/20 system.

■ CHAPTER ONE ■

GOING FOR THE CHECKERED FLAG

JOEL ROBBINS

■

JOEL ROBBINS

Joel Robbins is founder and President of Robbins Trading Company (RTC), a well-known Chicago brokerage firm. A former floor trader and broker at both the Chicago Board of Trade and the Chicago Mercantile Exchange, Mr. Robbins was one of the original members of the Index and Options Division at the Chicago Mercantile Exchange, trading in the S&P 500 pit.

Mr. Robbins has become well-known for his efforts in searching out some of the best traders and technicians in the industry. To accomplish this goal, he originated the Robbins World Cup Championship of Futures Trading®, the premier annual competition among futures traders. In his never-ending search for excellence, Mr. Robbins has gathered some of the best-known names in the futures business as money managers and advisors for clients' accounts and for commodity funds sponsored by Robbins Trading Company. Through the World Cup Championship, he has discovered several traders who have subsequently gained fame and stature as members of the Robbins World Cup Team.

Always the innovator, RTC publishes *Futures Market Alert*, a monthly newsletter which is widely recognized in the industry and is read by individual futures investors as well as market professionals.

High Performance Futures Trading reflects Mr. Robbins' commitment to excellence and integrity in the futures industry.

■ CHAPTER ONE ■

Rushing into the Future:
The Changing Face of Futures Trading

IN 1848 A SMALL GROUP OF GRAIN TRADERS gathered in Chicago to form the Chicago Board of Trade (CBOT). None could have realized at that time the far-reaching consequences of their action. Organized for the sole purpose of bringing some order to the chaotic grain markets of the period, the CBOT soon established rules for the trading of grain futures and, in 1865, became a full-fledged futures exchange. From the start, the CBOT attracted an independent breed of individuals, many of whom believed strongly in the principles of a free market and, with fortunes made in the pits at the CBOT, managed to keep government regulation at a respectful distance for many decades—decades during which very little changed in the business called commodity futures trading. Sometime in the late 1960s and early 1970s, however, the futures business took a turn, and a few seemingly inconsequential changes in the rules led to a spiraling transformation of the entire industry.

We live in an era when time seems to be compressing ever more tightly and change is occurring with a rapidity that seems beyond comprehension. Computers have become miniaturized and increasingly powerful; automobiles add ever more electronic gadgetry to improve handling, stretch mileage and increase horsepower while decreasing size; telephones are being installed in cars, trucks, boats, airplanes, and purses; world-wide communication has become much more accessible; robots build cars and computers solicit customers by phone and scientists measure matter in units called quarks. Change seems to have become the natural order of things—the expected, the comfortable.

"Revolutionary" seems inappropriate to describe this frenzy of development. The industrial revolution changed a basic agrarian society into an automated, economically specialized, and interdependent social structure. That was revolutionary. What has occurred since then has been a steady increase in the rate of change, so that one identifiable era quickly blends into the next and all of us seem to expect rather than anticipate the next generation of change. (Before buying an electronic gadget, don't we often hesitate, wondering whether we shouldn't wait for the next model, which will have even more power, smaller size, and a greater number of features?)

In the midst of this frenetic activity, the concept of high performance is steadily being redefined, tested, and restructured. There was a time when high performance meant simply a'64 GTO or Chuck Yeager breaking the sound barrier or a well-oiled 30-ought-6 hunting rifle. Now, high performance can mean a laser disc pumping out nearly distortion-free sounds through high-powered amplifiers and finely tuned speakers. High performance can mean a 200 m.p.h. Ferrari Testerossa or an 800 m.p.h. supersonic airliner or a lap-top computer capable of nearly unimaginable functions.

In an era marked by change, the futures industry is both the recipient of the fruits of change and a pacesetter in the frantic and headlong rush forward. It is difficult for us to remember that the first foreign currency futures contracts were traded as recently as 1972. (Haven't there always been Swiss Franc futures?) T-bonds were first traded in 1977 and the S&P 500 index in 1983. Volume in all of these new-comers has significantly outstripped that in the older, more traditional commodities. In 1986, for example, T-bonds alone traded more than twice the total number of all contracts in all markets in 1972.

In a rush to satisfy the needs of mushrooming growth in potential speculators as well as an ever-growing need to reduce risk in various segments of a developing international economy, the futures industry continues to create new and more esoteric contracts as well as new exchanges on which to trade the new contracts.

In 1979, the year Larry Williams wrote his classic *How I Made One Million Dollars Last Year Trading Commodities,* soybeans was the most actively traded futures contract, accounting for 4.04 million of a total 18.33 million futures contracts traded. That same year Commodities (now Futures) magazine published its first issue and the International Monetary Market (IMM) was formed at the Chicago Mercantile Exchange, opening the way for currency futures, interest rate futures, and stock index futures, all of which came along later.

In 1974, Congress passed the Commodity Futures Trading Act, creating the Commodity Futures Trading Commission (CFTC). This act established the first major step toward Federal regulation of the commodities trading industry. Each renewal of the act—in 1978, 1982, and 1986—provided for increased Federal regulatory control over futures market activity.

At the time the CFTC was established, 38 futures contract markets existed. By 1975, the commission had approved 44 additional contracts in metals, forest products, currencies, and international commodities. In 1975 the first interest rate future, the Government National Mortgage Association certificates (GNMAs), began trading at the Chicago Board of Trade, followed by 90-day Treasury bills at the Chicago Mercantile Exchange.

In 1977, total volume in futures contracts had more than doubled from that of 1972, with 42.88 million contracts traded. The volume leader was still soybeans. Five years later, however, T-bonds led the pack with a total volume of 16.7 million of a total 112.4 million contracts traded. That year—1982—the CFTC approved the first stock index futures contract, the Value Line average, which was traded on the Kansas City Board of Trade. This was followed by the S&P 500 and the NYSE indexes the next year. In 1986, Japanese government bond futures, traded on the Tokyo Stock Exchange, became the most actively traded futures contract in the world, eclipsing U.S. Treasury bonds.

Now nearly 40 futures exchanges exist world wide, trading an ever-broadening number of contracts. Five of the foreign exchanges are entirely electronic, eliminating the activity in the pits that marks the older exchanges and gives them their unique identity and romance. Many of the older exchanges are experimenting with evening trading and 24-hour trading, pointing to the inevitability of a 24-hour world-wide electronically traded futures market.

Rushing into the Futures: The Changing Face of the Commodity Trader

The precipitous rise in volume in the new futures contract markets reflects an influx of new traders who were virtually nonexistent less than 20 years ago. In 1972, most traders could be classified into three distinct categories: floor traders, commercial interests (producers and users), and individuals who traded on the advice of a full-service broker. Most of the brokers' advice in those days was based on a limited knowledge of the fundamentals of the commodity, combined with basic charting. Many brokers seemed to have a spe ciality that they traded in, and their uncanny ability to pull profits out of those specialty markets was often next to incredible.

A few of the old-timers were still around in 1972—individuals who were watching for opportunities to corner a market, thereby controlling the price of a particular commodity. The last such attempt occurred in 1980, when the Hunt brothers tried unsuccessfully to corner the silver market. In recent years, however, CFTC regulations limiting the total number of positions that any one person or company may hold in a particular commodity has made it virtually impossible for an individual to corner a market, a practice that had led to huge profits for several of the legendary grain traders earlier in the century.

One need only read *The Grain Traders*, by William G. Ferris (Michigan State University Press, 1988), to understand how great the changes have been in the futures industry during this century. Written by a journalist who reported on the activities at the CBOT for many years, *The Grain Traders* reveals the raw power and great wealth accumulated by a few speculators willing to take huge risks by accumulating vast positions in a particular commodity. While some succeeded and others failed, many fortunes were made around the turn of the century by manipulating the various markets. For many decades, government chose to turn its eyes away from practices that, if not illegal, bordered on the unethical.

With the advent of currency futures, interest rate futures, and stock index futures, the commodity futures industry came of age. No longer a midwestern novelty, futures trading assumed its place as an integral part of the world economy. At the Chicago Board of Trade, employment jumped from a staff of 80 in 1972 to well over 450 full-time personnel in 1988, the year the first volume of Larry Williams' book *The Definitive Guide to Futures Trading* was published. In 1972, the total number of contracts traded on all exchanges was just over 18,000. In 1988, the volume of contracts traded annually was approaching 190,000,000. A new type of trader had appeared on the scene, whose numbers eclipsed those who had formerly relied heavily on brokers' advice.

On the trading floor, the new pits filled up with young, aggressive traders just out of college, looking to make quick fortunes in the volatile new contracts. In 1981, the joke was that the cost of renting an associate membership at the CBOT, then $600 a month, was cheaper than the cost of renting a taxi in Chicago. The newer markets, which opened earlier and closed later than the traditional agricultural markets and tended to be much more volatile day in and day out, aged the young traders quickly. Many locals in their 30s and 40s complained that they were too old for this kind of trading.

Off the floor, the new traders had sophisticated computers, real-time quote systems, and software capable of producing nearly instantaneous technical analysis of huge amounts of historical price data, and they were generally well-capitalized, having transferred from successful careers in various professional fields. Not needing a broker's advice, they did not want to pay large commissions to support a research department, most of which would be useless to them anyway. To cater to this group, discount brokers opened shop and drove the price of commissions into the 'teens.

In the past few years, yet another group of traders has surfaced: individuals who are often poorly capitalized and who are looking to risk $3,000 to $5,000 for a shot at the huge profits available from the futures markets. These traders, wary of the risks involved in futures trading but itching to take their chances, are particularly attracted to options trading, with its promise of limited risk. To satisfy their desires, another variety of broker has arrived on the scene—the options broker. Although many options specialists are undoubtedly very honest and straightforward, a few charge huge commissions—up to 40 percent of the option premium—with the promise of limited risk, and establish an initial investment of capital so high that the chances of recouping—not to mention showing a profit—are very slim.

Rushing for the Checkered Flag:
The Futures Trader as High-Performance Race Driver

Few experiences can match the exhilaration of punching a 500 horsepower engine and feeling the raw, turbocharged power mash you to your seat, watching the road ahead hurtle toward you at speeds well over 200 m.p.h. At those speeds, only objects directly ahead are in focus; everything on the periphery is a blur of colors and shapes.

No one would dispute that the sport of high-performance auto racing, while exciting, is also dangerous. Yet how is it that, in a sport where danger lurks only a fraction of a second or a fraction of an inch away, so many drivers are able to compete year after year, race after race, without serious mishap? Of course, there are the well-publicized crashes and occasional deaths, but the number of fatalities and serious injuries is surprisingly small compared to the risks being taken.

When A. J. Foyt or Rick Mears or any of several dozen other well-known and successful race drivers push their cars to speeds in excess of 200 m.p.h. on the high-speed oval at Indianapolis, two factors directly contribute to their success and safety: their own skill as a driver and the engineering and construction of the race car.

Year after year, the same drivers return to Indianapolis to try again to win the race that is probably the best-known of all auto races in the country. Every now and then a new name appears, as a younger generation of drivers slowly takes the place of those who have become nearly legendary. But the great ones seem to stay on forever—A. J. Foyt, the Unser brothers, Mario Andretti.

The curious thing about racing at Indianapolis is that some of the car owners become nearly as well-known as the drivers themselves, particularly to anyone who watches the race with more than half an eye. The reason is that Indy-car racing, as with any high-performance competition, can't be run with a car somebody slaps together in a backyard garage, no matter how good a mechanic he or she may be. High performance auto racing is a high-stakes venture, involving millions of dollars in backing and many specialized skills—only one of which is skill at high-speed driving. Engineering the engine for maximum power is complemented by aerodynamic engineering to provide the most effective "ground effects" and chassis engineering to provide the best handling.

The best car owners know how to pull together the best drivers and car builders—and how to raise the necessary money to support the effort, because they know that high-performance automobile racing requires three essential ingredients: a skillful and disciplined driver, a precision-engineered car, and adequate capital to fund the operation and to keep it going when set-backs occur. The average spectator, of course, gives most of his or her attention to the driver and very little to the other two parts of the equation. Ask any spectator why a certain driver won the race and you will likely hear, "Because he (or she) drove the best." Yet, ask a driver of great skill why he (or she) did not win a race and the answer will likely involve some part of the car that was not performing properly.

The factor that often separates first place from second place (or fifth place, for that matter) is some small adjustment in the air foils, or the fuel injection system or the tires. Top performing drivers understand how vital a well-designed and precision-tuned car is to the winning of races. No one would deny, however, the equal importance of the driver.

If, for example, for some sadistic reason one were to invite a randomly selected driver from the streets and highways around Indianapolis to get behind the wheel of one of these high-powered cars and attempt to duplicate the performance of the professional drivers, the outcome would be decidedly tragic. Envision the potential for disaster if an unskilled driver, who has no understanding of the judgment and discipline required of high speed driving, were to attempt to race one of these cars. The probability of a crash would be enormous.

In high-performance racing, the total racing effort is what wins races—not the driver, not the car, not the money backing it up. It is the synthesis of all three that creates a winner.

High-performance futures trading likewise demands three essential elements: a skillful and disciplined trader, a well-designed trading plan, and adequate capitalization to keep the trading plan going when set-backs occur.

Jake Bernstein has often said that an undisciplined trader can make a failure out of the best-designed trading system, but a consistent, disciplined trader can make even a mediocre system work. The key, it seems, is following a plan religiously and unemotionally, all the while observing the rules of careful money management.

That is why, when we first envisioned gathering a group of master trading strategies and compiling them in a trader's handbook to be called *High Performance Futures Trading*, we felt obligated to present more than simply a collection of trading plans. Consequently, the reader will find within these pages, in addition to some excellent trading strategies, several chapters dealing with topics such as discipline, money management, education, managed futures accounts, how to develop and test trading systems, and how to use advisory services. Just as a synthesis of ingredients leads to successful auto racing, so will the incorporation of each of these elements lead to successful futures trading.

Synthesizing the Ingredients: The Master Strategies

Recognizing the equal importance of each part of the equation: trading plan, capitalization, and trader discipline, contributions to *High Performance Fu-*

tures Trading were sought from each of the three areas. As with any project that purports to gather the best from a particular field, however, the decision as to what to include and what to exclude was a difficult one. In this case, we had to define for ourselves what we meant by a master strategy. Although many of the contributors are recognized masters in futures trading, a master strategy, we decided, is not necessarily the strategy of a master. Consequently, the reader will recognize many of the names included in our collection, while other contributors will be quite unknown.

A master strategy, we decided, is most simply a strategy that works. But it can't have worked only a short time. It must be a strategy that has worked consistently over time in actual trading. We were not looking for hypotheticals. Additionally, a master strategy must be adaptable to an individual trader's style. The key word, of course, is *strategy*. *High Performance Futures Trading* is not a collection of canned, mechanical systems. It is, rather, a set of strategies that can be incorporated, adapted, modified, and blended into a trader's own plan.

The master strategies we finally chose are not the only trading strategies that work. Just as it would be difficult to identify the best from among a group of Indy-car drivers, so is it difficult to identify the best from among trading strategies. We do know, however, which drivers are consistently competitive. Similarly, we know that the master strategies we chose will, if properly used, help a trader be consistently competitive in the markets.

High Risk versus High Performance:
The Futures Trader as Auntie Mame

Although the S&P 500 contract had been in existence less than five years when the stock market crashed in 1987, it nevertheless was already being traded in such high volume that it became the whipping-boy upon which experts and laymen alike tried to hang the unprecedented fall in stock prices. This one incident typifies the ambivalence with which the futures industry continues to be viewed in spite of its claims to legitimacy. On the one hand, futures trading offers legitimate risk transfer and profitable speculative opportunities; on the other, the legitimate investment community still tends to view commodities trading as the Auntie Mame of the investment family— seductive but unstable; glamorous but not reliable.

The wash-out rate in futures speculation tends to support this perception. Generally held to be 90 percent, research tends to put the number of losers at 80 percent, still not a lot different, one would think, than the numbers in Las Vegas. Yet there is a distinction—and an important one.

When Evil Knievel decided, some years back, to jump the Snake River Canyon with a rocket-powered cycle, he really did nothing more than strap himself to an oversize roman candle and blast off. Although he is a man of great athletic skill and a fair degree of intelligence, neither of these two attributes gave him any edge where his chances of success were concerned.

The least athletic or the least intelligent among us would have stood an equal chance on that flight—just get in and hold on. The rocket was certainly a high-powered, but not a high performance, machine. Evil Knievel's rocket cycle was little more than a high-stakes gamble, while Indy-car racing, by contrast, is a high-performance sport, where the degree of risk can be controlled—up to a point.

So it is with futures trading. Those who are without adequate preparation or skill, like the driver plucked unprepared from the street and told to cruise the Indianapolis speedway at 200 m.p.h., will surely crash, if not immediately then ultimately. For such traders the activity of futures trading is little more than gambling. The trader who takes the time to lay the necessary groundwork, however, will find himself or herself in the company of professionals. Having discerned most of the markets' mysteries and reduced the tasks to manageable proportions, the high-performance futures trader will discover the secret that high-performance race drivers have known for years: the thrill of victory does not have to come at the expense of unmanageable risk or at the whim of unpredictable fate.

To you who have chosen to prepare yourselves for high-performance futures trading, we offer these Master Strategies and entrust them to your repository of trading expertise. Some among you, however, after reading this fine collection of articles, may decide that the effort required to prepare yourself fully for successful trading is impracticable, yet you still wish to participate in the futures markets. For you, there exist the options of investing in a limited partnership fund, asking a professional to trade your account for you, or subscribing to an advisory service. These alternatives can provide valuable diversification, as well, for the individual futures trader. Every approach to the futures market, however, requires careful professional and businesslike study and preparation. *High Performance Futures Trading* is dedicated to that goal.

REVIEWING
THE BASICS

■

■ SECTION ONE ■

PERIODICALLY, THE NATION'S SCHOOLS encounter a strong public outcry to "return to the basics." This usually follows a period during which educators and school reformers have instituted excessive alternative educational approaches aimed at alleviating rote learning and encouraging development of the "whole person." Then, when reading and math scores suffer, critics suddenly cry out for a return to the basics.

So it is that futures traders, in their search for the perfect system, often neglect the basic skills they first learned while being introduced to futures trading. Or perhaps there are many traders who never were introduced to basic concepts, but who skipped right to the level of seeking sophisticated systems. Regardless of the reasons, a review of some of the basics of trading seems essential to laying an adequate foundation for high performance trading.

Included in this section are chapters dealing with two of the three elements of successful trading: trading discipline and capitalization. We place them first because of their importance. Otherwise, such unsexy topics might well be overlooked in the search for the diamonds and nuggets among the trading stategies.

The section begins, by design, with two chapters by Jake Bernstein, "On Discipline" and "Twenty-One Tools for Successful Trading," in which Jake reminds us that discipline and following the rules are essential to surviving in the markets. Mark Silber then takes us back to the basics of following the trend, suggesting that a trader who continues to be whipsawed by the market may be remiss in identifying and diligently paying attention to price trends. Don Sarno asserts that a solid education, attained through reading books, periodicals, and market reports, attending seminars, studying the discipline and skill necessary for success in the markets. Section 1 ends with a treatise by Ken Upshaw that reminds every trader of the need to conserve capital if they are to preserve their freedom to trade.

■ CHAPTER TWO* ■

ON DISCIPLINE

JAKE BERNSTEIN

■

* From Jake Bernstein, *Facts on Futures* (Chicago: Probus, 1987), 131-144, by permission of the author and publisher. Copyright 1987 by Jake Bernstein

JAKE BERNSTEIN

Jake Bernstein is President of MBH Commodity Advisors Inc., based in Northbrook, Illinois. He is a noted author, lecturer, and commodities trading advisor, and publisher of the *MBH Weekly Commodity Letter*. His books have been highly acclaimed by the financial community. *The Investor's Quotient: The Psychology of Successful Investing in Commodities and Stocks*, is a comprehensive self-improvement manual geared to help investors learn the psychological tools of success. It has been called a "modern classic" by many in the field. In 1982, he published *The Handbook of Commodity Cycles: A Window on Time*. *Seasonal Commodity Spreads* was published in January 1983. All of Jake's books have received highly complimentary reviews from the financial press. In 1987 *Short-term Trading in Futures* was published by Probus. The book incorporates many of the tools that Jake has taught short-term traders over the past several years.

Mr. Bernstein is recognized throughout the world as a leading expert on commodity cycles and seasonal trends. He has lectured to capacity audiences in the Far East and throughout the United States. He has appeared on major financial radio and TV programs, including *Wall Street Week*.

He is one of the principals of Futures Symposium International. He also publishes the *MBH Commodity Advisors Newsletter* with a twice daily updated hotline, along with the *K-Wave Survival Tapes*, a monthly 90 minute tape along with charts that provide specific long-term economic analyses. And last, but not least, an exhaustive monthly study called *Letter of Long Term Trends*, which consists of over 20 pages of charts, indicators, and comments designed and evaluated for its long-term status, potential for change, and price projections.

■ CHAPTER TWO ■

LTHOUGH THERE ARE MANY THINGS I could tell you about different trading approaches and the lessons I have learned through long and hard experience, none of them would be more meaningful, ultimately, than the lessons I have learned about discipline. The advice I can give you about this single most important area of success in futures trading is the most important knowledge I can impart. If I were to suggest that you read only one chapter in this book, this would be it!

When asked what is the single most important variable to success in futures trading, my reponse is not "trading sytems" nor is it "the type of computer you have" nor is it "the type of inside information to which you might be privy." It is not "the amount of capital you have" or "the broker with whom you are trading." The simple fact of the matter is that what ultimately separates winners from losers, commercial, speculative, short-term, long-term, or otherwise, is discipline and its many facets.

To most traders discipline is just another well-worn topic in futures trading. They have heard the word, they've studied the preachings and they believe they have learned the lessons. My observations and experiences with futures markets and futures traders lead me to the irreversible conclusion that *the lessons have not been learned!*

To most traders the word "discipline" merely signifies something they know they need and believe they have. In their hearts of hearts, however, most traders know they are sorely lacking in discipline, and that they will probably never have it.

Discipline is virtually impossible to teach and to learn from anyone else. It is complex, elusive, evasive, and often camouflaged. It is the *sine qua non* of success in virtually every form of human achievement, in every field, and in every generation. To the best of my knowledge, there is no simple way to define discipline, nor is there any simple way to acquire or teach it.

There are futures traders who have virtually no objective trading system to speak of, but who, through the application and development of discipline, have achieved success. On the other hand, there are many futures traders with excellent trading systems, that, for lack of discipline, have remained unsucessful, in spite of massive statistical evidence to suggest that their techniques are indeed valid and capable of producing tremendous profits.

17

Discipline can transform a marginal trading system into a highly successful one. Lack of discipline can transform a potentially successful trading system into a consistent and persistent losing approach. In reviewing the history, literature, and facts about virtually any form of investing or speculating, I have found that a key element of success is discipline. It is impossible for me to overstate the fact that discipline is probably the main difference between winners and losers.

The purpose of this chapter is twofold: first, to underscore the importance of discipline, and second, to suggest a number of ways by which discipline can be developed and improved. First, let's look at the fashion in which discipline functions and its ramifications in the successful trading approach.

Why Discipline is Important

As you know, there are many different approaches to futures trading. Some are potentially more profitable than others. Some are simple, some are complex, some are logical, and some not so logical. Regardless of the trading approach one employs, all trading systems and methods have certain elements in common. These are as follows:

1. Specific signals (rules) for entry and exit.
2. Specific parameters, methods of calculation of timing signals.
3. Specific action that must be taken as a function of 1 and 2.

When systems and methods are tested by computer in order to generate hypothetical or "ideal" results, they are not tested in real time, but rather in theoretical time, with perfect adherence to the trading rules that have been programmed into the computer.

What gets tested is a series of specific parameters. What comes out is a listing of trades and hypothetical results based on *the perfect execution of the rules that were programmed into the machine.*

The output of the system test will yield many different types of information, including such things as percentage of trades profitable, percentage of trades unprofitable, percentage of trades that break even, average winning trade in dollars, average losing trade in dollars, performance for given markets, average length of time per trade, etc. All of the data derived from the computer test of a trading model is based upon perfect follow-up, implementation and execution of trading signals according to the parameters programmed into the computer. There is no room for error!

There is no room for lack of discipline! Some systems are profitable only 55–65 percent of the time. Other systems show higher percentages. But such statistics can be misleading. I have rarely seen systems that are profitable more than 80 percent of the time. Certainly you can imagine that a trading system that is correct 90 percent of the time, making a $100 profit on the average each time, and then losing $900 on the occasion that it is wrong, would certainly not be very profitable. Furthermore, the individual trading the system would give back all of the profits made on nine trades on one losing trade! One losing trade would bring the account back to even. Should there be another error due to lack of discipline, the account would show a net loss.

Conversely, a trading system may show eight losers for every two winners. If, however, the average profitable trade is much larger than the average losing trade, even a system having nine losers out of every ten trades could be profitable, if the bottom line per trade were higher on the winning side. Nevertheless, such a system would be thrown astray if lack of discipline resulted in much larger losses than expected for the eight losing trades. If lack of discipline interfered significantly with the profits on the two profitable trades, then the net results might be much worse than anticipated.

A third scenario would be a marginal trading system. Assume that a trading system is profitable about 65 percent of the time. In such cases, we can figure that approximately 65 out of every 100 trades are winners and 35 are losers. You can see that only 30 percent separates the winners from the losers. In other words, the trader must have sufficient discipline to keep the losses as small as possible, and to maximize the profits. This is where discipline enters into the formula.

Discipline is the machinery that can make or break any trading system. There are some conditions under which discipline will not be the important variable; however, *in most cases it is the significant variable*. All of the glowing trading statistics for your trading system will be totally uselss if you are not capable of duplicating the exact statistics generated by the computer test of your trading system. In other words, you must stick as close to the averages as possible or one or two losses, much larger than the average, or one or two profits much smaller than the average, will be sufficient to ruin your results. Sometimes this can occur strictly as a function of market behavior (i.e., limit moves against you); however, more often than not, as I have stated before, it is the trader who is responsible for maintaining the discipline of a system.

Doing Your "Homework"

It is uncanny how many times markets will begin major moves in line with the expectations of many advisors, analysts, and speculators, without these various individuals being on board for the big move. Why do things like this happen? How often has this happened to you? I know from personal experience that many individuals have good records at predicting where prices will go. I also know that when it comes to doing their homework, they have especially poor records.

What do I mean by doing your homework? I mean, very simply, keeping up to date on the signals generated by the system or systems you are following. In order to keep in touch with the markets according to your system, you will need to have a regular schedule for doing the technical or fundamental work your system requires. Whether this consists of simple charting that may take only five minutes per day, or complex mathematical calculations which may take considerably longer, the fact remains that the discipline of doing your homework is one of the prerequisites for successful trading.

If you have a system and do not follow it, you are guilty of poor discipline. If you have a system and fail to do the work which generates your trading signals, then you are just as guilty of lacking discipline. As you can see, and as you can well appreciate, it is a sad but true fact that most traders don't even get past the first step.

Can you identify strongly, or even partially, with some of the things I am saying? How often have you been in the situation of missing a move because your charts or systems were not up to date? How many times has this frus-trated you into making an unwarranted decision in an effort to compensate for your first error? If the truth were fully known, we would know that many of us are guilty. The sad fact about the situation is that its rectification is a very simple matter. In fact, the steps one must take in order to rectify virtually any problem resulting from lack of trading discipline are very specific, easily understood and exceptionally elementary to implement.

It is, unfortunately true that the discipline required to trade consistently and successfully is the same type of discipline that is required in virtually every aspect of human life. Whether it is the discipline that is required to lose weight, stop smoking or to develop a successful business, the roots and basics of all discipline are the same.

If you develop discipline in your trading, I am certain that it will spread to other areas of your life, including your personal affairs. Unfortunately, however, discipline in other aspects of your life may not necessarily spread very quickly to your trading. The nature of futures trading provides serious challenges to discipline developed in other areas of life. Suggestions for improving discipline will be provided later on in this chapter.

How Lack of Discipline Grows Stronger

Lack of discipline is not confined to any one situation, any one trade, or any one trader. Lack of discipline, for all intents and purposes, is a way of life, albeit a bad one. Individuals who achieve success without adhering to certain disciplined practices do so as a stroke of good fortune and stand the chance of forfeiting their wealth through a lack of disciplined action. Unfortunately, lack of discipline is not a simple matter, but rather it spreads like a cancerous growth through the trader's behavior. Lack of discipline tends to result in a compounding of errors that result in a far greater tragedy than that caused by the initial mistake itself. Yet, it should come as no surprise to those who understand relationships, whether they are those between individuals or those between the individual and the marketplace. In an interpersonal relationship, lack of discipline and specificity can cause negative interaction. Negative interaction will then result in further tests of discipline and self-control. These will; in turn, result in other problems, failures, and negative experiences until the entire relationship is threatened. The same is true of one's trading.

Lack of discipline in instituting a trade may frustrate the trader into a further display of poor discipline. After several such incidents, the trader will become frustrated, causing further errors to become likely. The net result is usually a succession of errors, each compounding upon the other and each likely far worse than the previous. It is for this reason that one must take great care to avoid making even the first mistake due to a lack of discipline. The first mistake will lead to the second, the second may lead to four others and four others may lead to 16 others. This is the manner in which a lack of discipline tends to spread. Frequently it can grow at an exponential rate.

Suggestions for Improving Your Discipline

Certainly I don't have all the answers for improving your discipline. However, I do have a number of very cogent, time-tested techniques to help you improve. All of the suggestions will require action and thorough implementation if they are to have a beneficial effect on your results.

1. *Make a schedule.* In order to help you keep your trading signals up to date, set aside a given time of the day or week during which you will do the necessary calculations, charts, or other market work. Doing the same work every day of the week will help you get into a specific routine, and this, in turn, will eliminate the possibility (or greatly reduce it) of not being prepared when a major move develops.

2. *Don't try to do too much.* Attempt to specialize at one particular trading approach. If you try to trade in too many markets at one time or with too many systems at one time, your work will become a burden, you will not look forward to it, and you will be more prone to let your studies fall behind. Ideally, seek to work in no more than three to five markets at any given point in time, and attempt to specialize at only one specific system.

3. *Use a checklist.* One of my favorite analogies for the trader to consider is the similarity between the trader and the airplane pilot. Before take-off a good airplane pilot goes through his or her checklist, marking off all of the various items that must be completed or checked prior to take-off. I certainly would not want to fly in a plane with a pilot who was sloppy in this procedure—would you? The trader who wishes to eliminate trading errors should also maintain such a check-list, consulting it regularly or preferably before each trade is made. Of all of my suggestions the checklist is probably the best one for all traders. I would suggest that even after your checklist has become automatic, you still maintain it, since lack of discipline is likely to attack you at almost any time. It can strike without notice and often does.

4. *Do not accept third-party input once your decision has been made.* I have come to respect the fact that good traders are usually loners. They must do their work in isolation, and they must implement their decision in isolation. A pushy or talkative broker, a well-intentioned friend, or a very persuasive newsletter can often sway you from a decision that only you should make. There are times when your decisions will be wrong, but these are part of the learning experience, and you alone must make your decisions based upon the facts as you see them. If you have decided to follow your trading system, then by all means follow it and forget about other input. If, however, your system is based upon deriving input from other sources, then strive to implement your decisions without being swayed from them once your mind has been made up. The benefits of deciding on your own far outweigh the potential benefits of having too much input.

5. *Evaluate your progress.* Feedback is a very important part of the learning process. Keep track of how you are doing with your trading, not only in terms of dollars and cents, but in terms of specific signals, behavior, and techniques. This will give you an idea of how closely you are staying with the rules, which rules you are breaking, and how often you may be breaking them. It is important to know when you make mistakes, but is is more important to know what kind of mistakes you made and how often you made them. This will help you overcome the lack of discipline that causes trading errors to occur.

6. *Learn from every loss.* Losses are tuition. They are expensive and they must be good for something. The something to which I am referring is, of course, learning. Learn from each loss and do your very best to avoid taking the same loss twice or more for the same

reason. Do not repeat the same errors. To do so indicates that your discipline is not improving.

7. *Understand yourself.* This is certainly a big job and not one easily accomplished. It is extremely important that you understand your mo-tivation and your true reasons for trading the markets. Frequently individuals will do poorly in the markets because their objectives and goals are not well-established.

8. *Work with your trading system and remain decicated to it.* If you are like most traders, you will have done considerable research on a trading method or system. Some traders, however, become quickly disen-chanted with their systems and hop from one technique to another. This is one of the worst forms of poor discipline. It does not allow sufficient time for a system to perform. In so doing, the speculator takes considerable more overall risk than he or she should.

9. *Check your objectives.* At times, poor trading discipline can be a function of unclear objectives. If you have decided that you want to trade for the short term only, then you have a very clear objective. How-ever, if you are not certain about the time frame of your trading, about the trading system you plan to use as your vehicle, about the relationship you wish to have with your broker, about the quotation equipment you plan to use (if any), then you will be prone to make mistakes and have poor discipline. My suggestion is to make all major trading decisions before you even get started with your trading. Some corrections can be made along the way, but a majority of decisions must be made prior to any serious trading.

10. *Know when to quit.* In order to improve your trading discipline, it is important to have an objective measure of when you will terminate a given trade, profitably or unprofitably. Whether this is done at a particular price or a particular dollar amount is of no consequence. The fact remains that you must know when you have had enough.

11. *Make commitments and keep them.* In trading it is important to make and keep commitments in the markets just as it is in every phase of human endeavor and interaction. If, however, you do not make a commitment, or if the commitment you make is not clear, then you stand the chance of not following through on an important phase of your trading. For this reason, I encourage all traders to make specific commitments, not only in terms of such things as trading systems, trading approach, available capital, maximum risk, etc., but also in terms of each and every trade they make.

Do not make the trade unless you are fully committed to it. What does this mean? It means that many individuals are prone to establish a position in the market based on what "looks like" a good signal or when it "looks like the market wants to turn higher." In other words, commitments are made on the basis of vague indications.

In order to make a commitment that will serve you well, do not make commitments that are based upon sketchy information. What you get when you make such a decision will be enough to let you know that you are not making a commitment based on correct procedures.

There are many more ways to improve your discipline, but quite a few of these are probably very specific to your individual situation. One good way to determine how, where, when, and what type of commitment you wish to make is to examine your individual situation by using a checklist or questionnaire designed to ascertain your situation.

TWENTY-ONE TOOLS FOR SUCCESSFUL TRADING

JAKE BERNSTEIN

■

* From Jake Bernstein, *Facts on Futures* (Chicago: Probus 1987), 179-188, by permission of the author and publisher. Copyright 1987 by Jake Bernstein.

JAKE BERNSTEIN

See the biography at the beginning of chapter 2.

■ CHAPTER THREE ■

THE STUDENT OF FUTURES TRADING has a very clear and concise goal. This goal is not primarily to beat the market or to become skillful for the sake of skill alone. The true speculator is, first and foremost, interested in profits and success.

As you can tell from your own experience, from other aspects of life, and from my many caveats elsewhere, there is no surefire simple road to success in the markets. With so many techniques to choose from, with so many different orientations, and with so many trading systems available to specu-lators, what you ultimately develop will be an individual approach tailor-made (by yourself) to suit your purposes.Whether what you end up with is a purely mechanical approach based upon the research of others, or a primarily subjective approach based upon your own interpretations and studies, the fact remains that the ultimate decision-making task is yours and yours alone.

Yet, regardless of what you select or how you select it, you can readily see from what you have already read in this book, and from what you may already know, that there are some general similarities and common threads that interweave every approach to futures trading. These commonalities influence and regulate the success or failure of virtually every trader.

While it may very well be true that some individuals can and do achieve success by breaking all the rules, it is also true that such individuals are clearly in the minority and that their success is the exception rather than the rule. Unless you are an individual blessed with fantastic luck, you will need to achieve success in the futures markets the good old fashioned way, you'll have to earn it. The only way to earn lasting success is through the diligent and disciplined application of specific techniques and methods, few of which are directly related to systems, and most of which are clearly the function of attitudes, psychology, and discipline.

You may not want to hear this, but the fact is that it matters little what system or systems you select, how tremendous their hypothetical performance may be or how well others may have done with these systems. What ultimately matters, as you very well know, is how you apply the systems, and the consistency with which you can put the techniques into operation.

Understandably, the human being is not a computer, and he or she cannot achieve the same level of perfection that may be required to institute a trading system in complete accordance with the ideal conditions under which it was tested. The degree of slippage, drawdown and trader error is often significant. Furthermore, it frequently seems that real-time market conditions deteriorate the performance of most systems and, in fact, no system based on hypothetical, or computer-simulated or -tested results can be taken as worth-while unless these results can be replicated with reasonable similarity in the markets themselves.

It is for these reasons, among others, that the steps toward trading success do not rest exclusively, or for that matter heavily, upon selection of a trading system. Though I know that the selection of a system is important, I suspect that its value has been overstated, particularly by those with a vested interest in selling systems or in managing a fund based on such systems. In order to achieve success it will be necessary for you to follow most, if not all, of the time-tested rules of profitable trading.

Though I will begin my "List of Twenty-One" with items related to system selection, you will observe that these items do not dominate the list. Remember also that variations on each item in the list are certainly possible in order to adapt them to your particular situation.

Twenty-One Tools for Better Trading

1. *Find or develop a trading system that has a real-time record (or computer-tested record) of 70 percent or more winning trades, with a ratio of approximately 2 to 1 in terms of dollars made versus dollars lost per trade (including commissions as losses).* In the absence of real-time results, computer results are acceptable, provided you have made provisions for the limitations. Though the figures just given need not be replicated exactly, attempt to get close.

2. *The system you find or develop should be consistent with your time limitations or availability (with or without a computer system).* If the signals are generated by an advisory service, then make certain you have familiarized yourself with the basics of the system, its trading approach and other details of the system as described earlier in the text.

3. *Select a brokerage firm that will be compatible with your needs.* If you are an independent trader wishing no input whatsoever, then select a discount firm that gives good service and prompt order executions. If, however, you are a novice trader requiring a full-service firm, then be willing to pay higher commissions in order to have your needs fulfilled.

4. *Select a broker within the firm, or specify your needs to the firm if you will not be working with one particular broker.* Make certain that both you and the broker are aware of each others' needs, and keep the lines of communication clear.

5. *Make certain you have sufficient risk capital to trade the system you have selected.* Be certain that your risk capital is truly risk capital and not funds upon which you are otherwise counting for some future purpose.

6. *Develop and formulate your trading philosophy.* As you know, your perceptions of trading, your expectations, your goals and your market orientation (i.e., long term, short-term, etc.) are all factors that contribute either to success or to failure.

7. *Plan your trades and follow through on your plans.* Attempt not to trade on whim. Rather, work from a trading plan each and every day so you will avoid the temptation of making spur-of-the-moment dec-isions that are not based on any system or method you are using.

8. *Be an isolationist.* There is great value in being an isolationist when it comes to speculation. You don't necessarily want anyone else's input. You don't necessarily want anyone else's opinions. As time goes on, as the lessons you learn begin to accumulate, you will realize that your own good opinion is just as valuable, perhaps more so, than the opinions of any others, experts or novices.

9. *Make a commitment—take the plunge!* Make a commitment to trading. The commitment should consist of rules, organizational procedures, goals and expectations. Delineate these carefully, with consideration and with forethought. By making your plans, you will avoid costly errors that are not consistent with your plans.

10. *Once you've decided—act!* Don't hesitate one moment once your trading decisions have been made (whether the decision is to get into a trade or to get out of a trade). It matters not whether you are taking a profit or closing out a loss. As soon as you have a clear- cut signal to act, don't hesitate. Act as soon as your system says you must act—no sooner, no later.

11. *Limit risk and preserve capital.* The best way to limit risk is to trade only in three to six markets at once and to avoid trading markets that have swings much too large for your account size. Once you have decided to limit risk to a certain dollar amount or to limit risk using a specific technique, make certain you take your losses as soon as they should be taken. Do this on time—not too soon, not too late!

12. *Don't anticipate.* Many traders go astray when they anticipate signals from their trading system. The trading system is your traffic light. The traffic is always heavy. Stop on the red, go on the green, be cautious on yellow. If you anticipate trading signals from your system, you might as well not have a system at all.

13. *The market is the master, you are the slave.* Like it or not, you cannot tell the market what to do. It will always do what it wants and it is your job to figure out what it is doing. Once done, you must follow the market through its many twists and turns. If it is zigging and zagging, then you must zig and zag. If it is trending higher, you must trade from the long side. If it is trending lower, you must trade from the short side. It may be instructive for you to review, from time to time, which side of the market most of your trades were on. If you find that you have been bucking the trend of the market, then you must review either your system or your discipline. One of the two (perhaps both) are not functioning properly. Many traders have gone astray by failing to follow the market, thinking that it is their job to forecast the market. The job of the trader is to follow, not to forecast. Let's leave forecasting to economists.

14. *Do your homework.* Whether you are using a computer, whether you are a novice or a seasoned veteran, you must keep your research current. Futures markets move so fast that there is precious little time to update your trading signals once a move has occurred. You must be there at the very inception of a move or shortly thereafter. Otherwise you will have difficulty getting aboard for the bigger move. The only way to do this is to keep your homework up to date. If you have a computer it may be easier. You can program your computer so it will automatically update your signals or system every day at a certain time. Regardless, discipline is always involved and you must keep current.

15. *Avoid emotion.* It is paradoxical that the greatest friend of the speculator is the emotion of others, yet emotion within the speculator is one of his or her greatest enemies. When trading, emotions must be under control and they must be ignored. Regardless of the trend of emotions, their consequences can be exceptionally dangerous to the speculator since they can result in unwarranted actions.

16. *Don't take tips, "sure things," or inside information.* The temptation in all of us is to find the easy way. You know that the easy way is rarely the best way. There will always be lottery winners, but your odds of winning any lottery are slim, indeed. Therefore, avoid the temptation of taking tips, following inside information, listening to the opinions of other traders or believing that the person you are listening to or talking to knows more than you do. Sometimes they do, but most of the time they don't. Collective opinions are, of course, helpful in the case of contrary opinion studies, but individual opinions or tips are basically useless to the trader.

17. *When you make money, take some of it away from the market.* When you have been doing well, remember to systematically remove money from your account. Whether you do this on a profitable trade basis or on a time basis (i.e., daily, weekly, monthly) is not important. What is important is to do it. Traders have winning and losing periods. During the winning times, profits will accumulate rapidly and before you know it you may become impressed with your own success. You will examine ways to expand your trading in view of your tremendous profits. You will look at how much money there is in your account and you will be tempted to trade larger positions. While there will be a time for this, it is usually not right to do so when you are feeling exceptionally euphoric about your performance. One way to reduce euphoria and put profits away for a rainy day is by having a systematic method of withdrawing profits.

18. *Develop winning attitudes and behaviors.* You can do this by reading the writings of the great traders. Spend more time developing yourself than you do developing your systems. The key variable in the trading success equation is the trader and not the system. I maintain that a good trader can make virtually any system work.

19. *"The trend is your friend."* This old expression is known to all, but used by few. Whether you allow the major trend to filter signals from your system as the final deciding factor, or whether you use a system that is based entirely upon trend following principles, always be cautious when your trades are not consistent with the existing trend. Naturally, there will be times when your signals are against the trend. There will be times when the trend is apt to change. However, you should always be careful about trades and signals against the trend since they will most often be wrong.

20. *Don't try to trade too many markets.* There are many different markets, but most move together. There are only a few major market groups. Take one market from each group, preferably the most active, and focus on it. Few traders can be involved in all markets at once.

21. *Don't lose sight of your goals.* Your goal in futures trading is to make money. There is no goal greater than this in futures trading. Though there may be other benefits such as self-satisfaction, the thrill of trading, and the sublimation of hostility and competitive instincts, these are all secondary. If you seek revenge against the market or other traders, if you wish merely to compete for the sake of competition or to trade only for the thrill of trading, then the primary goal of speculation will be lost and so will your money!

Conclusions

The rules presented in this chapter are based upon my many experiences and observations in futures trading since 1968. Though some rules may be more important to you than others, I know that at one time or another, all of these will be important to all traders. The best way to employ these rules in your trading program is to study them, to keep them at your disposal and to review them regularly. They will help keep you on the right track, and they will help keep you honest with yourself.

Perhaps one of the greatest errors a speculator can commit is self-deception. The markets are brutal and the pain of losses is omnipresent. No trader or speculator is immune to losses. I might even go so far as to say that what ultimately separates the winners from the losers is the ability to be honest with one's self. From this rare quality arises clear perception. From a clear perception of reality emanates the ability to use only what is effective and to discard all that is not.

ONE STEP BACK— HOW BASICS ARE IMPORTANT

MARK SILBER

■

MARK SILBER

Mark Silber's experience in the futures markets dates to 1974 when he started his career as a floor trader on the Mid-America Commodity Exchange. In 1975, Mark joined a major futures brokerage firm, eventually becoming its Senior Analyst.

As a result of this extensive experience, Mark has developed a keen understanding of the different phases of the futures industry. His knowledge and talents are many and varied, including such vital skills as order entry procedures, contemporary technical analysis, money management, compliance, regulatory matters and technical trading systems.

In 1988 Mark entered into partnership with Jake Bernstein and Joel Robbins forming Bernstein Futures. Mark is responsible for the supervision of full service brokerage operations and technical research.

■ CHAPTER FOUR ■

O NE OF THE MOST FREQUENT COMPLAINTS I've heard from traders is that their trading systems work well in trending markets but not in trading ranges or, perhaps, only work well in trading ranges but not during trends. After while I began to realize that most of these same traders had no effective method(s) for determining market trends. It was more a matter of perspective than ignorance. Because market participants trade in different time frames, at different levels of need and varying levels of stress, most are forced by the realities of trading to lose sight of the so-called big picture or major trend.

The scalper, trading in the shortest of all time frames, sees each new tick as an opportunity. Profits are earned by accumulating and trading large positions for a price fluctuation as small as one tick. Stress is generated by the competition in the pit for the right to buy the bid or to sell the offer and by the speed at which the scalper must compute and react to changes in prices. On this level, the trader may feel very little need to recognize the major trend beyond the realities of the last few ticks.

The average speculator, on the other hand (if one exists), seeks to isolate longer-lasting opportunities while tatooing the office walls with effete epigrams about bulls, bears, slaughtered pigs, and trends. Yet in spite of their pure intentions, most are forced to lose sight of the major trend either by the high degree of leverage in futures trading (which we all know can work either for us or against us) or by a lack of discipline prompted by a host of extraneous variables.

High leverage necessitates correct trading decisions or a prompt loss will result. Lack of discipline may lead traders to hold a losing position too long. The once daily phone calls to the broker become once hourly, then once every few minutes, forcing the trader to focus even more on the minor trend. Of course, shortly after the trader can no longer endure the anxiety and the trade is exited, the market frequently turns back in the direction previously expected. The trader, now armed with the benefit of 20/20 hindsight, offers all sorts of prayers to the gods of "woulda-coulda-shoulda" and vows to pay even closer attention next time, thus exacerbating his or her already high level of stress. And stress tends to facilitate further losing behaviors.

Virtually all types of traders may fall into the anxiety trap. Those on a winning streak may surmise that trading more often will lead to more profits. They then proceed to see opportunities that just don't exist. Perhaps a trader successful at playing the major trend will decide he or she, too, can walk on water, attempting to catch each of the minor waves. But now let's look at some potential solutions.

First, Define the Trend

Perhaps those traders currently less than satisfied with their results would do well to take a step back, redetermine the major trend of the market, and use their systems in conjunction with the trend. But how does one properly define trend, and how can one further differentiate between trend, reversal, and consolidation?

Let's first examine some of the most common definitions. L. Dee Belveal in the classic book *Charting Commodity Market Price Behavior* notes that a "price trend down characteristically presents a succession of lower highs, as reflected by the daily bar chart. An uptrend shows a consistent tendency to higher lows, as reflected in the daily price bars." In *The Commodity Futures Market Guide*, Kroll and Shishko add another dimension to the definition: "An uptrend is characterized by prices fluctuating in a succession of higher highs and higher lows; a downtrend by a succession of lower highs and lower lows."

Perhaps one of the most complete studies of trend can be found in *Technical Analysis of Stock Trends*, written by Robert D. Edwards and John Magee in 1948 and revised many times since. In this "bible" of technical analysis, the authors contend that there are three phases to a major trend: the primary trend, which is the broad movement encompassing most of a time span; the secondary swings, which last for a period of several weeks to a few months, moving in a direction opposite the primary trend; and the minor waves, which only last a few days and are essentially meaningless. Edwards and Magee compare the three phases of the trend to the tide, a wave and a ripple of the ocean.

Beyond a simple definition, Magee and Edwards examine various types of reversal and continuation chart patterns in order to help the reader determine where the market stands in each phase. A brief examination of some of these patterns reveals the most important factor in trend analysis: *the major trend will continue in one direction, although pausing or consolidating at several levels, until the previous minor low made before the last new high in an uptrend or until the previous minor top made before the last new low in a downtrend is violated.*

Figure 4-3A shows December live hogs on August 26, 1988. The market has rallied in a series of higher highs and lows from the level but has yet to penetrate the high of 44.30 made before the low of 40.90 on August 29, 1988. While the minor trend may be in an uptrend as defined by the common definitions, this market is merely consolidating the primary trend, which is still pointing to lower prices. As you can see, this chart also suggests the

Figure 4-1

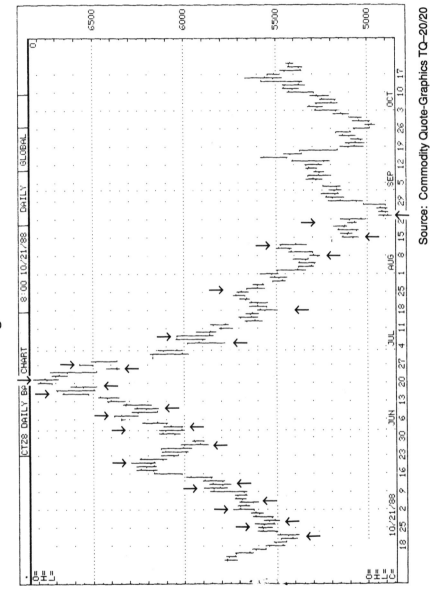

Source: Commodity Quote-Graphics TQ–20/20

Figure 4-2

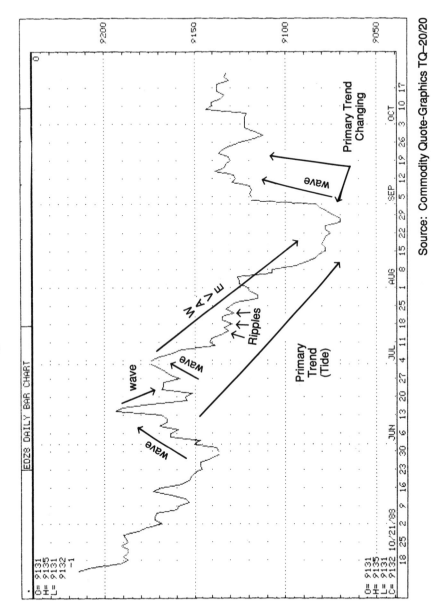

Source: Commodity Quote-Graphics TQ–20/20

Figure 4-3A December Live Hogs, August 26, 1988

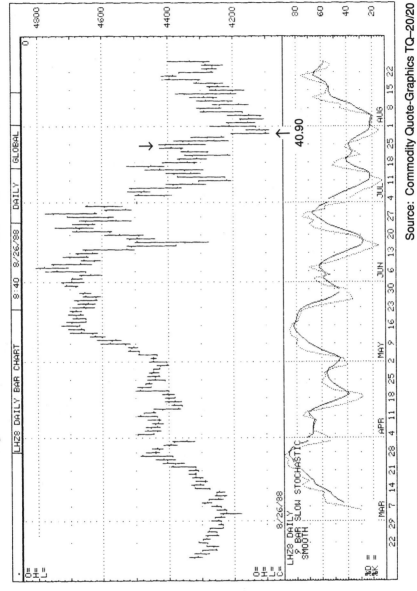

Source: Commodity Quote-Graphics TQ-20/20

probability of new lows for this move. Figure 4-3B shows that on September 9, 1988 the market actually did make a final low of 39.15.

Note in Figure 4-4 the triangle of consolidation on the December corn chart just prior to a major upside move. In this case, the low of 2.20 3/4 made just prior to the new high at 2.44 1/2 was never violated, allowing one to see this pattern clearly as consolidation. The breakout of this pattern led to a rally in excess of $1 a bushel for those lucky enough to have understood what the market was trying to imply.

Looking at the series of small pennants on the December cocoa chart (Figure 4-5), one sees several instances of minor up-trends indicated by higher highs and higher lows. None of these has taken out a high made prior to the most recent low, so that the down-trend is still intact. As you can see the market continued to drop in dramatic fashion.

Reversal Patterns

Now let's examine the same concept in regard to definite reversal patterns. Figure 4-6 shows a definite head-and-shoulders top in the market. Notice how the head represents the last high made in the move, while the minor bottom just before that high, when violated, indicates a definite change in the primary trend. The same holds true for the downward violation of a symmetrical triangle. Earlier we showed the triangle in corn which led to continuation. But in Figure 4-6 a violation of the low made before entering the congestion phase led to much lower prices.

As in many trading systems or philosophies, situations exist where this may not work. Such is the case in markets where a broadening formation takes place (Figure 4-7). This seems to occur because a broadening formation is generally found in those situations where there is no trend to the market, because of a lack of leadership by either the bulls or the bears. That small drawback, however, is a small price to pay for such a logical understanding of trend, congestion, and reversal.

Chart Systems

If you are like most traders, you have spent either great sums of money or considerable time and effort on those systems or mathematical formulas that attempt to ascertain the direction of the market trend. We all try to find the best fit in moving averages or stochastic time frames, or we purchase as many trading systems as economically feasible in order to gain a trading edge. Many of these work well on their own or in conjunction with the market trend, yet they, at times, are subject to lead or lag factors. Most have been created with the benefit of hindsight and are based on hypothetical

Figure 4-3B December Live Hogs, September 9, 1988

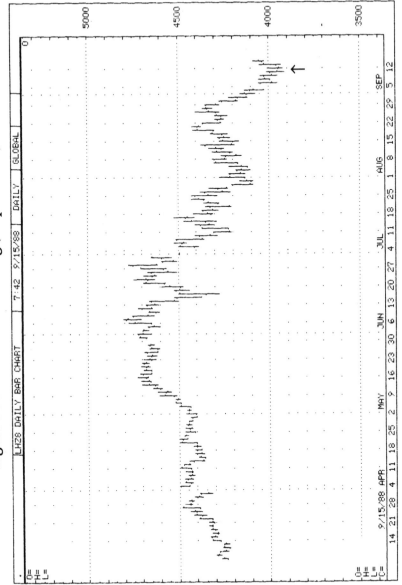

Source: Commodity Quote-Graphics TQ–20/20

Figure 4-4 December Corn

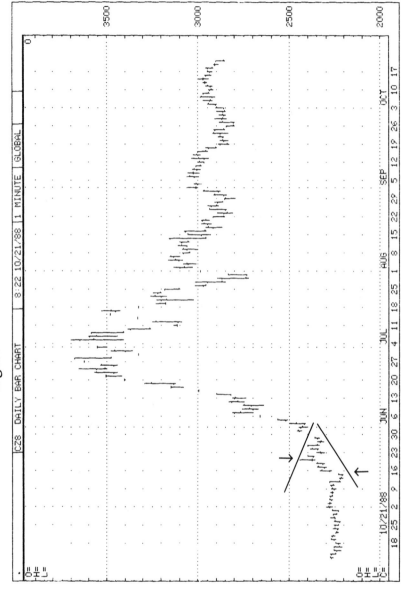

Source: Commodity Quote-Graphics TQ-20/20

Figure 4-5 December Cocoa

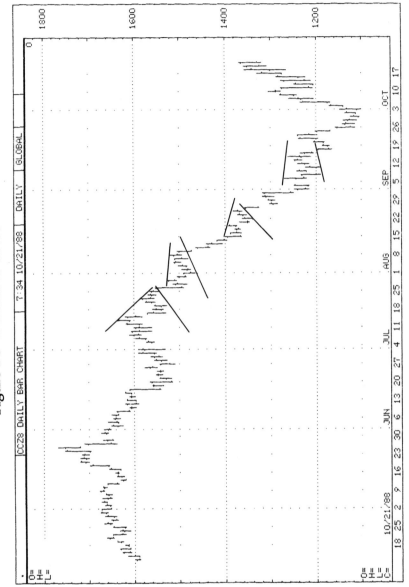

Source: Commodity Quote-Graphics TQ–20/20

Figure 4-6 Reversal Patterns

Source: Commodity Quote-Graphics TQ–20/20

Figure 4-7 Broadening Formation

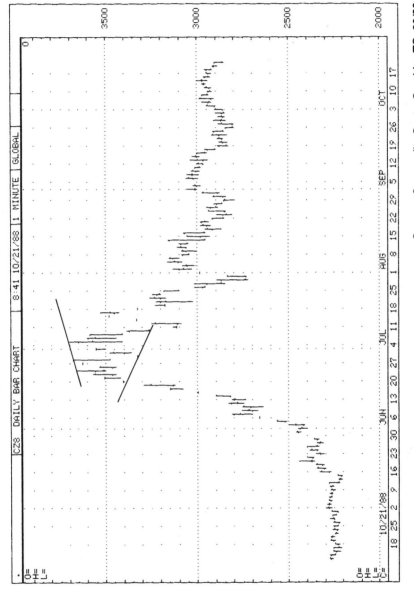

Source: Commodity Quote-Graphics TQ–20/20

results rather than real time trading. In my experience, the most successful traders use these tools to their advantage, but only after first gaining a true understanding of the language of the market and after learning how to pause and take the one step back necessary to visualize the major trend.

But please don't take my word for it. Review chart after chart until you can determine trend at a glance. Then combine that understanding with the other methods you may use. See how many whipsaw losses you could avoid by not taking signals against the trend in a congestion phase.

Just one more suggestion: visualize the trading profits you might have accumulated had you the foresight to establish positions early in each trend, as well as the discipline to hold those positions until a reversal of trend was signalled. With more confidence, you can learn to overcome the stress that comes from not only holding a losing position but also a big winner.

EDUCATION: THE WAY TO SUCCESS IN THE FUTURES MARKETS

DON SARNO

■

DON SARNO

Don Sarno graduated from Northwestern University, Evanston, Illinois, with a degree in Radio-TV Broadcasting. He also taught courses in broadcasting at Northwestern. Following a three year stint at the University of Missouri Medical School in Columbia, Missouri, Mr. Sarno began his business career in 1967 as an account executive for Merrill Lynch. As a senior account executive, he was actively involved in the firm and raised considerable equity for managed accounts. In 1975, he joined Dean Witter as associate Vice-President, and then joined Clayton Brokerage Company of St. Louis as national director of advertising. He developed all of Clayton's advertising and marketing literature, as well as being extensively involved in all aspects of seminar development and presentation.

In 1977, Mr. Sarno was among six instructors who started a commodities school known as Commodities Educational Institute. In 1980, he bacame Executive Director of CEI, a position he held until recently. He has conducted schools and seminars throughout the world and has trained thousands of new brokers and traders on how to use futures markets. He also developed specialized training programs for major brokerage firms and financial institutions. Mr. Sarno stepped down as head of CEI in January 1989, but continues to be an instructor at their schools.

Mr. Sarno pioneered a syndicated radio program, called "The Gary Wilhelmi Show," which is the largest futures market program in the U.S. Originating live from the exchange floors in Chicago, it is currently heard on 625 radio stations, in 24 states, each market day.

He has appeared frequently on financial radio and TV talk shows and is a regular participant on Financial News Network (FNN).

Using his marketing and seminar skills, he serves as Coordinator of Futures Symposium International (FSI), which holds major futures seminars throughout the U.S.

■ CHAPTER FIVE ■

I N JAPAN, THE HIGH-SPEED SHINKANSEN races into the station at more than 50 miles per hour. Waiting passengers stand a mere two feet from the edge of the platform. Yet, in the history of these bullet trains, not one person has ever fallen—though many have jumped—to his or her death.

The confidence and sure-footedness that come from experience seem to have saved the lives of millions of Japanese. Compare that to the tens of thousands of players worldwide who plunge into futures markets each year, only to meet certain disaster. Fortunately, most leave the futures arena able to continue in their prevailing lifestyle. Too many others, however, are not so fortunate.

Having been on virtually every side of the futures market these twenty years—as broker, speculator (both winning and losing), brokerage firm officer, and, ultimately, futures market educator—I find it particularly dismaying that the losing players keep making the same mistakes. The game has changed, but the faces haven't.

Many players are currently entering the futures game from the equities side for the first time—perhaps because they were so badly and quickly burned during the October 1987 chapter and now need to play "catch-up" in the futures. The number of casualties is increasing at a staggering rate. What possibly can be the new player's incentive to trade futures when the odds against success, like a stuck stochastic indicator, remain at nine to one?

It's possible that hungry brokers have contributed to the massacre by not conditioning their new traders to the feasibility of positioning within the strict constraints of a game plan. But if the broker isn't going to educate the new trader about the perils of venturing aimlessly into the pits, who will?

Should the NFA, for instance, require a "futures literacy test" of all new players? Hardly likely. Should the brokerage firm go the extra mile to tell all new clients on their new account forms, "Congratulations. . . you're about to join a very privileged club. As many as 90 percent of your fellow members with this firm are likely to lose most, if not all, of their trading capital in the futures markets."

Among brokerage firms, the discounter (by definition) ought to be serving those who shouldn't lose. After all, these are the players who don't want to pay $75 and up for the privilege of talking with a real, live broker instead of an order desk clerk. These are the players who are paying $400 each year for a chart service or $6,000 each year for an on-line quote service that guarantees they will see every single price change in their favorite markets. If they're called away, their computers will assure that their indicators will be poised to generate a new buy or sell signal when they return. Unfortunately, however, discount brokerage firms, which were virtually nonexistent a mere decade ago, now take orders also from those who have been turned away by full-service firms primarily because they weren't big enough accounts or because they couldn't justify paying the high commissions.

In some respects, the large wire houses are the smart guys in the futures brokerage game. They've conceded that area of commission business that contains the most market fatalities—the small speculator. As a result, the contingency of brokers out there who will help the neophyte through initial futures shock is dwindling.

On the other hand, the number of new firms that will help anyone and everyone to cash-in on the greatest moves in the history of the sugar or silver or soybean markets has skyrocketed. In 20 years as a participant in this business, I've never witnessed such a proliferation of new brokerage firms as I'm finding today in the various financial media. Through slick TV spots and "brochuresmanship," these firms, with their questionable sales tactics and even more dubious credentials, are taking millions of dollars from customers each month.

So, how do you learn right from wrong? How does someone who is generally excited about the opportunities offered by futures markets obtain the right tools, develop the proper discipline, and find the right match in the brokerage world to help him or her minimize the consequences of what will likely be a painful plunge?

Read Before You Plunge. . .

The first step to knowledge is to know that we are ignorant.
LORD DAVID CECIL

The futures industry can be a cruel temptress. After all, it looks so easy. We read about the fortunes that have been made with $5,000 of borrowed money. We hear about how easy it was to triple or quadruple your money in the big run-up in grains during May and June, 1988. What about the bull sugar market of 1987–88? If we had only bought a couple of call options back when. . . .

Most people seem to hear about futures trading through avenues that encourage that kind of dreaming: cocktail party conversations, sensational newspaper stories, someone bragging at the office. As a consequence, most individuals who approach futures trading do so with a false sense of confidence that leaves them vulnerable to failure and unprepared for the inevitable losses they will suffer. It is precisely this kind of ignorance that feeds millions of dollars into the futures market every year, there to be scooped up by those who understand the game and who have prepared themselves both emotionally and cognitively to play the game rationally and thoughtfully.

The futures game is not a game for dreamers—it is a business for realists. And a realist won't throw $5,000–$10,000–$15,000 or more at a business about which he or she has little more knowledge than rocket science or macroeconomics. The realist will recognize futures trading for what it is—a high-stakes venture that, with adequate study and preparation, can and does produce handsome profits consistently for the relative handful of traders equipped to make it work for them.

For anyone with a serious interest in becoming erudite regarding futures trading, a wealth of information is available. Much of it is very expensive, but a great deal of excellent, instructive material can be gotten at little or no expense.

The Exchanges

The first place to look for excellent information is the education division of each of the major exchanges. Here you will find information ranging from the most basic orientation to very sophisticated instruction. Most of the exchange publications are informative in nature, but provide little in the way of trading strategy. Nevertheless, as a source for developing a basic understanding of futures trading, none is better.

As an example, the Chicago Mercantile Exchange publishes a range of booklets and brochures designed to facilitate usable access to the exchange. A recent survey of titles available for the asking revealed the following.

The Merc at Work: A Guide to the Chicago Mercantile Exchange. This illustrated 20-page booklet is a quick introduction designed to enhance one's first view of the exchange from the visitor's gallery. As a quick synopsis of why and how people trade futures, it can be an invaluable aid to explaining to a spouse or members of the family just what you are doing when you sell a contract of oats that you don't own.

CME Traders Scorecard. This can be an excellent tool for tracking your performance as a trader. Set up as a blank form with instructions for its use, this straight-forward scorecard forces you to look at your trading performance with an objective eye, noting the losses as well as the wins and paying attention to patterns of behavior that may be leading to poor results (Figure 5-1).

A World Marketplace. Written in a style that is naturally somewhat self-serving, this 32-page illustrated publication is designed to publicize the role of the CME in the world marketplace, from agriculturals to financials and cur-

Figure 5-1 From "CME Trader's Scorecard"

TRADER'S SCORECARD

*O — to indicate a trade to open a position
L — to indicate a trade to liquidate a position

	BOUGHT						SOLD					POINTS MOVED (SALES MINUS PURCHASE)	LOSS	PROFIT
DATE	COMMODITY	MONTH	PRICE	QTY.	*	DATE	COMMODITY	MONTH	PRICE	QTY.	*			
9/6/8X	LIVE CATTLE	OCT.	57.05	1	O	9/26/8X	LIVE CATTLE	OCT.	60.85	1	L	+ 380		$1520
9/20/8X	T-BILLS	DEC.	90.83	2	L	9/12/8X	T-BILLS	DEC.	90.67	2	O	− 16	$800	
9/21/8X	S+P 500	DEC.	171.90	2	O	10/6/8X	S+P 500	DEC.	171.35	2	L	− 55	$550	
10/7/8X	DEUTSCHE MARK	DEC.	.3379	1	L	9/21/8X	DEUTSCHE MARK	DEC.	.3526	1	O	+ 147		$1837.50
10/7/8X	S+P 500 175-CALL	DEC.	2.35	1	O	10/10/8X	S+P 500 175-CALL	DEC.	2.95	1	L	+ 60		$300
10/25/8X	PORK BELLIES	FEB.	74.00	1	L	10/10/8X	PORK BELLIES	FEB.	71.50	1	O	− 250	$950	
10/15/8X	EURODOLLAR 90.50 PUT	DEC.	0.78	2	O	11/10/8X	EURODOLLAR 90.50 PUT	DEC.	1.16	2	L	+ 38		$950
11/1/8X	LIVE CATTLE 64 CALL	DEC.	0.92	2	O	11/20/8X	LIVE CATTLE 64 CALL	DEC.	0.41	2	L	− 51	$204	

rencies. Though limited in scope, it nevertheless is a quick introduction to the world of futures trading.

In Introductory Hedge Guide to Random Length Lumber Futures. A Self-Study Guide for Hedging with Livestock Futures. Want to really understand hedging? These are excellent source books.

Agricultural Options: The 10 Most Frequently Asked Questions. Options on Currency Futures: A Strategy Guide. Do you know what a call-ratio backspread is? A short butterfly? A long strangle? Better read these publications (Figure 5-2.)

Also available are individual brochures outlining the specifications for each of the contracts traded on the exchange. These are more complete than the usual tables that summarize contract specifications for a large number of commodities. (Figure 5-3.)

Advisory Newsletters

With hundreds of newsletters competing to provide the best advisory information for traders, there is no dearth of information and advice from this sector. It should be possible to find one or more that match your trading style and goals. Although the cost of advisory newsletters can be very high, most offer low-priced introductory subscriptions that make it feasible to shop around. As you read various advisories, however, note the following characteristics and beware of advice that might sound good but is relatively worthless.

Specificity. How specific are the recommendations? It really does not require a lot of market know-how to draw a few trendlines, note some support and resistance areas, and write some vague advisories that sound like this:

> We see a strong tendency for silver to break out of the present $7.00 to $7.50 range sometime in the next 2 months. When that happens, look for it to go as high as $9.00 before Christmas. Buy in the $7.60 to $7.70 range. If prices fall below $7.00, then look for a continued slide to as low as $6.30 before recovery.

Advice like this is available nearly everywhere in the industry, and can be worse than useless: it can be harmful. If provides only a vague 10¢ price range for going long. It offers no specific point to exit the trade—no specific stop-loss parameters. And worst of all, it carries with it a major hedge. If prices don't go up, they will likely go down, and this advisor will be able to say he or she called the move whichever way it goes.

Figure 5-2   From "Options on Currency Futures: A Strategy Guide"

Synthetic Long Put

Description: The construction of a position which includes a short futures position and a long call. This combination establishes a price at which the futures can be liquidated should the futures price rise. This is equivalent to being long a put option.

Characteristics: Unlimited downside profit potential, with pre-determined upside risk. The objective is to limit the risk of a futures price rise. The risk in this strategy develops in two ways. First, if the futures price remains stable, the extrinsic value of the call erodes. Second, if the futures rises, when using an out-of-the-money call, the position loses the difference between the original futures price and the call strike price, plus the premium paid, as a maximum. When an in-the-money call is used, only the extrinsic value is at risk. At expiration, the break-even is the original futures price less the premium paid for the call.

Determinants of Theoretical Option Value When Trade Is Initiated:

- Underlying British Pound
  Futures Price $1.2805
- Volatility   14.20%
- Interest Rate   9.85%
- Days to Option Expiration   121

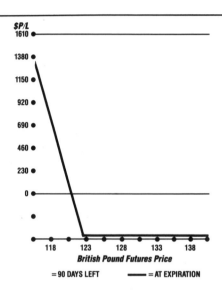

British Pound Futures Price

= 90 DAYS LEFT   ——— = AT EXPIRATION

	per contract		
Position	Point Price	Dollar Premium	Delta
Sell 1 futures	1.2805	—	−1.00
Buy 1 1.2250 call	730	$1825	+ .71
Position Net Debit	730	$1825	
Position Net Delta			− .29

Maximum Risk:	175 points or $437.50
Maximum Return:	unlimited on downside
Break-even futures price:	1.2075

24

25

Figure 5-3   From Livestock Futures and Options

Ticker Symbols	Calls CK; Puts PK	Calls CH; Puts PH
Trading Unit	One Live Cattle futures contract (covering 40,000 lbs.) of the specified contract month.	One Live Hog futures contract (covering 30,000 lbs.) of the specified contract month.
Strike Prices	Numbers in two cent intervals, e.g., 60¢, 62¢, 64¢, etc. When a new contract month is listed for trading there will be seven put and call strike prices: the nearest whole cent to the underlying futures price that is divisible by 2, the next three higher, and the next three lower. A new strike price will be listed for both puts and calls when the underlying futures price touches the third highest (or third lowest) listed strike prices. (No new options will be listed, however, with less than 10 trading days until expiration.)	
Premium Quotations	Quotations are cents per pound. A quote of $.0075 represents an option price of $300 (.0075 × 40,000 lbs.)	Quotations are cents per pound. A quote of $.0075 represents an option price of $225 (.0075 × 30,000 lbs.)
Months Traded	Feb., Apr., Jun., Aug., Oct., Dec.	Feb., Apr., Jun., Jul., Aug., Oct., Dec.
Minimum Price Fluctuations	$.00025 per pound ($10.00)	$.00025 per pound ($7.50)
Daily Price Limit	None	None
Trading Hours	9:05 a.m. to 1:00 p.m.	9:10 a.m. to 1:00 p.m.
Last Day of Trading	Option trading shall terminate on the last Friday that is more than three business days prior to the first business day of the delivery month of the underlying futures contract. If that Friday is not a business day, then trading shall terminate on the immediately preceding business day.	
Minimum Margin	No margin required for put or call option buyers, but the full premium must be paid in cash.[1]	
Exercise Procedure	Option buyers may exercise on any trading day.[1] Exercise results in a long LC or LH futures position for a call buyer or a put seller, and a short position for a put buyer or a call seller. The futures position is effective on the trading day immediately following exercise, and is marked-to-market to the settlement that day. If the futures position is not offset prior to the expiration of trading in the LC or LH futures contract, delivery of physical Live Cattle or Live Hogs will result or be required.	
Expiration	Options expire at 5:00 p.m. on the last trading day.[1] There is no automatic exercise of the expiring in-the-money LC or LH options by the CME clearing house.	

Ticker Symbol	LC	LH
Trading Unit[2]	40,000 lbs. choice grade live steers	30,000 lbs. USDA No. 1, 2, 3 barrows and gilts
Price Quote Means	$ per hundred pounds (or cents/pound)	$ per hundred pounds (or cents/pound)
Minimum Fluctuation	.025 = $10.00 (2.5¢/hundred pounds or .025¢/pound)	.025 = $7.50 (2.5¢/hundred pounds or .025¢/pound)
Maximum Daily Fluctuation From Prior Day's Close	1.50 = $600.00 ($1.50/hundred pounds or 1.5¢/pound)	1.50 = $450.00 ($1.50/hundred pounds or 1.5¢/pound)
Contract Months	Feb., Apr., Jun., Aug., Oct., Dec.	Feb., Apr., Jun., Jul., Aug., Oct., Dec.
Trading Hours (Chicago Time)	9:05 a.m. - 1:00 p.m.	9:10 a.m. - 1:00 p.m.
Last Day Hours	9:05 a.m. - 12:00 p.m.	9:10 a.m. - 12:00 p.m.
Last Day of Trading	20th of the contract month, (or prior business day if 20th is not a business day)[3]	20th of the contract month, (or prior business day if 20th is not a business day)[3]
Delivery Days[4]	Any business day of the contract month, except the day preceding a holiday	Any business day of the contract month, except Fridays or the day preceding a holiday

1. Consult your brokerage firm for additional information or specific requirements, policies and procedures.
2. Consult the CME rules for a more detailed definition of quality and par delivery.
3. If two or fewer delivery days follow the 20th, then the last day of trading will be two business days prior to the 20th calendar day.
4. Note that long positions outstanding during the contract delivery month may be assigned to take delivery.

Chicago Mercantile Exchange
30 S. Wacker Drive
Chicago, Illinois 60606
312/930-1000

Chicago Mercantile Exchange
27 Throgmorton Street
London, EC2N 2AN England
01/920-0722

Chicago Mercantile Exchange
67 Wall Street
New York, New York 10005
212/363-7000

Chicago Mercantile Exchange
2000 Pennsylvania Avenue N.W.
Suite 6200
Washington, D.C. 20006
202/223-6965

OA04/20M/287

Reprinted with permission of the Chicago Mercantile Exchange

A more helpful advisory will tell you:

Sell July 1988 Gold (CMX) on Tuesday, March 8, 1988 market on close. Buy July 1988 Gold (CMX) on Monday, March 14, 1988, market on close. Stop-loss: buy July 1988 Gold (CMX) stop close only at the March 8, 1988, settlement price plus $15.00.

The trade might be dead wrong, but the advisor has taken a specific stance that, along with his or her past recommendations, can be tracked and evaluated for long-term effectiveness.

Unfounded Hype. It is very likely that a year or so after writing the advice about silver from our first example, the advisor of the vague prophecies might well send a direct-mail circular announcing in bold script:

In 1988, we correctly predicted all ten of the major market occurrences. Prediction #1: Silver will fall to $6.30! In my May, 1988 advisory I predicted that silver could go as low as $6.30. Those who heeded my warning and got out of silver when it was trading at $7.50 saved a bundle. Anyone who sold short at $7.50 reaped a profit of $6,000 per contract!

Obviously, all claims made by an advisor must be checked out and, even if correct, must be compared with the overall performance of the advisory service.

Money Management. How much capital is required to trade the recommendations from the advisory with relative safety? What risk management parameters are established? Do these parameters fit comfortably with your particular trading style and capitalization limitations?

Practicality. If the advisory produces trading recommendations that require a close watch on market conditions during the day and your job requires most of your attention throughout the day, that particular advisory is impractical for your use. If your source of market quotes is your broker or the evening paper, better stay away from day-trading advisories.

Performance. It could be argued that performance is the only characteristic of an advisory that truly matters. If you find a high-performance advisory newsletter that sports a well-documented history of high profitability, why not adjust your life-style to the newsletter, put up all the money you can raise, and simply watch the profits roll in? Who needs a job that requires all your attention if you can get rich by following someone's advice in the markets?

As with all situations that sound too good to be true, this scenario is, unfortunately, also too good to be true and, therefore, highly unlikely. The reason is that past performance of an advisory is not a good predictor of future profitability. There are reasons for this. The major factor that contributes to low correlation between past performance and future performance is that all trading advisors, no matter how conservative, tend to have streaks. Woe to the trader who, because a newsletter has racked up mind-boggling profits for the past 18 months, jumps in with all his or her Christmas savings only to encounter a 3-month string of losses and consequently a lean Christmas season. So what if the advisory returns to profitable trades in the fourth month? Both the savings and the forbearance of the trader's family have been wiped out.

At the 1980 and 1981 mid-year seminars sponsored by *Managed Account Reports*, Polly Shouse presented the results of her study of managed futures accounts with the following conclusions:

How much or how little can past performance tell you?

1. A trading system always works over the period it was designed on.
2. A robust system works over subsequent periods.
3. The longer the system works, the more confidence one might have.
4. Past performance may have some connection with the future but is not reliable.[1]

In giving her reasons, Shouse asserted: "Impressive paper portfolios are intended to give you confidence in a system (every advisor has one)...Human nature is to expect that a good system will continue to be a good one...(however) the market picks the commodity manager just as often as the manager picks the market." Her final conclusion was that "the relationship between past and future results is weak at best, non-existent at worst."

Usefulness. If you can't have confidence in the past performance of advisory newsletters, then what good are they? The contention of this chapter is that education is the key to success in futures markets, and newsletters can be very educational. As you study the various publications, you will find the ones that are most useful to your trading circumstances, and you will synthesize the information and advice found there into your own unique approach to the market. You will learn not to follow blindly only one advisory. You will learn that diversification of advisories is just as important as is diversification in the markets.

Brokerage Firm Market Commentaries

Though less specific than most advisory newsletters, the commentaries produced by the various brokerage firms can be an invaluable part of your education as a trader. In many cases backed by highly sophisticated communications equipment and computer programs, the research information produced by the better brokerage houses will provide a "feel" for the market that can play a major role alongside your technical analysis in producing trading decisions.

Much of the commentary produced by brokerage houses is fundamental information that, contrary to the opinions of many technicians, should not be discounted and, in fact, can provide a valuable complement to mechanical trading programs. I would urge anyone serious about trading futures to get on the mailing list of as many brokers as possible. Although there is the risk of being inundated with too much information, some systematic cataloguing of the publications should allow a good synthesis of the material. Remember, the goal is not necessarily to obtain specific trading signals or recommendations, but rather to nurture a "feel" for the market.

To illustrate the importance of this intangible and elusive market sense, I offer the writings of Roy W. Longstreet in his classic *Viewpoints of a Commodity Trader* (New York: Frederick Fell Publications, 1967).

> If you had your choice between $1,000,000 and "the touch," which would it be? For many, probably for most, it would be the million. For me, it would be the touch. With it comes the ability to make that million and more in addition to having fun doing it.
>
> What is this touch? Call it what you will—a knack, a feel for what you're doing, an awareness. We sense its presence in many different activities, as well as in commodity trading.
>
> . . .So this touch is valuable. But what is it, really? To define it precisely would be difficult, and perhaps impossible. But I think I know what a man has when he has it. He has an extra portion of awareness, of sincerity, of comprehension of the world around him. He has foresight, as well as knowledge of past markets. . . .

This kind of touch can be developed, and, once acquired, can be worn as comfortably as an old pair of jeans or a favorite pair of shoes. The acquisition, however, is not easy; it requires a commitment to researching, studying and reading. And brokerage firms' commentaries can contribute significantly to that effort. Sample copies are always free for the asking.

Some of the better commentaries come from these firms:

A. G. Edwards & Sons
One North Jefferson
St. Louis, MO. 63103

Paine Webber
1285 Avenue of the Americas
New York, N. Y. 10271

Prudential-Bache Securities
100 Gold Street
New York, N. Y. 10038

Shearson Lehman Hutton
American Express Tower
New York, N.Y. 10048

Stotler & Company
141 West Jackson
Chicago, IL. 60604

Smith Barney, Harris Upham & Co., Inc.
333 West 34th Street
New York, N.Y. 10001

Chart Services

A great deal of "the touch" can be developed by a religious commitment to charting the markets. Subscribe to at least one chart service and update the charts daily. As patterns develop, learn to recognize them. Practice making predictions based on chart analysis. Do some paper trading and record your results. Coordinate your chart work with the advisory newsletters and brokers' commentaries you are receiving. Check your judgment against theirs. Most important, learn to recognize trend lines.

This kind of practice can be invaluable to the novice and the seasoned trader alike. There's nothing quite like the actual activity of marking price bars on a chart and drawing trendlines with a straight-edge and pencil to involve an individual in the markets on a basic level.

It is rather like the farmer who, after plowing all day in his air-conditioned diesel tractor, listening to his state-of-the-art stereo radio in the cab high over the long furrows, needs to climb down and touch the earth with his fingers, crumbling a few clods into loose dirt and smelling the freshly turned fragrance. Or again, perhaps an analogy can be drawn between the trader and the basketball star. Day after day, the basketball player practices the fundamentals of dribbling, passing, shooting so that he or she is able to thrill the crowd on game night. That is what charting is all about: practicing fundamentals, getting back to basics.

Recommended Chart Services. Here are some excellent chart services I would recommend. Some are more expensive than others. Some offer added attractions. Most have special trial subscriptions. Some have breakouts for those who only want the financial charts versus those who want agricultural only.

Commodity Price Charts
219 Parkade
Cedar Falls, IA 50613

Commodity Perspective
Suite 1820
30 S. Wacker
Chicago, IL 60606

Commodity Trend Service
1224 U.S. Highway #1
Old Port Cove Plaza
North Palm Beach, FL 33408

Order some samples of each and choose the one that best serves your needs.

Schools and Seminars

There is no substitute for learning from the masters. Once the basics have been covered through copious reading and disciplined practice, live instruction and the chance to engage in face-to-face dialogue with experts in the industry can hone emerging skills and provide specific strategies and systems for trading the markets.

There is no dearth of instruction available. In fact, the growth of the seminar industry seems to be accelerating in response to an expanding demand for such pedagogy. One need not search far to discover a wealth of seminars, symposia, classes, and schools. For the rawest of recruits to the most sophisticated trading veterans, instructional programs are available to teach new skills and fine-tune others.

Many such programs are publicized in *Futures* magazine each month. The exchanges offer courses and seminars through their educational departments and they publicize others. A majority of the publishers of advisory newsletters also offer periodic seminars, at which they teach their particular specialty—be it Gann's lines, Elliott's waves, Kondratieff's cycles, Steidlemayer's logic, or Mrs. Wilson's astrology and ESP. Here, too, the problem is not so much where to find instruction as how to sift through the available selection to find the best and the most helpful.

Price alone is not a valid indicator of value, in spite of the axiom, "you get what you pay for." One helpful technique is to talk with other traders about the skills they may have picked up at a seminar or two. Find out how well the skills paid off in real trading. Some seminars offer "real-time trading" during the final day, so you can watch the system applied to developing market conditions rather than carefully chosen charts of past market conditions. Other characteristics to watch for are specificity, hype, track record, practicality and usefulness. Usually, the advisors with the best advisory letters for your purposes can be counted on for the best seminars.

Commodities Educational Institute offers an intensive one-week course ten times each year in all major cities across the country. By bringing together a faculty of experts in each phase of futures and options, these schools offer valuable instruction and a comprehensive overview of the entire industry that can be valuable to novice and veteran alike.

Futures Symposium International (FSI) brings together many of the best trading advisors several times each year to share specific strategies and techniques that work for them. At their larger meetings, FSI offers a veritable smorgasbord of systems and trading styles to choose from.

The Electronic Age

Financial news wires offer a wealth of information or commentary that will amaze you. Particularly comprehensive and noteworthy are Reuters and the Dow Jones news services. However, if you want to weed out the unnecessary stories, two newswires are devoted exclusively to commodity news. Futures World News (FWN), 219 Parkade, Cedar Falls, IA 50613, is available directly via satellite and can interface with a personal computer. I particularly like this service because the headlines are coded so that if, for example, you only want commentary on the sugar or cocoa markets, you can eliminate all other stories from printing-out. The computer can also store the stories for later retrieval. A similar, but more costly, service is Commodity News Service (CNS) of Kansas City.

The higher priced quotation systems are a topic, in themselves, for an article. In general, you can spend a few hundred dollars each month to more than a thousand, depending on the services and computerized studies you want. One inexpensive service new in 1988 is Global Link, a satellite package available from Oster Communications, 219 Parkade, Cedar Falls, IA 50613. It includes news, quotes, and charts on active markets.

I can't recommend Financial News Network (FNN) highly enough. In spite of an excellent mix of programming, however, beware of the "paid propaganda" programming that may have the appearance of a bona-fide interview with a leading market expert, while actually consisting of nothing more than a commercial endorsement of a certain trader or system.

From droughts to monsoons, wars to peace demonstrations, fundamentals to technicals, international market conditions to third world buying habits—whatever moves the markets will be covered by one of the electronic media. Again, the problem will be sifting for the nuggets among the torrents of information, for there is no dearth of available news and commentary.

Trading Advisors, Commodity Funds and Pools

With so many to choose from, how can an educated choice be made? Because we live in an information age, wherever a need for news, advice, orientation, enlightenment, or instruction exists it seems some resourceful entrepreneur rushes to fill the gap. Thus, there are newsletters that rate the advisors and follow the performance of the funds and pools. If you want to know the percentage of profitable trades an advisor recommends, the size of the drawdown you might expect, the average profit per trade, the capitalization necessary to follow the advisory, and other such salient information, subscribe to the *Commodity Traders Consumer Report*, which follows many major advisors trade by trade and publishes the results. *Managed Account Reports* provides a similar service for commodity pools and funds. *Futures Truth* and club *3000* are other excellent publications that help you sort out the valid services from the trash and quick-buck artists.

Understand the Obstacles and the Odds

In the world of gambling, the best players understand that by shifting the odds only a bit a gambler can win significantly more often. The casinos know this and consequently establish rules and limits that reduce the individual's opportunity to shift the odds.

In futures trading, however, the opportunity does exist to shift the odds dramatically, which is what distinguishes futures trading from gambling.

Know that, rather than finding instant wealth, most traders wind up losing their entire grubstake. Only the most prepared and the most professional will consistently be profitable. Along with the recommended reading and the seminars, arm yourself for your foray into the futures wars with as much personal contact as possible with other traders and prospective brokers. Your relationship with your broker will be an important element in your success or failure as a trader. Learn what to look for in a broker. Spend some time asking questions about their services, their styles, their track record. Ask to see their personal trading records. Finally, check with the National Futures Association to find out what complaints might be pending against the firm.

Understand Yourself

To be at peace with self, to find company and nourishment in self, this would be the test of the free and productive psyche.

MARYA MANNES

A good education does not in itself guarantee success in the markets. A lack of self-discipline can sabotage the best trading system while a disciplined trader can often win with a less-than-perfect system. Don't just assume you have the discipline to be a good trader. Assess your potential and learn how many ways you can go wrong.

First, you must read *The Investor's Quotient* and *Beyond the Investor's Quotient* by Jake Bernstein. These are must reading. Jake, himself a psychologist and a trader, will map out for you where the behavioral and attitudinal traps lie. Injecting a liberal dose of Freud and modern behavioral psychology, he forces you to spend time in self-reflection and self-diagnosis. You will find that a thoughtful, contemplative reading of these two books will improve not only your trading but your personal psyche as well.

Next, read the chapter "School for Losers" in *The Commodity Futures Game: Who Wins, Who Loses, and Why* by Teweles, Harlow, and Stone. Buy the paperback edition for $7.95. This chapter alone is worth the price of the book.

Jeff Elliott of *The Elliott Report*, Dallas, Texas has long recognized that most people lose in the markets because of their own disposition and failure to recognize how and when to admit they are wrong. Consequently, he has developed the "Speculator Profile" to help traders assess their self-discipline as well as their potential to be successful speculators. This simple test has demonstrated an amazing correlation with one's ability to trade the markets successfully. If you are serious about trading, you should take this self–assessment.

A Business or a Gamble

Day after day, week after week, year after year, thousands of airplanes and buses converge on a small town in the middle of the Nevada desert, carrying millions of people to this glittering, though climatically inhospitable, spot in an otherwise barren and desolate land. They come not only willingly but eagerly, with dreams of the riches to be made on the gaming tables and in the slot machines of the casinos in Las Vegas.

Likewise, when the commodity markets make the front pages of the newspapers—as they did during the spring and summer of 1988, when grain prices reacted so dramatically to the drought that consumed so many billions of bushels of corn and soybeans—the phones in brokerage offices across the country ring almost nonstop with the calls of otherwise rational people who want to throw money into the pits and chase the quick bucks to be made there.

To the objective observer, it is very difficult to distinguish between these two groups of eager dreamers. Both are searching for the hot streak, and many will find it and make profits enough to fill many a later barroom conversation with tales of their exploits and masterful judgment.

Unfortunately but inevitably, almost every penny made on these hot streaks will return to the tables, the slots or the pits, probably taking other money with it. Very few dreamers can recognize when a streak has ended. Very few realize that it will.

For many astute speculators, however (and their numbers are growing every year), the commodity futures business is as far removed from gambling as Las Vegas is from Des Moines, Iowa. Because you are reading this chapter you number among this elite group. My final word to you is to keep studying, keep learning and keep expanding your horizon. As you follow my suggestions, you will encounter many educational opportunities that have not been covered in this brief chapter. Assess their value and then, if they have worth, give them your attention. But as you pursue your education, keep in mind the words of Tryon Edwards:

The great end of education is, to discipline rather than to furnish the mind; to train it to the use of its own powers, rather than fill it with the accumulation of others.

Endnotes

[1]Baratz, Morton S., *The Investor's Guide to Futures Money Management* (Columbia, Maryland: Futures Publishing Group, 1984) , p. 39.

PRESERVE THE FREEDOM TO TRADE: CONSERVE CAPITAL

KENNETH UPSHAW, Ed. D.

■

■

KEN UPSHAW, Ed. D.

After a successful 20-year career as an educator and school administrator, Ken Upshaw has recently become a full-time participant in the futures business. Nationally known in educational circles for his innovative ideas and numerous accomplishments, Ken has now applied his considerable analytical and creative skills toward a study of the futures industry.

Ken is editor of the monthly publication *Futures Market Alert* and has contributed the research for two of Jake Bernstein's forthcoming books.

He completed his doctoral studies at Loyola University of Chicago.

■

■ CHAPTER SIX ■

MANY FUTURES TRADERS seem to approach trading in much the same way they would approach gambling or motorcycle jumping: they roll the dice, crank open the throttle, close their eyes and hope for the best. The results, as one might expect, often fall short of the expectations. In motorcycle jumping, that can be particularly disastrous.

The consequences of a haphazard venture into futures trading will not be physically quite as debilitating as motorcycle jumping but, nevertheless, can be a real emotional and financial bloodbath. But it doesn't have to be that way. In fact, futures trading can be a relatively low-risk business venture if approached with the right attitude and the right planning.

As with any of life's ventures, proper planning requires that one establish goals. With futures trading, the range of possible goals is quite broad, and each different set of goals will introduce specific implications regarding preparation and strategy. At one end of the continuum is the trader in it primarily for the excitement, the huge profit potential, and the bragging rights associated with making some spectacularly profitable trades. (Such bragging, however, rarely mentions the long string of strikeouts that preceded each home run trade).

At the other end of the continuum is the very conservative trader who screens every trade several different ways to ensure it will be profitable. Although this trader enjoys a very high percentage of winning trades, most of the big moves elude him or her, resulting in an overall record of relatively low profitablility.

Somewhere between these two extremes lies every active or potential futures trader, who must ask him or herself: what is my goal? Am I doing this for the excitement or for the profits—or both? Is this to be a business venture or a side-line lark? Am I seeking prowess through beating the market, or am I attempting simply to pull reasonable profits from the market? And what is a reasonable profit? 20 percent? 30 percent? 100 percent? 200 percent?

It is amazing how many traders jump into the market without ever considering any of these questions. Without hard answers to questions like these, however, every venture in futures trading is doomed to ultimate failure. Without a specific goal, it becomes impossible to establish a plan. And without a plan, one simply wanders aimlessly in and out of the market, buffeted by the seemingly incomprehensible patterns of price movement that occur.

Successful futures trading requires a businesslike approach, which translates into a carefully developed and thoroughly conceived business plan. A good business plan always includes short-term, intermediate-term, and long-term goals. It includes projections of growth as well as capitalization needs. It establishes reasonable reserves in the event of unanticipated adverse circumstances. A good business plan demonstrates keen knowledge of the business one is entering and a realistic appraisal of the risks, as well as a strategy for managing them.

At the core of any good business plan is a carefully devised strategy for money management. In futures trading, a good money management plan involves at least four different strategic components:

1. Risk management
2. Capitalization
3. Leverage
4. Diversification

This chapter will deal with each of these components separately, making every attempt to offer as much insight and useful information as possible. It is not our intention to teach one particular "best" strategy for money management, because each reader's goals and purposes will be unique and individual. From the suggestions offered, however, each reader should be able to develop a money-management plan that will best serve his or her unique style of trading.

There are those who, because of the association between futures trading and gambling, attempt to apply specific strategies of money management that have developed around casino gambling, particularly roulette and blackjack. Such strategies, based on probability theory, have proven to improve the chance for success in gambling. Unlike gambling, however, futures trading is not purely a chance occurence, and therefore the application of probabilities is not as likely to produce an expected outcome as in gambling. Nevertheless, some space will be devoted to discussion of strategies used in gambling that have some applicability to futures trading.

Risk Management

The primary component in a responsible money-management plan is risk control. To establish acceptable risk control, one must first choose an acceptable trading system. What constitutes "acceptable," of course, varies significantly with the individual trader. What may be acceptable to one will scare the pants off another.

Some traders will not even approach the futures market unless they stand to show at least 100 percent return on their money no matter what the risk. Others are content to go for 20 to 30 percent a year and keep the risk lower. The first decision each trader must make when choosing a system is an acceptable level of profitability versus risk exposure, knowing that greater rewards usually require greater risk. At this stage it is essential that a person be completely honest and candid regarding his or her expectations from the futures markets and his or her motivation for trading futures. With so many trading systems available, as well as software to develop personalized trading systems and to evaluate systems for risk, a trader who approaches the task with candor should be able to adopt a system compatible with his or her goals and personal nature.

Once an individual decides on an acceptable parameter of risk versus profits, three specific factors must be examined when looking at a trading system. The first is the *frequency of profitable trades*. Many of the best trading systems show only a 40 percent accuracy rate, although it is possible to approach a 60 or 70 percent rate of accuracy. The advantage to having a high percentage of profitable trades is primarily the psychological benefit of being positively rewarded for making a good trade. High accuracy does not necessarily translate into high profits. In fact, some of the most profitable systems show a relatively low accuracy rate.

The second factor to consider is the *relative size of profits versus losses.* In futures trading the goal is net profitability—that total profits will be larger than total losses. A string of 10 minor losses can be offset by one large gain, resulting in a net profit. Conversely, one large loss can offset 10 small gains, resulting in a net loss.

The third consideration when evaluating a trading system is the *number of buy/sell signals* that are given. It is not uncommon to find a system so conservative as to filter out most trades. Although the accuracy of such a system may be high and the size of profits relative to the size of losses excellent, if a system provides very few opportunities to trade, its overall profitablility will remain quite low.

Once a system has been chosen that shows an acceptable ratio of profits to risk, that provides an acceptable rate of accuracy, that establishes net profitability by limiting the size of losing trades in relation to winning trades, and that signals trades with sufficient frequency, the rest is in the trader's own hands. Some trading systems, of course, are so comprehensive in establishing risk/reward parameters that nothing more need be done— simply trade the system mechanically. For most systems, however, some judgment is called for on the part of the trader when putting on a trade. In such circumstances, specific guidelines must be followed to control risk as much as possible.

First, every trader must acknowledge that losing trades will occur. Quite often, losing trades occur more frequently than winning trades. In fact, when perusing the advisory services that are monitored by *Commodity Traders Consumer Report* (CTCR), one finds that the vast majority of advisory services show less than a 50 percent rate of accuracy. What this means is that each time a trader puts on a trade, he or she must be prepared to suffer a loss and know that the odds favor it. The trick lies in managing that loss—both fiscally and emotionally.

Emotionally, a trader must learn to see losses not as a defeat or as a mistake, but as a necessary cost of doing business—part of the overhead, so to speak. Fiscally, one must learn to limit the size of the loss to a manageable level. "Cut your losses and let your profits run" is the trader's maxim.

Two excellent ways to cut losses exist. Both require the trader to establish, before a trade is made, an acceptable level of risk and then liquidate when that point is reached. Some traders advocate making a decision based solely on money management considerations—the reward/risk ratio. When using a purely mechanical trading system, such mechanical risk control procedures are useful to assure a specific degree of financial risk. A trader simply determines a profit objective and then establishes a loss limit in relation to that objective. A common ratio is 3:1. If the system indicates a profit objective of $.09 in corn, then the loss limit would be established at $.03 (Figure 6-1). Each trader, of course, will determine the most comfortable ratio for his or her trading style.

Figure 6-1 Mechanical Stop-Loss Using 3:1 Reward/Risk Ratio

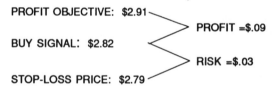

Other traders favor a loss limit based on logical relationships inherent in the trade itself. If a trade is based on seasonal tendencies, for example, a trader who places a high conviction trade might want to let the trade run its natural course without an artificial stop-loss, maintaining only a disaster stop in case of totally unexpected developments.

A mechanical system that indicates support and resistance levels provides another situation wherein logical relationships may establish risk parameters. If the trading system gives a buy signal in corn while corn is trading at $2.82, and trend line analysis indicates there will be resistance around $2.94 and support around $2.78, the reasonable point for a stop-loss would be just under $2.78 (Figure 6-2). The reward/risk ratio for the trade will be $.12: $.04 = 3:1, which is the same as the mechanical stop loss in the prior example. This time, however, the trader can be confident that the trade will not be as likely to be stopped out artificially and prematurely before it has a chance to work, which is a major drawback to using a purely mechanical stop-loss.

Figure 6-2   Logical Stop-Loss Using Support/Resistance Levels

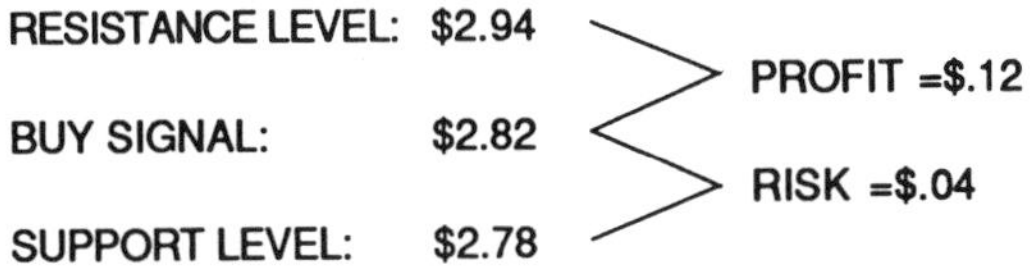

RESISTANCE LEVEL: $2.94

PROFIT =$.12

BUY SIGNAL: $2.82

RISK =$.04

SUPPORT LEVEL: $2.78

A system may give a sell signal in wheat, for instance, while wheat is trading at $3.26. The profit objective for the trade is established at $3.08. Arbitrarily, the stop-loss is established at $3.32, providing a 3:1 ratio of reward to risk (Figure 6-3). The trader ignores the fact there is resistance at $3.35. The trade is put on, and prices fluctuate a while before moving higher. They move to $3.35 1/4, pause a while, then fall all the way to $2.92. In this case, establishing an artificial risk level denied the trader a profitable trade. What if, on the other hand, prices had tested the $3.35 resistance level and broken out, going as high as $3.43? The trader would have congratulated him- or herself on a good job of risk control.

As this example so aptly illustrates, each strategy for establishing risk parameters has pluses and minuses. In choosing one or the other, however, a trader must do two things: be consistent with whatever strategy is chosen and always use a risk-control strategy.

The choice of whether to use a logical stop-loss or a mechanical stop-loss based solely on money management depends, of course, upon the individual trader's preference. In both cases, however, it is essential that the stop be placed concurrently with the trade. Many traders put on a trade knowing where they want to get out in order to limit their losses. Rather than placing a stop-loss at that point, however, they say to themselves, "I'll watch closely, and if prices get close to that point, I'll get out."

Two fallacies spoil that strategy. First, the market might move past the stop-loss point so quickly as to make it impossible to get out, resulting in larger losses than anticipated. Second (and probably even more potentially destructive) is human nature: it is very difficult to admit defeat, and therefore it is often difficult to "pull the plug" on a trade. And so when prices get close to the stop-loss point, a trader will tend to say, "O.K., let's watch it a little longer and see whether it turns around. Prices could still rally." The result is that the trader chases the trade, refusing to admit defeat until losses are so great that an inordinate number of winning trades is required to recoup.

As with every other aspect of futures trading, establishing limits on losses must be done in a rational, unimpassioned manner. Once done, no room exists for second-guessing or misguided hope.

Figure 6-3

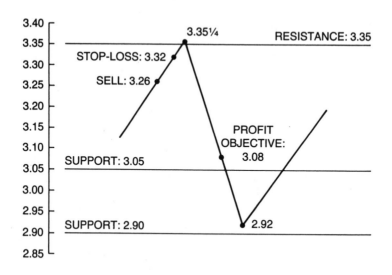

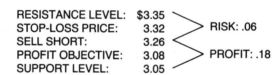

RESISTANCE LEVEL:	$3.35	
STOP-LOSS PRICE:	3.32	RISK: .06
SELL SHORT:	3.26	
PROFIT OBJECTIVE:	3.08	PROFIT: .18
SUPPORT LEVEL:	3.05	

Capitalization

All the risk management in the world will be useless in an undercapitalized account. The point has already been made that a majority of trades in a trading program will lose money. But what happens if the first five trades are losers? Even though all five losses are held to reasonable levels using the techniques discussed in the previous section, will there still be money in the account to place the sixth trade?

Almost no one begins trading expecting to lose. Most are disappointed if the first trade loses money. By the fifth losing trade in a row, however, even the most stoic trader may well be biting his or her lip a bit, wondering whether the system is malfunctioning and having doubts whether trading futures was such a good idea. At this point, most traders will be greatly disheartened. The trader who is prepared emotionally and fiscally, however, will still be ready to put on the sixth trade, while the undercapitalized trader will be forced out of the market. Because the undercapitalized trader did not expect to lose, the account was opened with the bare minimum necessary to begin trading, and after five losses, the trader has a choice: stop trading or put up more money.

A trader who has decided ahead of time to approach futures trading in a business-like manner will not be caught in such a dilemma. He or she will be prepared to withstand the inevitable losses that occur, realizing that staying power is an essential ingredient in any business plan or futures trading plan and that substantial reserves are necessary in the event of unexpected business losses.

The unrealistic trader who "saw something happening in the market" and opened a small account to grab the opportunity, or the trader who just knew he or she had the ultimate system—one that would give 90 percent accurate signals—and therefore wanted to start trading with bare minimum capital will, unfortunately, probably be forced at this juncture to retire prematurely from the trading—or commit some more trading capital.

What often separates the successful trader from the unsuccessful is the amount of financial reserves remaining in the trading account after a string of losing trades. For the business-like trader, a few simple rules regarding capital apply that, if followed religiously, will enhance the trader's overall plan. If violated, however, these rules will cause even the best trading system to fail.

Rule 1: As part of the original trading plan, before any trading occurs, establish the amount of capital to be risked. Then adhere firmly to that limit. The absolute minimum, nevertheless, should be $10,000.

To determine how much capital is a reasonable amount requires an examination of the trading plan as well as some simple homework. A review of the trading plan should establish these particulars: (1) how many markets are to be traded; (2) which markets specifically are to be traded; (3) how many markets at a time are likely to be traded; (4) how many contracts at a time are likely to be traded; and (5) whether trading will be intraday or overnight. Simple homework will determine the margin requirements for the markets to be traded. To establish minimum capitalization requirements, simply perform the numerical operations necessary to establish the following ratios:

1. The total amount of margin for all positions at any one time will be approximately 40 percent of the total capital in the account at that time.

2. Reserves in the account (unmargined capital) will be approximately 60 percent of the total capital in the account.

If the markets to be traded are quite volatile and subject to large swings, then a larger percentage of capital should be held in reserve. Conversely, if the plan is to trade less volatile markets, then a smaller proportion can be held in reserve. Similarly, if the trading system is subject to large drawdowns, the proportion of reserves to margin should be adjusted commensurately.

Rule 2: As the account balance changes, the 60/40 ratio between reserves and margin should be maintained. As the account balance increases, additional money can be allocated to margin—usually to trade more units at a time—but margin should never exceed 40 percent of the total account equity. Likewise, if the account decreases, the same ratio must be maintained—60/40—with the new account balance, not the original trading capital.

Rule 3: Don't meet margin calls. If a margin call is met, a trader is tacitly acknowledging that more trading capital was being held in reserve than was originally committed to the account. This is a violation of Rule 1. The established trading plan included a trading system with specific characteristics and a capitalization plan based on those characteristics. If more capital is infused to meet margin calls, no way exists to evaluate the original plan, and whatever happens next will be haphazard, undercapitalized, and not well planned. Such a circumstance, as has already been demonstrated, is subject to failure. Rather than meet a margin call, it is better to acknowledge that something was wrong with the original plan and take some time to restructure.

Rule 4: Maintain account reserves in T-bills. The inital Treasury bill must be $10,000, with additional bills in increments of $5,000. T-bills can be held as margin, so a trader need not worry that they will have to be cashed prematurely in the event that some losses occur in the account.

Undercapitalizing is probably the single most common reason why traders fail at futures trading. It is unfortunate, but most individuals simply do not want to admit that over half of the trades they put on will lose money, and therefore, they are very stubborn about how much money they want to commit to a trading account—never realizing that by undercapitalizing they significantly increase their risk.

An undercapitalized account does not allow for the development of a considered trading strategy. It provides only two avenues to a trader: either place one risky trade in an attempt to increase capital in the account (go for broke—which is, unfortunately, all too often the outcome) or place a series of trades with very low risk tolerance and small profit margins in an attempt to increase capital gradually. Here, too, the likelihood is that a series of losing trades will deplete the capital before the winning trades have a chance to work.

Leveraging

Leveraging is the characteristic that makes futures trading most attractive to speculators. If it weren't for the ability to trade futures contracts on a very small margin, futures trading would be no different than trading stocks or other similarly speculative vehicles. The very trait that is so appealing about futures trading, however, is also the trait that makes it so risky.

Many traders seem almost spellbound by the extreme profit potential avaliable through leveraging a futures contract and thus ignore the fact that it is not necessary to fully leverage a trading account. By accepting maximum leverage, however, such traders also assume maximum risk. Since this chapter is all about risk management, it will be helpful to demonstrate some alternatives to a fully leveraged account.

In the previous section on capitalization, the point was made that the initial capital in an account should include approximately a 60 percent reserve. This section demonstrates the efficacy of that strategy by analyzing various degrees of leverage in relation to profitability and risk.

Consider the case of an investor with $100,000 to invest in Treasury bonds. In looking for the optimum relationship between risk and return, he or she might consider a number of alternatives. The first alternative, of course, and the safest, is simply to purchase $100,000 worth of Treasury bonds. This option also offers the lowest return. The investor will receive an interest check every six months. If interest rates rise, the bond will decline in value; and if interest rates fall, the bond will increase in value. But the total potential change in value is a small percentage of the original investment. Conversely, there is no risk of losing the original investment.

An alternative is to use the futures market to purchase $100,000 contracts of Treasury bond futures. The question then is how many contracts to buy. The answer lies with the investor. How much risk is this investor willing to assume in proportion to the reward he or she hopes to gain? In other words, how much leverage is this investor willing to use?

If the investor chooses to buy two contracts of bonds, leverage would be 50 percent, and if bond prices moved five points, the profit or loss would double, from $5,000 to $10,000 (Table 6-1). With three contracts, leverage stands at 70 percent (30 percent capitalization) and profits or losses on a 5-point move are $15,000. Above 70 percent leveraging the profit/loss potential increases dramatically, as shown by the curve in Figure 6-4 on page 80.

Table 6-1 Leveraging $100,000 Trading Treasury Bonds

Leverage	Cost	Contracts	Profit/ Loss	% Profit/ Loss
0%	100,000	1	5,000	5
10%	90,000	1	5,000	5
20%	80,000	1	5,000	5
30%	70,000	1	5,000	5
40%	60,000	1	5,000	5
50%	50,000	2	10,000	10
60%	40,000	2	10,000	10
70%	30,000	3	15,000	15
80%	20,000	5	25,000	25
90%	10,000	10	50,000	50
95%	5,000	20	100,000	100
97.5%	2,500	40	200,000	200

If this investor maintains 60 percent reserves and 40 percent margin, there would be $40,000 available for capitalizing a purchase of bond contracts. At $2,500 margin, 16 contracts could be purchased, which would establish leverage for the entire $100,000 investment commitment at approximately 94 percent. A 5-point change in bond prices at this leverage rate would produce $80,000—or 80 percent—profit or loss (Table 6-2).

By contrast, if the entire $100,000 were placed on margin, 40 contracts could be purchased and a 5-point move would produce $200,000—or 200 percent profit or loss. The risk of ruin, however, has just been escalated to an untenable level, such that a move of 2 1/2 points against the investor would wipe out the entire account. With 16 contracts, it would require a 6 1/4-point move to wipe out the account. As with all investment decisions, risk must always be balanced against potential reward but, as this example illustrates, it is not necessary to fully margin a trading account to reap generous profit margins.

Table 6-2 Margining 40 Percent of $100,000 Account Trading Treasury Bonds

Total Committed	Margin	Contracts	Trading Capital	Total Value	% Leverage	% Profits On 5-Point Move
$40,000	$2,500	16	$100,000	$1,600,000	93.8%	80%

Table 6-3 looks at an account trading in three different markets from the perspective of leverage and its impact on potential for profit or loss. This table represents the total possible profits if all three markets perform as shown. If gold is bought at $350 per ounce and moves to $400 per ounce, the profit per contract would be $5,000 ($50 per ounce × 100 ounces). If corn was bought at $3.50 a bushel and moved to $4.00, the profit per contract would be $2,500 ($.50 × 5,000 bushels). Finally, if hogs were bought at $.50 per pound and moved to $.60, the profit on each contract would be $3,000 ($.10 × 30,000 pounds).

At 0 percent leverage, the value of one gold contract is $35,000 ($350 per ounce × 100 ounces); the value of one corn contract is $17,500 ($3.50 per bushel × 5,000 bushels); and the value of one hog contract is $15,000 ($.50 per pound × 30,000 pounds). In a $50,000 account, using no leverage, one contract of gold could be bought plus one contract of either hogs or corn. Because the hogs represent a greater profit potential they would be chosen. If the prices indeed moved as expected, the profit would be $8,000, representing a 16 percent gain on a $50,000 account. The gain remains constant until the 30 percent level, when it jumps to 21 percent. Even a very conservative trader would agree that the chances of losing the entire investment at a 70 percent capitalization rate would be very slim, so a trade at 30 percent leverage would be rather safe in exchange for the additional five percent potential in this example.

Each succeeding jump of 10 percent in the rate of leveraging represents an increase of five percent or six percent in potential profits or losses until the 70 percent level is reached, when the gains become increasingly larger—representing even higher potential for profit and for loss. At 95 percent leverage (five percent capitalization) a move in all three markets of the magnitude in this example would show a profit nearly triple the size of the original investment or a loss in which the original investment would be lost nearly four times over.

When the values from Tables 6-1 and 6-3 are plotted on a simple graph, they form a curve as in Figures 6-4 and 6-5. These two curves, very similar in form, represent the risk-reward relationship that exists with increasing leverage in any investment. Ordinarily, very little advantage or disadvantage results from leveraging an investment up to approximately 30 per-

Table 6-3 Leveraging $50,000 Trading Account in Three Markets

% Leverage	GOLD				CORN				HOGS				Total Utilized	Total Profit	% Profit
	Number Contracts	Cost	Utilized	Profit	Number Contracts	Cost	Utilized	Profit	Number Contracts	Cost	Utilized	Profit			
0	1	35,000	35,000	5,000	0	17,500	0	0	1	15,000	15,000	3,000	50,000	8,000	16
10	1	31,500	31,500	5,000	0	15,750	0	0	1	13,500	13,500	3,000	45,000	8,000	16
20	1	28,000	28,000	5,000	0	14,000	0	0	1	12,000	12,000	3,000	40,000	8,000	16
30	1	24,500	24,500	5,000	1	12,250	12,250	2,500	1	10,500	10,500	3,000	47,250	10,500	21
40	1	21,000	21,000	5,000	1	10,500	10,500	2,500	2	9,000	18,000	6,000	49,500	13,500	27
50	2	17,500	35,000	10,000	0	8,750	0	0	2	7,500	15,000	6,000	50,000	16,000	32
60	2	14,000	28,000	10,000	1	7,000	7,000	2,500	2	6,000	12,000	6,000	44,000	18,500	37
70	2	10,500	21,000	10,000	2	5,250	10,500	5,000	3	4,500	13,500	9,000	45,000	24,000	48
80	3	7,000	21,000	15,000	3	3,500	10,500	7,500	4	3,000	12,000	12,000	43,500	34,500	69
90	6	3,500	21,000	30,000	6	1,750	10,500	15,000	8	1,500	12,000	24,000	43,500	69,000	138
95	12	1,750	21,000	60,000	12	875	10,500	30,000	16	750	12,000	36,000	48,000	138,000	276

For Purposes of this illustration, the following prices were used:

Corn: Bought at $3.50 x 5,000 bushel = $17,500 per contract. Price moves to $4.00, profit per contract = $2,500
Hogs: Bought at $ .50 x 30,000 bushel = $15,000 per contract. Price moves to $ .60, profit per contract = $3,000
Gold: Bought at $350 x 100 ounces = $35,000 per contract. Price moves to $400, profit per contract = $5,000

cent. At that point, risk and reward begin to grow ever larger. Beyond 70 percent leveraging (30 percent capitalization) the risks and rewards grow exponentially.

A trader wishing to trade all three markets with a 40 percent margined account of $50,000 would have $20,000 available for initial margin. If the margin requirement for hogs is $500, for corn $500 and for gold $1,700, one possible mix of contracts would look like Table 6-4.

Table 6-4 $50,000 Account Trading Three Markets on 40 Percent Margin

Commodity	Margin	Number Contracts	Total Committed	Price	Value 1 Contract	Total Value
Gold	$1,700	5	$ 8,500	$350.00	$35,000	$175,000
Corn	500	10	5,000	3.50	17,500	175,000
Hogs	500	12	6,000	.50	15,000	180,000
			$19,500			$530,000

Total Contract Value	$530,000
Total Trading Account	$ 50,000
Leverage	90.6%

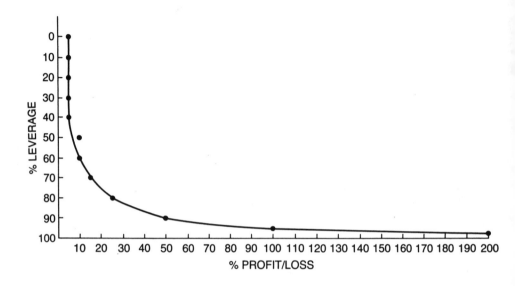

**Figure 6-4   Relationship Between Leverage and Profit or Loss
$100,000 Account Trading Treasury Bonds**

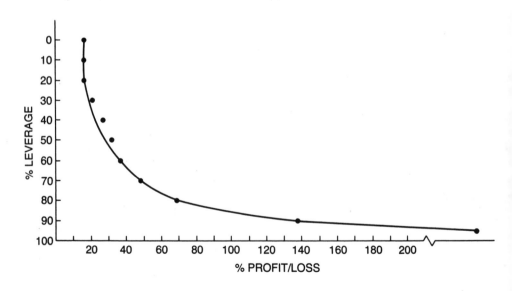

**Figure 6-5   Relationship Between Leverage and Profit or Loss
$50,000 Account Trading Three Markets**

Taking this position, a trader would be working at approximately 90.6 percent leverage, as compared to 96.4 percent leverage in a fully margined account, which might look like Table 6-5.

Table 6-5 $50,000 Account Trading Three Markets in 100 Percent Margin

Commodity	Margin	Number Contracts	Total Committed	Price	Value 1 Contract	Total Value
Gold	$1,700	12	$20,400	$350.00	$35,000	$ 420,000
Corn	500	29	14,500	3.50	17,500	507,500
Hogs	500	30	15,000	.50	15,000	450,000
			$49,900			$1,377,500

Total Contract Value	$1,377,500
Total Trading Account	50,000
Leverage	96.4%

Although the difference in leverage between a fully margined account and one that is only 40 percent margined is surprisingly small in this example, the difference in the potential for profit or loss is significantly large (Table 6-6).

Table 6-6 Comparison of   Profit/Loss Potential Between 40 Percent and 100 Percent Margin in a $50,000 Trading Account

MARGIN	LEVERAGE	GOLD		CORN		HOGS		TOTAL	%
		#CON-TRACTS	PROFIT/ LOSS	#CON-TRACTS	PROFIT/ LOSS	#CON-TRACTS	PROFIT/ LOSS	PROFIT/ LOSS	PROFIT/ LOSS
40%	90.6%	5	$ 25,000	10	$ 25,000	12	$ 36,000	$ 86,000	172%
100%	96.4%	12	$ 60,000	29	$ 72,500	30	$ 90,000	$ 222,500	445%

Here again, as leverage increases by a very small percentage change, the potential for profit or ruin increases dramatically. The smart trader, however, recognizes the value of caution and staying for the long haul as opposed to going for the big kill.

Pyramiding: Trading Multiple Positions

In hopes of milking a good trade for all possible profits, many traders add additional positions as the price moves in their favor. A favorite tactic is to *pyramid* from the original position. Two kinds of pyramids can be built—one that is upside down and the other right side up. Graphically, they look like the illustrations in Figures 6-6 and 6-7.

Figure 6-6   Pyramiding Contracts

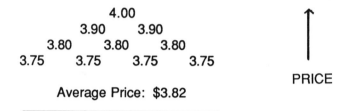

```
                   4.00
             3.90        3.90
        3.80      3.80        3.80
   3.75      3.75      3.75      3.75
```

Average Price: $3.82

PRICE

WHEAT MARGIN = $600   VALUE OF 1¢ MOVE = $50
TOTAL MARGIN = $6,000   PROFITS SHOWING = $9,000

Figure 6-7   Inverted Pyramid

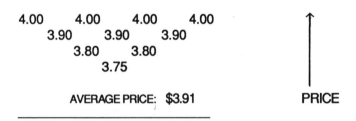

```
   4.00      4.00      4.00      4.00
        3.90      3.90      3.90
             3.80      3.80
                  3.75
```

AVERAGE PRICE: $3.91

PRICE

WHEAT MARGIN = $600   VALUE OF 1¢ MOVE = $50
TOTAL MARGIN = $6,000   PROFITS SHOWING = $4,750

In Figure 6-6, four contracts of wheat were bought on the original buy signal at $3.75. When prices began moving up, three positions were added at $3.80. As prices continued to rise, two more were added at $3.90 and finally one last contract at $4.00. If margin on wheat is $600, this trade is now margined at $6,000, but showing profits of at least $9,000. The average price of the total position is $3.82, which is not far from the original buy signal. As long as wheat prices remain above $3.82, the position is making money. In the case of an adverse price move, the price would have to drop below $3.82 before the position will lose money. In Figure 6-7, one position was taken on the original buy signal at $3.75. When the signal proved accurate, two postions were added at $3.80, three more at $3.90 and four at $4.00. In this example, the average price of the position is $3.91, which is $.16 higher than the original buy signal. If prices move below $3.91, the entire position will be losing money. Neither of these examples has significantly overleveraged the account. Both are using profits to create additional margin. In Figure 6-6, there is $9,000 in profits showing and in Figure 6-7 there is $4,750 showing. The problem is that the profits are all on paper. If prices run back down, the entire position can quickly be turned into a loser. In Figure 6-6, if prices fall to $3.73, the loss would be equivalent to holding 10 contracts at $3.82 and would amount to $4,500. In Figure 6-7, the loss would be equivalent to holding 10 contracts at $3.90 1/2, and would total $8,750. Figure 6-8 compares the performance of both pyramiding strategies if wheat prices were to go as high as $4.20 or as low as $3.73. Given this particular set of circumstances, the standard pyramid seems to outperform the inverted pyramid. Profit potential is greater—$19,000 versus $14,750—and loss potential is smaller—$4,500 versus $8,750.

If prices were to fall shortly after the first buy signal, however (if this were one of the 60 percent losing trades), then the inverted pyramid would provide less risk of loss. If prices fell to $3.60 prior to any additional positions being added, the loss using the standard pyramid strategy would be $.15 x $50 per 1 cent move × 4 contracts = $3,000. The loss in the inverted pyramid strategy would be $750 (1 contract × $.15 × $50). Thus, the initial risk is less using an inverted pyramid strategy that begins with only one contract and adds more only if the price moves in the right direction; but the ultimate risk, if both strategies are able to be carried to completion, is significantly greater with the inverted pyramid.

Given all this information, which pyramiding strategy should be used? The answer, for the trader who wishes to conserve capital and manage risk in a prudent way, is neither.

Averaging to the Market

Another form of pyramiding is a technique known as *averaging to the market*. If the first position that is put on turns out to be incorrect, the trader adds

Figure 6-8   Comparing Performance of Pyramid and Inverted Pyramid Strategies

	AVERAGE PRICE OF POSITION	TOTAL PROFIT AT $4.20	TOTAL LOSS AT $3.73
PYRAMID STRATEGY:	$3.82	$19,000	$4,500
INVERTED PYRAMID STRATEGY	$3.91	$14,750	$8,750

predetermined quantities of additional contracts at preset intervals. As the price continues to move against the original entry point, a pyramid forms—providing an average entry price that is much closer to the market price and thus establishing a position that will produce profits very quickly in the event of a reversal.

In Figure 6-9, the original buy signal is $3.75. This trader determines that each time the market price drops $.05, additional positions will be added as shown. When the market price reverses at $3.53, it requires only a move of $.11, to $3.62, before the trade breaks even. When prices reach $3.75 (the original entry point), the trade is showing $9,750 in profits.

Under ideal circumstances, this technique can produce large profits by anticipating a price reversal that is very likely to occur. After all, every time the market price drops $.05, it is just that much closer to an eventual reversal. The problem is that the reversal may not occur early enough. What if prices continue in a down-move or move lower and refuse to rally? At some point in an extended down-trend, the trader would be forced to cease adding positions because of escalating margin costs, at which point the average entry price would move farther and farther from the market price, making recovery less and less likely. If, in this example, prices dropped to $3.20, then traded in a range between $3.20 and $3.40 for an extended period, the best that could be hoped for might be to liquidate at $3.40, for a total loss of $24,000 (15 contracts x $.32 loss x $50).

It could be argued that the chance of such a large price slide is unlikely if the trading system is a good one and if the market conditions are monitored carefully, so that such a strategy is not used under highly volatile

Figure 6-9   Averaging to the Market

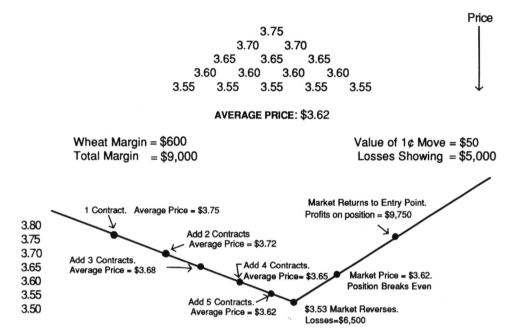

Price

```
                        3.75
                 3.70        3.70
            3.65       3.65        3.65
       3.60       3.60       3.60       3.60
  3.55      3.55       3.55      3.55       3.55
```

AVERAGE PRICE: $3.62

Wheat Margin = $600   Value of 1¢ Move = $50
Total Margin = $9,000   Losses Showing = $5,000

conditions. Nevertheless, the strategy of averaging to the market, like other pyramiding strategies, is simply too risky for the business-like trader who desires to manage risk carefully.

A good money management strategy handles the issue of multiple contracts only one way—and that way will assume (1) that a good trading system is being used, (2) that proper risk control has been used in setting stop-loss points, (3) that logical objectives have been chosen to take profits, and (4) that a reasonable analysis of trading capital has established the amount of margin money to be used and thus the number of contracts to be traded.

When the number of contracts has been determined using good money management techniques as described earlier, all of those positions are then put on when a signal is given by the trading system. A profit objective is established and a stop-loss point is chosen. If prices move favorably, one of several alternatives can be used.

1. All positions can be held until the profit objective is reached, then all positions are liquidated. If this strategy is chosen, the stop-loss is moved with the trade to lock in profits.

2. Some positions can be liquidated along the way to lock in profits. Again, a trailing stop is used with the positions left on.

3. At least one or more positions can be held if prices move past the profit objective, taking advantage of a larger move that may develop.

In Figure 6-10, a buy signal for wheat has been given at $3.75. An analysis of available trading capital indicates that $2,500 should be used for margin—enough to buy four contracts at $600 margin per contract. A technical look at the charts reveals a profit objective around $4.00. If the profit objective is $4.00, which produces a $.25 profit, then $.08 would be a reasonable amount to risk. Consequently, a stop-loss is placed at or around $3.67. The total being risked is now $1,600 (4 contracts × 8 cents × $50). The total profit potential is $5,000 (4 contracts × 25 cents × $50).

Figure 6-10   Managing Multiple Contracts in a Winning Trade

Strategy: Buy 4 contracts at $3.75.

Alternative 1: Sell all 4 at $4.00.

> **Profit:** 4 contracts x 25¢ x $50 = $5,000

Alternative 2: Sell 2 at $3.80. Sell 1 at $3.90. Sell 1 at $4.00.

> **Profit:** 2 contracts x 5¢ x $50 = $ 500
> 1 contract x 15¢ x $50 = $ 750
> 1 contract x 25¢ x $50 = $1,250
> Total $2,500

Alternative 3: Sell 1 at $3.80. Sell 1 at $3.90. Sell 2 at $4.00.

> **Profit:** 1 contract x 5¢ x $50 = $ 250
> 1 contract x 15¢ x $50 = $ 750
> 2 contracts x 25¢ x $50 = $2,500
> Total $3,500

Although this profit may not be as exciting as that generated by the pyramiding strategy, the lesser risk engendered by trading the plan is very attractive. After all, the concern in futures trading is often not how to make money—that seems easy. The real concern is how to keep the money that has been made.

As the trade develops, the trader has several alternatives. Rather than adding more contracts as prices move up, however, the trader this time takes positions off, locking-in profits along the way. Because four contracts are being traded, various combinations are available, three of which are covered in Figure 6-10. The choice of which strategy to follow depends on market conditions and the trader's willingness to withstand risk. The important point is that, rather than compounding profits and thus risk, this strategy for handling multiple contracts allows a trader both to take profits early on some contracts and to stay in the market to take advantage of any larger moves that may occur.

This technique for handling multiple positions offers another advantage: if prices move past the original profit objective, the trader can stay with the move, having already locked-in profits with the earlier liquidating of part of the position. By leaving one contract on and trailing it with a stop, a trader can take full advantage of a large move that may develop without incurring significant risks.

It is clear that the strategy of putting on mulitiple positions initially, with some destined to be "trading" positions while others are "trading" positions, offers a number of interesting alternatives to a trader. Each trader will adapt the basic concept to his or her own trading style, depending on how aggressive he or she wishes to be. No matter which alternative is chosen, the results over time will be far superior to pyramiding techniques for preserving capital and managing risk.

In the delightful book *Viewpoints of a Commodity Trader* (Frederick Fell Publisher, 1973), Roy Longstreet quotes two successful traders in regard to this issue. One said, "When I am long with a large profit, I get in my car and leave town. At each town I come to, I call back to the office and reduce my position." Another, when questioned as to what he owed his success replied, "I always took my profits too soon."

Diversification

Very few traders would deny that diversifying into several markets reduces the level of risk in a trading account. Common sense says that spreading risk among several commodities is safer than concentrating risk in one or two. A reduction in risk almost always is accompanied by a corresponding reduction in profits, however, and this is particularly true when diversifying. As with all risk management, the key is to balance the two so that risk is reduced more than profitability.

Diversification works to a trader's advantage in two ways. First, losses in one market are offset by profits in another. It is rare indeed that concurrent losses would occur in all the markets being traded. Second, by trading in several markets, a trader will be positioned to catch major moves when they occur in the various commodities.

As with all strategies associated with futures trading, diversification brings with it several potential pitfalls. The most obvious is that a trader can attempt to trade too many markets and by so doing dilute his or her efforts. To trade effectively in any given market requires careful study and focused concentration, as each market has its own unique characteristics. An important consideration for each trader is to assess the number of markets he or she can realistically follow with the degree of expertise necessary to see success. Some experts recommend that traders limit themselves to trading four to six markets. Others recommend as many as 10 to 14. Within that range is a number that will work well for each individual. The actual number chosen will depend on subjective considerations as well as an objective assessment of how much time can be devoted to trading, how much electronic equipment a trader has available to help study the markets, and the amount of trading capital in the account.

Weiss Research has carefully studied the issue of diversification as it relates to risk management in a large portfolio and has published the results in the book *Timing the Market* (Probus, 1986). Their studies indicate that an account trading only one market requires $4.00 in reserve for each $1.00 margined. In other words, risk management in a nondiversified trading account would require that no more than 20 percent of the capital be margined, while 80 percent be held in reserve. A portfolio that trades nine markets, on the other hand, requires only $1.20 in reserves for every $1.00 in margin. This corresponds very closely to the 60/40 ratio recommended previously.

If an account is to be truly diversified for the purpose of limiting risk, it is important that limits be placed on the amount to be committed to any one market. Generally, no more than 15 percent of the total trading capital should be obligated to one market, while the total risk in one market should not exceed 5 percent of trading capital. If more than one market is being traded within a closely related group (i.e., grains, metals, indexes, etc.), the amount committed to the group should not exceed 25 percent of trading capital, since markets within a group tend to move together.

The Theory of Runs and Contrary Opinion

A trader cannot be long involved with the futures industry without encountering the theory of contrary opinion. In its simplest form, it says that when everyone around you is bullish, be a bear, and vice versa. A great deal of objective data supports this theory, which is also appealing on a common-sense level—appealing, but difficult to implement. Supporting contrary opinion as a concept is the theory of runs—based on probability theory and originally applied to the game of roulette.

As presented by Perry Kaufman in *The New Commodity Trading Systems and Methods* (Wiley, 1987), a set of 256 spins on a roulette wheel produces the possibilities for runs of red shown in Table 6-7.

Table 6-7 Probability of Various Lengths of Runs Occurring

Length of Run	Probablility of Occurrence	Expected Number of Occurrences	Total Appearances of Red
1	1/8	32	32
2	1/16	16	32
3	1/32	8	24
4	1/64	4	16
5	1/128	2	10
6	1/256	1	6
		Total Appearances:	120

Because the total number of appeerences of red is only 120, the remaining eight can lead to runs of greater than six, or more occurrences of any of the shorter runs. Statistically, there is one chance of a run greater than six occurring in 256 tries, the average length of which is eight.

If the commodity market is seen as a roulette wheel in which each day's trading has an equal chance of going up or down, then this theory of runs can have some applicability to the market as well. Kaufman studied 21 different commodity markets and determined that, though similar, the markets produced different probability levels than simple red or black probabilities—nearly twice the probability of pure chance. Moreover, in commodities there are fewer runs of one and more frequent runs of two. (Table 6-8.)

To a trader wishing to manage risk, this information can be very valuable in mapping out a strategy. When considering capitalizing an account, the theory of runs makes it very clear that an account must be capable of withstanding at least one run of eight losing trades in a row. Any less than that is flirting with possible ruin. Another implication of the theory of runs is that after a losing streak of three or four trades, the probability is high that the streak will end. Therefore, the next one or two trades can be made perhaps a bit more aggressively. The tendency, of course, would be to become more conservative—trade fewer contracts; set stops a lot closer—but the theory of runs (and contrary opinion?) would recommend the opposite. Needless to say, after a run of three or four winning trades, the opposite tack should be taken—trade fewer contracts; set stops closer; be more conservative. Again, this goes against the grain of most traders.

In the section on trading multiple contracts, the recommendation was made to avoid pyramiding or adding to positions. The theory of runs, as can be seen, verifies that conservative advice. The farther market price has run in

Table 6-8 Length of Commodity Runs

Length of Run	Expected Probability of Occurrence	21 Combined 1976 Occurrences		Cotton (6 years)		Copper (6 years)		Potatoes (6 years)	
		Expected	Actual	Expected	Actual	Expected	Actual	Expected	Actual
1	$\frac{1}{2}$	1225	1214	369	346	382	380	329	295
2	$\frac{1}{4}$	612	620	185	183	196	229	165	177
3	$\frac{1}{8}$	306	311	92	111	98	92	82	90
4	$\frac{1}{16}$	153	167	46	50	49	44	41	42
5	$\frac{1}{32}$	77	67	23	21	24	18	21	28
6	$\frac{1}{64}$	38	41	12	12	12	11	10	7
7	$\frac{1}{128}$	19	16	6	8	6	4	5	9
8	$\frac{1}{256}$	10	5	3	5	3	4	3	7
9	$\frac{1}{512}$	5	3	1	1	2	1	2	2
≧10	$\frac{1}{1024}$	4	5	1	1	1	0	1	1
Total Tested			2449		738		783		658

Kaufman, Perry J., The New Commodity Trading Systems and Methods, New York, New York, John Wiley and Sons, 1987, p. 370.

a particular direction, the higher is the probability it will reverse itself. A business-like trader will always be cognizant of that fact and avoid going after the low-probability runs in an aggressive manner.

Conclusion

In their book *The Commodity Futures Game* (McGraw-Hill, 1974), Teweles, Harlow, and Stone advocate risk management when they make the statement "...a trader with less probability of success but trading conservatively can actually have a better chance of long-term success (winning the game) than a trader with a higher probability of success who chooses to trade more aggressively." The focus of this chapter has been on managing money by managing risk in a conservative fashion. Along the way various high-powered strategies have been discussed (e.g., pyramiding) but cast aside. In the section on leverage, it was revealed that incredibly high returns are possible if an account is fully margined, but the recommendation was made to margin only 40 percent of the total trading capital.

Many traders will read this chapter and conclude that the recommendations that have been presented are simply too conservative. They have heard stories of traders who have pyramided themselves to a fortune nearly overnight and that's what they want to do. All that can be said to such traders is "good luck." Some few of them will accomplish their goal. A few people every year will also win millions in various lotteries across the country. The only real difference is that the risk of ruin involved in buying a lottery ticket is much less than the risk of ruin attached to an overly aggressive futures-trading strategy.

Many other traders who read this chapter will recognize the efficacy of a more conservative trading style that limits risk at every possible juncture. These are the traders who, as children, understood the message behind the old fable about the hare and the tortoise: "Slow and steady wins the race."

The best trading system in the world can lose money if certain very specific steps are not taken to manage trading capital carefully. First, the account must be adequately capitalized initially. Second, a trading system must be adopted that limits risk in very specific and predictable ways. Third, the trader must constantly be aware of the extent to which trades are being leveraged—and not overextend the account. Fourth, the trading program must be diversified into several markets. Following these simple dictums of money management will assure a trader that, no matter how bad the trading goes at times, he or she will be around to trade another day.

Roy Longstreet has summed up the case for risk management very simply yet passionately:

"Risk control is not denial of freedom. On the contrary, it is the only thing that does permit freedom to act. Without capital, courage to act is diminished as is the power to act. Freedom is the existence of choices. No capital—no choice."

■ SECTION TWO ■

MASTER STRATEGIES

■

■ SECTION TWO ■

THE ESSENCE OF ANY TRADING SYSTEM, whether it be technical, fundamental, or some other approach, is timing. As we so often have heard, timing is the common denominator of all the master trading strategies, and the element around which they all are grouped.

Waves and Retracements

The most commonly used timing indicator, of course, are price patterns as revealed by bar charts. Section II begins, fittingly, with a chapter by Dan Rahfeldt that reviews the basic formations that occur as the market reveals itself through price movement. Charts, they say, are the maps that help a trader navigate through turbulent markets. Using charts, Joe DiNapoli presents a very specific timing strategy that he developed, based on Fibonacci ratios, which uses price retracement to establish logical profit objectives. Designed to capture profit rather than give it back to the market, Fibonacci expansion analysis requires great discipline, but can pay off handsomely in the form of personal satisfaction and profits. Bob Prechter, well-known to most traders for his work with Elliott Wave Analysis and as publisher of one of the most successful market advisories, demonstrates how price patterns can be studied and trading signals can be generated by locating the price waves as originally identified by Ralph Nelson Elliott. For the trader who cannot watch the markets all day, or who simply prefers trading for the longer term, Ed deLanoy reveals some potentially profitable strategies for trading long term market moves based on inverse markets and major breakouts. Based on many years of trading and learning, Ed's strategies are brilliant in their simplicity.

Seasonal Patterns and Signals

Most commodity traders are familiar with the seasonal tendencies of commodity prices. Jake Bernstein has studied these tendencies exhaustively and, through the years, has make the results available. Now, he offers a unique timing strategy based on an even more thorough analysis of seasonal price tendencies: high probability seasonal trades. After analyzing copious amounts of historical price data, Jake was able to identify many specific seasonal trades that historically have done well a high percentage of the time—in many cases 70 percent or better. Some have performed profitably 100 percent of the time! In this chapter he presents the tables that display the results of his extensive research effort, as well as a detailed explanation of how to read the tables and use the information for placing trades.

Traders who master chart analysis often find that price patterns alone are insufficient to provide the precise timing they need. Adding moving averages and stochastics, in many cases, still does not fill the bill. To further enhance timing proficiency, many traders look to other elements of the markets.

With the Cambridge Hook, Jim Kneafsey demonstrates the efficacy of combining volume, open interest, and the relative strength index with the standard hook or key reversal pattern to signal major turns in the market. Not a mortgage-your-house indicator, the Cambridge Hook nevertheless enables a trader to respond immediately to changes in trends in most markets.

Bill Eng looks even further beyond price data to two dimensions he calls time-sensitive and volume-sensitive strategies. By combining these with price-sensitive strategies, he has developed a "periodic table," from which he has been able to identify "bridging" market conditions. These are markets that bridge bear markets of bull markets to trading markets, or trading markets to bull or bear markets. By identifying and quantifying the various stages of the market, Bill imparts some understanding to the behavior and misbehavior of technical indicators.

The Market Profile®, as it reflects market logic, organizes price auctions into half-hour time segments and establishes value by measuring trading volume at the various prices throughout the day. By identifying when a commodity is undervalued or overvalued, a trader can more accurately make specific trading decisions. Jim Dalton and Eric Jones introduce the reader to an admittedly difficult stategy—one that might take as long as two years to master, but provides the trader off the floor with some of the same tools available to the floor trader.

The Market Personality Profile, as developed by Bill Williams, adds yet another dimension to the Market Profile® by adding volume and value area indicators to a system that utilizes open and close prices to assess the market's personality. Intended to simplify the amount of information obtained through the Market Profile®, Bill's system should help a trader bet-ther know when to "pull the trigger" on a trade.

Larry Williams tells how to pick a trade with ten to one odds by watch-ing for premium markets, then combining open interest, price gaps, contrary opinion, and moving average. Each part of Larry's plan contributes sig-nificantly to raising the odds of picking a winning trade. Unlike Jim Kneafsey's Cambridge Hook, which picks major market turns, Larry's strategy will not identify tops and bottoms, but will allow the patient trader to call profitable trades with confidence.

Veteran traders of futures and securities have long known that a consensus of opinion regarding market condiditons, particularly among less sophisticated traders, is often a predictor of exactly the opposite of that which is expected. Mark Lively tells how he quantifies market sentiment on a daily basis and how that sentiment can be an important timing indicator. Mark also explains how his "market sentiment" is unique in its approach to measuring consensus.

Weather and Timing

Common wisdom among traders is that fundamental information is too complex, too difficult to obtain, and too late in coming to be of practical benefit to the average trader. Jim Roemer demonstrates that the common wisdom may be wrong. With access to timely and accurate weather information and more than a passing knowledge of the supply\demand characteristics of a particular commodity, the average trader can trade successfully on the fundamentals. Jim tells us how to turn a far-away drought or a near-by hurricane into a profitable trading opportunity. He cautions us, however, that the key is not to pay a lot of attention to the evening TV weather forecast.

WAVES AND
RETRACEMENTS

CHARTING YOUR COURSE TO PROFITS

DAN RAHFELDT

■

■

DAN RAHFELDT

Dan Rahfeldt is currently publisher and editor of a real-estate newsletter. He is also the co-author of the national best sellers: *Timing the Market* (Probus, 1986), *Who Can You Trust in Coins* and *Winning with the Insiders*. His articles have appeared in *Barron's* and *Financial Planner* and other national publications.

During the last 10 years he has written for or been advisor to the following publications or publishers: *The Granville Market Letter* (Joe Granville); *The Professional Tape Reader* (Stan Weinstein); *MBH Commodity Journal* (Jake Bernstein); *Money and Markets; New York Institute of Finance* (Simon and Schuster); Probus Publishing; Windsor Books; Money Forecasts; Wow Indexes; *RHM Survey of Low-Priced Stocks and Warrants; Heritage Tangible Investments; Commodity Trend Service* (Joe Van Nice); Investors' Research (Chris Starkey); Mega Research (Bill Cruze); and has been contributing editor to the *Holt Advisory* (T. J. Holt) for the last year.

As a nationally syndicated television producer, he has produced numerous segments of "Real Estate Action Line," over 50 "Investor's Action Line" programs and all of the "World Business Review" programs ever produced and aired.

■

■ CHAPTER SEVEN ■

MOST INVESTORS have felt that technical analysis in general, and specifically its most visible and useful manifestation, charts and graphs, were something perhaps best left in the hands of professionals. That to construct, and most important, successfully interpret, charts was something simply out of their reach, perhaps requiring years of practice and training to be useful.

Absolutely nothing could be farther from the truth! Whether you choose to "do-it-yourself," subscribe to a good chart service, or a combination of both, you will find that charts will be your most useful, profitable, and cherished investment tool. As you will shortly see, they are not difficult to understand, construct, or update. After reading this chapter, we're sure that you'll be well on your way to charting your own course to profits.

Charts: They Helped Columbus Get Here and They'll Help You Get Where You Want to Go

Charts have been used in different forms for hundreds of years. The best and perhaps easiest to understand historical example is a navigational chart. Columbus used whatever charts he could get his hands on to help discover America (never mind that he was looking for India!), and today's mariners rely on charts constantly for safety as well as directional information.

Navigational charts give mariners an accurate, multidimensional picture—how deep is the water, and how far is it across, for example—of his physical environment. The exact same thing can be said about today's investment charts. They give investors an accurate picture—how high and/or low are prices, where have they been, and where are they going—of today's investing environment.

Even the most primitive navigation chart had the same utility to ancient mariners that a modern investor finds with his charts: to simply and successfully get from point A to point B without killing yourself. And in both cases, it's all the better if you're able to learn from your mistakes (or those of others) and repeat the process!

Although there are several kinds of charts—bar charts, circle (pie) charts, etc.—for our purposes, we will be most interested in modern bar charts and point-and-figure charts.

Since human psychology tends to repeat itself, a key to understanding the future lies in a study of the past. Price chart patterns reveal the bullish and bearish psychology of the market. By studying chart patterns, commercials, speculators and producers can anticipate future prices.

The two primary methods of price forecasting are fundamental and technical. Fundamental analysis is based on the traditional study of supply and demand factors causing prices to rise and fall. In financial markets, the fundamentalist looks at corporate earnings, trade deficits, and changes in the money supply, to name just a few. In the ag markets, fundamentalists study weather, crop conditions, planted acres, etc.

A Picture Is Worth a Thousand Words

While fundamental analysis studies the reasons and causes for prices going up or down, technical analysis studies the effect, the price movement itself. That's where the study of charts comes in. Technical analysis is the study of market action, primarily through the use of charts, for the purpose of forecasting future price trends. The basis of the technical analysis philosophy is the belief that all fundamental factors influencing market price action are quickly reflected in market activity. In other words, the impact of these factors will quickly show up in some form of price movement. It follows, therefore, that a study of price action is all that's required.

All technicians are really claiming is that price action should reflect shifts in supply and demand. If demand exceeds supply, prices should rise. If supply exceeds demand, prices should fall. This action is the basis of all economic and fundamental forecasting. If prices are rising, for whatever reason, technicians conclude that the fundamentals must be bullish. If prices fall, the fundamentals must be bearish. Technicians are indirectly studying fundamentals. Chart analysis, therefore, is simply a shortcut form of fundamental analysis. Charts obviously do not cause market to go up or down. They simply reflect the bullish or bearish psychology present in the minds of the market participants.

Generally, chartists don't concern themselves the the reasons why prices rise or fall. Technical analysis is a "what" business, rather than a "why" business. Fundamentals are always the most bullish at tops and most bearish at bottoms. But some of the most dramatic bull and bear markets in history have begun with little or no known perceived change in fundamentals. In the early stages of a changing trend, at the critical turning point, no one really seems to know exactly why a market is performing a certain way.

While the technical approach may sometimes seem overly simplistic in its claims, the logic behind its first premise—the market discounts everything—becomes more compelling. By studying charts and a host of supporting technical indicators, the chartist lets the market tell him or her which way prices are most likely to go.

Obviously we can't teach you about charts and other technical indicators without examples. Careful independent research of all the possibilities has brought me to the conclusion that the most complete chart service available for all the futures markets is *Futures Charts*, published by Commodity Trend Service in North Palm Beach, Florida. There are, of course, others, but none with all the features offered by *Futures Charts*. All the following charts have been furnished by Commodity Trend Service, and I'd like to thank them for their efforts on our behalf. This series of charts has been carefully chosen to illustrate several critical areas of interest and important principles to beginning and advanced chart students.

As you go through the various subjects, please study, and constantly refer to, the annotated charts provided.

Here's what I'll be covering in this chapter:

- Bar Charts: The Basic Foundation for Technical Analysis
- Volume and open interest (p. 107)
- Support and resistance congestion areas (p. 109)
- Daily reversals (p. 109)
- Continuation patterns—Flags and pennants (p. 110)
- Triangles (p. 110)
- Gaps: common, breakaway, runaway, and exhaustion (p. 110)
- Islands (p. 116)
- Cycles (p. 116)
- Spreads (p. 117)
- Head-and-shoulders (p. 117)
- Moving averages (p. 119)
- Average directional movement index (ADX) (p. 119)
- Market sentiment (p. 120)
- Commitment of traders report (net trader position charts) (p. 120)
- Relative strength index (RSI) (p. 122)
- Stochastics indicator (p. 125)
- Intraday Bar Charts (p. 127)
- Point-and-figure charts (p. 128)
- Double tops and bottoms (p. 128)
- Previous highs and lows (p. 130)

Ok, here we go!

Bar Charts: The Basic Foundation for Technical Analysis

Charts are widely used by commercial interests, speculators and producers to determine where and in which direction present momentum is moving prices, one may be able to anticipate future prices.

Bar charts or vertical line charts are the most popular method of graphing commodity prices. Bar charts are simple to construct and easy to maintain.

On the daily chart, each vertical line represents one day's price range. the horizontal has mark on the left side of the bar is the opening price. The right horizontal hash mark is the closing price. Weekly and monthly charts are constructed the same way. Daily charts are used to identify short-term price movements, while weekly and monthly charts show the longer-term picture.

The whole purpose of charting price action is to identify trends in the early stages of development for the purpose of trading with the trend. The entire trend-following approach is predicated on riding an existing trend until it shows signs of reversing.

The trend frequently follows a straight line within parallel lines (called a channel, as shown on page 108). There are many types of information used by the chartist, but the trend line is the most basic and most reliable.

A chartist should first determine the trend. A trend is defined in one of the following three ways:

1. An uptrend (or down trend) is considered to be intact as long as intermediate-term highs (or lows) are higher (lower) than the preceding highs (lows). This is the basic Dow Theory definition of trend given in the early years of the twentieth century by Charles Dow, one of the primary founders of modern-day technical analysis.

2. An uptrend (or downtrend) prevails as long as prices do not penetrate the upward (downward) sloping line connecting successive intermediate-term lows (highs). This is a commonly used definition which is a more stringent requirement than used in Dow Theory.

3. An uptrend (downtrend) remains in force as long as the settlement price is above (below) a moving average that is computed by averaging the settlement prices for a predetermined number of the most recent trading sessions. This is the most sophisticated definition of a trend, and it also involves the greatest subjectivity, since the analyst must decide such things as the number of days to average and whether and how to weigh the different days being used.

NOTE: There are two schools of thought about commodity price movement; random walk and non-random predictable price movement. Random walk theorists argue that there is no predictability into the future about commodity price movement. However, the fact that there are purely mechanical trading models that produce profits, indicates that prices are not random, but do continue to repeat past price patters.

Some chartists introduce further refinements to these definitions of trend, but the choice of a particular definition remains largely subjective.

Whatever criterion is chosen, traders should always try to take positions in the direction of the basic trend. This is the most elementary rule of technical analysis because it allows you to profit from the sustained moves that represent the most significant deviations from randomness.

Volume and Open Interest

Market technicians use several analytical tools to predict price movement. One of these tools is an analysis of volume and open- interest data. Volume figures, plotted as a bar for each trading day at the bottom of the chart, are the total number of contracts (all contract months) for that commodity. (Figure 7-1.)

The Basic Rules of Volume Analysis

1. When prices are rising and volume is increasing, prices will continue to rise. The up-trend is said to be technically strong. During the spring period, total soybean volume was generally increasing until the June high. This confirmed the up-trend was intact.

2. When prices are rising but volume is decreasing, the up-trend is losing momentum and may be near the end. The price rise will slow and possibly reverse. Soybean volume at the June high was lower than the volume during May, warning that the trend may be ending.

3. When prices are falling and volume is increasing, prices will continue to fall. The down-trend will persist. Heavy soybean volume in late June and early July pointed to lower prices.

4. When prices are falling and volume is decreasing, the down-trend is losing momentum and may be near the end. Soybean volume began to dry up in August as prices began to form a bottom.

As a rule of thumb, volume tends to expand rapidly as prices reach a major high. When a market takes a long time to form a bottom, such as a rounding bottom, volume is usually low for an extended period, as it was on the soybean chart during August.

The Basic Rules of Open Interest

An analysis of open interest is somewhat more complex. Open-interest figures are the total number of contracts (for all contract months) not yet liquidated. Increases in open interest during periods of rising prices indicate new buying, and almost inevitably signal technical strength. In our illustra-

Figure 7-1

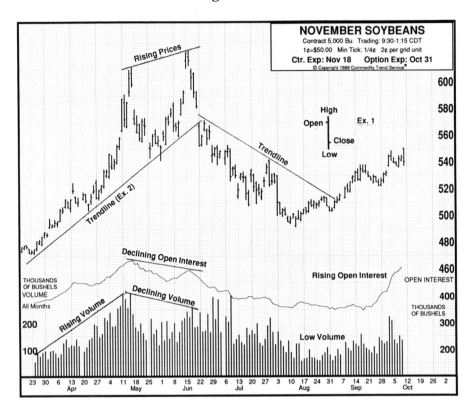

NOVEMBER SOYBEANS
Contract 5,000 Bu. Trading: 9:30-1:15 CDT
1¢=$50.00 Min Tick: 1/4¢ 2¢ per grid unit
Ctr. Exp: Nov 18   Option Exp: Oct 31
© Copyright 1988 Commodity Trend Service

tion, until the June high, total soybean open interest was rising with prices, which is a sign of technical strength.

Decreasing open interest during a period of rising prices suggests that shorts (holders of short positions) are liquidating. This is not a sign of strength, because prices are advancing primarily on short covering, not new buying. This partially explains what was happening in the soybean market at the June high. When soybeans made their high in June, the open interest was less than it was in May.

When prices are falling, an increase in open interest represents short hedging and short selling. Again, this is a technical signal that the downtrend will persist. Falling prices with declining open interest implies longs are liquidating, which indicates the downtrend is losing the strength to continue. The declining soybean open interest during the June-August decline told you the downtrend would not persist.

In summary, a market is technically strong when both volume and open interest are moving in the same direction with prices. Specifically: during a period of rising prices, an increase in volume and open interest suggests new buying and a technically strong market.

Support and Resistance Congestion Areas

A congestion area is simply a price range where prices have traded for a few weeks or longer. (Dristan will not relieve it under any circumstances!) These areas act as support when they are approached from above or as resistance when approached from below. To understand this behavior, consider what happens during the formation of a congestion area. Bullish and bearish forces are in balance, and approximately equal positions are established on both sides of the market.

If prices break below the established trading range, a return rally does two things:

1. It allows longs who entered the market in the congestion area to liquidate near breakeven.
2. It allows those who missed the original move to go short at a level that had previously proved profitable.

Similar reasoning governs the approach to congestion areas from the topside. The strength of a congestion area as support or resistance is usually related to the length of time and volume of activity in the price area.

Daily Reversals

The daily reversal is the simplest top and bottom formation. A down-side reversal occurs when prices reach new high ground for a move and then close substantially lower for the day. In Figure 7-2, April feeder cattle left a downside reversal on January 28. After a sizable rally, such action usually marks a significant top when it is accompanied by large volume. Reversal tops are often followed by abrupt collapses. Reversal bottoms are the opposite of reversal tops. Weekly and monthly reversals should also be noted on long-term charts.

Continuation Patterns—Flags and Pennants

Flags are small parallelograms that often form just after a rapid price move. They represent breathing spells in the midst of substantial rallies or declines and usually persist for three to seven days. Volume tends to decrease when a flag is forming, reflecting a pattern of a hiatus in a recently active market. A rule of thumb often used by chartists is that a flag marks the approximate half-way point of a price move. Both a bull flag and bear flag are shown in the British pound chart (Figure 7-3).

Pennants are similar to flags, except they are small triangular formations rather than parallelograms. Some chartists consider flags and pennants to be among the more reliable chart formations. Since they are easily identifiable and develop only after a clear short-term or intermediate-term trend has been established, they can be an especially valuable chart formation. The weekly gold chart (Figure 7-4) has a good pennant formation with the "pole" for the pennant extending down to the 1986 summer low.

Triangles

Triangles form when there are simultaneous short-term up-trend and down-trend lines that intersect. Their meaning is similar to flags and pennants, but triangles may take several weeks or more to form on daily charts. There are three types of triangles: (1) ascending, (2) descending, and (3) symmetrical.

The usual interpretation is that a breakout is likely to occur in the direction of the steeper trendline. Thus, an ascending triangle is considered bullish, a descending triangle is bearish, and a symmetrical triangle usually indicates that an impending large move in either direction is possible.

Volume usually declines during the consolidation period but increases substantially during a breakout. Both descending and ascending triangles are shown on the April feeder cattle chart. The early 1986 consolidation on the weekly gold chart (Figure 7-4) is a symmetrical triangle.

Gaps

Gaps are simply price ranges on a chart where no actual trading took place. There are four types of gaps.

Figure 7-2

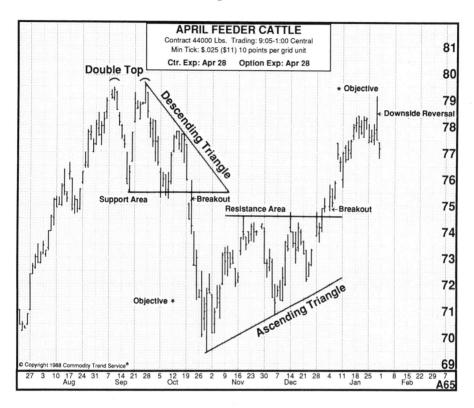

APRIL FEEDER CATTLE
Contract 44000 Lbs. Trading: 9:05-1:00 Central
Min Tick: $.025 ($11) 10 points per grid unit
Ctr. Exp: Apr 28   Option Exp: Apr 28

Double Top

Descending Triangle

★ Objective

← Downside Reversal

Support Area   ← Breakout

Resistance Area   ← Breakout

Objective ★

Ascending Triangle

© Copyright 1988 Commodity Trend Service®

81
80
79
78
77
76
75
74
73
72
71
70
69

27 3 10 17 24 31 7 14 21 28 5 12 19 26 2 9 16 23 30 7 14 21 28 4 11 18 25 1 8 15 22 29 7
        Aug   Sep   Oct   Nov   Dec   Jan   Feb

A65

Figure 7-3

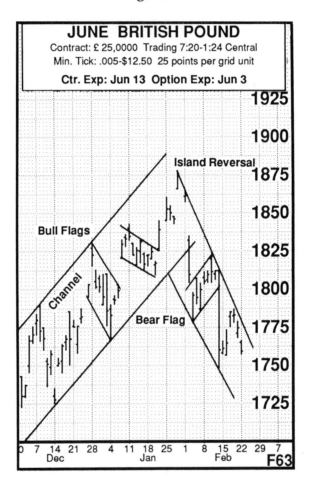

Common Gaps. These gaps are usually assumed to have no special meaning. Prices return to fill common gaps, usually within a few days. On the May silver chart (Figure 7-5), there are several common gaps during the August-September consolidation period.

Breakaway Gaps. The breakaway gap often accompanies a breakout from a congestion area or a consolidation pattern. If it is a real breakaway gap, it signals the beginning of a rapid price move or at least a sustainable trend. Breakaway gaps are not filled for several weeks or months. In this instance, silver's breakaway gap from the ten-week congestion area was left on October 20.

Figure 7-4

GOLD - WEEKLY
Nearest Futures Contract through Friday's Close
© Copyright 1988 Commodity Trend Service®

Figure 7-5

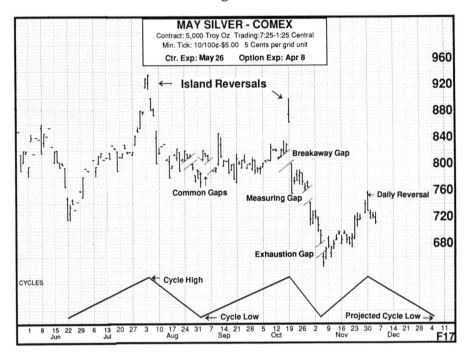

MAY SILVER - COMEX
Contract: 5,000 Troy Oz Trading:7:25-1:25 Central
Min. Tick: 10/100¢-$5.00   5 Cents per grid unit

Ctr. Exp: May 26   Option Exp: Apr 8

← **Island Reversals**

Breakaway Gap

Common Gaps

Measuring Gap

← Daily Reversal

Exhaustion Gap

CYCLES

← Cycle High

← Cycle Low

Projected Cycle Low →

960
920
880
840
800
760
720
680

1 8 15 22 29 6 13 20 27 3 10 17 24 31 7 14 21 28 5 12 19 26 2 9 16 23 30 7 14 21 28 4 11
Jun   Jul   Aug   Sep   Oct   Nov   Dec   F17

Figure 7-6

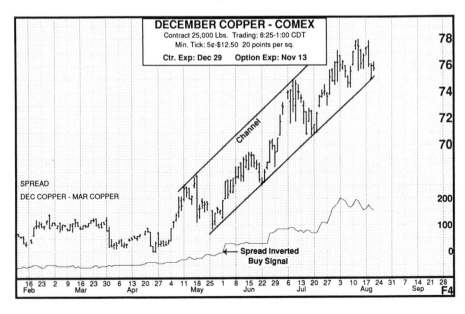

DECEMBER COPPER - COMEX
Contract 25,000 Lbs. Trading: 8:25-1:00 CDT
Min. Tick: 5¢-$12.50 20 points per sq.

Ctr. Exp: Dec 29   Option Exp: Nov 13

Channel

SPREAD
DEC COPPER - MAR COPPER

← Spread Inverted
Buy Signal

78
76
74
72
70

200
100
0

16 23 2 9 16 23 30 6 13 20 27 4 11 18 25 1 8 15 22 29 6 13 20 27 3 10 17 24 31 7 14 21 28
Feb   Mar   Apr   May   Jun   Jul   Aug   Sep   F4

Runaway Gaps. These gaps occur after a trend is already established. A specific runaway gap called a measuring or midpoint gap is the most important runaway gap, because it often accurately marks the midpoint of the move. A measuring gap for the October-November silver break was left on October 29. Runaway gaps indicate a strong underlying trend, especially when accompanied by high volume or a limit move.

Exhaustion Gaps. This gap occurs during the final stages of a move. An exhaustion gap usually occurs within a couple of days of a climax top or bottom. The November 5 exhaustion gap marked the end of silver's decline. An exhaustion gap reflects a market that simply runs out of steam with a final gasp.

The key to recognizing an exhaustion gap is often the intraday action. If a point-and-figure chart, 30-minute chart, or some other very short-term indicator shows labored and unsuccessful rally attempts following a gap opening, the possibility of an exhaustion gap and an impending reversal should be considered.

Islands

An island top or bottom is a small formation, often just a single day's action set apart from the other price action by a "see-through" exhaustion gap, signaling the end of a move. Two island reversal tops are on the May silver chart (Figure 7-5).

The day or days forming the island reversal are isolated, like an island, from all previous and subsequent price action. Islands frequently signal abrupt trend changes and are characteristic of volatile markets such as the yen, sugar, and cocoa. An island reversal often occurs following a sharp move that contains a series of runaway gaps and limit moves.

Cycles

Repetitive cyclical patterns in the futures markets may help you in your timing. Most markets have a short-term cycle that repeats once a month. This short-term cycle may be as short as three weeks or as long as five weeks. For example, grains, meats, and interest-rate futures have a short term cycle averaging about 28 calendar days.

Combining two or more of these short-term cycles forms an intermediate-term cycle, which runs from eight weeks to as long as 26 weeks, depending on the market. Cattle and silver, for example, have two 28-calendar-day cycles that combine to form the dominant eight- to nine-week cycle, which is the cycle shown in *Futures Charts.*

Cycles are seldom symmetrical, and their patterns differ in bull and bear markets. In a bull market, the crest of the cycle leans to the right because the highs are to the right of the cycle's midpoint. This is called right translation. In strong bull markets, cycle lengths tend to contract (shorten) slightly. Look for just the opposite in bear markets. The cycles tend to be slightly longer than they were in bull markets. Cycles in bear markets tend to peak early in the cycle to the left of the midpoint, which is called left translation.

Cycles are projected on the charts into the time period (not the precise day) for the next most likely time for a cyclical high or low. Because of the differences in bull and bear markets, the projected time period for the lows will be more accurate than the projection of the highs.

Once a cycle high or low has been confirmed, the cycle line is redrawn to match actual highs and lows. This lets you see how consistent the cyclical pattern has been. If the cycle is reasonably consistent, it will be helpful in your timing. But when the cycle is too irregular, use other tools for timing your trades.

Spreads

Whether you trade spreads or not, spread relationships are excellent lead indicators of major moves. Unlike other chart services, *Futures Charts'* spreads are plotted on a futures chart, lining up with prices. When the nearby contract goes to a premium over a deferred, it is a sign of a strong bull market. Note the buy signal on the December copper chart (Figure 7-5) when December climbs to a premium over March. That signal was given during May when copper was in the 60s. Copper's price doubled by the end of the year.

Spreads are plotted as the first contract minus the second one listed in the title. With an upward trending spread, profits are made with a long position in the first contract and a short position in the second contract. If the spread is trending downward, be short the first contract and long the second.

Head-and-Shoulders

This is one of the best known and most reliable reversal patterns. It consists of a left shoulder, head, and right shoulder to form a top formation at the end of an extended advance or a bottom formation terminating a decline. A head-and-shoulders bottom is just the inverse of a top formation. In a textbook-perfect top formation, left and right shoulders are about the same height, although few formations are symmetrical. At a minimum, the head must be higher than either shoulder. Volume is heavy on the right shoulder but lighter during the formation of the head and left shoulder.

On a head-and-shoulders bottom formation, the neckline is drawn across the tops of the left shoulder, head, and right shoulder. September eurodollars formed a head-and-shoulders bottom on the chart shown in Figure 7-7. The formation is completed when prices penetrate the neckline.

In addition to signaling a trend reversal, head-and-shoulder formations also make price projections. Measure the vertical distance from the top of the head to the neckline. Project this same distance from the point where the neckline was broken for the price target. The Eurodollar head-and-shoulders bottom projected a price target of 9300, which was achieved before Eurodollars resumed their downtrend.

Moving Averages

The use of moving averages to determine price trends has been very popular. This method, often used by professional portfolio managers, is popular because the trend can be determined mathematically, making computer analysis of price trends a reality.

Figure 7-7

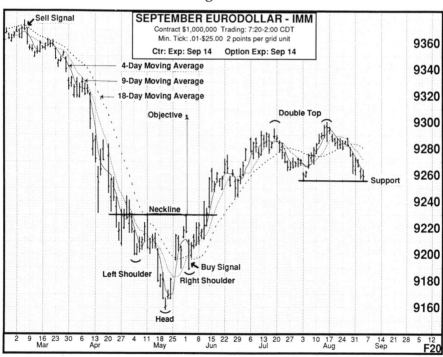

A simple moving average is constructed by adding the closing prices of a certain number of days and then dividing by that number. Each day, the oldest price in the series is dropped and the most recent closing price is added. When these numeric values are plotted, a very smooth trend can easily be seen, as shown in the chart in Figure 7-7.

One successful trading model with an excellent track record uses the four-, nine-, and 18-day moving averages. A buy signal is generated when the four-day average is greater than the nine-day average, and the nine-day average is greater than the 18-day average. All three averages must be increasing. A profitable moving average buy signal on the September Eurodollar chart is given in early June, and this long position is held until late July when the moving averages give a couple of whipsaws.

A sell signal is generated when the four-day average is less than the nine-day average, and the nine-day average is less than the 18-day average. All three averages must be decreasing. The first moving average ell signal on the September Eurodollar chart is given in March for a profitable ride down to the May low.

Average Directional Movement Index (ADX)

As a longer-term indicator, the ADX (Average Directional Movement) line on the weekly chart will help you filter out a lot of false oscillator signals on the daily chart. The ADX line will be climbing when a market is trending (either up or down).

With the ADX indicator, a longer-term trader can stay with a trending market by following this simple rule: *A climb by the ADX line above 40 followed by a down-turn signals an imminent end to the current trend.* When the ADX line climbs above 40 and turns down, traders should take profits on their positions. This is the signal to exit the market. It does not necessarily signal a move in the opposite direction.

As an example, there are four ADX signals on the weekly gold chart. The ADX tells you to take profits on short positions in March 1985. Following ADX signals, profits on longs in gold are taken in October 1986, May 1987 and January 1988. All of gold's ADX signals accurately marked the end of an intermediate-term move. Other indicators must be used to re-enter the market.

While the ADX signals an end to the existing trend, a move in the opposite direction is not necessarily predicted by the ADX. Prices may enter a consolidation phase like gold did following ADX signals in 1986 and 1987. The ADX is not helpful during a sideways market.

The ADX is part of the directional movement system introduced by J. Welles Wilder in his book, *New Concepts in Technical Trading Systems.*

Market Sentiment (Percent Bullish)

Bullish consensus figures are compiled and published by Earl Hadady's organization in California. They arrive at their figures by polling on a daily or weekly basis, a very large group of financial advisors, on whether they are bullish or bearish on various markets. The figure is then weighted, depending on how many subscribers, or clients each has. The theory being that the greater number of people that will be influenced by any advisor or organization, the greater the chance that the advisor's bias will be acted upon, and subsequently reflected in price movements in the markets. It, over time, has proven to be an accurate and valuable indicator for investors to consider when making market timing decision.

One reverses from a long or short position, whenever the consensus reaches overbought, or oversold conditions. This may be easily visualized by imagining water vapor in the air. The air absorbs as much water as it possibly can. But, at some point it is saturated, and rain begins to fall. Market prices rise until the rally can no longer be sustained, and then fall like the rain in our example.

Market sentiment, as shown on the weekly chart, plots the percentage of advisory services and traders who are bullish on that commodity. Trade with the trend of market sentiment until it reaches an extreme. When market sentiment numbers are between 30 percent and 70 percent, odds favor a continuation of the existing price trend. Prices enter an overbought condition when market sentiment numbers climb above 80 percent; an oversold condition exists below 25 percent. Consider a contrarian position when market sentiment rises above 80 percent or drops below 25 percent.

The overbought and oversold zones will vary by commodity. By looking at the historical chart of market sentiment published in *Futures Charts*, you can see what market sentiment numbers typically mark tops and bottoms over the past four years. This provides you with the best guide for judging the current market sentiment readings.

Net Trader Position Charts

The Commodity Futures Trading Commission (CFTC) releases a report each month on the positions held by traders. When a new report is released, we publish this data in the table in Figure 7-4 and also show the net position of each group (excluding spreads) in a net trader chart below the weekly chart for most actively traded markets.

Figure 7-4 shows each group's percentage of the total long and short position and the change from the previous month. Example: If the numbers for copper are:

Large Speculators

% Long	% Short
29 – 3	11 – 4

This means large speculators held 29 percent of the total long position (down three percent from last month's report), and large specs held 11 percent of the total short position (down four percent from a month ago). Total longs and shorts for all three trader groups may not total 100 percent because spreading is not included in these figures. (In the example shown of the net trader charts, commercials are plotted as a solid line, large speculators are a dashed line and small specs are the dotted line.)

Subtracting a group's short positions from their long positions produces this net figure. Net short positions are plotted as a – (minus) while net long positions are charted as a + (plus). For example, if small specs are long 25,000 contracts and short 5,000, this would be plotted as +20,000. Or if a group held 2,000 longs and 12,000 short contracts, this would be plotted as -10,000.

Changes in a group's net positions may give clues to price direction. But certain groups may have a tendency to favor one side of the market. Commercials are often net short because they probably own the physical commodity, and they are protecting the value of their inventory. On the other hand, small speculators tend to favor the long side because of their bullish bias.

The movement of a group's positions gives clues to price direction. Small specs are too bearish at bottoms and too bullish at tops. Large speculators are usually on the right side of the market. Watch the movement of commercials, because they should be the most knowledgeable about the fundamentals.

Note on the weekly gold chart that commercials held their largest net long position as the gold market turned up in 1985. In 1987, as the gold market approached a top, commercials held a heavy net short position.

Net trader position charts will be published for the two weeks following the release of the monthly CFTC report. Then they publish the weekly volume and open interest chart until the next CFTC report is released.

Relative Strength Index

Relative strength index (RSI) values range from 0 to 100. While this indicator follows the movements of closing prices on bar charts, the RSI can warn you when a market is near a top or bottom. In an up-trending market with prices making new highs, a RSI climbing above 70 warns of a trend reversal if the RSI peaks below its previous high. This is called bearish divergence. A reversal is confirmed when the RSI drops below its previous low. (This RSI failure to make new highs followed by the RSI dropping below its previous low is also called a failure swing.)

An example of bearish divergence is shown at the August high on the S&P 100 (OEX) chart in Figure 7-8. The RSI's failure to exceed the previous RSI high while prices made new highs on August 25 is bearish divergence. Confirmation of the top was the RSI drop below its August 18 low.

Bullish divergence is shown on the December T-bond chart in Figure 7-9. After making a short-term bottom in September, T-bonds continued to plunge into October, but the RSI managed to stay above its September low at 20, creating bullish divergence. This bottom was confirmed when prices exploded during the third week of October.

The RSI can be used as an oversold/overbought indicator. Generally, values over 70 indicate overbought and values under 30 are oversold. In strongly trending markets, this indicator may stay at an extreme level for an extended period. RSI reversals at these extremes may give you better signals.

To begin a new RSI chart, list the price changes for 14 consecutive days, putting the up (+) changes in one column and the down (-) changes in a second column. Total the column of up changes and divide by 14 to calculate the up average. Total the column of down changes and divide by 14 for the down average. Then proceed with this formula:

$$RSI = 100 \times \frac{U}{U + D}$$

U = up average
D = down average

To help you update the RSI values until the next issue of their service arrives, they list the "up average" and "down average" as of Thursday on each RSI chart. To incorporate the next day's price change, multiply each average by 13, add the day's up or down amount to the respective average, and divide this total by 14. Then proceed with the above formula.

By using the up and down averages published in *Futures Charts* to calculate your RSIs, your results will closely duplicate their RSI charts. Since the RSI is an exponential moving average, the early data carries less weight as each new day is added, but is never completely eliminated. This data creates a smoothed momentum oscillator, as described in J. Welles Wilder's book *New Concepts in Technical Trading Systems*.

Stochastics Indicator

Like the relative strength index (RSI), stochastics is another popular oscillator to judge price momentum. Stochastics is not a new oscillator, but it has

Figure 7-8

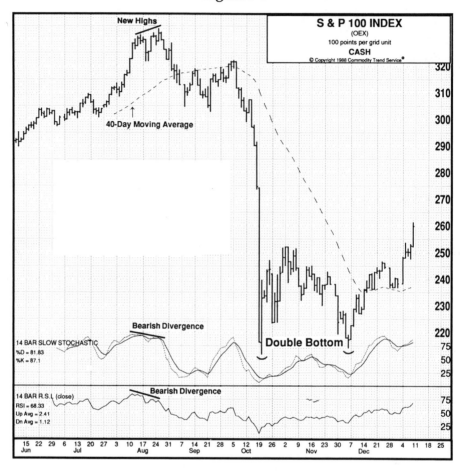

New Highs

S & P 100 INDEX
(OEX)
100 points per grid unit
CASH
© Copyright 1988 Commodity Trend Service®

40-Day Moving Average

320
310
300
290
280
270
260
250
240
230
220

Bearish Divergence

14 BAR SLOW STOCHASTIC
%D = 81.83
%K = 87.1

Double Bottom

75
50
25

Bearish Divergence

14 BAR R.S.I. (close)
RSI = 68.33
Up Avg = 2.41
Dn Avg = 1.12

75
50
25

15 22 29 6 13 20 27 3 10 17 24 31 7 14 21 28 5 12 19 26 2 9 16 23 30 7 14 21 28 4 11 18 25
Jun   Jul   Aug   Sep   Oct   Nov   Dec

Figure 7-9

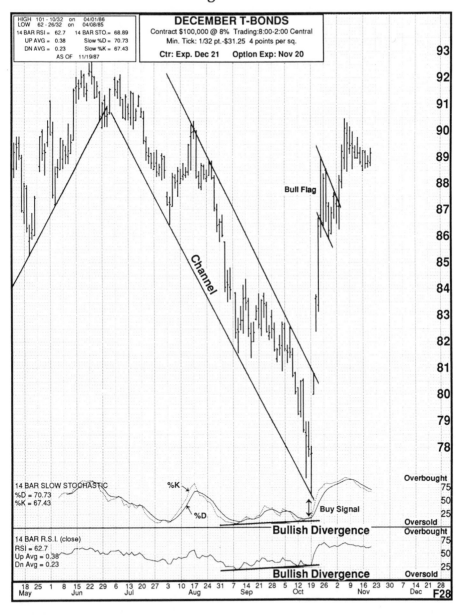

DECEMBER T-BONDS

HIGH 101 - 10/32 on 04/01/86
LOW 62 - 26/32 on 04/08/85
14 BAR RSI = 62.7   14 BAR STO.= 68.89
UP AVG = 0.38   Slow %D = 70.73
DN AVG = 0.23   Slow %K = 67.43
AS OF 11/19/87

Contract $100,000 @ 8% Trading:8:00-2:00 Central
Min. Tick: 1/32 pt.-$31.25 4 points per sq.
Ctr: Exp. Dec 21   Option Exp: Nov 20

Bull Flag

Channel

14 BAR SLOW STOCHASTIC
%D = 70.73
%K = 67.43

%K

%D

Buy Signal

Bullish Divergence

14 BAR R.S.I. (close)
RSI = 62.7
Up Avg = 0.38
Dn Avg = 0.23

Bullish Divergence

Overbought
Oversold
Overbought
Oversold

become especially popular during the 1980s. The stochastics indicator is undoubtedly the most popular tool used by technical traders today.

While the RSI measures momentum based on the changes in daily settlement prices, stochastics has two lines, and its calculations are based on the rate of change in the daily high, low, and close. The concept for stochastics is based on the tendency that as prices move higher, the daily closes will be closer to the high of the daily range. The reverse is true in downtrends. As prices decrease, the daily closes tend to accumulate closer to the lows of the daily trading range. This concept also holds true to daily, weekly, and monthly charts.

Stochastics is a measurement of where prices are within the period used to calculate the stochastics value. If the current price is near the top of the 14-period range, stochastics numbers will be high. If prices are near the bottom of the 14-period range, stochastics values will be low.

To update a stochastics chart, we need to calculate three values—the raw value, %K, and %D. These values are plotted on a scale from 0 to 100. When the raw value and the %K are plotted on the same chart, the result is "fast stochastics," which shows many up and down swings in a very short period of time. When the %K and the %D are used, as in *Futures Charts,* you have "slow stochastics," which smoothes the data.

In the example, they plot the %K line as a dotted line and the %D as a solid line. The %K line is the faster moving line; %D is a smoothed three-day moving average of %K.

In the upper left-hand box on each daily chart, they publish the numbers for the raw stochastics (14-bar sto.) value, %K and %D as of Friday. The formula for calculating the daily updates for stochastics is as follows:

$$\text{Raw Value} = 100 \times \frac{\text{Last Close} - \text{14-Day Low}}{\text{14-Day High} - \text{14-Day Low}}$$

The formulas for updating the new %K and %D are as follows:

$$\text{New \%K} = 2/3 \text{ Prev. \%K} + 1/3 \text{ New Raw Value}$$
$$\text{New \%D} = 2/3 \text{ Prev. \%D} + 1/3 \text{ New \%K}$$

Note that we must have 14 days of information before we can begin calculating the raw value. For clarity, the 14-day high is the highest price for the commodity during the last 14 trading days, and the 14-day low is the lowest price for the last 14 trading days, not the high or low 14 days ago.

Stochastics Signals

Traders use the action on the stochastics charts in several ways, including the following.

Divergence. Like the RSI, stochastics lines may diverge with price action to warn of a potential top or bottom. If prices make a new high but the stochastics does not exceed its previous high, a top may be near. The opposite is true at bottoms. Bullish stochastics divergence is shown on the December T-bond chart in Figure 7-9. Bearish divergence warns of a top on the S&P 100 (OEX) chart in Figure 7-10.

The more times a market shows divergence, the more likely a profitable signal will be given when the stochastics lines cross. Some patient traders wait for double or triple divergence before taking a stochastics buy or sell signal. You won't see divergence very often on long-term charts. Divergence is much more common on daily charts.

Overbought/Oversold Zones. Markets seldom go straight in one direction without a pause or correction. When prices move up and appear to be ready to correct, the market is called overbought. When prices have been moving down and appear to be ready to rebound, the market is oversold. As a mathematical representation of a market's overbought or oversold condition, stochastics tells you when prices have gone too far in one direction.

Values above 75 indicate the overbought zone. Values below 25 indicate the oversold zone. (Some traders prefer using 80 and 20 as the parameters for overbought and oversold markets.) In sustained moves, stochastics values may remain in the overbought or oversold zones for extended lengths of time.

Trend Identification. One of the reasons *Futures Charts* includes the stochastics indicator on weekly and monthly charts is for trend identification. With the help of stochastics, you will know the longer-term trend and when there's a major trend change. When both %K and %D are moving in the same direction, they confirm the existing trend. When the lines cross, especially after first rising above 75 or dropping below 25, they signal trend reversals. Knowing the long-term trend gives you confidence to trade in its direction.

Buy/Sell Signals. There are several ways traders use stochastics for buy and sell signals. In the July, 1986 issue of *Stocks and Commodities* magazine, the results of a research report were published where buy and sell signals were generated every time %K crossed %D, similar to the buy and sell signals of two moving averages. Not surprisingly, the results were "poor to mediocre."

Stochastics is not a trading system by itself, but rather a tool for you to use in making trading decisions. The key to using stochastics successfully is filtering out as many of the unprofitable signals as possible. Here are a couple of suggestions:

1. One method to reduce the number of unprofitable stochastics signals is requiring that both stochastics lines must first enter the overbought zone or oversold zone before recognizing a %K line

crossing the %D line as a buy or sell signal. This filter requires that both lines be overbought or oversold before there's a legitimate buy or sell signal.

2. Another way to filter out bad signals is to take the daily stochastics signals only in the direction of the longer-term trend. The problem with stochastics is the same problem traders have with a lot of oscillators: they are notoriously unreliable in signaling a trade against the major trend. After identifying the long-term trend with the stochastics on the long-term charts (as discussed earlier), follow only buy signals on the daily stochastics charts in uptrends and only sell signals in bear markets.

Once you have determined the major trend, a more aggressive approach is using all the crossings in the direction of that trend, regardless of where the stochastics lines cross. When the major trend is up, you take all the upturns by the daily stochastics as additional buy signals, or to pyramid, regardless of whether %K or %D reached the oversold zone. Stochastics sell signals are ignored, except to take short-term profits.

On the other hand, when the major trend on the long-term charts is down, take all down-turns on the daily stochastics as signals to sell or pyramid short positions. Stochastics buy signals are ignored, except to take short-term profits.

Stochastics is a very useful technical indicator that helps you with your timing, especially when it is used in conjunction with the other trading tools described in this chapter.

Intraday Bar Charts

Futures Charts includes 30-minute bar charts on the most actively traded futures markets and a 60-minute bar chart on the Dow Jones Industrial Average. These charts show price action plus support and resistance levels that are not apparent on daily bar charts. If you have access to intraday data, you can update these 30-minute and 60-minute charts, although it can be very time consuming. An on-line computer with graphics capability is obviously the preferred method for updating intraday charts.

Each bar on a 30-minute chart represents the open, high, low, and close for that 30-minute period. Using the accompanying T-bond chart as an example, there are 12 30-minute periods per day, and the past ten days, or 120 bars, are shown on the chart.

All technical analysis techniques that are used on daily bar charts can be applied to the intraday charts, resulting in greater accuracy for those who want to fine tune their signals. To make your trading decision, analyze the monthly chart first, the weekly chart next, followed by the daily chart and finally the intraday chart.

Point-and-Figure Charts

Intraday point-and-figure charts were the first known method of constructing charts and are still popular with floor traders today. Point-and-figure charts reflect pure price movement, disregarding a time scale. They are constructed using columns of X's representing rising price, and columns of 0s for declining prices. The reversal amount is the distance prices must retrace before the next column is plotted. (See Figure 7-10.)

Point-and-figure chartists believe there is a direct relationship between the width of the horizontal congestion area and the extent of the subsequent vertical move following a breakout in either direction. This is based on the theory that congestion-area activity results in a steady build-up of buying and selling pressure, which is likely to dissipate only after a commensurate price move. This is probably the most widespread use of point-and-figure charts.

Figure 7-10

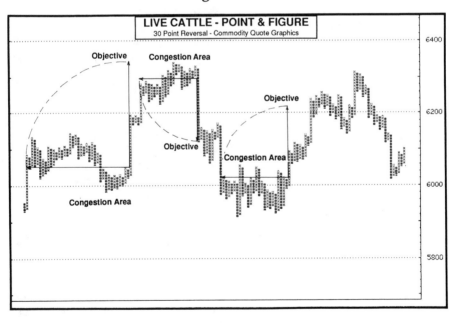

Double Tops And Bottoms

A double top is formed when consecutive rallies stop at approximately the same level, and the second decline falls below the previous low, completing an "M" on the chart. Technicians usually allow for a three percent or four percent difference between the two highs of this formation. Volume during the final rally should be less than it was during the first peak since the market is losing momentum.

A double top formed on the September Eurodollar chart (Figure 7-7) in the 9300 area, and this top formation was completed later when prices fell below the August 10 low. April feeder cattle (Figure 7-2) also completed a double top during the fall, projecting a price drop equal to the distance of the shortest "leg."

A double bottom is just the inverse, forming a "W." A double bottom formed on the S&P 100 chart (Figure 7-8). Double tops and bottoms are more common but not as reliable as head-and-shoulders formations.

Previous Highs and Lows

Previous highs and lows can act either as resistance or as support. An earlier low tends to slow declines because many traders reason that prices had once before rallied from that level and may do so again. These traders are likely to go long or cover shorts as the previous low is approached, thus lending support to the market. But if prices slip below the old low, the role of this price level is reversed and it becomes resistance.

Those who went long before the breakdown in anticipation of a turn-around would view a return rally as a chance to get out close to breakeven. Those who had taken profits on shorts would be more likely to reinstate their shorts near the level where they had previously covered their positions. When large numbers of traders behave this way, identifiable support and resistance are created. April feeder cattle (Figure 7-2) registered a downside reversal when prices tested previous highs made the during the fall.

The Spider Strategy

As I wrote in *Timing the Market*, there is no one perfect approach to the markets. Rather, I recommend that all traders adopt my *spider strategy*.

A spider does not need to "feed" every day. He is content to wait until a morsel comes his way, patient and secure in the knowledge that he has taken the steps necessary for his survival.

His carefully crafted web transmits to him all sorts of information. But he knows how to identify the false signals—the wind vibrating his web, a drop of rain—from the real thing enmeshed in it.

Why does he know it so intimately? Because he has carefully constructed his web himself. No one else can build it for him. As a result, the configuration of his web is unique. Most importantly, the spider is patient. He waits until he sees a convergence of most or all of his indicators before he acts; but when he does, he pounces aggressively and without hesitation.

Therefore, with your newfound knowledge about charting I urge you to build your own web of knowledge, and catch some huge profits! Just remember to be patient and thorough as you chart you way to profits!

FIBONACCI EXPANSION ANALYSIS:

A Method to Determine Logical Profit Objectives

JOE DiNAPOLI

■

■

JOE DiNAPOLI

Joe DiNapoli is an active, independent trader and is President of Coast Investment Software, Huntington Beach, California. His primary activity for the past twenty years has been centered around investment market research and trading for his personal account. His area of expertise includes such diverse markets as real estate and other tangibles, stock, stock options, cash bond transactions, commodities, financial futures, and options on futures. Since 1980, he has devoted himself primarily to the financial futures markets, particularly the stock market indexes since their advent in 1982.

Mr. DiNapoli's years of involvement in a variety of markets as both a fundamental and technical trader has led him to definite conclusions in the trading of highly leveraged instruments. His belief in computerization as the key to consistent profits led to his development of specific computerized trading tools which he now uses daily in his trading and markets through his company, Coast Investment Software. He has taught the application of computer trading tools as well as risk management techniques in investment seminars. Mr. DiNapoli graduated with honors from Lowell Technological Institute with a Bachelor in Science degree in electrical engineering and a minor in economics.

■

■ CHAPTER EIGHT ■

HOW MANY TIMES HAVE YOU SEEN A MARKET SHOOT UP, charge ahead, add hundreds if not thousands of dollars to your equity. You think this is the big one! Then, in a few hours, minutes, or even seconds you watch all that equity wash away, only to end up with a loss when your stop is hit. Sound familiar? It's all too familiar to many of us. It was to me. After watching it happen time and again to my own account, I went about the task of doing something about it. The result is a specific technique I've researched, developed, and use daily, called Fibonacci Expansion Analysis. Through deceptively simple calculations, Fibonacci Expansion Analysis tells me with a reasonable degree of certainty where up and down moves in the market are likely to end. That way I have my orders in place waiting, and as a consequence, usually avoid the kind of anguish described above.

It was Fibonacci Expansion Analysis that gave me the 2702 Dow profit objective I called for on national television two weeks before the August 1987 high. That particular profit objective was the result of a simple calculation that I'll teach you in this chapter.

Before we get into specifics of the method, however, I first want to cover some basic ground so that we all start from the same gate. The information I will cover assumes that you are an initiated investor with some level of experience in the stock or futures markets. I also assume that you are familiar with and have used at least one reasonably accurate entry technique and that you have learned both the value and the cost of using protective stops.

Essentially, only three ways exist to exit any position. The first is to be stopped out at either a profit or a loss. The second is to get out at the market, sometimes for rational reasons, other times, (unfortunately) for emotional reasons. The third is to set predetermined logical profit objectives, preferably executed by OB ("or better") or MIT ("market if touched") orders. The first two exit procedures are the ones most commonly seen in the marketplace. The focus of this chapter is on the third procedure: establishing logical profit objectives.

Just What Is a Logical Profit Objective?

To answer that question, we'll begin by first considering what it is not. A logical profit objective is not necessarily the top (if you're long) or the bottom (if you're short) of a given market swing. It is not arbitrary; it is not capriciously selected. *Logical profit objectives are price objectives that are specifically set ahead of time at a point where valid indicators tell you significant orders will be placed against the direction you are trading in.*

The logical profit objectives I use are largely independent of any market entry technique. Although a highly accurate entry technique will provide superior results over time, almost any good entry method will work. I recommend you use one you are familiar with and have confidence in.

Why are logical profit objectives important? Logically predetermined profit objectives have been one of the most critical factors in boosting bottom-line equity for me, as it has been for hundreds of speculators I have taught and known. Consistently capturing profit on at least 50 percent of all positions can mushroom account equity over time into proportions that the uninitiated trader might otherwise consider unrealistic. Also, profit-capture techniques can provide the individual player with a very high percentage of winning trades, which in turn produces the advantage of high morale and the incentive to keep going—not a minor consideration.

What are some of the problems involved with establishing logical profit objectives? First, you must become familiar with the techniques involved. You must gain experience applying the techniques to the market and develop specific trading tactics based on the methods used. These problems, however, can be overcome by study and practice. A far greater problem may be your psychological predisposition to trading. Since this could be the major prob-lem, you need to consider it first.

If, for example, you take 100 points per contract out of the market *where you should* on a specific trade and the market keeps going, are you likely to punish yourself mentally? Will you feel as if you played poorly? I can tell you, if *I* take 50, 100, or 1000 points out of the market and it goes on without me, I don't feel the slightest regret, regardless of the extent of the total move. Instead, I'm pleased—as I should be—that the plan was executed properly. If you do not feel capable of congratulating yourself on a job well done just because the market happens to continue on, maybe logical profit objectives are not for you. If you're the type of individual who is in the game to "catch the big one" with maximum margin, then again, logical profit objectives may not be for you.

Of course, a few well-capitalized, highly disciplined, experienced traders say that the real money is earned by letting the market take you out, usually through stops. These traders, who tend to get a lot of publicity, have at their disposal excellent systems that they have researched and have full confidence in. They are characteristically prepared to suffer large drawdowns and a high percentage of losing trades while waiting to catch the big moves. I am not. I know that about myself, because I have taken the time to find out about myself. It's up to you to know yourself. When you know where you fit into the market psychologically, you can trade accordingly.

You must have confidence in any method of trading to consider using it; but beyond that, you should feel comfortable with the process of a method as well as the perceived outcome. Establishing logical profit objectives through Fibonacci Expansion Analysis is a method of trading with inherent advantages and disadvantages. It requires the emotional ability to cut short a *potentially* huge gain in the interest of a long-term profitable plan. If this fits your temperament, then Fibonacci Expansion Analysis may be for you.

Fibonacci Expansion Analysis

Anyone who has been involved in the market for long has probably heard about Fibonacci numbers and ratios. We know that they somehow mysteriously affect the market; however, most of us seem to resist trying to understand how they work. My primary resistance came from the misconception that Fibonacci numbers, wave analysis, and related systems were very difficult concepts to learn. Eventually, however, my desire to perfect my understanding of the market and to be a bigger winner overcame my previous prejudice. I quickly discovered that the application of Fibonacci techniques to the market is not very difficult. More important, I discovered that one definitely does not need to be an Elliott Wave technician to apply Fibonacci concepts.[1] I, for one, am not.

The Fibonacci number series (1, 2, 3, 5, 8, 13, 21...) and the resulting Fibonacci ratios (.146, .382, .5, .618, 1, 1.382, 1.5, 1.618, 2.618, etc.), form the heart of all Fibonacci analysis. For the purposes of Fibonacci Expansion Analysis as I use it, however, we can ignore most of the ratios as well as the entire number series from which the ratios are derived. In the basic calculations to determine logical profit objectives, we need be concerned with only three ratios: .618, 1, and 1.618.

Objective Point Equations

These are the three simple equations I use to establish logical profit objectives. Note that A, B and C are specific points in a market move (see Figure 8-1). The first objective is the contracted objective point (COP). It uses the Fibonacci ratio .618.

$$COP = .618 (B - A) + C$$

The second objective is the objective point (OP), which uses the Fibonacci ratio 1.

$$OP = B - A + C$$

Figure 8-1 Fibonacci Objective Points

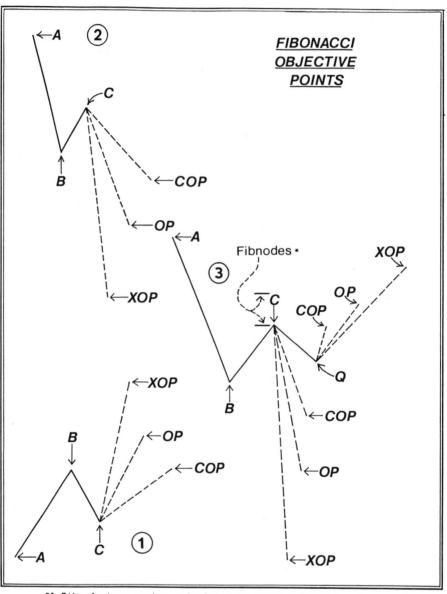

*A Fibnode is a number calculated by using Fibonacci retracement
analysis. A Fibnode is generally a market entry number.

The third objective is the expanded objective point (XOP), which uses the Fibonacci ratio 1.618.

$$XOP = 1.618 (B - A) + C$$

This simple set of equations has allowed me to calculate—days, weeks, sometimes months ahead—the major turning points in a variety of markets, including the 2702 stock market objective mentioned earlier.

In Figure 8-1, example 1, A marks the beginning of an up-move, B marks the *highest high* of that move, and C marks the *lowest low* following point B. In example 2, point A marks the beginning of a down-move, B marks the *lowest low* of that move, and C marks the *highest high* following B. Once all three points have been located on a bar chart, their respective values can be entered into the above equations, and all three profit objectives can quickly be determined.

The strategy of Fibonacci Expansion Analysis, then, is to locate points A, B and C on a price-versus-time chart, determine the values of each point, and enter the values into the objective point equations, producing three different profit objectives at varying distances from point C. Once you have located the three profit objectives, your strategy for taking profits can include any combination of the objective points. You might choose to take all of your profits at one objective point, for example. Or if you were holding a multiple-contract position, you could peel off contracts at each objective point. As you work with the concept, you will likely develop other workable strategies as well.

Three targets, or logical profit objectives, can thus be calculated from any ABC market swing, whether the thrust is up or down, using intraday highs and lows. A software program called Fibnodes[2] can perform these calculations and others, but all you must have is a pencil or perhaps a calculator to do the figuring. A programmable calculator can provide additional assistance. Profit objectives can also be located on a price-versus-time chart with an architectural tool called a proportional divider or precision ratio compass. The resulting numbers are extended from point C in the same direction as wave AB (Figure 8-1).

In Fibonacci Expansion Analysis, negative numbers are not recognized. It should be noted also that the analysis does not use time to locate profit objectives. Wave D is shown in Figure 8-1 reaching the various price objectives at different times for clarity only. It is possible for the wave that occurs after wave ABC to reach all three objective points (COP, OP, XOP) after experiencing a reaction at the previous profit objective. It is also possible that the first objective could be the end of the move.

In understanding the nature of logical profit objectives, note that *significant* selling will be manifest at all three objective points in an up move, while *buying* will occur in a down move. One is not sure of the extent of the resulting reaction, only that the aforementioned activity will ensue. As alluded to earlier, nothing is wrong with exiting partial positions at each objective as it is met. An important rule to observe when using Fibonacci Expansion Analysis, however, is to use objective points primarily for exiting established positions. That way, you are always trading with the trend of wave AB and not against it. (A strategy of purchasing options against objective points is also acceptable but more risky than flowing with the trend.) After exiting a position, I usually wait for outright entry signals before taking new positions.

Whether you use a COP, OP, or an XOP as a profit objective is a judgment call taking into consideration other tools in your technical arsenal—for example, overbought/oversold oscillators, strength and thrust of the move indicators, previous length of base, trend in the next higher time frame, and volatility. It should be recognized now, however, that having three logically identified areas available in which to capture profit is substantially better than an infinite number of arbitrary guesses.

Examples of Fibonacci Expansion Analysis in the Market

Figure 8-2, which displays one month of S&P prices, shows wave AB and minor retracement C. It will be helpful if you exercise your imagination somewhat and pretend you do not see price action after point C (26480). In other words, pretend the last four days of price action haven't happened yet. We will assume we are long in the market due to "Key of the Day" (3 × 3) price penetration on January 2 (see *Notes from a Trader*)[3] or some other entry method, and we are looking for a logical place to take profits. Point A is located at the bottom of the up-thrust (24060). Point C is located where shown because it is the first day a previous low was penetrated. Point B is simply the highest high prior to point C (26880). Using these points, our calculations provide us with the COP, OP, and XOP as shown. Our nearest sell point is the COP, at 28222. (Note: If subsequent price action had carried the S&P prices lower than the existing low at C, point C would have been located wherever the lowest low occurred. In fact, market action continued up, so ABC had to be located as shown. It should also be noted that for fast intraday action on a 30-minute, five-minute, or even a one-minute chart, point C can change rather rapidly before being definitively established. Therefore, although the calculations are simple, they may take a bit of effort to keep up with.

Strategy: The move comprising AB is almost unprecedented in its rise. Since a substantial pull-back seems imminent, and the COP is the first logical profit objective, it is the preferred objective. As it turned out, the COP projection gave an almost perfect point to take profits and, for more adventurous and experienced souls, to buy put options or even to go short. The other un-

Figure 8-2   Determining Profit Objective Points for March S&P
(12/23/86 to 1/23/87)

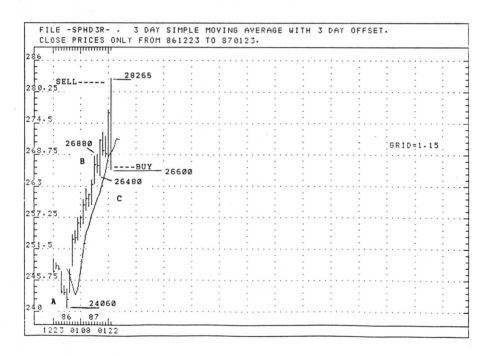

```
     Point Value        Objective Points        File  SPH01191.OP
     ---------------------------------------------------------------

       A = 24060          COP = 28222
       B = 26880   .       OP = 29300
       C = 26480          XOP = 31042


   Focus Number    File SPH01232         Focus# (High for the swing)
   Point Number    Support Fib Nodes   Point# (Enter highest reaction low first)
   --------------------------------------------------------------------------------
   28265          1
                ===>  26658    *
                ===>  25666    *
   24060                 .
   ------------------------------------------


      End ....
```

```
     FILE -SPHD3R- .   3 DAY SIMPLE MOVING AVERAGE WITH 3 DAY OFFSET.
     CLOSE PRICES ONLY FROM 861223 TO 870123.
286
        .SELL-----       28265
280.25

274.5

268.75    26880                                           GRID=1.15
        B
                   ----BUY
263                       26600
                   26480
                   C
257.25

251.5

245.75

240   A      24060
        86    87
   1223  0108  0122
```

realized objectives, OP and XOP, are not negated. They continue to exist for later consideration as long as point C is not taken out. Remember however, that they must be recalculated at contract rollover, since the numbers for A, B and C will obviously be different.

Figure 8-3, which displays intraday T-bond prices, depicts a break in the bond market (AB). If we assume that we are short or got short at the throw-back rally (BC) using Fibonacci Retracement Analysis, our next problem is where to take profits. The logical profit objectives have been calculated by the Fibnodes Program and appear in the lower left-hand corner of the chart.

Strategy: The COP objective (10110) is our preferred profit objective, be-cause in this example, we are an intraday trader and will not hold our posi-tion overnight. So the fact that it is late in the day has a bearing on our choice of a logical profit objective.

Figure 8-4, which displays a month of the Dow Industrial Index, is analogous to Figure 8-2. In Figure 8-4, however, we have two sets of profit objectives for the Dow. The first set, calculated from points ABC, is similar to the example given in Figure 2. In other words, this is the Dow equivalent of the S&P example in Figure 2. On January 19, we calculated a COP objective of 2179, which was exceeded intraday on January 23 by 31 points. The OP from that calculation was 2256 and the XOP was 2378. Make note of that XOP value. Now look at the A'B'C' wave, where B'=2210 and C'=2079. This wave was the first dramatic pull back of the bull run that began in January. The OP' objective of 2399, which was calculated on January 23, is very close to the XOP objective (2378) of the earlier calculation. Two objectives so close to one another from such important market swings as these tend to confirm each other and provide logical profit objectives of high accuracy. In fact, as Figure 8-5 reveals, the Dow 2400 area later marked a significant high from which large reactions in both the cash and futures markets occurred.

The last example is Figure 8-5, which includes over five months of the Dow Industrial Index. This is the chart that I used to calculate my 1987 projection of 2702. I am concluding the chapter with this chart, because I want to show you how things can sometimes go wrong—although in this case, the error was not large and not due to any failure of the concept.

The chart shows support of the industrials at approximately the 2210 area, which was an *entry* level calculated from Fibonacci Retracement Analysis (point C and C'). Notice that price action came down to that area of confluence three times, but never closed beneath it. From there, the index embarked on a thrust to 2700. In Figure 8-5, we again see two sets of objec-tive point calculations. The first calculation (ABC') is wrong because of incor-rect data I received indicating a low of 2169 on May 20 (see the cursor). The actual low on May 20 was 2192. Remember my call of 2702 that I mentioned earlier? It was calculated incorrectly! Since the actual intraday low of the move occurred at 2192 on April 27, 2192 had to be used for point C, resulting in the calculation ABC, which produced a profit objective (OP) of 2725, not

Figure 8-3   Determining Intra-Day Profit Objective Points for March Bonds

```
            OBJECTIVE POINTS CALCULATOR
            ============================


Point Value        Objective Points     File  BDHINDY2.OP  /in 32nds/
-----------------------------------------------------------------------

A = 10202             COP = 10110
B = 10115              OP = 10103
C = 10123             XOP = 10023
```

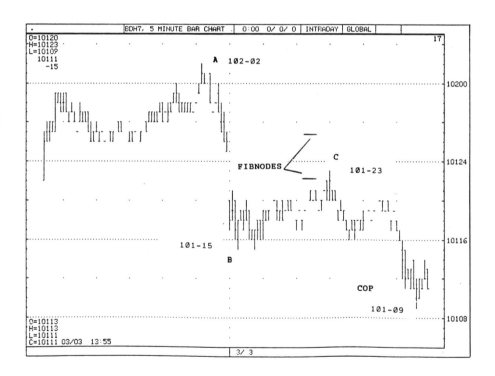

Figure 8-4   Determining Profit Objective Points for Dow Industrials
(12/23/86 to 1/23/87)

OBJECTIVE POINTS CALCULATOR
============================

Point Value	Objective Points	File DJIO1191.OP

```
  A = 1890        COP = 2179
  B = 2089         OP = 2256
  C = 2057        XOP = 2378
```

Point Value	Objective Points	File DJIO1231.OP

```
  A  = 1890       COP = 2276
 (B) = 2210        OP = 2399
 (C) = 2079       XOP = 2596
```

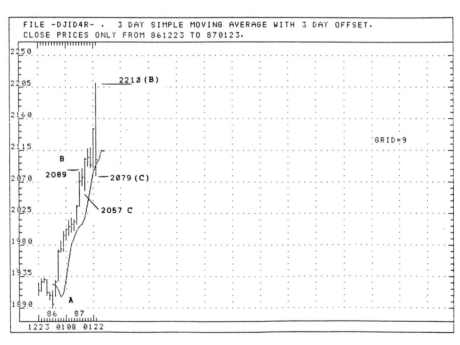

Figure 8-5   Determining Profit Objective Points for Dow Industrials
(12/30/86 to 6/11/87)

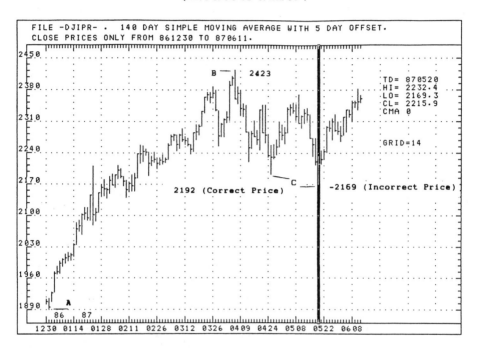

```
Point Value        Objective Points       File  DJI05201.OP
-------------------------------------------------------------------

   A = 1890           COP = 2498
   B = 2423            OP = 2702
   C = 2169           XOP = 3031
(INCORRECT POINT C)


Point Value        Objective Points       File  DJI04271.OP
-------------------------------------------------------------------

   A = 1890           COP = 2521
   B = 2423            OP = 2725
   C = 2192           XOP = 3054
(CORRECT POINT C)
```

2702! For Dow projections, actual point values must be used, NOT averaged values as appear in certain popular publications.

Tying Up Loose Ends

So far we have covered only one procedure for determining logical profit objectives, but a variety of other methods can be used. I use one other method, a study I pioneered called the *oscillator predictor*, which uses a computer program to generate a profit objective. Looking at price data over time, the study identifies previous overbought and oversold levels by means of a detrended oscillator. Through a series of calculations, it determines the price necessary to achieve an overbought or oversold condition *tomorrow*. At times I have attempted to teach the calculations but have given up the idea, since they are too cumbersome and complex to do by hand—unlike Fibonacci Expansion Analysis. For the oscillator predictor study, you must have the computer program. Although the numbers generated by the Oscillator Predictor are not hit as frequently as those generated by Fibonacci Expansion Analysis, the Predictor has been known to make some amazing calls. As with all logical profit objectives, however, orders must be in place ahead of time, as the price levels (especially with the predictor) are highly unstable and usually not available for long.

When I work with logical profit objectives, my stop placement techniques involve time as well as price. Although my stops are specific, they may *initially* be twice the size of the profit objectives I calculate. This reflects the confidence I have in my entry techniques rather than my desire to incur risk. I hide my stops behind a specific displaced moving average or behind Fibnode confluence numbers or both. On a position trade, I raise them to a comfortable margin below these points, depending on volatility and the time frame in which I'm trading.

Although in my teaching I usually suggest using profit objectives for 50 percent of all trades, in my trading I use profit objectives for virtually all of my positions. That's because I have run parallel accounts and have always done better using profit objectives on every trade. My results, however, could have been due to my psychological need to trade shorter term and capture profit. A different approach may better suit your temperament. I suppose the point again is that you ultimately have to decide to trade in a manner consistent with your psychology. There is another reason, however, that I love to capture profit: I have full confidence that my entry techniques can get me back into any market move I want to participate in, so I don't fret about losing my position.

As I said earlier, one of the reasons I can take profit objectives and ignore further market movement is that I am sure over time that I'm ahead that way. For you to be sure, you have to do your own research—past and real-time. Prove to yourself that this technique works. If you depend on my research, you will probably be uncertain and ultimately will have regrets. Use my work as a source of knowledge—a bit of insight to feed your own thought process.

The cheapest way to use Fibonacci Expansion Analysis is to take a pencil and start calculating moves based on the equations described earlier. The next step (and one I highly recommend) is to purchase a proportional divider—an architectural tool that quickly identifies expansions and retracements on a chart. The divider is available through Coast Investment Software, along with a 60-page professionaly illustrated applications manual, which answers many of the questions that you will have regarding the most effective use of this tool. The booklet also covers entry as well as exit techniques. Once you have the divider and the manual, a reasonable next step is the purchase of a programmable calculator.

The ultimate tool, however, for those who really want to master the concepts of both Fibonacci Expansion and Retracement Analysis and effectively apply them to the market on an active, intraday basis, is the Fibnodes program, also available through CIS. This program took a year and a half to develop and is the same program I trade with. The ultimate for speed and reliability, it provided all of the calculations that were detailed in the examples we covered earlier. Fibnodes calculates both entry and exit signals, and the Fibnodes manual contains additional theoretical information as well as practical applications of Fibonacci Expansion Analysis.

As with all trading tools, Fibonacci Expansion Analysis, with its use of logical profit objectives, is only as good as the trader who uses it. It is an approach that has the potential to reap large profits over time, but only if you, the trader, are disciplined enough to stay with it.

The market will not always look as ideal as I have presented it in my five examples. There will be times when you see strange things happening, and you'll be tempted to bail out. Other times, when you see prices move right past your first profit objective, seemingly to go on forever, you'll be tempted to pull your remaining exit orders—or worse yet get back in the move by entering "at the market" without waiting for a proper entry signal. Just remember, when you encounter these situations that many professional traders who are now earning a living vending lottery tickets faced those same circumstances and gave in to their emotions. To succeed with this or any other trading technique, don't make that mistake.

I have presented you with a valuable technique that doesn't require mystifying calculations to set up and that has the potential to reward you with large profits. Please use it wisely.

Endnotes

[1] For an excellent presentation of Elliott Wave theory, I recommend *Elliott Wave Principle* by A.J. Frost and R. R. Prechter, Jr. New Classes Library, P.O. Box 1618, Gainesville, Georgia 30503.

[2] Fibnodes is a software program created by Joe DiNapoli and available three Coast Investment Software, 8851 Albatross Drive, Huntington Beach, California 92646. (714) 968-1978. It calculates profit objectives as well as entry points (Fibnodes) by creating a retracement series.

[3] *Notes from A Trader* is also authored by Joe DiNapoli, and available through Coast Investment Software, 8851 Albatross Drive, Huntington Beach, California 92646. It discusses trend following techniques including "Key of the Day," as well as the use of detrended oscillators.

BASIC TENETS OF THE ELLIOTT WAVE PRINCIPLE

ROBERT R. PRECHTER & A. JOHN FROST

■

ROBERT R. PRECHTER, JR. & A. J. FROST

Robert R. Prechter, Jr. attended Yale University on full scholarship and graduated in 1971 with a degree in psychology. After several years of self-education in the field of technical analysis, he joined the Merrill Lynch Market Analysis Department in New York and for four years specialized in market timing, technical research, computer output, cycles and wave phenomena.

Mr. Prechter is author of *The Major Works of R. N. Elliott*, a reprinting of Elliott's original writings, and editor of *The Elliott Wave Theorist*, a financial forecasting letter covering the stock market, interest rates and precious metals. Mr. Prechter has been labeled the "foremost" Elliott Wave practitioner by *Barron's*, "the champion market forecaster" by *Fortune* and "the nation's leading proponent of the Elliott Wave method of forecasting" by the *New York Times*. Independent rating services have ranked *The Elliott Wave Theorist* #1 in the country for timing accuracy so often that the Financial News Network recently named him "Guru of the Decade."

A.J. Frost, C.F.A., is a graduate of Queens University, Kingston, Ontario. He started his career as a legal accountant. He was admitted to the Ontario Institute of Chartered Accountants in 1934 and called to the Ontario Bar in 1937. He served as Chairman of the National Capital Commission (Canada) for two years and later sat on the bench as a member of the Tax Appeal Board, Tax Review Board, and Anti-Inflation Appeal Tribunal. Mr. Frost was introduced to the Elliott Wave Principle in 1960, and later wrote three of the annual Elliott Wave supplements for the Bank Credit Analyst. He has delivered numerous lectures on the subject to professional groups.

■ CHAPTER NINE ■

R ALPH NELSON ELLIOTT DISCOVERED that the ever-changing stock market tended to reflect a basic harmony found in nature. From this discovery he developed a rational system of stock market analysis. He postulated that the price movement of the DJIA (Dow Jones Industrial Average) formed discernible patterns that were repetitive in form, but were not necessarily repetitive in time or amplitude. Elliott claimed predictive value for "the wave principle," which now bears the name "The Elliott Wave Principle."

Essentially, the Elliott Wave Principle is a system of empirically derived rules for interpreting action in the major stock market averages. The Wave Principle is a tool of unique value, whose most striking characteristics are its generality and its accuracy. Its generality gives market perspective most of the time, and its accuracy in pointing up changes in direction is at times almost unbelievable. Many areas of mass human activity also tend to follow the wave principle, but since the stock market (as reflected by the DJIA) was the basis for Elliott's studies, it is there that the principle is most popularly applied.

While Elliott had theories regarding the origin and meaning of the patterns he discovered, it should suffice for now that the rules herein have stood the test of time and that market action can be perceived within the context of Elliott's principles. As in much of technical analysis based on chart patterns, it is not necessary to understand immediately the *why*, as long as the tools are workable.

In the bull market, the basic objective of Elliott's rules is to follow and to count correctly the development of a five-wave advance in the averages, three up, with two intervening down. This concept should be divorced immediately from the currently popular "all bull markets have three legs" idea, which appears to be a muddled mixture of Dow's three phases and Elliott's five waves. What one might conclude to be a market "leg" in general terms may have any number of different definitions in Elliott terms and may not be a bull leg at all. Conversely, a series of legs may be interpreted under the wave principle to be the completion of only one.

Often one will hear several different interpretations of the Elliott Wave status, especially when cursory, off-the-cuff studies of the averages are made by latter-day experts. However, most uncertainties can be avoided if hourly charts are kept, both on arithmetic and semi-logarithmic chart paper, and if care is taken to avoid breaking any of the rules of wave identification.

149

In a series of articles published in 1939 by *Financial World* magazine, Elliott pointed out that the stock market unfolded according to a basic rhythm or pattern of five waves up and three waves down to form a complete cycle of eight waves. The three waves down are referred to as a "correction" of the preceding five waves up. The basic concept of five waves in the direction of the main trend followed by three corrective waves is shown in Figure 9-1.

Figure 9-1 The Basic Pattern

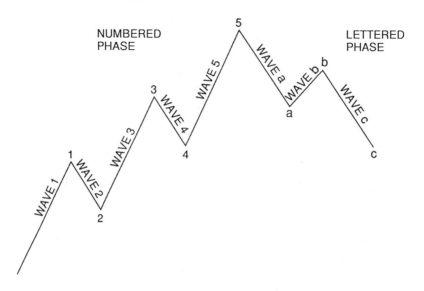

Waves 1, 3, and 5 are termed *impulse* waves and waves 2 and 4 *corrective* waves. Wave 2 corrects wave 1, wave 4 corrects wave 3 and the entire sequence 1, 2, 3, 4, 5 is corrected by the sequence a, b, c. One complete cycle consisting of eight waves, then, is made up of two distinct phases, the numbered phase, sometimes referred to as a "five," and the lettered phase, sometimes referred to as a "three."

Following this cycle, a second similar cycle of five upward waves begins, followed by another three-waves-down pattern. A third and final advance then develops, consisting of five waves up. At this juncture a major five-wave "up" movement has been completed and a major three-wave "down" movement takes place. These three major waves down "correct" the entire movement of five major waves up. Each of the numbered and lettered "phases" then is actually a wave itself, but of one degree larger than the waves of which it is composed.

This concept is illustrated in Figure 9-2, which shows that two waves of larger degree can be broken into eight waves of the next lower degree, and those eight lower-degree waves can be further subdivided in exactly the same manner to produce 34 waves of the *next* lower degree. The Elliott wave Principle postulates, then, that waves of any degree in any series can always be subdivided and re-subdivided into waves of lesser degree or, conversely, expanded into waves of higher degree. Thus we can use Figure 9-2 to illustrate two waves, eight waves, or 34 waves, depending on the degree to which we are referring.

Figure 9-2

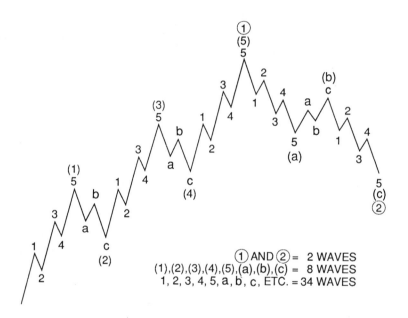

(1) AND (2) = 2 WAVES
(1),(2),(3),(4),(5),(a),(b),(c) = 8 WAVES
1, 2, 3, 4, 5, a, b, c, ETC. = 34 WAVES

The (a)-(b)-(c) corrective pattern illustrated as wave 2 in Figure 9-2 subdivides into a 5-3-5 pattern. Wave (2), if examined under a "microscope," would take the same form as we show for wave 2. Waves (1) and (2) in Figure 9-2 always take the same form as waves 1 and 2, illustrating the phenomenon of constant form within ever-changing degree.

The entire phenomenon of *form* and *degree* is carried one step further in Figure 9-3. Figure 9-3 illustrates the theory that in a complete stock market cycle, waves will subdivide as follows:

Table 9-1 Impulse Waves—Variations

	Cycle Bull Market	*Cycle Bear Market*	*Complete Cycle*
Cycle Waves	1	1	2
Primary Waves	5	3	8
Intermediate Waves	21	13	34
Minor Waves	89	55	144

Figure 9-3

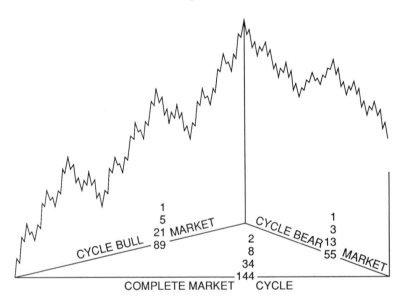

Extensions

For the most part, five-wave formations have clear-cut, wavelike characteristics with infrequent irregularities, except for what are known as extensions. Extensions occur quite often. They are exaggerated or elongated movements that generally appear in one of the three impulse waves (1, 3, or 5). At times the subdivisions of an extended wave are nearly the same amplitude and duration as the other four main waves, giving a total count of nine waves of similar size rather than the normal count of five for the sequence. In a nine-wave sequence, it is occasionally difficult to say which wave extended, although it is usually irrelevant anyway, since under the Elliott system a count of nine and a count of five have the same technical significance. The diagrams in Figure 9-4, illustrating extensions, should clarify this point.

Figure 9-4 Extensions

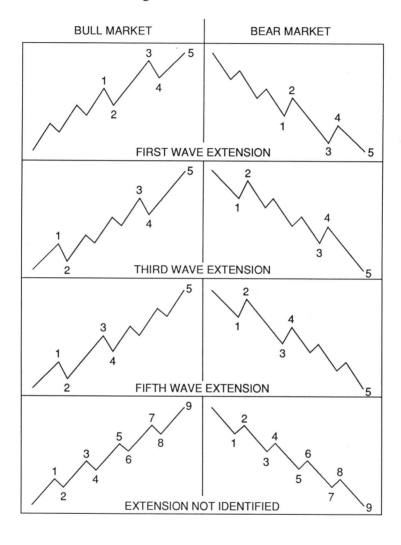

The fact that extensions exist can prove a useful guide to the expectable lengths of upcoming waves, since in our experience the majority of waves do contain extensions in one, and only one, of their three impulse waves. Thus, if the first and third waves are of about equal length, the fifth wave will likely be a protracted surge, especially if volume on the fifth wave is greater than volume on the third wave. Conversely, if wave three has extended, the fifth should be simply constructed and resemble wave one.

Extensions may also occur within extensions.

While extended fifths are not uncommon, extensions of extensions occur most often within third waves, as Figure 9-5 illustrates.

Figure 9-5   Extension of Extension in the Third Wave

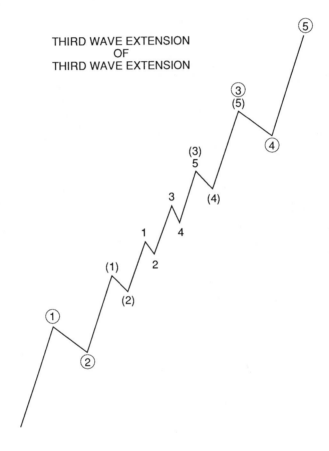

THIRD WAVE EXTENSION
OF
THIRD WAVE EXTENSION

Diagonal Triangles

Diagonal triangles occur in fifth-wave positions, usually after the preceding move has gone "too far too fast," as Elliott put it. They are a special type of fifth wave, which indicate exhaustion of the larger movement. Diagonal triangles are essentially wedges formed by two converging lines, with each subwave, including the impulse waves, subdividing into a "three" as illustrated in Figures 9-6 and 9-7.

Figure 9-6   **Figure 9-7**

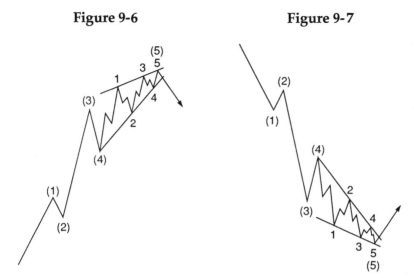

A rising wedge is bearish and is usually followed by a sharp decline, retracting at least back to the level where the diagonal triangle began. A falling wedge, by the same token, is bullish, usually giving rise to an upward thrust. Diagonal triangles are the only five-wave constructions in the direction of the main trend within which subwave four may, and usually does, fall to a level that is below that of the peak of wave one. Diagonal triangles are fairly rare phenomena and must not be confused with the more common variety of corrective triangles that develop in fourth wave positions of impulse waves and wave B positions in corrective waves.

Diagonal Triangle Type 2 (A Variation)

By far, most diagonal triangles occur in the wave-5 position. A small percentage occur in the wave-C position, but in either case they are phenomena that are found at the *termination points* of larger patterns. When diagonal triangles occur in the wave-5 or wave-C position, they take the 3-3-3-3-3 shape that Elliott described.

It has recently come to light that a variation on the diagonal triangle will be found in the wave-A position in very rare cases. The characteristic overlapping of waves 1 and 4 *and* the convergence of boundary lines into a wedge shape remain as in the standard diagonal triangle. However, the wave subdivision is different, tracing out a 5-3-5-3-5 pattern. The structure of this formation (see Figure 9-7A) does seem to fit the spirit of the wave principle in that the five-wave subdivisions in the direction of the larger trend communicate a different message from the termination implication of the three-wave subdivisions in a normal diagonal triangle.

Figure 9-7A

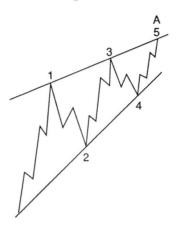

This pattern must be noted, because it implies only B and C waves ahead. The analyst could mistake this pattern for a more common development, a series of 1's and 2's, which would imply an acceleration of the trend and substantial price movement.

Failures

Elliott used the word "failure" to describe a five-wave pattern of movement in which the fifth impulse wave fails to move above the end of the third. It can usually be verified by noting that the presumed fifth wave contains the necessary five subwaves, as illustrated in Figures 9-8 and 9-9.

Failures are not uncommon, especially in waves of small degree. Failures give warning of underlying weakness or strength in the market and tell us more about the reality of stock-market life than most of us care to hear. Just when we think we have it all wrapped up in a neat Elliott package, along comes a failure to cut short our expected target.

We have two classical examples of failures since 1932. The first occurred in October, 1962 at the time of the Cuban crisis and preceded an unusually strong and persistent advance consisting of over five years of uninterrupted bull market.

The second occurred in the move up from November to December, 1976 and indicated underlying weakness in the stock market. This second failure is a fine example of what an upside failure implies. In the ten months following the failure, the DJIA lacked the strength to mount even one five percent rally, almost an unprecedented event. The underperformance of the DJIA compared to the rest of the market was just as striking and persisted through to the final bottom.

Figure 9-8   Bull Market Failure

BULL MARKET FAILURE

Figure 9-9   Bear Market Failure

BEAR MARKET FAILURE

Corrective Waves

Stock market swings of any degree tend to move more easily with the trend of one greater degree than against it. Since corrective waves are generally less clearly identified and subdivided than impulse waves, which flow in the direction of the larger trend, it becomes difficult at times to fit corrective waves into recognizable patterns until they are completed and behind us. As the terminations of corrective waves are less predictable than those for impulse waves, the Elliott analyst must exercise more caution in his analysis when the market is in a meandering corrective mood than when prices are in a positive bull trend. As we shall illustrate, corrective waves are quite a bit more varied than impulse waves.

The single most important rule that can be gleaned from a study of the various corrective patterns is that *corrections can never be fives*. Only impulse waves can be fives. In other words, an initial five-wave movement against the larger trend is never the end of a correction, but only part of it. The following discussion should serve to illustrate this point.

Corrective patterns generally fall into four main categories:

1.   Zigzag (5–3–5. Includes the variation "double zigzag").
2.   Flat (3–3–5. Includes "irregular").
3.   Triangle (3–3–3–3–3. Four variations: ascending, descending, contracting, expanding).
4.   Double three and triple three (combined structures).

Zigzags (5–3–5)

A zigzag in a bull market is a simple three-wave pattern that subdivides into a 5-3-5 affair with the top of wave B noticeably lower than the start of wave A, as illustrated in Figures 9-10 and 9-11.

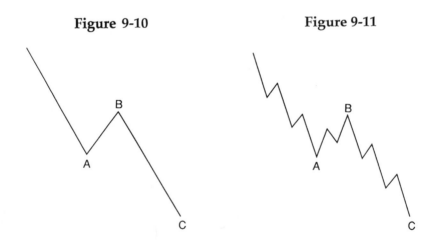

Figure 9-10   **Figure 9-11**

In a bear market, an A–B–C zigzag pattern will be in the opposite direction, as shown in Figures 9-12 and 9-13. The position is inverted, and for this reason a zigzag in a bear market is often referred to as an *inverted zigzag*.

Figure 9-12

Figure 9-13

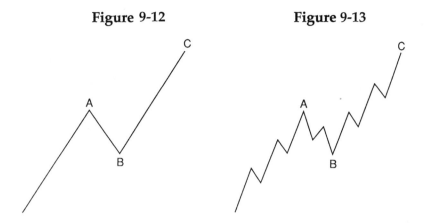

Occasionally, in larger formations zigzags can occur twice in succession with an intervening three, producing what is called a *double zigzag* (see Figure 9-14). Double zigzags are not common but occur often enough that the analyst should be aware of their existence.

Figure 9-14

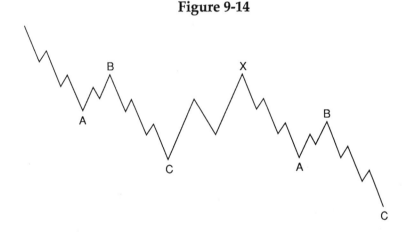

Flats (3–3–5)

A flat type of correction differs from a zigzag in that the subwave sequence is a 3–3–5 affair as shown in Figures 9-15 and 9-16. Since the first decline, wave A, lacks sufficient downward force to unfold into a full five waves as it does in a zigzag, the B wave seems to inherit this lack of countertrend pressure and, not surprisingly, often terminates at or above the start of wave A.

Figure 9-15   **Figure 9-16**

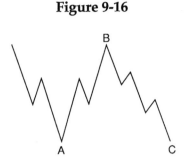

In a bear market the pattern is the same, but inverted as shown in Figures 9-17 and 9-18. In inverted flats, of course, the B wave will terminate at or *below* the start of wave A.

Figure 9-17   **Figure 9-18**

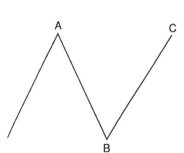
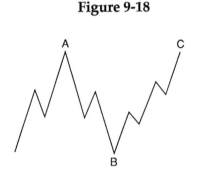

Wave C in any flat generally terminates at or just below the end of wave A rather than significantly below as in zigzags. Thus flat corrections, in their entirety, do less damage to the broader trend.

The word *flat* is often used as a catch-all name for any A-B-C correction that subdivides into a 3-3-5. In a normal flat correction, wave B terminates at about the level of the beginning of wave A, as we have shown in Figures 9-15 to 9-18.

In an irregular flat correction, wave B of the 3-3-5 pattern terminates *beyond* the starting point of wave A, and wave C beyond the end of wave A, as shown for bull markets in Figures 9-19 and 9-20 and bear markets in Figures 9-21 and 9-22.

The formation in the DJIA from August to November, 1973 was an irregular correction in a bear market, or an inverted irregular correction.

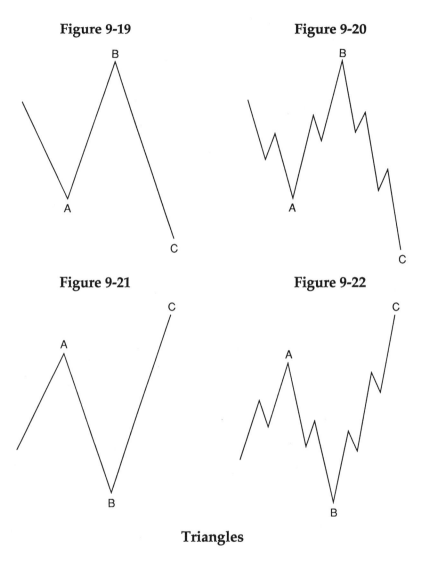

Figure 9-19

Figure 9-20

Figure 9-21

Figure 9-22

Triangles

Triangles as a general rule occur only in positions prior to the final movement in the direction of the larger trend. For the most part, they are
protracted waves and reflect a balance of forces that creates a sideways
movement that is usually associated with lower volume and volatility. Triangles are five-wave affairs that, in turn, subdivide 3–3–3–3–3. They fall into
four main categories as illustrated in Figure 9-23.

After a triangle is complete, the final impulse wave is generally swift
and travels approximately the distance of the widest part of the triangle. El-
liot used the word "thrust" in referring to the swift, short impulse wave following a corrective-wave triangle.

Figure 9-23 Corrective Wave (Horizontal) Triangles

CORRECTIVE WAVE (HORIZONTAL) TRIANGLES

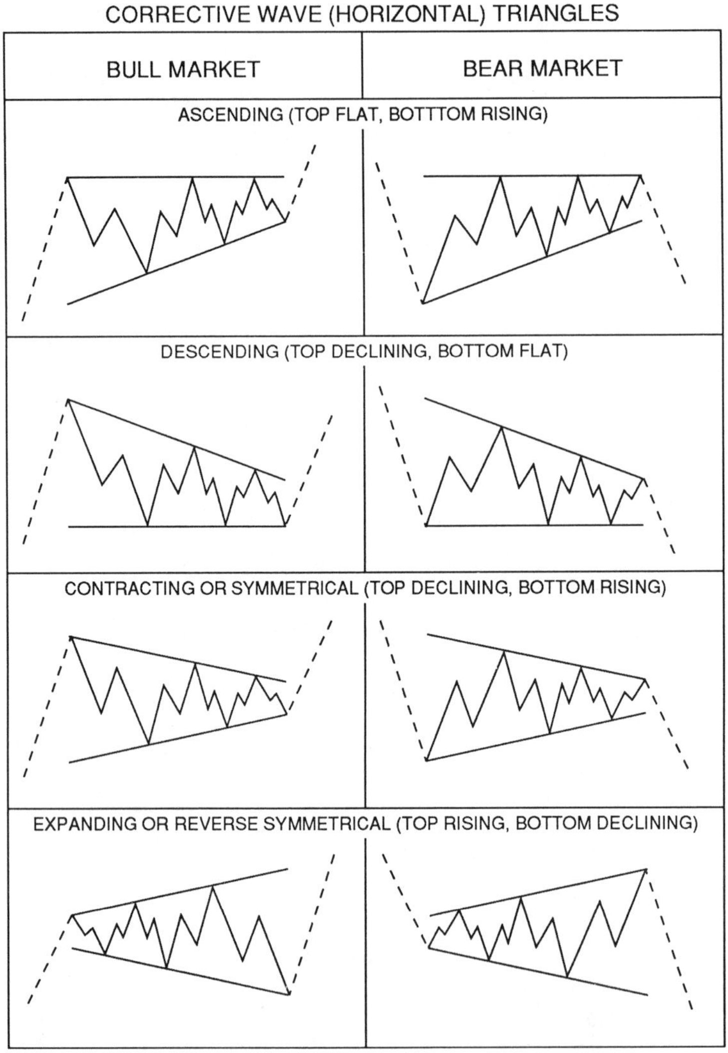

Generally, the trendlines containing the triangle are phenomenally accurate in that touch points rarely fall short of or exceed the boundaries of the lines. Only the fifth subwave can be expected to undershoot or overshoot the triangle boundaries, and, in fact, our experience tells us that it tends to happen more often than not, especially in contracting triangles and expanding triangles.

Double Threes and Triple Threes

A single three is any zigzag or flat. A double three or triple three is a less common type of corrective pattern that is essentially a combination of simpler types of corrections, including zigzags, flats, and triangles. A double three is composed of seven legs and a triple three of eleven. Combinations of threes were labeled differently by Elliott at different times, although the illustrative pattern always took the same shape. In Figure 9-24, the double three is composed of seven waves, which can be mentally counted as if saying "a-b-c and a-b-c" or as one through seven.

Figure 9-24

A triple three is illustrated in Figure 9-25.

Figure 9-25

In these cases, the market is hesitating and acts as if one three weren't enough, as if more time were needed to straighten out whatever reasons the market had for pausing in the first place. Sometimes stock prices seem to be waiting for economic fundamentals to begin to catch up with the market's expectations. For the most part, double threes and triple threes are horizontal in character, although Elliott indicated that the entire formations could slant against the larger trend. These formations frequently give rise to strong subsequent action.

As far as we know, these pages list all wave formations that can be constructed in the price movement of the broad stock market averages. Under the Wave Principle, no other formations than those listed here will occur, indeed, the authors can find few examples of waves above the subminor degree that cannot be counted satisfactorily by the Elliott method.

If the reader wishes to move on to some of the finer points of analysis under the Wave Principle, we suggest *Elliott Wave Principle—Key to Stock Market Profits* and *The Major Works of R.N. Elliott*, both published by New Classics Library, P.O. Box 1618, Gainesville, Ga 30503.

A LONGER-TERM APPROACH TO COMMODITY FUTURES TRADING

EDWARD T. deLANOY

■

EDWARD T. deLANOY

Ed deLanoy is an independent commodity trader. He has operated a private commodity pool for more than 15 years, as his principal avocation in addition to his full-time outside employment. Mr. de-Lanoy holds a B.S. in Business Administration from the University of California, Berkeley, Califorina, an M.B.A. from the University of Santa Clara, California and is a registered C.T.A.

■ CHAPTER TEN ■

THIS CHAPTER IS WRITTEN for the independent trader who recognizes the important economic benefits commodity futures markets provide to the trade, (i.e., the actual holders and users of commodities) and who has resolved to trade for speculative profit in an equally business-like way.

The methods discussed are especially suitable for traders who wish to make their own trading decisions but who cannot devote any significant amount of time during market hours for trading. For such traders, a longer-term approach to profitable trading is recommended.

For this longer-term trading approach, no computers or computer-based data services are needed. For data analysis, only daily, weekly, and monthly charts of historical commodity prices, trading volume, and open interest are required; these are readily available from several publishers. The trader must have access to each day's commodity futures prices, trading volume, and open interest found in any metropolitan or financial newspaper. Last, the trader must be able to devote a specific amount of time for analysis after every market day. In general, the time required should compare with that needed for any serious hobby or avocation.

This chapter is limited to the trading of contracts for physical commodities. It is assumed that the trader has no specialized knowledge about the fundamentals that govern supply and demand for these commodities. Therefore, the technical or market approach to analysis is used. The premises underlying this method of analysis are discussed in the Addendum.

The trading suggestions presented are limited to picking potentially profitable trades after extensive prospecting, taking trading positions in the market, and abandoning the position if unprofitable. The trader must make his or her own study of how to manage a profitable trading position and where to take profits. This will depend on the trader's emotional tolerance for risk and on his or her familiarity with technical behavior of market prices. Assistance with the latter can be found in the References.

Normal and Inverted Markets

Cash commodity prices are determined by current actual supply and demand for a commodity, while commodity futures prices are determined by current perceptions of the trade (i.e., the holders and users of commodities) and speculation as to what supply and demand will cause commodity prices to be for future contract months.

This is the essence. From a technical viewpoint, it makes no difference why prices are what they are. The day's closing prices represent a consensus by all traders, knowledgeable or otherwise, of what prices prevail on that market day for the various contract months. Refer to the Addendum for justification of this view of prices. The Addendum also explains why the trade uses futures markets to minimize risk to their commercial profit margins. Experience shows that if the trade develops other ways of eliminating this risk, the affected futures markets atrophy and disappear through lack of participation. Speculative trading alone will not sustain such markets.

Therefore, the trading actions of commercial interests are the principal determinants of futures prices, even though speculative over-enthusiasm or excess pessimism may cause exaggerated price movements from time to time, which are soon adjusted. Occasionally, of course, commercial interests may be wrong in their perceptions, but it is wiser not to count on this happening.

Normal Markets

A normal (sometimes called a *contango*) futures market for a commodity indicates adequate supplies or a surplus. Schematically, futures prices for a commodity in a normal market will appear as shown in Figure 10-1.

Figure 10-1

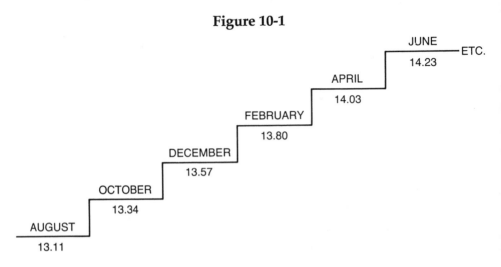

Note that the contract price of each later contract month is higher than the previous month's price. This indicates adequate supplies at current futures price levels. For commodities in storage, the progressively higher prices reflect the carrying charge (i.e., costs of storage, insurance, and interest) that must be paid by the buyer. For commodities delivered out of current production (e.g., the meats, soybean oil, and meal), a progressively higher price is the charge for holding a call on production, which has approximately the same price effect as a carrying charge. In the case of basic agricultural contracts (wheat, cocoa, cotton, etc.) the above price relationship can only be relied upon for contracts in the same crop year. Prices for new crop contracts will depend on how traders perceive the size of the new crop. Crop year dates are available in any standard commodity futures text. For example, the cocoa crop year runs from October through September.

Although not covered in this chapter, interest rate futures contracts, taken as a group, show the same normal market characteristics when the supply of money is adequate. The Treasury yield curve, which appears each market day in *The Wall Street Journal*'s credit market section, extends 30 years into the future. When money is plentiful, the curve will slope upward, showing a progressively higher cost of money (interest rate) as time goes on. If we wanted to take the trouble, we could arrive at a similar curve by calculating the interest rate implied by futures prices of Treasury bills, five-year and ten-year Treasury notes and 20-year Treasury bonds at any given time to see if these contracts, taken as a group, showed a normal market or not. The main point is that all futures markets work in about the same way.

Price Movements in Normal Markets

Aside from downside price breakouts (covered later in this chapter) normal markets are less suitable for long-term traders because price movements tend to be more random and, therefore, less predictable. Prices can move up and down, apparently with equal ease, and are probably better analyzed using computer-based, short-term trading systems. Of course, major economic forces such as the general price inflation that began in the mid-1970s resulted in profitable long-term (buy) positions in normal markets. Similarly, a major price deflation would result in profitable short (sale) positions.

In general, though, and lacking statistical proof, I believe that under stable economic conditions normal markets tend to have a downside price bias because:

1. Cash prices are lower than futures prices. (Occasionally, cash prices may be higher because of cartel price support action such as occurs in crude oil, cocoa, and coffee from time to time.)

2. Supplies are adequate at current price levels.

In the above circumstances, the trade would tend to be short on balance, hedging against the risk of lower prices.

True downside breakouts are very tradeable, given that a normal market prevails. As shown in Figure 10-2, a fine example occurred in pork bellies.

Figure 10-2 Pork Bellies CME

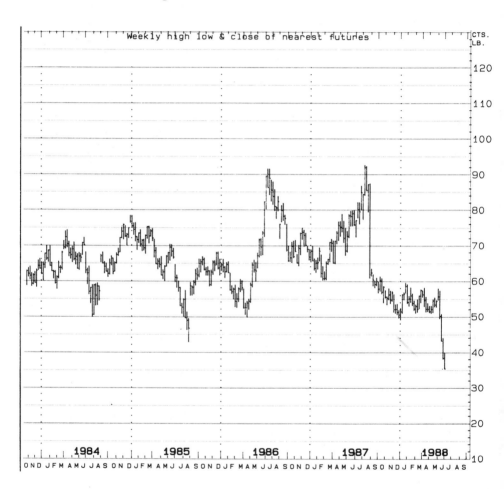

An open stop order to sell the August 1988 at just under the $ .50 lows occurring early in 1986 and at the end of 1987 would have been immediately profitable and would not have caused the trader a moment's worry until prices stabilized at approximately $ .32. Note that the breakout occurred at a round number, $ .50. Of course, not all major declines are so persistently orderly. But they are worth the patience and effort required to track them. Order placement recommendations are covered later in the discussion on break-out markets.

Crude Oil

Another fine down-side price breakout is shown in Figure 10-3.

Figure 10-3   Crude Oil NYMEX

An open stop sell order in January 1986 just under the $25 low price in early 1985 would again have been immediately profitable. Note again that the breakout occurred just below a round number.

Inverse Markets

Such markets are pregnant with meaning for the long-term buyer of futures contracts. The term "backwardation" is sometimes used instead of inverse, probably because they tend to be the opposite of a normal market. Such markets shout shortage.

Schematically, prices for a commodity in an inverse market, within the same crop year if it applies, will look like Figure 10-4.

Figure 10-4

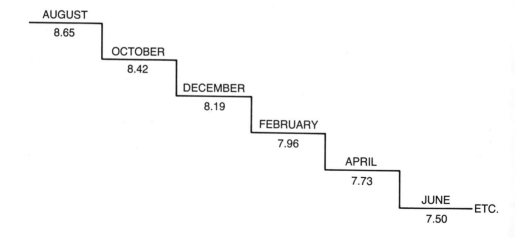

Note that the contract price of each later contract month is lower than the previous month's price. This is the tip-off to near-term shortage, because demand is outpacing supply. We reason as follows:

1. As explained in the previous section, markets exist for the trade, i.e., the holders and users of commodities. Like any other business, the trade can make money only if its profit margin can be maintained.

2. We can, therefore, expect trade buyers to buy at the lowest possible price. Yet in an inverted market, commodity prices indicate that buyers are willing to pay higher prices for nearby delivery, even though they could buy at lower prices later on. As the Chicago Board of Trade's *Commodity Trading Manual* puts it, the buyer says "We will pay you a premium for your commodity if you deliver it to us now."

Before going on, note that:

1. Price inversion occurring in basic agricultural contracts applies only within the same crop year.

2. Interest rate contracts covering maturities over a 20-year period (from Treasury bills to Treasury bonds) can show higher interest rates for Treasury bills, indicating near-term money is in very short supply. See Chicago Board of Trade quotation in the previous paragraph.

Detecting the beginning of what may prove an inverse market is often quite a leisurely process. Since ordinarily most markets are of the normal variety, all we need to do initially is to be observant and search for the unusual as we look at current closing commodity prices in a metropolitan newspaper or *The Wall Street Journal*. Serendipity—an apparent aptitude for making fortunate discoveries accidentally—will be our goal at this stage. Big price moves take time to develop. Here are some examples of the process.

March 1988 World Sugar. Let's see what conclusions we could have drawn from the price actions of the world sugar contracts in 1987. (The contract expired at the end of February 1988). For our purpose, let's begin with May 1, 1987, May being the first full month in which both the March 1988 and May 1988 contracts first appeared in *The Wall Street Journal*. In Figure 10-5 are month-end prices for these two contracts.

Figure 10-5   Sugar "11" NYSCS

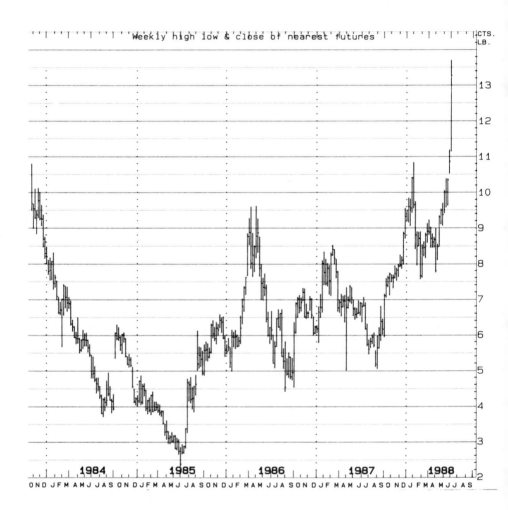

Reprinted with permission, © 1988 Commodity Research Bureau, 30 South Wacker Drive, Suite 1820, Chicago, Illinois 60606.

Date	March 88	May 88	Difference (spread)	Price Trend
(May 1)	7.43	7.63	+20	Down
May	7.52	7.68	+16	Down(?)
June	7.39	7.56	+17	Down
July	6.71	6.87	+16	Down
August	6.56	6.74	+18	Down
September	6.96	7.20	+24	Up(?)
October	7.59	7.66	+ 7	Up
November	8.01	8.05	+ 4	Up
December	9.49	9.41	- 8	Up
January	9.64	9.45	-19	Up
	May 88	*July 88*		
February	7.91	7.85	-6	Down
March	8.88	8.80	-8	Up
	July 88	*Oct. 88*		
April	8.51	8.70	+19	Down
May	9.47	9.45	-2	Up
June	13.32	12.63	-69	Up

Through August (actually starting in March), world sugar prices have been in a down-trend. The price difference (spread) between the two contracts is wide. This is a *normal* market, indicating adequate supplies.

Prices moved higher in September. But is this just a minor reaction in a bear market? The spread is still wide indicating ample supplies. Patience! Better wait and see.

October prices add a new dimension. The trend is still up, but now the spread has narrowed. The market is significantly less "normal." Are supplies now less ample than last month? Is the price uptrend for real? If it is, at what price should we buy?

The November and the December year-end prices show that the price uptrend has continued. In December, the carrying charge (spread) has turned negative, suggesting some shortage of supply for the March contract. In fact, world sugar has changed from a *normal* to an *inverted* market. As we know, inverted markets indicate necessitous buying.

Going back to the end of October, where the possibility of a trend change is still in doubt, a trader's analytical perceptions can often be sharpened by actually entering the market. This transports the trader from the academic to the real world, thereby also stimulating the adrenaline. A spread position (in this case, long March/short May) can serve this analytical purpose and doesn't pose a serious financial risk if the spread should prove unprofitable. The important thing is to try to be in the market at this stage.

We can now prepare to take a long (buy) position. Let's place an open (i.e., good till cancelled) stop buy order above a previous high price, thereby letting the market confirm our judgment if the order is filled.

Such a breakout occurred at about 8.60 as shown on the weekly chart in this case, earlier breakouts on the daily chart would have worked equally well.

Some other indicators also can be helpful in predicting a bull market. But try to think of commodity prices in commercial terms. It will make your analysis more meaningful, and your trading more profitable. The key points are:

1. An inverted market in which prices of the nearby contracts are higher than the more distant ones.
2. Chart indications that a price uptrend may be starting.
3. A noticable drop in open interest. In depressed markets, a sharp drop in open interest can be considered an indication that holders of commodities are less fearful of lower prices and may actually expect higher prices. Therefore, they feel it less necessary to take short positions to hedge their profit margins.

1987 December Copper. Using the same method of analysis as for world sugar, above, following are 1987 month-end copper contract prices (except as indicated).

1987 Date	Nearest Contract	Next Contract	Difference (spread)	Price Trend
	May 87	July 87		
(Jan 2)	61.90	62.30	+40	Down
January	60.95	61.45	+50	Down
February	63.40	63.45	+ 5	Up
(Mar 10)	63.40	63.35	- 5	Up
(Mar 25)	64.50	63.70	-80	Up
(Mar 31)	62.45	62.00	-45	Down(!)
April	62.30	62.15	-15	Down
	July 87	Sept.87		
May	65.90	65.15	-75	Up
June	72.55	71.45	-90	Up
	Sept.87	Dec.87		
July	78.15	76.35	-190	Up
August	77.05	75.10	-195	Up

	Dec. 87	March 88		
September	79.75	78.55	-120	Up
(Oct.20)	74.60	73.10	-150	Down
October	82.15	78.70	-345	Up
November	114.80	107.00	-780	Up
	March 88	May 88		
December	127.40	108.20	-1920	Up
(Jan. 88)	95.75	85.85	-990	Down
(Feb. 88)	90.90	86.30	-460	Down

Figure 10-6   Copper COMEX

Reprinted with permission, © 1988 Commodity Research Bureau, 30 South Wacker Drive, Suite 1820, Chicago, Illinois 60606.

Notice first the excellent correlation between the spread and the price uptrend in an inverted market.

Copper prices entered 1987 in a minor down-trend as part of a larger irregular uptrend that started the previous September. During this period, the spread was normal (+) and open interest was rising, indicating adequate supplies. But February revealed some possible shortages, as indicated by the strengthening spread and some reduction in open interest. On March 10, the spread turned negative, and the copper market became inverse. But both the price and the spread weakened after strong closes on March 25, and prices fell back at the end of March. Still, copper prices remained inverse, suggesting the possibility of still more interesting developments ahead.

As the later data show, the upward price movement resembled a space launch from Cape Canaveral. Open interest dropped significantly as this bigger move began. Even the backlash from Black Monday (October 19, 1987) didn't disturb the spread, although copper low closes occurred the next day).

Preparation for buying copper could have involved placing open stop buy orders for the nearest nondelivery month contract at prices slightly above the March 1986 high price or above the March 1984 high. Note that there was no real risk in being stopped out had you bought above the higher 1984 high price, unlike such possibility if buying above the 1986 high price.

1988 July Soybean Meal. The dynamic 1988 bull markets in the grains and soybean complex stand out on our charts. But most of these contracts were normal markets during the 1-1/2 year period from 1987 thru mid-1988. And since prices in normal markets usually move less predictably, they must, for planning purposes, be considered less trustworthy for sustained upward price moves than our inverted markets. Aside from oats and wheat which made occasional forays into inverse price territory, the only contract that was consistently inverse was soybean meal, as shown in Figure 10-7, thereby providing long-term advance notice of possible important price rises ahead.

In preparation for placing an open stop buy order, we would ordinarily prefer placing it above a longer-term high than the $223 high of November 1987 that occurred only six months previously. However, since the November 1987 price was still a long-term high for several years, and since the grain and soybean markets were moving dynamically higher, order placement above the November 1987 high would have been prudent. As it turned out, the Soybean contract was the stellar performer, but soybean meal was the more orderly market, providing the opportunity for a more certain profit.

Platinum. Practically everyone, whether trading commodities or not, is aware of the majestic bull market in precious metal that started in 1979. It seemed to spring from nowhere. But inverse market watchers would have observed that, of all the precious metals, only platinum suddenly shifted from a normal to an inverse market. For precious metal traders, it provided a trader's edge" of enormous proportions. Like soybeans, gold and silver were never inverse markets throughout this period.

1987 Date	Nearest Contract	Next Contract	Difference (spread)	Price Trend
	March '87	May '87		
Jan. 2	144.30	145.30	+ 1.00	—
January	144.20	140.00	- 4.20	Down
February	141.40	136.90	- 4.50	Down
	May	July		
March	143.10	142.20	-0.90	Up
April	160.90	159.40	-1.50	Up
	July	August		
May	168.10	166.40	-1.70	Up
June	170.90	167.80	-3.10	Up
	August	September		
July	165.20	161.60	-3.60	Down
	September	October		
August	159.90	155.40	-4.50	Down
	October	December '87		
September	174.70	169.40	-5.30	Up
	December '87	January '88		
October	181.90	175.00	-6.90	Up
November	219.40	208.30	-11.10	Up
	January '88	March		
December '87	201.50	192.60	-8.90	Down
	March	May		
January '88	178.20	178.10	-0.10	Down
Februrary	189.60	188.60	-1.00	Up
	May	July		
March	193.80	192.40	-1.40	Up
April	203.50	203.10	-0.40	Up
	July	August		
May 16	225.90'	225.60	-0.30	Up
May	241.20	239.70	-1.50	Up
June	293.20	291.50	-1.70	Up

Figure 10-7   Soybean Meal CBOT

Profitable Trading in "Breakout" Markets

Using weekly and monthly charts in conjunction with daily charts, a simple way to trade when prices are rising is to consider buying when prices for a commodity rise into all-time high ground or above a high price not seen for a year or more, preferably longer. Similarly, when prices are falling, consider selling short when prices fall below a previous low price not seen for a year or more, preferably longer. (Several examples of this technique appear in the previous section.) That's all there is to *picking* possible winning trades this longer term way. But disciplined trading and patience are paramount requirements.

Many traders may feel uncomfortable, at least conceptually, with the idea of buying at high prices and selling short at low prices. Perhaps a bit of personal history will help illustrate how I learned to trade breakout markets early in my trading career.

Attracted by tales of good profit possibilities trading commodities, I started daily charting in 1972. In 1973, I felt confident enough to open a small account at a local single-office brokerage firm in California's Silicon Valley.

Conveniently located on the way to work, I used to stop by in the morning to watch the opening and first hour of trading (a benefit when living on Pacific time) and in the evening to copy the teletyped record of the day's prices for my charting that evening.

It was an unusual office. The 30-year-old owner was usually not present until after the markets had closed for the day. But the occasional late afternoon bull sessions in which he often participated were the firm's most noteworthy feature. Usually, these involved discussion of trading principles, illustrated by recent market actions. It quickly became apparent that the owner had very fixed ideas about how to trade based on technical considerations. He welcomed questions about his ideas, but any contrary opinion was brushed aside, thereby making it clear that we were there to learn and not to exchange ideas. (It wasn't until much later that I discovered, quite by accident, that the owner was already a millionaire due to his trading acumen. But he valued anonymity in this regard more than recognition. In retrospect, it was as though I was a golf novice being tutored without charge by Jack Nicklaus.)

During these discussions, he emphasized attention to inverse markets as an important indicator of possible dynamic bull markets. Given such a dynamic market, he felt strongly that a trader should consider buying only when the nearby contract of a commodity broke out either into all-time high ground or to a new high price not seen for several years. There were similar policies for selling when prices broke out on the down-side, notably that it must be a normal market, never an inverse one.

These ideas threw me. Didn't everybody know that to make money you had to buy low and sell high? Yet here I was being told to buy high and sell higher, and to sell low and buy (cover) even lower.

Shortly thereafter, the firm advertised in *The Wall Street Journal*. The ad said "Sugar—39 cents." It created amusement and even ridicule in some commodity circles. The previous all-time high price of about $ .13 occurred in 1963. Prices then fell to five cents or less where they remained for eight years. In 1972, prices jumped to ten cents but quickly fell back to five cents. But in early 1973, prices were again rising to the ten-cent range, and contract prices were inverted. Because of the price inversion, I had to buy some sugar. But prices quickly returned to the seven-cent area (see Figure 10-8). This caused the all-time low balance in my personal trading account.

Discussing this deplorable situation with my mentor, he pointed out that I had not waited for the price breakout above $ .13. Instead, I had anticipated by buying too early (read "greed") and this can often get traders in trouble. Wait for the breakout before buying, he emphasized, and "don't diddle in the middle" of a trading range. It took some time for me to grasp the logic of this trading policy. As a market (technical) analyst, I could infer that an all-time high price would indicate real supply problems in the sugar market that required necessitous buying, especially as sugar was an inverted

Figure 10-8 Sugar (World) NYSCS N.Y.

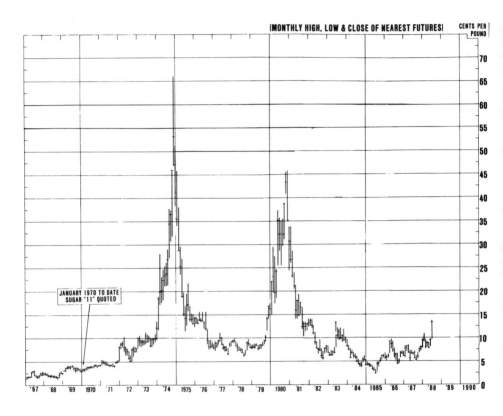

(MONTHLY HIGH, LOW & CLOSE OF NEAREST FUTURES)   CENTS PER POUND

JANUARY 1970 TO DATE
SUGAR "11" QUOTED

Reprinted with permission, © 1988 Commodity Research Bureau, 30 South Wacker Drive, Suite 1820, Chicago, Illinois 60606.

market. Moreover, given that prices had broken out, all speculators with short positions would have losses, requiring them to buy to cover their short positions. These two buying forces can move prices decisively higher.

With my depleted capital, I belatedly "followed the rules" and the rest is history. The world sugar bull market of 1974 topped at $ .66. I caught portions of the upmove which restored capital and then some. It made me a believer in the excellent profit potential of trading breakout markets—and in a business-like way to boot. Such opportunities are not uncommon in today's markets, as weekly and monthly charts show.

In 1974, *Commodities* (now *Futures*) magazine started a monthly feature interviewing "Young Market Millionaires." The first interview was with my anonymous benefactor, now reportedly worth $3 million. (Incidentally, the second trader interviewed is a contributor to this volume, none other than Larry Williams.)

In planning your trades this "breakout" way, keep in mind that prices can often become quite volatile as they approach previous long-term highs or lows. At highs, previous buyers may sell to bank their profits. Other traders will attempt to out-guess the market by selling short because they feel prices are too high, thereby trading against a strong uptrend with all its hazards. At lows, previous sellers may buy (cover) their profitable short positions. Other traders may attempt to out-guess the market by buying because they feel prices are much too low, thereby trading against a strong downtrend with all its hazards.

Now, we "breakout" traders are trend lovers, not trend fighters. We believe that unusually high prices in an inverted market indicate far too little of a commodity, and unusually low prices in a normal market as too great an abundance. We place our open buy stop order slightly above a previous long-term high, and our (short) open sell stop order slightly below a previous long-term low. This way, we don't anticipate what we hope the market will do. Rather, we wait and let the market tell us if our trading judgment is correct. If prices break out as we expect, well and good. That's the good part. Moreover, prices may break out faster than expected because trend fighters are now rushing for the trading exit to salvage what they can of their trading capital.

The bad part is that, more often than not, prices will react against us after our order has been filled. In addition to the profit takers and trend fighters mentioned previously, it is always possible that the trade (holders and users of the commodity) believe that prices are either too high or too low, and must correct. Therefore, to protect our capital from these lurking predators, we must enter an open stop-loss order at the time we are notified that our original buy or sell order is filled. We should plan our potential loss to a small amount, say, no more than $100 or so per contract.

If stopped out, capital is still essentially intact, and we can try to get right back in again by placing a buy order above the now new higher price or a sell order below the now new lower price. We may have to do this several more times before prices really move dynamically in our desired direction. But often the third time's a charm, and the resulting profit is usually well worth it.

Of course, in some cases, current prices may not exceed a previous long-term top or bottom price or may exceed it only slightly and then react significantly. In such cases our current buy or sell order will not be executed, and should be cancelled. Here are some additional suggestions:

1. Buy the nearest nondelivery-month contract.

2. Sell a farther-out contract with relatively high open interest when the nearby contract price falls into long-term low ground.

3. Breakouts seem more reliable when they occur more or less simultaneously on both daily and weekly/monthly charts.

4. Open interest should be relatively flat. (Refer to any standard futures text for implications of unusually high or low open interest at market tops and bottoms.)

5. Use of open (good-till-cancelled) stop orders for entering trades and for stop-loss purposes is recommended. But they must be cancelled promptly when no longer needed. When it applies (open orders must usually be renewed on the first trading day of the month), check with your broker.

In evaluating the above "system" in terms of Jake Bernstein's "Twenty-one Tools for Better Trading" in this volume, you'll find it measures up very well, notably:

1. We have a winning trading system, albeit a simple one.

2. Our trading plan is to trade with the trend, not against it.

3. We wait for market prices to reach the price at which we are willing to trade. We do not second-guess the market by trying to anticipate what we hope will happen.

4. We protect capital zealously. We are willing to take a risk for an important profit, but we are unwilling to take a significant loss if wrong.

If you're a reader of books and periodicals about commodity speculation, you may be impressed as I am with the wide variety of computer-based systems that use intricate formulation and indices to arrive at trading decisions. By contrast, the above- described long-term trading method may seem a quantum leap backward, more resembling tactics of a medieval knight attacking the market with lance and shield. Trading this way can cause many small losses. But as you already know, it made my original futures teacher a millionaire three times over. And it has the important advantage of keeping your trading simple—a real benefit for those of us who trade as an avocation.

Finally, recall that *contango* refers to normal markets and *backwardation* to inverse markets. From that definitive source of English usage, the *Oxford*

English Dictionary, here is a couplet that originated in the London Stock Exchange:

"The bear a good contango loves.
The bull, a backwardation."

Anonymous

That says it all!

Addendum

Oh, ye'll take the high road and I'll take the low road..."

Confused when the experts discuss pros and cons about fundamental versus technical analysis techniques? Let's see if we can help clear it up.

But first, let's get back to the basics. A commodity speculator is one who "attempts to anticipate commodity price changes and to profit through the sale and purchase (short position) or purchase and sale (long position) of commodity futures contracts" (*Commodity Trading Manual,* Chicago Board of Trade).

More basics: commodity markets exist not for speculation but to permit producers and users of commodities (the trade) to hedge, i.e., to protect their profit margins from the risk of anticipated unfavorable price changes. Thus, producers will hedge against lower prices and users against higher ones. If such changes do not result in a significant way, net profit is still protected; hedging costs are business expenses.

Speculators must not only try to forecast price changes but the price changes must actually result for the speculator to profit. There's a big difference. So how do we speculators forecast? Our trusty CBT *Commodity Trading Manual* defines the two traditional approaches:

Fundamental analysis: An approach to market behavior that stresses the study of underlying factors of supply and demand in the commodity, in the belief that such analysis will enable one to profit from being able to anticipate price trends.

Charting (Technical analysis): The use of graphs and charts in analysis of market behavior, so as to plot trends of price movements, average movements of price, volume and open interest, in the hope that such graphs and charts will help one to anticipate and profit from price trends.

Here are two distinct possible "roads to riches." One speculator may like vanilla while others might prefer strawberry or chocolate. Nothing wrong with that.

Yet, I think fundamental analysis has greater acceptance simply because the term has its roots in the stock market. Biased to the buy side, stock market research emphasizes a firm's overall prospects—emphasizing a well-reasoned, logical *why* to promote discretionary buying by the investing public. In this situation, it is normally assumed that share prices will rise, dividends will be increased, etc. The opposite occurs when stock prices fall, and the *why* may help stockholders feel better in the knowledge that they are losing money intelligently.

But fundamental analysis for speculative commodity trading seems less pertinent, because the *why* is less important. At any given time for a commodity, there is either too much inventory (as reflected in falling prices) or there is too little (causing prices to rise). Any grocery shopper understands this line of reasoning when he or she finds that the meat market is now charging 25 percent more for chicken than last month. It can be of no financial benefit to the shopper to know that the higher price was caused by actual or expected higher feed costs due to drought, a producer marketing decision, or any number of other reasons. If the shopper must have chicken, he or she must pay the price asked.

For their own analytical purposes, commodity and stock technicians alike take our shopper's view of prices. Technicians assume that, in a free market, the commercial impact of all present and anticipated fundamental data is encapsulated in current price(s), supported by trading volume and, for commodities, open-interest data. The *why* is imbedded in the price and is not stated separately.

In essence, then, commodity speculators as a class must take trading positions with an uncertain result to try to make a profit. Fundamentalists must base their trading judgments on subjective assumptions about supply and demand, while technicians base them on factual data, i.e., price, volume, and open interest. It seems to me that in a supply and demand milieu, the closer a speculator stays to facts the better—let the trade use fundamentals for making its hedging decisions.

So for commodity speculation, the term *fundamental* seems misleading and *technician* too superficial. Let's adopt some new labels. Using the above definitions, let's rename the two concepts:

1.   Fundamental analysis becomes *product analysis,* and
2.   Technical analysis becomes *market analysis.*

Then lets add a third category—*facts.* This would primarily include reports from governments and other bodies considered to be authoritative. Examples include livestock, crop, GNP, trade reports, etc. Product analysts would use report information to update their supply/demand studies, while market analysts might be more interested in how market prices react to the report.

So choose the analytical approach that suits you better. Then stick to it for a fair trial. Using bits of both approaches can be confusing—too many variables—and can be costly.

One quick example of possible confusion: if you as a market analyst were long world sugar or coffee when prices dropped dramatically the last week in July 1988 (factual), would you sell your contracts promptly to protect capital? A prominent financial newspaper said during this period that prices were dropping contrary to positive fundamentals (subjective). If you had thereby been persuaded to stay long, you would have sustained crippling losses. It happens.

So stick to one "flavor" and leave the "Neapolitan" for the experts. But product analysts should be cautioned that many experts are leaning more toward the market analysis approach. Chances are they'll "get to Scotland before ye."

■ REFERENCES ■

Bernstein, Jacob. *Beyond the Investor's Quotient.* New York: John Wiley & Sons, 1986. Fine insights on trader psychology.

Commodity Trading Manual. Chicago: Chicago Board of Trade, 1985. Definitive source of factual data about all aspects of commodity markets.

Edwards, Robert D. and John Magee. *Technical Analysis of Stock Trends.* 5th ed. Definitive source of principles for analyzing price movements and trading volume for stocks traded in a free market. Equally applicable to trading commodity futures contracts. Open interest is not covered.

Hieronymous, Thomas A. *Economics of Futures Trading,* Commodity Research Bureau, Inc. Authoritative treatment of the economic functions performed by commodity futures market. Excellent background reading for speculative traders.

Teweles, Richard J. and Frank J Jones. *The Commodity Futures Game: Who Wins? Who Loses? Why?* New York: McGraw Hill Book Company, 1987. Good general text on all aspects of trading commodity futures. Open interest is also covered.

Williams, Larry R. *How I Made. . . One Million Dollars Last Year. . . Trading Commodities,* 1973. Very sound treatment of technical trading basics, especially on behavior of prices and open interest in inverted markets.

PATTERNS
AND SIGNALS

TRADING WITH SEASONAL PRICE PROBABILITIES ON YOUR SIDE

JAKE BERNSTEIN

■

■

JAKE BERNSTEIN

See biography in the beginning of chapter two.

■

■ CHAPTER ELEVEN ■

THE USE OF SEASONALITY IN THE COMMODITY MARKETS is not new. During the last few years, a number of books and studies dealing with the technique have been published. In 1977, MBH released *Seasonal Chart Study 1953–1977—Cash Commodities*. This was one of the first serious attempts to quantify seasonals in the commodity markets. In 1979, MBH published *Seasonal Chart Study II—Commodity Spreads* and in 1988 MBH published *Seasonal Cash Charts—1988 Edition*. This report provided a week by week seasonal analysis of commodity spreads and isolated many highly reliable trends in a number of markets. Williams and Noseworthy (1977), in their *Sure Thing Commodity Trading*, provided speculators with a list of specific seasonal trades having high reliabilities over the previous ten years or so. This study was a pioneering effort in the isolation of specific seasonal trades in the futures market on a market by market basis. The combined effect of these and other efforts has been to increase markedly the use of seasonals!

Despite all the available information, however, it is unfortunate that few traders can use seasonal concepts to their advantage. Very often, speculators will seek to justify an already established position by referring to seasonals. But when the seasonal does not agree with their opinion, they ignore it. If there is agreement, they may double up on the position. Then there are those traders who understand the concept of seasonality and are aware of key seasonal trades, but who do not have the patience to trade them effectively. These are all primarily problems of discipline, however, and will not be discussed in this report.

The goal of this brief introduction is twofold:

1. To isolate and present in graphic form seasonal patterns in the futures markets.

2. To present possible uses for futures seasonals, both in conjunction with trading systems and independently.

In the hope of facilitating the rational use of my results, I have provided specific instructions as to how they may be employed. If you have any questions about uses not covered, contact me at MBH.

What is a Seasonal?

Futures and cash markets move in fairly regular price patterns. To most traders, these cyclical movements are neither obvious nor meaningful. This is truly unfortunate, since regularity and repetition are the cornerstones of profitable trading. All trading systems seek to isolate signals or indicators that repeat themselves with sufficient frequency and reliability to permit profitable trading. Seasonals and cycles are the ultimate factors underlying market regularity. Those who have read my 1978 study, *Commodities Now Through 1984* and my 1988 study, *Futures—Now Through 2001*, should be familiar with the underlying long-range cycles in each market. (Although some of the specific forecasts I made have not yet come to pass, some of the more radical expectations have indeed become realities. This attests to the validity of cycles.) Within the cyclical patterns, we find shorter-term repetitions in price trend. Among these are seasonals.

The price of virtually all futures and cash markets is affected by weather, season, and growing conditions, because supply and demand are closely related to seasonal fluctuations. When crops are large following harvest, it would be natural to assume that prices may be low because of farmer selling. When demand for grain feeds is high during winter months, we might expect prices to be high. If we knew all the factors that affect the market, it would permit errorless forecasting of prices because the markets themselves are perfect. Unfortunately, our ability to recognize and use all of the price inputs is imperfect. Hence, our forecasting ability is limited.

A seasonal pattern is the tendency of a given futures market to trend in a given direction at certain times of the year. Because seasonal factors affect prices, it should be possible to determine whether and when a given market will move up or down because of seasonality. We do not always know the reasons for seasonal price movement. Personally, however, I have no need to know why a market moves up or down at a given time of the year. Certainly, knowing why makes some traders more secure. But my concern is not with the Why of things; rather, it is with the That of things. I know not why a given market moves up 90 percent of the time during November, but I do know that it makes the move. My security comes from the profit I can reap by having this knowledge. "Ours is not to reason why, ours is but to sell and buy."

How to Read the Charts

No price charts are 100 percent accurate. I have, however, validated the data used in the charts for this study both in real time and on computer to test for accuracy. To the best of my knowledge, the data is reliable and reflects the true seasonal situation for each commodity.

Note that the weekly up and down percentages for a given contract month are applicable only to that contract month. I do not suggest, for example, that you use the plot for November beans to trade July beans.

Before Using These Charts . . .

Before you use the charts in this study, it's important to understand exactly what they mean and what they are saying. For this reason, I urge you to read the instructions and explanations provided below prior to using these charts. My main caveat is that you understand what you're looking at so that you will not misuse the information by reading too much meaning into this study of seasonals. By reading the instructions, you'll also save yourself a great deal of frustration and confusion. The old saying "if all else fails, read the instructions" comes to mind. In this case, I'd like you to read the instructions *before* all else fails.

I have provided a sample chart at the outset that lists specific details to observe in each chart to follow. More refined uses of the chart patterns will be discussed later. PLEASE READ THESE INSTRUCTIONS CAREFULLY. You will save considerable time and frustration if you read the instructions before attempting to use or understand the charts. I have listed the key points in order. Refer to the sample chart (Figure 11-1) as you read these instructions.

1. This line lists the *contract month and market*, which is plotted below.

2. *Years covered for this seasonal chart* are listed accordingly. For example, 67–88 means that 22 years' worth of data were used in preparing this chart.Where a market has been actively traded for only a few years, there is less of a data base.

3. *The scale or index* is shown along the left and right axis. Note that this is a normalized rate-of-change index and does not have any direct bearing on actual price. It merely shows, on a relative basis, the magnitude of move from one week to the next. If, for example, the move from week 23 to 22 is very high, compared to previous weeks, and if the percent reading is 85 percent, we can expect a large weekly up-move 85 percent of the time during the week under study. A drop under the zero line merely indicates that a rather persistent bear trend usually occurs. There is not special significance associated with a market crossing above the zero line or below it. It is just another reference point.

4. *The weekly average change plot* shows the average net change, up or down, for a given week.

Figure 11-1

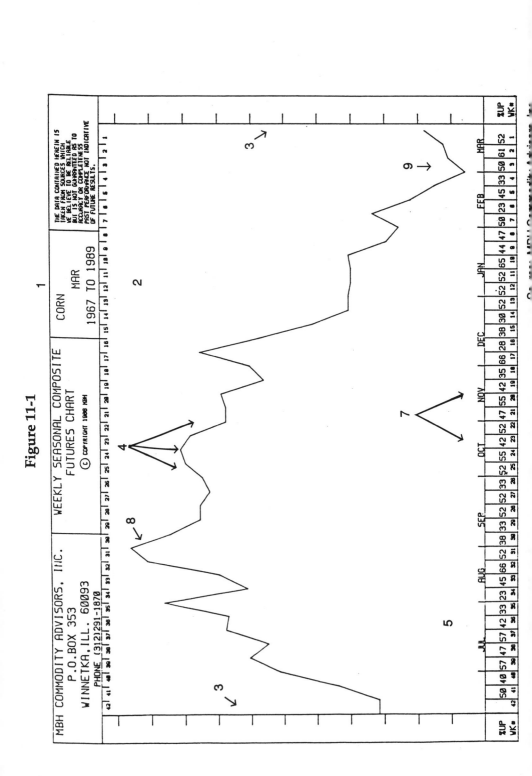

MBH COMMODITY ADVISORS, INC.
P.O.BOX 353
WINNETKA,ILL. 60093
PHONE (312)291-1870

WEEKLY SEASONAL COMPOSITE
FUTURES CHART
© COPYRIGHT 1988 MBH

CORN
MAR
1967 TO 1989

5. These figures represent the *weekly upside probability,* on a percentage basis for the specific week numbered under the reading. If the data plot for a given week is up from the previous plot and the reading is 80 percent, for example, this is an indication that 80 percent of the time for the years under study prices have tended to rise during this week. This is a strong indication of seasonality. If the percentage figure is under 65 percent and the plot is up, the seasonal is not particularly reliable.

    If the plot is down and the percent reading is above 65 percent, it means that, although the market tends to move up more years than it moves down, the net down-move is much larger than the net up-move, thereby accounting for the down entry. If you buy, you stand to make only a small profit.

    If the plot is down and the percent reading is below 35 percent, it means that for the years under study the market is down 65 percent or more. In this case, the downside reliability would be 100 percent minus 35 percent. For downside reliabilities, subtract the indicated figure from 100 to arrive at the reading. A down-move that has a reading of 10 percent, for example, indicates that the market has been down 90 percent for the years studied. Remember this simple rule for calculating down-move reliability—it is important.

    If plot is up and the percent reading is below 35 percent, it is an indication that even though most years have been down for this week, those years which were up were very strong. If you sell short on this type of combination you may take a very large risk for a potentially small but reliable profit. If the plot is unchanged (sideways) from the previous week, this indicates that the magnitude, or size, of the move for this week is in equal balance between up or down. This does not necessarily mean a sideways trend for the week. Trend can only be determined by the accompanying percent reading. If it is 65 percent, you can expect generally higher prices. If it is under 35 percent, you can expect a down move. The sideways plot means only that the total magnitude of all the up moves is about equal to the total of the down moves.

6. *Week number is indicated under the percent probability reading.* The week number tells you how many weeks are left until contract expiration. These are full weeks. The last week of trading would read 1 since it is the final week in the life of this contract. A reading of 34, for example, means that figures are important in order to calculate the week and month number according to exchange expiration dates for any given year. Note that the week numbers will allow you to determine relative time for any year.

7. *Month and week are indicated by the listings shown.* Please note that the number of weeks in any given month (using Friday as the last day of a week) will vary from year to year. Sometimes November will have five Fridays, and other years it will have four. The dates listed on these charts are for 1988. If you wish to adapt your chart for other trading years, simply determine when the given contract is due to expire and work backward using the trading week as a guide. Once you have learned to use these charts, you will find it unnecessary to pinpoint the exact week. If a given market is conforming well to its seasonal trend, you can superimpose actual weekly price onto the seasonal chart to see whether there is a time lead or lag. A clear acetate sheet can be used for this purpose.

8. *Usual seasonal high is indicated by the highest plot on the chart.* During the years under study prices have tended to hit their contract high around this week and/or month. If a high is made during the last few weeks of a contract, prices may move even higher several months thereafter and the next contract month should be checked for this possiblity. If a seasonal high occurs with high percent readings followed by a move to the downside with equally reliable readings, this is most likely a highly reliable seasonal top.

9. *The same holds true for seasonal lows, only in reverse.*

More Details About the Charts

You must remember that these charts are a composite or distillation of typical activity. As such, extreme highs and extreme lows during the same period of time in different years tend to balance each other out, resulting in a relatively even line on the seasonal chart. Such a formation provides valuable information, because it indicates that the market is not seasonal at those times. During such periods, you can safely look to trend as the single most reliable indicator. You can also assume that once a trend starts, it should continue, making it best not to rely on seasonals while the trend remains.

Note also that relative highs and lows within the composite chart are not necessarily repeated in the market during any actual year. Some years may look exactly like the seasonal composite charts, while others may not. A low may or may not occur at a given time period, but this does not mean that the seasonal chart is incorrect. In using these charts, there are five specific patterns you should look for:

1. *Very strong up or down weeks.* When I say strong, I mean reliabilities in excess of 70 percent over ten years or more. These weeks will probably bring quick profits on short term trades.

2. *Long-term up or down trends.* These can be seen in many markets. Copper and cattle are two notable examples. If a trend begins and is accompanied by high reliability readings at the start and high readings interspersed within the trend, it is most likely a highly valid seasonal tendency. The same is true of down-moves. Reliable trends or "runs" have been marked off with arrows on each chart.

3. *Seasonal highs and lows .* These can be estimated by referring to the chart, in accordance with the guidelines outlined in items 8 and 9 above.

4. *Contra-seasonal moves.* Such moves in the actual market can be spotted. If a market shows highly reliable seasonality on the composite that fails to appear in the actual market for any given year, a further move in the contra-seasonal direction can be expected. This is perhaps one of the most important uses of a seasonal chart.

5. *Market turns.* This is just another term for "trend changes" and can be expected at certain times of the year. If the market has been moving down and the seasonal chart shows a high reliability down-move followed by a high reliability up-move, one should be on the lookout for a major trend change in the market.

How Can Seasonal Composites Be Used With Your Trading System?

Since I am not familiar with any of your individual systems or needs, I can only offer some suggestions as to how this information might be useful in your particular program. Here are a few general guidelines:

1. *Point and figure charting, bar charting, close only charts, moving averages.* I find that seasonals tend to help most traders do their best work. When seasonals are in solid and reliable trends, other indicators will be effective. If you get a signal to buy during a time frame that is clearly bearish on the seasonal composite chart, take great care. You might want to test the history of your trading system against the seasonal indications. If you find that most of your losses and incorrect signals come during seasonal moves in the opposite direction (as I believe you will), you might do well to build a seasonal factor into your system.

2. *Moving averages.* These can help isolate the start of a seasonal. If there has been a fairly consistent up-trend, for example, entering a period of seasonal highs, you can be quite certain that the moving average signals will be reliable as soon as the seasonal composite shows the start of a reliable down-trend.

3. *Hedging and spreading.* Hedgers may wish to use the seasonal highs and lows as points for market entry and exit. Spreaders can determine the relative relationship between two contracts in a given market at similar times of the year, as well as the relationship between different markets during the same time frame (e.g., corn vs. wheat from October through December).

4. *Fundamentalists.* Bearish news at seasonal lows does not necessarily bring lower prices and vice versa at seasonal highs. Inasmuch as seasonality is, in my opinion, a prime fundamental factor, all those who trade from such an orientation must keep seasonals foremost in their awareness. Do not buck the seasonal trend, regardless of fundamentals, if that seasonal pattern is highly reliable.

5. *When to buy and sell.* It is not the intention of this chart study to make recommendations. Rather, it is the intent of this study to help you make profitable decisions. The chart points were calculated on a Friday-to-Friday basis (last trading day of the week through last trading day of the next week). If a given week shows strong upside reliability, one might consider buying on the Friday just previous to the week and selling out on the next Friday. In so doing, your results will most likely reflect the idealized chart results. There are those, however, who will use the seasonal data for market entry at key turning points. Their overall results may be better than those of individuals who trade only the weekly moves.

How Were Seasonal Charts Developed?

You do not need a background in computer programming to understand how the Seasonal Futures Charts were prepared. To appreciate more fully the results as well as the amount of work that went into their production, you should familiarize yourself with the methodology. Here, step by step, is the procedure that was followed in the computer analysis:

1. Take the daily history file for a given market for each year on file, e.g., June live cattle '67, '68, '69, '70. Read this data from tape to a disk file.

2. Line up each contract by date. The last day of trading is treated as day 1, the second-to-last day as day 2, etc. This is done because not all contracts terminate on the same calendar day. There are, however, specific rules for determining last day of trading that are set by the exchange, and most contracts will, therefore, terminate on or about the same week.

3. Calculate the price change for each week using the Friday price as the last price (or the Thursday price, if Friday was not a trading

day). In so doing, we end up with a weekly price change for each market and year.

4. Standardize or normalize the price changes for each year. This is done to limit the effect of unusually wide or unusually small price swings. We are primarily interested in direction of move, or trend, from one week to the next.

5. Once data has been normalized, take the algebraic average for each column of weeks. This yields an index of average weekly fluctuation per week of the year.

6. Determine the percentage of years during which price was up or down for each week.

7. Dump data to plotter, and plot cumulative price trend line.

There are other ways in which the data could have been massaged. If you plan to replicate this study on your own data base, you may wish to experiment with different indexing arrangements. Those who wish to use our software to replicate results on different markets may purchase a copy of the program. It is written in Fortran 4 for Data General systems and a Houston Instrument incremental plotter. Write me for price and availability details.

Use of Asterisk (*) in Reliability Readings

There are some weekly reliability readings of 100 percent on several of the charts. This has occurred where the number of years under study was relatively small (e.g., currencies). I have inserted an asterisk (*) where the reliability would read 100 percent to alert you to the fact that:

1. The reading for this week is 100 percent.

2. The number of years under study is small. If we have only five years of data for any given market, a reading of 100 percent is not as meaningful as it might be for a market with 14 years under study. The same holds true for readings of "O" in the reliability box.

The Weekly Percent Reading
and How It Relates to Current Time

As I indicated previously, the weekly readings were obtained by lining up contract data from last trading day to first trading day. The month and week readings, which have been included along the bottom of each chart, may not necessarily apply to every market year. They are primarily for 1982–83 expirations. In future years, or in past years, there may be a shift of one to two weeks in the timing. In such cases, you can calculate the period of time by working backward from the current contract expiration date, counting the weeks back to the current year. This is not a difficult task. Simply determine from exchange rules when a given contract is due to expire. Once you have determined the number of the current week from expiration date, line it up with the same week on the chart. After several months of use, you will find it possible to isolate the time frame rather easily. Then, in studying actual market behavior compared to the seasonal composite, you will know whether there has been a lead or lag in the current contract, which can occur during individual years. A major seasonal low, for example, because of various fundamentals, could come several weeks ahead of time. Be on the lookout for early tops and bottoms.

High-Reliability Weekly Runs

From time to time, the seasonal composite shows a series of high reliability readings that spans several weeks. This is typically a good period for seasonal trends. I have marked such trends with arrows on the chart (Figure 11-2) to make spotting these moves less difficult. A run of high reliability weekly percent readings— 69, 75, 68, 45, 78, 69, 50, 33, 78, and 67 percent — represents a very strong seasonal up-trend, interrupted only by a few low reliability readings. The longer term trader might establish and hold a position through this seasonal up- or downtrend. They are often large profit makers.

In studying the seasonal futures charts, you will note that I've marked some of the seasonal run periods with arrows. Arrows pointing up indicate an upside seasonal run, whereas arrows pointing down indicate a downside seasonal run. You'll also note that I've marked some seasonal runs that have a few smaller readings within them, e.g. 60–64 percent or 36–40 percent. These are not necessarily strong seasonals; nevertheless, I've marked them because they have validity and should be looked at by higher risk traders. Note further that I've not considered anything less than a three-week period as a seasonal run. You should also note that there are many one- and two-week readings that carry high reliability. These can be used to the advantage of short term traders. REMEMBER: the idea is to use seasonal trend as indicated by chart and percent reliability readings.

Seasonals as Part of Long-Term Cycles

Seasonal price patterns are by no means the only reliable market cycles. Longer term cycles, as discussed in *Commodities Now Through 1984* and *Futures—Now Through 2001*, are important in the overall accuracy of seasonals. At major long-term tops and bottoms, seasonal cycles become distorted. If you are aware of the long-term patterns within which seasonals function,

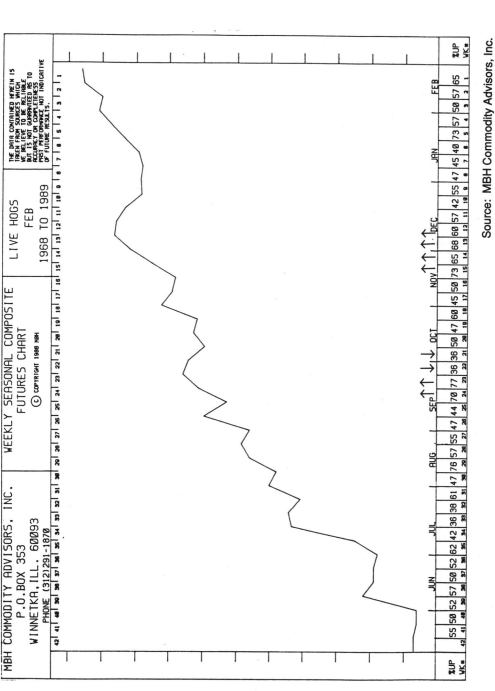

you can be prepared well in advance for a period during which seasonals may become unreliable. You must remember, above all, that when a part is dissected from the whole an unnatural distortion takes place. Consequently, when the analysis is over and the necessary information has been gleaned, the part must be replaced within the whole. A total picture is necessary in the formulation of any long-range decision. A student of seasonals must also be a student of all cycles.

One Final Word

Regardless of what the seasonals say, maintain a sound trading strategy—use stops! One of the worst errors a trader can make is to become totally dependent upon a method or technique. We do not as yet have trading tools that are totally reliable; therefore, I urge you to use good sense when making trades.

Suggestions for Further Study and Reading

Bernstein, J. *Seasonal Concepts in Futures Trading*. NY: Wiley & Sons, 1987.

Bernstein, J. *Cyclic Analysis in Futures Trading*. NY: Wiley & Sons, 1988.

Bernstein, J. *MBH Seasonal Futures Charts—1988 Edition*. P.O. Box 353 Winnetka, IL 60093.

Bernstein, J. *MBH Seasonal Cash Charts—1988 Edition*. P.O. Box 353 Winnetka, IL 60093

Williams, Larry and Michelle Noseworthy. *"Sure Thing" Commodity Trading*. Brightwaters, NY: Windsor Books, 1977.

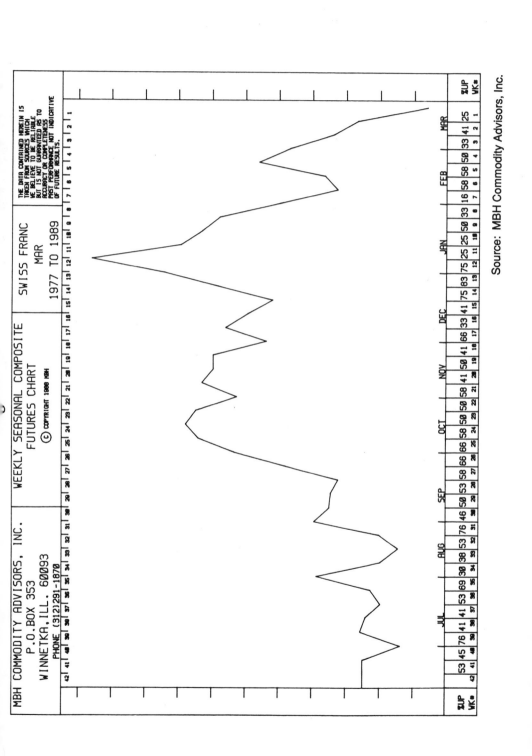

Source: MBH Commodity Advisors, Inc.

Figure 11-4

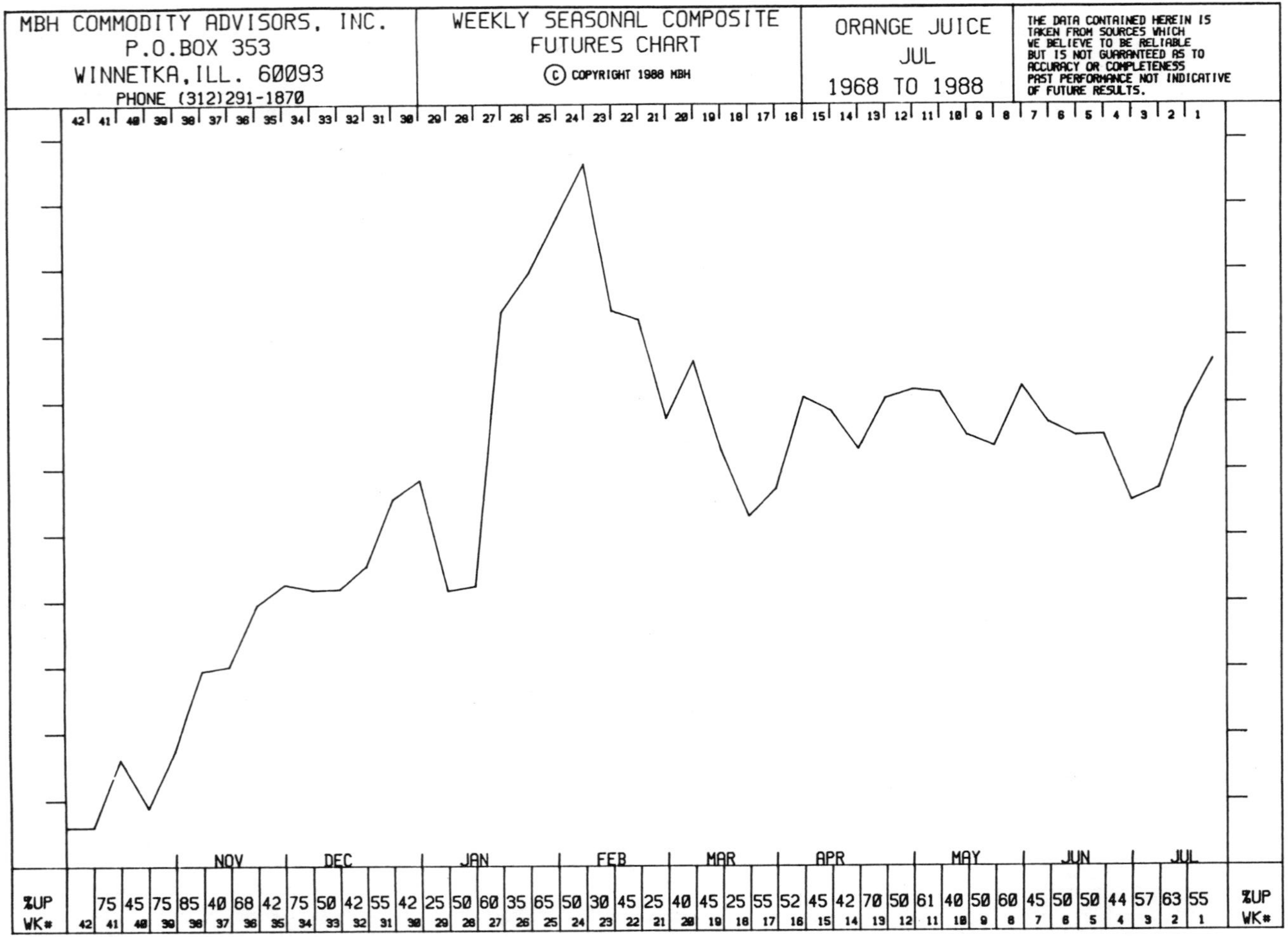

MBH COMMODITY ADVISORS, INC.
P.O.BOX 353
WINNETKA, ILL. 60093
PHONE (312)291-1870
WEEKLY SEASONAL COMPOSITE
FUTURES CHART
© COPYRIGHT 1988 MBH
ORANGE JUICE
JUL
1968 TO 1988
THE DATA CONTAINED HEREIN IS TAKEN FROM SOURCES WHICH WE BELIEVE TO BE RELIABLE BUT IS NOT GUARANTEED AS TO ACCURACY OR COMPLETENESS PAST PERFORMANCE NOT INDICATIVE OF FUTURE RESULTS.
NOV
DEC
JAN
FEB
MAR
APR
MAY
JUN
JUL
%UP
WK#
75 45 75 85 40 68 42 75 50 42 55 42 25 50 60 35 65 50 30 45 25 40 45 25 55 52 45 42 70 50 61 40 50 60 45 50 50 44 57 63 55
42 41 40 39 38 37 36 35 34 33 32 31 30 29 28 27 26 25 24 23 22 21 20 19 18 17 16 15 14 13 12 11 10 9 8 7 6 5 4 3 2 1

Source: MBH Commodity Advisors, Inc.

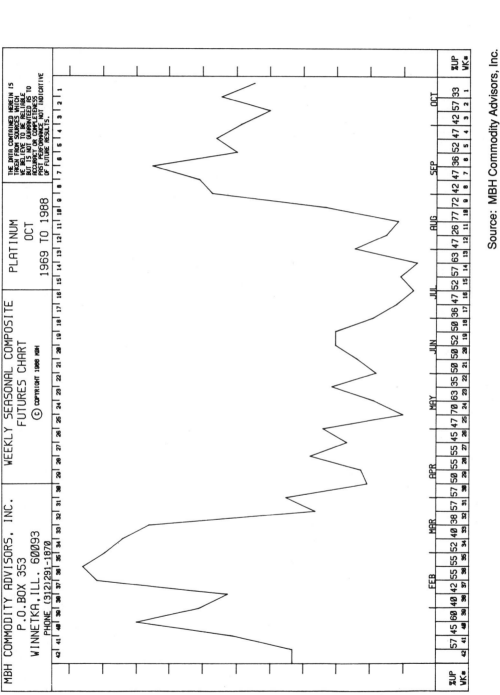

Source: MBH Commodity Advisors, Inc.

Figure 11-6

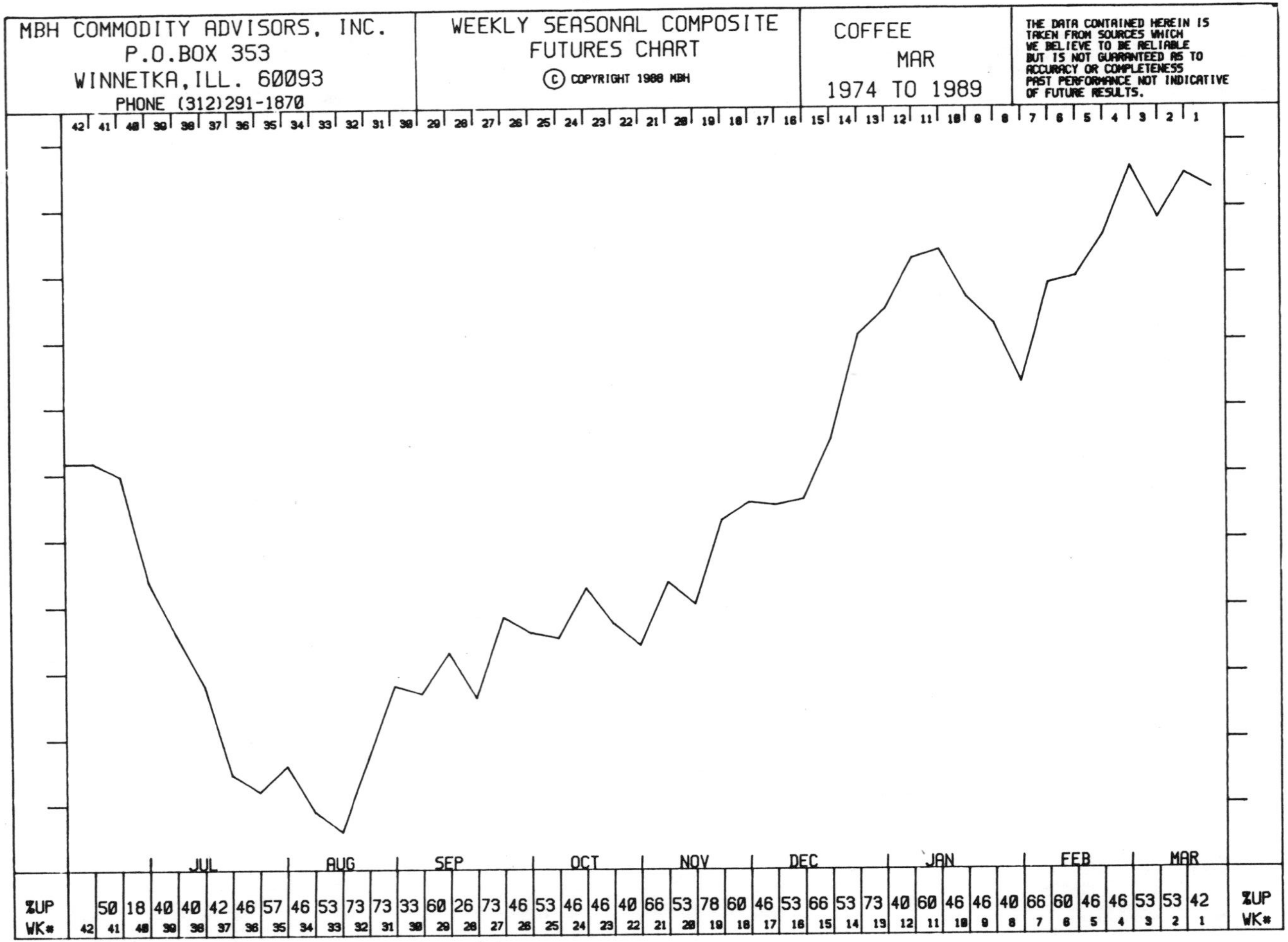
MBH COMMODITY ADVISORS, INC.
P.O.BOX 353
WINNETKA, ILL. 60093
PHONE (312)291-1870
WEEKLY SEASONAL COMPOSITE FUTURES CHART
© COPYRIGHT 1988 MBH
COFFEE
MAR
1974 TO 1989
THE DATA CONTAINED HEREIN IS TAKEN FROM SOURCES WHICH WE BELIEVE TO BE RELIABLE BUT IS NOT GUARANTEED AS TO ACCURACY OR COMPLETENESS PAST PERFORMANCE NOT INDICATIVE OF FUTURE RESULTS.
JUL AUG SEP OCT NOV DEC JAN FEB MAR
%UP 50 18 40 40 42 46 57 46 53 73 73 33 60 26 73 46 53 46 46 40 66 53 78 60 46 53 66 53 73 40 60 46 46 40 66 60 46 46 53 53 42
WK# 42 41 40 39 38 37 36 35 34 33 32 31 30 29 28 27 26 25 24 23 22 21 20 19 18 17 16 15 14 13 12 11 10 9 8 7 6 5 4 3 2 1

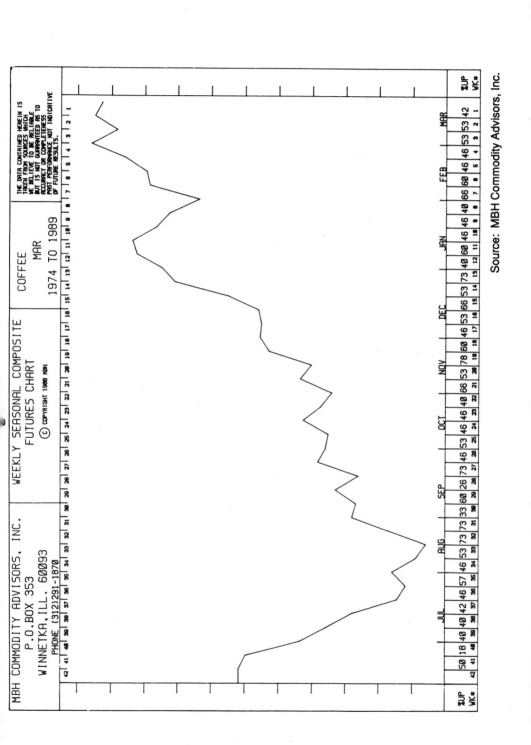

Source: MBH Commodity Advisors, Inc.

THE CAMBRIDGE HOOK

JAMES T. KNEAFSEY, Ph.D.

■

JAMES T. KNEAFSEY, Ph. D

Dr. Jim Kneafsey is the founder and president of Cambridge Financial Management, Inc. (and Cambridge Commodities Corporation), an internationally recognized research and investment advisory firm known for its accurate market forecasts, state-of-the-art research and innovative trading methods in stocks and futures. As advisor to several profitable investment programs and public funds, Dr. Kneafsey has earned a reputation for consistent management which produces significant rates of return. Dr. Kneafsey has formulated investment strategies for investors of major brokerage firms, corporations, and federal agencies. He is also the author of *The Cambridge Marketletter (with Hookline)* which is ranked among the most profitable financial newsletters by *Commodity Traders Consumer Report*. As a noted authority on the futures markets, Dr. Kneafsey is widely quoted in *The Wall Street Journal*, and *International Herald Tribune, Consensus Futures Magazine* and other media periodicals. He is also a commentator on several New England radio and TV shows and is a frequent guest on the Financial News Network's "Moneytalk" program. Dr. Kneafsey received a Ph.D. in economics from Ohio State University in 1971 and has lectured at the University of North Carolina, Princeton, and Harvard Universities among others, and has served on the faculties of the University of Pittsburg and M.I.T., where he occasionally lectures.

▪ CHAPTER TWELVE ▪

HE CAMBRIDGE HOOK IS A CONFLUENCE or coming together of several technical indicators coupled with a very specific chart pattern. The concept is simple, as is the application. The Cambridge Hook allows a trader to maximize profits on winning trades but, more important, to keep losses small. While these are not revolutionary features, they are the principal attributes necessary for a trading system to produce consistent profits.

Not that the Cambridge Hook is a guaranteed, never-fail, mortgage-your-house type of an indicator. But it does enable a trader to respond *immediately* to changes in trends in most markets, as well as to tighten stops and to move effectively into new trends.

At the time we discovered the Cambridge Hook, we had been acting as an advisor to managed account programs for more than seven years. Although our trading performance was successful, we were not satisfied that it was as good as it could be. The missing element appeared to be the ability to determine with a degree of confidence when an existing trend had turned and when a new trend was forming. Many of our indicators were providing daily trading signals, and, as economists, we were able to generate very acceptable long- term price forecasts. But we needed a signpost—something that would indicate the right direction at critical turning points and something that could continue to assure us that we were headed the right way during seemingly trendless intervals. While trend-following tactics were useful, we felt we needed something more.

The first clues to putting together the Hook were found in the peaks and troughs of historical price charts. An examination of all of the information available at each major turning point resulted in filtering out many false signals, and we thereby arrived at a set of indicators that, in tandem, generated the Cambridge Hook. Once isolated, the particular pattern of the Hook showed up an incredible number of times at critical turning points.

While the various components of the hook have been customized for each commodity, there is nothing particularly esoteric about each of the three elements. They are simply volume, open interest, and the relative strength index (RSI.) The chart pattern used is the standard hook or key reversal. What differentiates the Cambridge Hook from a standard hook or key is that the RSI, open interest, and volume must be at certain values when the chart pattern occurs. The major benefit of the Cambridge Hook is that it allows a trader to recognize that the odds for a reversal in the primary trend have increased enormously on the day that a *reversal occurs*. In this way, the trader can get a jump on other systems, which need time (often several days or even weeks) to identify that a trend has changed. Even if the Hook signal is wrong, the loss is minimized by placing a protective stop just one tick outside the extreme point of the daily range of the "Hook Day." It's amazing how often this stop will not be touched. The reason for the safety of this particular point is that when the Hook signal is correct, which it has been more than 75 percent of the time since 1985, it implies a distinct change in market psychology.

The Cambridge Hook Formula

To identify the components of the Cambridge Hook formula, first examine the bar chart of your favorite contract and locate a *contra-trend* reversal, i.e., the daily reversal must be *against the trend*.

It is important to ascertain at the outset whether the market is in an uptrend, downtrend, or moving sideways—perhaps a quantitative measure should be used (e.g., Wilder's Directional Movement indicator or even simple moving average crossovers). Hook or key reversals per se may be important in their own right—but for a Cambridge Hook signal, the price reversal must be *against* the prevailing trend.

The two possibilities for a reversal-down are classic hooks and keys (as shown in Figure 12-1, A & B). Similarly, for a reversal up, the two possibilities are shown in Figure 12-1, C & D. Note that a reversal in the same direction of the trend does not count—we are looking only for signs of a trend reversal.

For a *Cambridge Hook Down*, the following formula must prevail:

- In an uptrend, look for a contra-trend reversal. Also,
- The high must be higher than the previous day's high.
- The close must be lower than the previous day's close.
- The RSI must be overbought.
- Volume and Open Interest must be increasing.
- A non-confirmation between the previous close and the RSI must exist.

For a Cambridge Hook Up, these are the criteria that must be met:

- In a downtrend, look for a contra-trend reversal. Also,
- The low must be lower than the previous day's low.
- The close must be higher than the previous day's close.
- The RSI must be oversold.

Figure 12-1 The Cambridge Hook

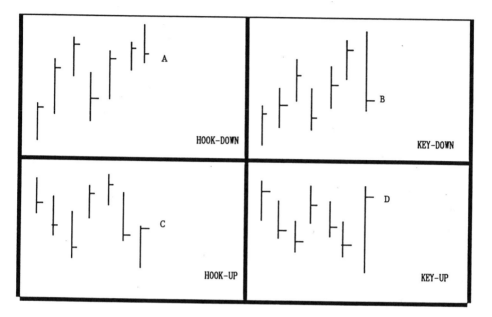

- Volume must be increasing and open interest must be declining.
- A nonconfirmation between the previous close and the RSI must exist.

There are several advantages and limitations of using the Cambridge Hook. Among the advantages, it can determine whether a trend reversal is likely. It can signal the reversal of a trend on the day that the peak or trough occurs. It indicates an excellent spot to place stops when a position is established. It provides the additional confidence to stay with a trend.

There are, however, limitations to the Hook. It does not catch every trend reversal. It does not always provide another hook to indicate when to get out of the position. It does not provide ongoing stops—another system must be used to determine profit protection stops (i.e., parabolic stops, trend lines, or moving averages).

A word of caution: the Cambridge Hook is designed to be effective *only* when all of the elements are present and operative. Also, remember that not every top or bottom of a market is depicted by a Cambridge Hook—in fact, only a few are. But, when a Hook does occur, watch out!

A good example of a Cambridge Hook occurred on February 27, 1987 in the July soybeans (range: $4.77 – $4.81 3/4). Note from the soybean chart (Figure 12-2) that a lower low was reached that day than the previous day,

Figure 12-2   July Soybeans

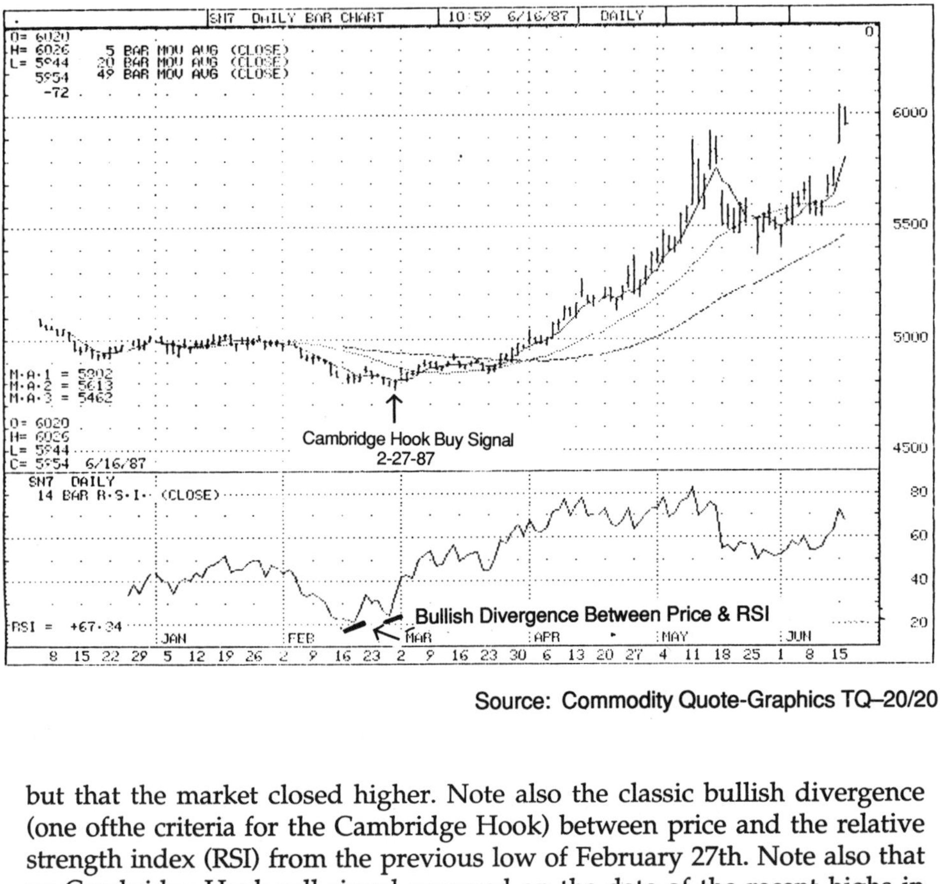

Source: Commodity Quote-Graphics TQ–20/20

but that the market closed higher. Note also the classic bullish divergence (one ofthe criteria for the Cambridge Hook) between price and the relative strength index (RSI) from the previous low of February 27th. Note also that no Cambridge Hook sell signal occurred on the date of the recent highs in May or June, suggesting that bean prices should move higher. Usually, a Cambridge Hook sell signal does not follow a buy signal in such a short period of time.

Another Cambridge Hook example appears on the monthly Treasury bond chart (Figure 12-3), where a major sell signal was given during April, 1986.

The monthly chart gives a long-term view of where interest rates have been and where they are likely to trend. The Hook sell signal at 105–15 on April 17, 1986 (with the bellwether 30-year Treasury bond yielding 7.10 percent) suggests that it should be a long time before such low yields are again seen.

Cambridge Hooks based on key reversals (the closes are lower than the previous day's low or higher than the previous day's high) are even more powerful than Cambridge Hooks based on simple hook reversals. Also,

Figure 12-3 Monthly Treasury Chart

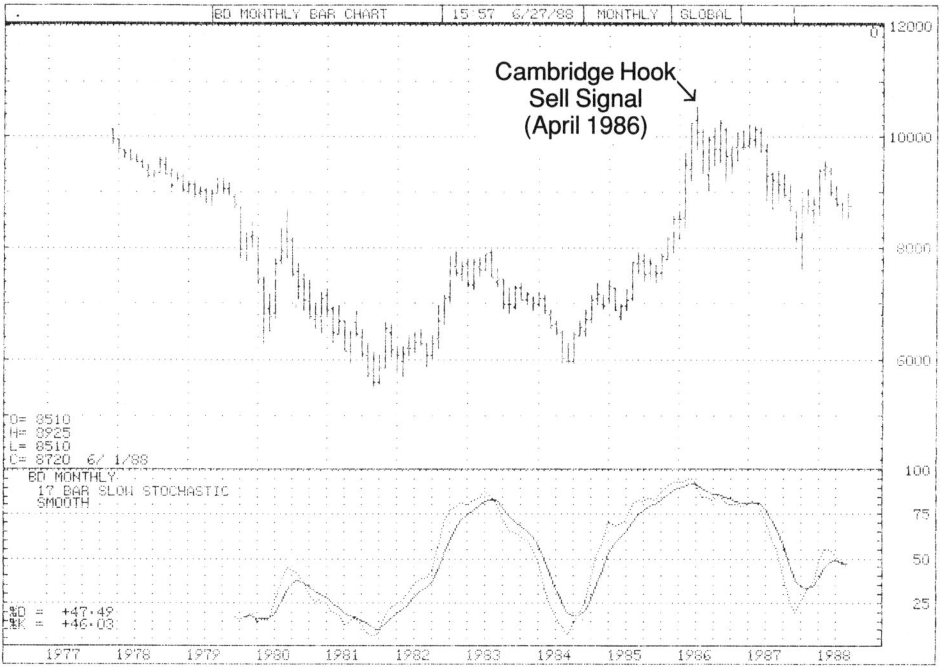

Source: Commodity Quote-Graphics TQ–20/20

Hooks that appear in several futures contracts of any given group (metals, financial futures, currencies, stock indices, etc.) are more powerful, as they reflect a stronger shift in market sentiment.

The Hook works because it is based on market psychology. On the day that a Hook takes place, say in an up-trend that has existed for some time, people are buying into the market with great enthusiasm—establishing a new high. At some point during the day, attitudes begin to shift—what looked like a great value earlier is beginning to look somewhat tarnished. Some of the buyers become sellers, and new sellers enter the market believing prices to be overvalued. By the close of the day, the market sentiment has completely reversed, pointing the way to lower prices the next day. When this chart formation is created against a backdrop of a high RSI (indicating an overbought situation) and rising volume (reflecting great market momentum suddenly reversed), it is reasonable to believe that the time is right for a trend reversal.

In many cases that we researched, however, the trend reversal was not always immediately apparent. In many cases, as daily price data were added to the picture over time, the pattern became clear, but only after several weeks had passed. Moreover, in the sideways markets that often prevail after a peak or trough, it is often not evident that the highs are not breaking new ground or that the lows are trending slightly lower. Cambridge Hooks can add a new dimension to this scenario in that they alert one to start watching—to begin considering that whatever factors created an uptrend, for instance, are gradually changing and now may be contributing to a downtrend.

Cambridge Hooks occur sporadically; they do not take place at every peak or every bottom. They sometimes occur in groups, but there are also times when the required combination of signals that constitute a Cambridge Hook do not converge for a long time. On the other hand, it is not uncommon for an apparent Hook to be proven false. The highs can sometimes be taken out—maybe even with a Cambridge Hook up. The probability that a Hook is valid is not 100 percent. As long as a Hook is in effect, however, a position should not be established that goes counter to it (unless it is on an extremely short-term, day-trading basis).

The Cambridge Hook concept continues to be an immensely useful tool in our daily trading. It has provided us with the extra element we were searching for, and it has provided new insights into many market movements that we might otherwise have failed to identify.

Since we have been using the Hook signal to enhance our trading, we have established the following statistics for our trades, based on realized profit/loss including commissions and fees:

- Average gain $785
- Average loss $322
- Thirty percent of gains over $1,000
- Ten percent of losses over $500—only two percent over $750
- Largest drawdown—23.9 percent

The important benefits available through the use of the Cambridge Hook are consistency and confidence. In many cases, knowing the direction of the trend will allow a trader to limit losses and avoid the whipsaws of market shifts. Trading should then become more consistent. Furthermore, knowing that a trend is in effect should provide confidence to hold on to winning trades. These two elements, in combination, can have a profound effect on profitability and market equanimity.

Figure 12-4 Weekly Japanese Yen

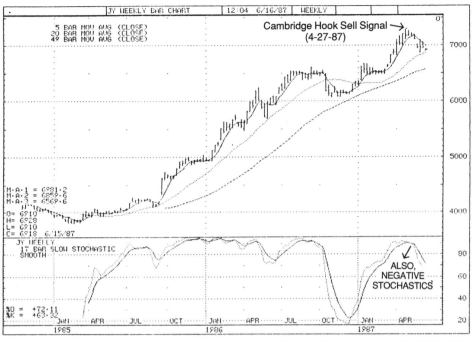

Source: Commodity Quote-Graphics TQ–20/20

Figure 12-5 Weekly Dow Jones Industrial Average

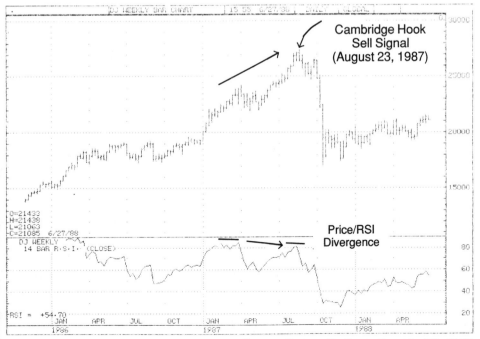

Source: Commodity Quote-Graphics TQ–20/20

Figure 12-6 Monthly Treasury Bonds

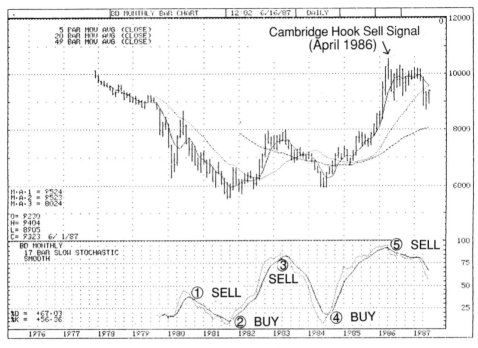

Source: Commodity Quote-Graphics TQ–20/20

BEHAVIOR OF TECHNICAL INDICATORS IN MARKET STAGES

WILLIAM F. ENG

■

■

WILLIAM F. ENG

William F. Eng is the President and founder of Financial Option Consultants, a Chicago-based financial consulting firm. Eng is a graduate of Northwestern University and did postgraduate work at the University of Chicago. He advises clients on trading strategies and policy implementation.

His best selling book, *The Technical Analysis of Stocks, Options and Futures* (Probus, 1988) has won wide critical acclaim as an invaluable guide for traders and investors.

His second book, *Trading Rules: Strategies for Success* (Longman Financial, 1990) follows on the heels of the first book in its useful and profitable information for readers.

■

■ CHAPTER THIRTEEN ■

I N TRADING VARIOUS MARKETS over the past decade and a half, I have arrived at a trading strategy that has made substantial profits for me. In a nutshell, my strategy involves the evaluation and interpretation of market stages and the implementation of various technical trading tools that allow me to position on the right side of the market to capitalize on potentially profitable moves.

Please note that I indicated that I must be on the "right side of the market" to make money. Despite this successful approach, I also discovered that I lost money at certain times of my trading career. I discovered that when I traded in the direction of the trend, I would make profits; i.e., if the market was bullish, then I would be a continual buyer. When the trend changed, I often found myself still positioning in the direction of the trend that was now on the verge of exhaustion and ready to reverse itself. When the trend reversed, I found myself on the wrong side of the market.

After I sustained losses, the new trend asserted itself, and again I would be on the right side of the market's move, but not until some damage had been done to my trading equity.

With my developing precision in trading, I found it disconcerting that I couldn't pick the point, either in time or price, where the bull or bear moves ended. In regard to making substantial money in the markets, it isn't absolutely necessary to be able to pick the tops and bottoms. Electricity exists despite the fact that we have never seen it with our own eyes, and we all use it without giving it second thoughts. However, as a professional in a business in which most people fail I couldn't allow the market to hide this ultimate secret from me. I had to learn to anticipate when and how the markets reversed.

Quantifiable Methods of Technical Analysis

Thus began my years of observing the behavior of the market's movements. I initially had to find the right tools to observe market action. Market action had to be numerically quantifiable. Watching market action without isolating those movements into quantifiable values is first, a nebulous task, and second, a task not easy to repeat. For future market students to know what I am talking about, they must be given values and numbers to compare and project with their own market examples and trading experiences.

I latched onto the easily quantifiable methods of technical analysis (please note that I mentioned "easily quantifiable" methods to distinguish them from the more nebulous technical analysis approaches) as my tools of market interpretation. In the past the popularity of technical analysis could be attributed to the recognition of basic chart patterns as advanced by Robert Edwards and John Magee in their classic work, *Technical Analysis of Stock Trends*. In the 40 years that this book has been in the public eye, technical analysts who are disciples of this approach have been trading the markets always with a subjective eye open to interpretation of chart patterns. More often then not, the chart patterns manifested themselves only after considerable time elapsed and the patterns themselves were more than half to three-quarters formed. The trading edge, as defined by correct market action *anticipation*, therefore, was limited or nonexistent in the case of some developing patterns. The analysis became after-the-fact—considerably after the fact that that pattern had formed and that market price was moving away from that pattern.

With the advent of more volatile markets, the old tried-and-true methods of conventional bar-chart pattern analysis exposed the practitioner of such techniques to greater and greater capital risk. What value is after-the-fact recognition of a double-top formation in the Dow Jones Industrials Averages in July and August 1987, when the market then drops a mere 508 points in one day? With current volatility, the role of *anticipatory* trend-reversal analysis is more crucial to successful trading than *confirmatory* analysis of trend-continuation. A time will come when the pendulum swings the other way, but until then, the hottest game in town is to pursue trend-reversal analysis.

The Three-Dimensional Approach to Market Analysis

Using a three-dimensional approach to quantify market analysis, I came upon a correct beginning formulation for anticipatory trend-reversal analysis. In my approach to market analysis, I discovered that market action can be viewed in three dimensions or, more correctly, with three aspects of the same puzzle formula: price, time, and volume.

In evaluating market action, I discovered a basic truism: no matter what technical analysts can or try to do, there is a limited universe of data to work from. Unlike fiction writers, the technical analyst, unfortunately, is reality bound: there is no deus ex machina for the forecasting analyst who finds himself boxed into the corner of lost excuses when he discovers that his methods don't forecast future market activity.

This universe of data comprises the following pieces of information for each respective time period: the high price, the low price, the opening price, the closing price, the date of trading, and the volume (and its derivation where existent—open interest) that make up market action. No other data are available for evaluation or analysis. Not only is the phrase, "what you see is what you get," valid, but also "what you don't see, you shouldn't defy," is doubly valid.

With man's penchant to justify losses in the face of unknown variables, he manipulates this limited universe of data with an unlimited array of statistical techniques. This, then, is the deus ex machina. Cornered analysts might think to themselves that, now that their analysis is incorrect and there is only a finite set of data to work form, the key to their salvation is more and more statistical massaging techniques, of which there are an infinite variety. While attempting to achieve the immortality of correct analysis, one finds that the purpose of these techniques—to arrive at correct buy-and-sell decisions—is lost in a mountain of statistical analysis approaches: crossovers of moving averages, normalizing oscillating values, %K values and %D values, ad absurdum.

Price-Sensitive Indicators

Most technical analysis tools are price-sensitive and are based on the high price, low price, opening price, and closing price. Since the superficial analyst uses this information because it is readily available (who ever heard the statement that you are deficit today because today is the fourth day from the previous cycle top—a time-sensitive approach; or that you must get out of the market because of the extremely light volume and declining open interest—a volume-sensitive approach?), you should find that what is ignored is the time and volume-sensitive tools of analysis.

Because of the abundance of technical tools to massage price-sensitive data, you mustn't be too ready to believe that, in order for you to trade successfully, you merely need to analyze price data. To the contrary, this "red herring" is the downfall of most unsuccessful traders. Using price-sensitive indicators *only* in arriving at a valid decision to buy or sell is similar to looking at a three-dimensional world with only one eye opened. If the trader can open the other eye, he will find the world so much richer in information (let's keep this analogy on a two-eyed example!). Unfortunately, with so many price-sensitive massaging techniques, it is only natural that a trader who is not inclined to mathematical techniques will be conversant with some price-sensitive techniques and have no knowledge of time-sensitive or volume-sensitive techniques. In a sense, it is a blessing to successful traders that most traders keep only one eye opened. (Back at the ranch, we're feverishly trying to clone a third eye, while you laypeople have a hard enough time keeping both eyes opened!)

The body of price-sensitive techniques is rich in depth of analysis and even richer in sheer numbers of such gain. The caveat to traders is: just because it's always there doesn't mean you use it exclusively. Among the many price-derived techniques are moving averages, banded moving averages, exponential moving averages, weighted moving averages, oscillators, regular stochastics and slow stochastics, relative strength, momentum studies, percent R, directional movements, price rate of change, weighted closes, spread analysis in a more perverse form of looking at numeric relationships, demand index, and something as insidious sounding as the "moving-average-crossover-divergence" technique. I'm sure that if I sat down and pored over the vast literature available, I could dig up more price-sensitive indicators. I'm also absotively and posilutely sure that most of these indicators were created with great emotional fervor after a bad trading day.

In applying these price-sensitive indicators to market action, the bottom line is that we are all trying to figure out the answer to the following question: will the market continue in its main trend or will it reverse?

The price-sensitive indicators are merely another way, out of a minimal total universe of three (price and volume being the other two), to answer the above question. Experience has shown me that price-sensitive indicators are better used to show market price continuation, i.e., the basic moving averages and the crossovers of varying time duration of moving averages. Yes, there are attempts, and very good ones at that, to manipulate price data to extract overbought and oversold signals for ultimate trend-reversals, but they are not that accurate, for they depend on circuitous logic for their validity. For example, in bull markets, the abundance of overbought indicators are to be ignored. Unless you are foolhardy enough (and there are plenty among us in this lopsided world) to sell into a bull move, this piece of information begs the following question: what is a bull market when defined by overbought and oversold indicators? Since overbought indicators in bull markets are to be ignored, for what purposes are the indicators if they show overbought conditions and you can't really act on them? Or, conversely, what about using oversold signals to go long in bear markets?

Time-Sensitive Indicators

For trend-reversal probabilities, I found that time-sensitive indicators are more appropriate. Time-sensitive indicators, to the conventional analyst, are created through research with various cycle lengths. The implied validity of cycles is not appropriate. In attempting to forecast future events and, in this particular case, to forecast future price movements, I have sifted through these three dimensions of the forecasting puzzle and have discovered that of price, time, and volume, only the dimension of time can be forecasted well in advance of the actual occurrence.

The superficial analyst will look at cycles and try to recreate them showing troughs and peaks in price movements. This approach, to the extent that it works, depends absolutely on the observed phenomena of price activity: a peak in price movement signals a cycle top and a trough in price movement signals a cycle bottom. In attempting to define cycles, the analyst uses an unpredictable variable, price, as a gauge of cycle beginnings and endings! (When do we tell the fox to stop guarding the hen house?) When projecting into the future with these price-derived time cycles, the analysts often encounter future price tops and bottoms that are not predicted by these observed time cycles. To justify the continued validity of these errant time cycles, the analysts bring in concepts named "left and right translations," which basically are excuses to explain why the tops and bottoms were not forecasted by the time cycles and why it is acceptable forecasting techniques to create a concept to accommodate imprecise forecasting. . .as long as the rest of the analysis is usable.

I study pure time movements as defined by physical phenomena: planetary motion. Independent of what the price action is, time is measured on an ongoing basis by planetary revolutions around some central point. We know that the moon revolves completely around the earth between 28-29 days. We also known that the earth revolves around the sun in 365 1/4 days. These are known revolutional periods, and they are as predictable to us as knowing that night follows day. No exceptions. In a sense, the knowledge that time is absolute and that it is the most reliable aspect of the time, price, and volume equation should instill in bewildered traders a very good feeling of confidence. (God is in the heavens and all's right with the world.) This is a very powerful piece of information. I affirm this knowledge to be even greater than knowing the following dictum: trade with the trend. This is absolute, and to study time correctly you must observe planetary motion.

In attempting to create tools that can first be used to duplicate past results, you must be conversant with astronomical terms. From the study of planet-timed movements, the trader can then extend out into less predictable data: price and volume projections.

Volume-Sensitive Indicators

The third dimension of forecasting is that concerning volume-sensitive techniques. Volume figures, as data to be analyzed and studied, is the most difficult facet of the three-variable equation. Volume is a reflection of trading activity, and, as such, volume numbers are disclosed only after the day's trading. There are sophisticated time-analysis techniques that purport to project time periods when trading activity is prone to be more volatile and when, (with a high probability) more volume activity exists. Volume numbers cannot be predicted in advance. However, this does not imply that you can't analyze the data that is created on a daily basis after the markets are closed. In this regard, this type of analysis is used more often to confirm analysis from other analytical techniques and cannot be used to forecast and project.

I have observed that, because of this tenuous position of volume analysis in the framework of definitive technical analysis, volume-sensitive indicators are bipolar in their benefits to the trader: they can be used, but rarely, to forecast correctly price reversals at certain price levels and stages of market action, and they can also be used to confirm price continuation in other types of markets.

My book, *Technical Analysis of Stocks, Options and Futures: Advanced Trading Techniques and Systems,* is a compilation of the many technical analysis techniques. What sets this book apart from the others is the fact that detailed trading examples are used to illustrate each of the trading techniques.

What makes this book so helpful is that all of the trading techniques are brought together into one chart, a "periodic table" if you will: a continuum of market ideology is evoked. In order to thread all these multidimensional, multiaspect trading techniques dealing with time, price, and volume into one cohesive framework, it was necessary, on my part, to redefine market activity types. It is common knowledge that markets can be classified into three types: trading market, bull market, and bear market; but these are static interpretations. The markets, however, are dynamic, constantly moving from one level of market activity to another level, and it is this dynamism that is brought forth in the chart. What is crucial to integrating these technical analysis techniques into one periodic table is the discovery of *bridging* market conditions, and I classify these under "transition markets."

Transition markets are markets that bridge bear markets and trading markets, that bridge bull markets and trading markets, that bridge trading markets and bear markets, and finally that bridge trading markets and bull markets. These are the four additional markets of transition that I discovered. I have classified the various technical analysis techniques in the chart reproduced from the book, *Technical Analysis of Stocks, Options and Futures.*

The intuitive professional traders understand that these transition markets exist but cannot pinpoint when and how they come into existence. They only know that after a market pauses in a trading range after a significant sell off, somewhere they will accumulate positions. They only know that after a market turns up for a period of time, the market must pause and reverse direction and that they can benefit when they position for an eventual reversal to the downside. Now, with the advanced trading techniques available to the retail trader, he or she can discern with more quantifiable accuracy what these innately professional traders only feel. The retail trader can observe how various technical indicators behave correctly in certain market situations and misbehave in other market conditions. What the intuitive trader senses when the markets misbehave, the retail trader can now observe quantitatively. Market misbehavior creates vital decision-making information. It is the intelligent trader who can see the misbehavior for what it really is: ongoing, continuing clues to future market activity.

OB = Overbought

OS = Oversold

Analysis	Indicator Group	Indicator	Trading Markets	Trending Markets: Bull	Trending Markets: Bear	Changing Markets: Trading to Bull	Changing Markets: Trading to Bear	Changing Markets: Bull to Trading	Changing Markets: Bear to Trading
Micro Analysis	Price Sensitive Indicators	Moving Averages	Many false breakouts and whipsaw action	Valid breakouts and continuous confirmation	Valid breakouts and continous confirmation	Excellent behavior	Excellent behavior	Excellent behavior	Excellent behavior
Micro Analysis	Price Sensitive Indicators	Relative Strength	OB/OS indication excellent	Skewed number of signals to more overbought	Skewed number of signals to more oversold	Increasing signals to OB	Increasing frequency of OS signals	Equal number of OB/OS signals from OB skew	Equal number of OB/OS signals from show OB
Micro Analysis	Price Sensitive Indicators	Percentage R	OB/OS signals are valid	False OB signals valid. Use modified OS	False OS signals valid. Use modified OB	Valid signals give way to false OB	Valid signals give way to false OS	False OS to valid signals	False OB to valid signals
Micro Analysis	Price Sensitive Indicators	Oscillators	OB/OS signals are valid	False OB signals valid if using modified OS	False OB signals valid if using modified OS	Valid signals give way to false OB	Valid signals give way to to false OS	False OS to valid signals	False OB to valid signals
Micro Analysis	Price Sensitive Indicators	Stochastics	Crossovers OB and OS are valid	Crossovers from OS only are valid	Crossovers from OB only are valid	Crossovers of OB/OS valid to only OS indicators valid	Crossovers of OB/OS valid to only OB indicators	Only OS area crossovers are valid to both OB/OS valid	Only OB area crossovers are valid to both OB/OS valid
Micro Analysis	Price Sensitive Indicators	Point-and-Figure	False breakouts whipsaw action	Valid breakouts	Valid breakdowns	Can project counts to likely tops	Can project counts to likely bottoms	Cannot forecast	Cannot forecast
Micro Analysis	Hybrid Indicators	Market Profile®	Normal distribution	Can observe and tell upside breakouts	Can observe and tell downside breakdowns	Can see buildup of buying pressure	Can see buildup of selling pressure	Great appearance of non-trend days	Great appearance of non-trend days
Micro Analysis	Volume Sensitive Indicators	Tic Volume	Very good accumulation indicator	Can use to possibly pyramid	Valid signals but because of briefness hard to pyramid	Excellent accumulation indicators	Too late to signal volume distribution	Flattening of OBV breakouts	Flattening of OBV breakouts
Micro Analysis	Volume Sensitive Indicators	On-Balance Volume	Very good accumulation indicator	Too long to use to pyramid	Valid but impractical signals	Excellent accumulation indicators	Too late to signal volume distribution	Flattening of OBV breakouts	Flattening of OBV breakouts
Micro Analysis	Volume Sensitive Indicators	Bar Charts	Valid, recognizable pattern	Valid, recognizable trend lines, channels	Valid, recognizable trend lines, channels	Reversal patterns valid	Reversal patterns valid	Reversal patterns valid	Reversal pattern valid
Macro Analysis	Time Sensitive	Astronomical Cycles	No good	Not applicable	Not applicable	Excellent turning points	Excellent turning points	Excellent turning points	Excellent turning point
Macro Analysis	Composite	Elliott Wave Theory	Hard to show beginning and end—just that it is occurring	Can project market to take out previous highs	Can project market to take out previous lows	Probability can be determined that this will happen	Probability can be determined that this will happen	Probability can be determined that this will happen	Probability can be determined that this will happen
Macro Analysis	Composite	Gann Analysis	Whipsaws	Long for the upmove	Short for the downmove	Can get you long but whipsawed first	Can get you short but whipsawed first	Whipsaw first then profits	Whipsaw first then profits

From William F. Eng, *The Technical Analysis of Stocks, Options and Futures: Advanced Trading Systems and Techniques* (Chicago, IL: Probus, 1988) by permission of the publisher and author. Copyright 1988 by William F. Eng.

TRADING LOGIC AND THE MARKET PROFILE®

An Introduction to Technical Applications

JAMES F. DALTON
&
ERIC T. JONES
BARTON J. HANSON, Contributor

■

■

JAMES F. DALTON
&
ERIC T. JONES
BARTON J. HANSON, Contributor

Prior to becoming President of Dalton Capital Management, Inc., Mr. Dalton was President of J.F. Dalton Associates, a leading discount brokerage firm. He has served as Senior Executive Vice President of Transmarket Group, Inc., Director of Options for Paine Webber, Inc., and Executive Vice President of the Chicago Board Options Exchange, responsible for marketing and education during its early years of primitive growth.

Eric T. Jones is a principal and Director of Market Information for Dalton Capital Management, Inc. Mr. Jones is also editor of *The Profile Report*, a bi-monthly Market Profile® education and research journal.

Barton J. Hanson is Senior Editor of *The Profile Report*.

■

▪ CHAPTER FOURTEEN ▪

THINK BACK, FOR A MOMENT, TO YOUR CHILDHOOD, to those joyous days when school was closed because of snow. Remember the frozen toes and the snow down your back and in your ear that so often accompanied the playful snowball battles in the afternoon.

Oh yes, let's think about those "harmless" snowballs. After being pelted with a few, we soon learned that although they may look the same, no two snowballs are created equal. Some were made of soft powder—others had rocks in the middle. Some were lobbed with the strength of a mouse, and some were virtual bullets hurled by a juvenile Dizzy Dean. Our snowball fighting strategy, and hence the amount of damage done to our bodies, depended on a careful evaluation of these factors. Being mere children and not yet our mature, intelligent selves, we often (unfortunately) discovered the substance and velocity of snowballs by stepping into their path or not escaping fast enough.

A few of the more intelligent among us would take cover for a moment, observing the effects the snowballs had on our teammates. By observing their responses it was possible to evaluate the significance of the snowballs thrown and who threw them, and then decide upon the best strategy to avoid unnecessary physical harm. Regardless of the strategy eventually chosen, it was clearly necessary to first determine the composition of the snowballs if the battle was to be won.

No two prices are created equal. Like snowballs, prices are formed by different types of market activity and by different market participants. Some prices are simply more important or more significant, whether it be because they elicit a strong response or demonstrate a blatant lack of interest. The Market Profile® is the first market analysis and trading approach to recognize that the forces behind a commodity bought for $5 are much different than those behind one sold for $5—even though the price may look the same. In a sense, the Market Profile® tells us what a price is "made of," and therefore may improve our chances of winning the futures battle.

Section One: Trading Logic and the Market Profile

We begin this chapter with a brief introduction to the Market Profile®. While many readers no doubt are already familiar with trading logic and the Market Profile®, the fact that it is still so new to the financial industry practically requires that we give it some introduction. The Market Profile® is not an ap-proach that can be taught in a chapter—there are whole books and extensive training courses for that. Rather, our aim here is to introduce it in concept, providing just enough background to support the "meat" of our discussion. Then, we quickly move on to using the strengths of the Market Profile® to enhance and complement current technical systems.

It is our hope that from this discussion traders will come away with an appreciation of the powers of trading logic, and the realization that, once learned, trading logic is precisely what it says it is: logical—practically second nature. Trading logic in its highest form is truly a one-on-one understanding of the market—an ability to understand at any time the operative forces at work in the marketplace. True, reaching such a level of understanding requires a lot of work (six months to a year, minimum). But, like learning to walk, once mastered it is an innate ability that sticks with you for the rest of your trading career.

Introduction

When J. Peter Steidlmayer, a career floor trader on the Chicago Board of Trade, introduced the Market Profile® to the world of futures trading, a new era of market analysis was born. Floor traders used to be the only individuals who actually knew just who was active in the marketplace, when, and at what price levels. Now, through an understanding of trading logic and with the aid of the Market Profile® graphic, off-floor traders have access to the same information formerly only privy to the trader standing in the pit. The Market Profile® is considered by active traders to be a major breakthrough in market analysis and trading, since it offers a logical and organized set of price and volume data from which traders can base trading decisions.

The Theory

Trading logic theory is based on a few basic principles of trade—principles common to all organized markets, be they the futures market, stock market, the automobile market, real estate or even your local supermarket. It involves the understanding that all competitive, free markets continually auction in search of those price levels at which to conduct the greatest amount of business, or in trading logic terms—facilitate trade.

Fundamental to trading logic is the assumption that a product, commodity, or security that trades at a specified price or range of prices for an extended period of time begins to be perceived as having "value" at that price(s). For example, if milk sells at $1.05 per gallon in your local grocery store for two consecutive months, what is the value of a gallon of milk?—$1.05. But, suppose that your friendly grocer receives a new shipment of milk, only to realize that he still has milk left over in the coolers. Milk spoils quickly, so he has to move it fast or face a loss. So, the grocer puts the older milk on sale for 89 cents a gallon. What is the value of the milk now?—It's still $1.05, or it would not be viewed as a bargain. Naturally, you buy two gallons instead of the usual one, to take advantage of the sale price.

This is the crux of trading logic. The grocer auctioned price down below value to move his inventory. You, recognizing that milk was priced below value, not only accepted the lower price, but also increased your volume in the process. With the old milk gone, a day later milk was selling at $1.05 again. This same concept of value applies to all financial markets.

The Market's Battleground

Every market is composed of producers, consumers, and middlemen. The producer, a large dairy farm, for instance, is continually searching for information regarding the condition of not only its competitors but also the end consumer. How much product is available? How badly do consumers want it? How much are they willing to pay for it? Meanwhile, consumers, such as you, me, and all others desiring a natural source of vitamins A and D, go through the same evaluation, but from the opposite perspective. None of these participants are willing to share their information, for it is a valuable tool in their negotiations.

The dairy farmer will attempt to price its milk as high as possible, while grocery shoppers (collectively) will try to buy as cheaply as they can. In the end, each participant must make a buy or sell decision and enter the market to conduct his or her business. Each consumer's desire for a product, as well as each producer's willingness to sell, is reflected by the market's auctions, the prices traded and how much was traded at that price. Each new buy/sell decision adds one more piece of information to the marketplace. The only collective source that holds the key to all of this information lies within the market's auctions themselves.

A key concept in trading logic is the fact that it is primarily the longer timeframe participants (producers and consumers) who are responsible for price movement. Logically, middlemen (floor locals, grocers, etc.) are not interested in moving price, since all they want to do is "mark it up" and move it out the door. Thus, it is the longer time frame participants who move price. When price trends, it is because longer time frame participants are in control of the market. The Market Profile®, through its reflections of the market's auctions, identifies which participants are in control of price—the key to successfully trading any market.

The Market Profile® Graphic

The Market Profile® graphic helps traders monitor and observe price in terms of time. The graphic organizes the market in half-hour time periods and uses the letters of the alphabet to plot price activity occurring in a specific half-hour time period. For example, in treasury bonds, the letter "A" indicates that a particular price traded between 8:00 and 8:30 CST, "B" represents 8:30 to 9:00, "C" from 9:00 to 9:30, and so on. Foreign currency futures, on the other hand, open at 7:20 on the International Monetary Market (IMM) in Chicago. Here, the first period runs from 7:20 to 7:50 and is designated by the letter "Y." "Z" spans from 7:50 to 8:10, "A" from 8:20 to 8:50, and so forth (see Figure 14-1).

Figure 14-1   The Construction of a Market Profile®
June Japanese Yen, March 8, 1988

```
7882    .   .   .   .   .   .   .   .   .   .   .                    .
7880    .   .   .   .   .   .   .   .   .   .   .                    .
7878    .   .   .   .   .   E   .   .   .   .                        E
7876    .   .   .   .   .   E   .   .   .   .                        E
7874    .   .   .   .   .   E   .   .   .   .                        E
7872    .   .   .   C   .   E   .   .   .   .                        CE
7870    .   .   .   C   D   E   .   .   .   J                        CDEJ
7868    .   .   .   C   D   E   F   .   .   I   J   K                CDEFIJK    ◄─── Close
7866    Y   .   .   .   C   D   E   F   G   .   I   J                YCDEFGIJ
7864    Y   .   .   .   C   D   E   F   G   .   I   J                YCDEFGIJ
7862    Y   Z   .   .   C   .   .   F   G   H   I   J                YZCFGHIJ   ⎫ Value
7860    Y   Z   .   B   C   .   .   .   G   H   I   .                YZBCGHI    ⎬ Area
7858    Y   Z   .   B   C   .   .   .   G   H   I   .                YZBCGHI
7856    O   Z   .   B   .   .   .   .   G   H   I   .  Open ───►     OZBGHI
7854    .   Z   A   B   .   .   .   .   G   H   I   .                ZABGHI
7852    .   Z   A   B   .   .   .   .   .   H   .   .                ZABH
7850    .   Z   A   B   .   .   .   .   .   .   .   .                ZAB
7848    .   .   A   .   .   .   .   .   .   .   .   .                A
7846    .   .   A   .   .   .   .   .   .   .   .   .                A
7844    .   .   A   .   .   .   .   .   .   .   .   .                A
7842    .   .   .   .   .   .   .   .   .   .   .   .                .
7840    .   .   .   .   .   .   .   .   .   .   .   .                .
```

Once again, the key to interpreting trading logic lies in organizing the market's price auctions in terms of time, so that one can arrive at an assessment of where price is—at any time—relative to value. The end result is a normal distribution curve displaying price on the vertical axis and time horizontally. The graphic in Figure 14-1 illustrates these concepts, as well as the construction of a Japanese yen Market Profile® throughout the trading day.

Like the gallon of milk that traded at $1.05 for two months, if the market spends a large amount of time at a particular price or range of prices, then by deduction, a large number of transactions are occurring at that price. That price is therefore considered to be accepted and to have value. In Figure 14-1, the value area for the day's trading spans from 7854 to 7868.

Conversely, if the market spends very little time at a given price, very little trade is conducted at that price. Since little trade is conducted, that price was rejected by the market as being either too high or too low. Referring once again to Figure 14-1, at 7844 price is below value and was rejected early in the day, since the market traded at 7844 in just one half-hour period (A). By roughly 10:30, price rose to 7878 (in "E" period). At 7878 price is above value. For the trader, the question is: at 7878 is price leading value (that is, will value rise to equal price) or will price drop back down to equal value? When price and value diverge, the market creates trading opportunities. Only through an understanding of trading logic can one begin to identify and capitalize on these opportunities.

The Concept of Value

The ultimate aim of all market participants, regardless of whether one is buying a house, a gallon of milk or 5,000 bushels of soybeans, is the discovery of value (i.e., getting a fair price). Value depends on a variety of economic variables, many of which are not known or understood when they are most affecting the market. Moreover, variables, by their very definition, change, causing value to change. However, all of the fundamentals do come together to be judged in one place—the marketplace. Through a daily evaluation—through real buy and sell decisions backed by real money—the market arrives at its best assessment of value. The Market Profile® provides the mechanism to determine value. With the Market Profile®, one can locate high volume price regions and thus determine current value, as well as project future value.

The Market Profile® is the bridge between value and the various prices paid by the market over time. In other words, Market Profile® locates value, using information (data) common to all markets—price, time, and volume. These price/time concepts are expressed by the equation developed by J. Peter Steidlmayer[1]:

$$Price \times Time = Value = Volume.$$

According to Steidlmayer's theory of auction markets, the value area for any point in time is determined to be where 70 percent, or roughly one standard deviation, of the volume was conducted. To calculate the value area, ideally one would like to have available data indicating the volume occurring at each price, since volume is the best measure of a market's ability to facilitate trade. However, when price/volume data is not available, estimating volume based on consistent units of time (called TPOs, or Time Price Opportunities) has been found to define the value area with a high degree of reliability.[2] When price is compared to its position on the distribution and the direction of the current trend, one can begin to develop an assessment of when price is above value, at value or below value for any time frame.

The Market's Auctions and the Trade Facilitation Process

The key to successful trading, of course, lies in being able to determine in which direction the market is headed, and perhaps more important, how determined it is to get there. Subtle, yet valuable, clues regarding market direction and conviction are embedded in the market's auctions and reflected by the Market Profile®.

We noted earlier that the primary purpose of the market is to facilitate trade—that is, to promote the continuous creation of activity among all market participants. When that activity stops or changes, old opportunities have ended and new opportunities are developing. The most successful traders will be those who recognize this change and *act*. (Many can recognize the change, but few can act.)

Market activity is created through a continuous *two-way* auction process, using price to auction from high to low and from low to high. The auction is the market's means for establishing a fair price to conduct business. The auctions also determine the shape of the Market Profiles®.

In an *up* auction, what is being purchased continues to rise in price until the highest bid is filled. In a *down* auction prices are offered down until the lowest offer is satisfied. As the auction continues, the bidders or offerers are either satisfied or stand aside until only one party remains. This last participant has either sold too cheaply or paid too dearly, establishing at least a temporary high or low price (hereinafter referred to as *excess*). Excess can develop in any period of time: one-half hour, one day, three days, one week, one month, one year or several years (we will subsequently refer to these periods as timeframes). The best trading opportunities will occur at the moment of excess and will diminish as price moves farther away from the excess. Figure 14-1 shows the day timeframe auctions transpiring in the Japanese yen future on March 8. Figure 14-1 also illustrates day timeframe excess occurring in "A" period on the lower extreme and during E period on the upper extreme of the yen Market Profile®.

The Role of Price and Time

The market uses price to advertise opportunity. Most traders misunderstand the purpose of price. Price excesses, extremes, or opportunities (these are all the same thing) are regulated through time. Thus, the market regulates itself through time. If a price offered or paid is truly a good opportunity, that price should not exist for very long.

Anatomy of a Market Profile®

The auctions reflect the attitudes of market participants, thus creating market-generated information. Figure 14-2 illustrates the salient features of a typical Market Profile®.

Section One: Summary

In the preceding paragraphs we have provided a thumbnail sketch of trading logic theory and the mechanics of the Market Profile®. Again, there is so much more to these powerful tools than space allows. Still, to best appreciate the technical discussions that follow, it is critical that you have at least a conceptual understanding of how to apply the Market Profile® to your trading.

If we can understand the structure of the market's auctions, then we can determine which participants are active (those who move price or those who do not), how much determination and control they possess, how much directional conviction is present in the market, and last, when that conviction is changing. Armed with this information, one can then determine with a relatively high probability which way the market is attempting to go, how badly it wants to go that way and, most important, how good a job it is doing. These are the answers that an understanding of trading logic can provide. Knowing these answers, the trader is well equipped to trade any market, regardless of the approach he or she is using.

Next, we demonstrate how blending the strengths of the Market Profile® with technical analysis can improve the results of technical systems.

Section Two: The Market Profile® in Technical Combinations*

Many experienced technical traders have devoted a trading lifetime to developing their technical systems. In effect, they are expert market technicians. It would be unrealistic to suggest to these individuals that they throw their systems out the door and begin trading exclusively with the Market Profile®. But, it is also our belief that whether you trade using fundamental information, technical information, market-generated information, or just plain by the seat of your pants, you will not be able to trade with maximum effectiveness unless you truly understand the market. If you under-

Figure 14-2   Anatomy of a Market Profile®
September Treasury Bonds, July 25, 1986*

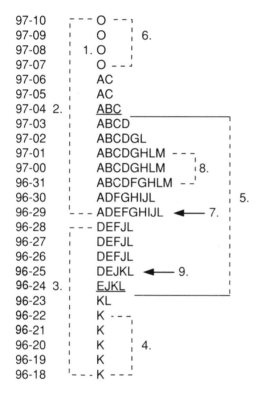

```
97-10   r - - O - -,
97-09   i     O   i 6.
97-08   i  1. O   i
97-07   i     O - -'
97-06   i     AC
97-05   i     AC
97-04  2. i    ABC
97-03   i     ABCD
97-02   i     ABCDGL                    i
97-01   i     ABCDGHLM - - -,           i
97-00   i     ABCDGHLM       i 8.       i
96-31   i     ABCDFGHLM - -'            i
96-30   i     ADFGHIJL              i 5.
96-29   '- - ADEFGHIJL  ◄— 7.           i
96-28   - - - DEFJL                     i
96-27   i     DEFJL                     i
96-26   i     DEFJL                     i
96-25   i     DEJKL  ◄— 9.              i
96-24  3. i    EJKL
96-23   i     KL
96-22   i     K - - -,
96-21   i     K     i
96-20   i     K     i 4.
96-19   i     K     i
96-18   '- - - K - - -'
```

1. *Opening range*—Important reference point for day time-frame traders.

2. *Initial balance*—Activity in first two time periods (for bonds). Market attempting to locate a range that will allow two-sided trade to take place.

3. *Range extension OT seller*—Activity extending below the initial balance.

4. *Single print OT buying tail*—Price advertisement be-low value area accepted, to enter on the extreme.

5. *Value area*—Where 70 percent of the day's business was conducted. The market identifies a fair area for the day time-frame only.

6. *Single print selling tail*—Initial opening was too high and attracted attention of OT seller, who entered voluntarily and caused price to fall away quickly.

7. *Point of control*—The longest TPO/price line closest to the center of the range. In a balanced market, the point of control represents the point at which control shifts from the buyer to the seller, and vice versa.

8. *Closing range*—Used only as a reference point.

9. *A TPO–Time Price Opporturnity*—TPOs are the basic unit used to measure market activity.

---

*Data courtesy of Commodity Quote Graphics. © CBOT 1984. OT represents "Other Time-frame," or longer time-frame)

stand trading logic, you are much better equipped to take advantage of the strengths and overcome the weaknesses of any approach you are using.

Almost any trading approach will make money at one time or another. The problem is, there are also plenty of times when they do not. And we are willing to admit that trading logic—like any other approach or system—has certain advantages and disadvantages built right into it. In a perfect world, we would all develop a way to use the Market Profile® that takes advantage of its greatest strengths. Even more, we would find a way to funnel together the greatest strengths of the Market Profile® along with those of other high-powered techniques such as technical trading systems.

In this section we attempt to demonstrate how the powers of two starkly different trading approaches—trading logic and technical analysis—can be fused together to produce superior trading results. Specifically, we combine the "zoom-lens" capability of the Market Profile® with the discipline provided by a technical system.

Before we jump into an illustration, let us first point out a few important distinctions between technical analysis and trading logic—important differences that, when the two approaches are combined, can lead to a very useful trading approach indeed.

Price

Technical systems, for all of their strengths in discipline, have one universal drawback—they are largely based on price, or some formulation of price. Consequently, a technical trend-following system will almost always be late getting in and out of a move. Likewise, an oscillator-based system may ultimately pick the top or bottom, but how many false peaks or valleys did it pick before it got the right one? And, do you have any money left when it is found? What is lacking from price-oriented systems is market understanding or logic. Through an understanding of trading logic, the trader can determine when a market is truly overbought or oversold, and when a trend is beginning and ending. The fundamental difference between market logic and technical analysis is that through trading logic, one can identify who is in control of price, and when that control is changing. A price oriented system makes no assessment of the behavioral forces responsible for the existence of that price.

---

*Note: Regretfully, the discussions in this section may include trading logic terminology and concepts that are beyond the material presented in the introductory portion of the chapter. While an understanding of these higher level topics is not crucial, readers desiring greater definition of a particular topic may refer to the trading logic glossary at the end of the chapter.

Timing

Because technical indicators are based on price and hence something that has already happened, the indicator is inherently *late*. Rather than a sound basis in understanding, the timing of technicals is left to mathematical and statistical formulae. Technical indicators are largely derived from a specific set of historical price data, data that has already had time to have an impact on the marketplace. Technical indicators are, therefore, inherently late. The Market Profile®, on the other hand, reflects the current market dynamics responsible for price. Given the ability to "see" the market participants in action—their strength, activity level, anxiety, etc.—the trader is equipped to see change occurring in the present tense, not after it has happened.

Flexibility

Aside from the theoretical differences, the Market Profile® adds another powerful human dimension to technical indicators—flexibility. Because technical indicators are usually mathematically derived, they tend to be rigidly structured systems. However, all traders are individuals, with different time- frames, levels of aggressiveness, and so on. To be truly effective, a trading approach needs to account for and take advantage of each individual's "trading personality." Technicals are generally unable to do this; through the Market Profile® you can.

On the flip-side, however, too much flexibility can lead to disaster for the trader without discipline. It is in the area of discipline and consistency that the technicals shine and can be most beneficial to a trader using trading logic. Technical systems have a built-in time frame and a consistent strategy, a strategy that looks at the market the same way, every day. For the trader who is easily absorbed by the market, using a technical approach can mean the difference between financial life or death.

Work

The Market Profile® reflects the continuous creation of market activity every second of the trading day. And with the increase in market-generated information provided by the Market Profile® comes an increase in the amount of time needed for the trader to absorb that information. While some traders may desire no other decision-support tool, others no doubt find the Market Profile® to be much more than they need. If you are going to fly only from Philadelphia to New York City, you probably do not need an Air Force jet.

By combining the Market Profile® with other technical systems, how-ever, the trader need only monitor activity during those periods that the system is generating a signal. Then, they can "zoom-in" with the Market Profile® and determine whether the signal is valid. Not everyone has the luxury (or wants) to sit in front of a computer screen all day, every day.

Moreover, since the vast information provided by the Market Profile® approach tends to narrow the trader's focus to smaller and smaller timeframes, it may prove helpful for traders to use long-term technical indi-cators to keep that long-term perspective in focus.

An Illustration

To demonstrate the melding of trading logic with technical analysis, in this section we will examine the Market Profile® in tandem with three- and five-day moving averages, and one well-known oscillator, the Relative Strength Index (RSI).

Illustrated in Figure 14-3 is June and September S&P 500 activity over the May 31 to June 21, 1988 period. The daily bar charts, Market Profiles®, three and five-day moving averages, as well as the RSI for each market day are detailed fully. The signals generated by the moving averages and RSI are summarized for each day in Figure 14-4. Our aim is not to show how each approach differs, but rather to show where and when one approach might complement the other. Let us begin, then, to assemble in a workable way the unique strong points of the Market Profile®, moving averages, and the Relative Strength Index.

Assumptions

The trading timeframe assumed for this discussion is relatively short, sim-ilar to that of a swing trader (three to five days). Thus, a three- to five-day Moving Average Crossover model is used to generate short term signals. Similarly, a 5-day RSI is used for top and bottom timing. Since the Market Profile® is the freshest among these three trading approaches, we feel it safe to assume that our readership is fairly acquainted with moving averages and the RSI. Not wishing to offend (or bore) anyone, we briefly present a few definitions.

About Moving Averages

When calculating a three-day and five-day moving average, an average is made of the three most recent—and five most recent—days' closes. With

Figure 14-3   Daily Bar Chart, Market Profile®, MA1 and MA2 and RSI for June and September S&P 500, May 31–June 21, 1988

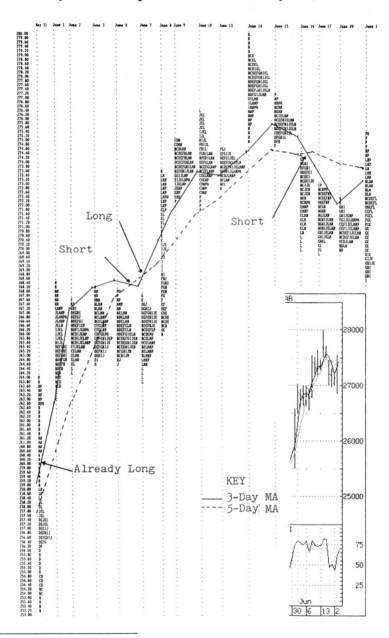

Data courtesy of Commodity Quote Graphics. Market Profile® ©CBOT 1974.

**Figure 14-4 Summary of Recommendations
generated by Moving Average Cross-Overs and by the RSI
for June and September S&P 500, May 31–June21, 1988**

Date	MA1	MA2	Sentiment	RSI	Sentiment
5/31	259.10	257.83	Long	75.02	Short
6/01	262.90	260.37	Long	80.67	Short
6/02	267.23	262.86	Long	77.95	Short
6/03	268.28	264.96	Long	75.41	Short
6/06	268.58	267.84	Long	79.22	Short
6/07	268.43	268.46	Short	66.06	Neutral
6/08	270.57	269.56	Long	80.31	Short
6/09	271.78	270.57	Long	74.55	Neutral
6/10	273.55	271.62	Long	73.17	Neutral
6/13	273.35	272.42	Long	74.77	Neutral
6/14	274.48	274.20	Long	82.17	Short
6/15	275.77	274.74	Long	82.69	Short
6/16	275.25	274.50	Long	48.43	Neutral
6/17	273.93	274.43	Short	51.77	Neutral
6/20	272.12	274.00	Short	44.79	Neutral
6/21	273.22	273.74	Short	63.83	Neutral

each subsequent trading day, the current day is added, and the earliest dropped, providing a moving representation of the average closing price.

A comparison of the two averages (three versus five) gives an assessment of the market's momentum. If a market is trending, the three-day will move faster than the five, since it is composed of a smaller sample of prices. When the three-day moving average crosses above the five-day moving average, a long is signaled. Conversely, when the three-day moving average (of the closing price) crosses below the five-day moving average, a short is triggered. The strength of looking at moving averages is that they can help determine and follow a trend. Moreover, since they smooth-out short-term price fluctuation, they also help us remain objective about the market's longer term direction.

About the RSI

The RSI is basically an oscillator, or timing device, that determines when the market has gone beyond what it has determined are normal oscillations of the market—when the market has exceeded its norm. The idea is that, based on recent history, the market should sooner than later return to its usual movements.

An RSI reading of 75 or greater indicates that a market is overbought and, therefore, triggers a sell signal. An RSI of 25 or less denotes oversold conditions and generates a buy signal.

One drawback of the RSI is that it may read a buying trend as an abnormally high oscillation and therefore keep selling all the way up an up move. And, while the RSI will eventually call the correct top or bottom, you may not have enough money left to take advantage of it. However, an RSI used in collaboration with an approach that more accurately evaluates when a trend has ended can be a very powerful combination indeed.

It may very well prove helpful to use these other systems in conjunction with the Market Profile® to help us stay on track with the larger trend (moving averages) and to help time the market turns suggested by oscillators. If these other approaches offer a panoramic view of the market, the profile provides the zoom-lens needed to justify or confirm them.

The following is a brief dissection of S&P market activity from May 31 to June 21, 1988, using the Market Profile®, moving averages, and the RSI.

May 31. Referring to Figure 14-3, the Market Profile® for May 31 exhibits a multiple distribution buying trend day an initiating break-out of an overlapping value region. According to the Market Profile®, this is no doubt a day to buy the S&P. The three-day moving average was already above the five-day—a standing buy signal lasting from May 24 at the 256.00 level. The RSI reads 75 as of the close, a sell signal. As we've mentioned, this sell signal will be correct, one of these days. A more "artistic" approach lies in realizing the meaning generated by such an RSI reading and then using the market-generated information of the Market Profile® to confirm whether selling is currently appropriate. Obviously, after so strong a trend day, it might not be.

June 1–7. As we can see (Figure 14-3), June 1 through 7 continues to allow value to be accepted above the late-in-the-day buying spike of May 31. Given these five days of overlapping value and rotating, two-time-frame trades after such a strong buying trend day, a case can be made from a trading logic stand-point for both buyers and for sellers. On one hand, there has been little continuation of the buying move (May 31). But, on the other, price has slowed to allow volume to catch up. Further, buyers have not given anything back. The key is that the Market Profile® finally provides the needed clue in the form of selling excess at 263.80 on June 7. Having established this excess—seen through the Market Profile® and not through the moving average (MA) or the RSI. On June 7, the three-day MA crosses below the five-day, reversing and going short. The RSI continues to generate consistent sell signals. After five days of overlapping value, the short advice of the MA and RSI are not surprising. Still, the Market Profiles® tell us to wait, be patient and ready to go with the break-out.

June 8. Activity finally breaks up and away from the 264.50 to 267.00 overlapping value balance. The three-day moving average crosses over the five-day on this day, telling us to reverse and go long. The RSI continues to generate selling signals as the S&P pursues its buying move. One of these days, it may be right.

June 9–13. On June 9, after the June 8 rally, value begins to overlap the June 8 buying spike rather than building above it, as was the case on May 31 through June 1. This overlapping value within the spike indicates that the buying auction may be slowing. According to the Market Profiles® of June 10 and 13 as well, anyone holding long should begin to consider exiting. The MA is still telling us to hold long. And the RSI continues to tell us to keep selling.

June 14. On June 14, the S&P gaps higher at the open, reaching as high as 280.00 early in the session, only to see responsive sellers enter and leave potential buying excess at the 280.00 level. Structure shows that subsequent auction rotations are down during most of the remainder of the session. The day's substantially higher volume on such a day trying to move lower definitely indicates renewed seller strength and reliability of the 280.00 excess level. Market Profile® structure says we should consider exiting. From a moving average viewpoint, all that is seen is the day's higher values. Therefore, the MA says "hold long." The RSI reading is 82—a strong selling signal—which is, of course, finally correct. On June 14, then, the RSI's higher-than-usual reading of 82 is actually confirmed by trading logic. The bullish, value-based MA is overridden by trading logic, which recognizes that the day's activity is most likely a sign of excess.

June 15. The June 15 Market Profile® shows a day not really able to facilitate trade well in either direction. Its narrow value, lower volume and inability to challenge the June 14 280.00 buying excess all suggest that anyone still long should exit and reverse short. The exit for such shorts would be the 280.00 level. Not sufficiently gauging the lower values yet, our moving average still generates a bullish sign. The RSI reading is at 83, at last coinciding with the Market Profile®'s signals.

June 16. There is an open in the upper quadrant of the day's range—a selling-composite day, complete with lower values. Higher volumes and lower value generally mean "hold short." The moving average stubbornly tells us to remain long. On the 16th, the RSI plunges from 83 to 48, confirming the June 15 signal of 83 saying the market is far off from its normal oscillations.

June 17–21. June 17 through 21 shows three nonconviction, balanced trading days. Four days of overlapping value indicate a potential break-out in either direction. Shorts should exit and traders should be flat. The June 21 rally creates potential short term selling excess at 268.50. A short term bracket begins to form between 268 and 280. The moving average finally reverses short on June 17, two days late. The RSI levels off and hovers between 45 and 65, suggesting that traders should exit shorts and stand aside.

Section Two Summary

It is true that stochastics, like the RSI, are effective tools for timing market changes, but they usually need some other system to tell them when a genuine turn is occurring. In other words, if the RSI is susceptible to false alarms, moving averages, with the smoothing effect of a larger sample size, do a good job of helping traders stay on track with longer time-frame trends. The Market Profile® can be useful in helping to override both the short-term (RSI) and longer-term (MA1 and MA2) overreactions inherent in the separate methods. The Market Profile®'s ability to zoom-in on the very thinking of the market and its participants is very likely what provides the crucial shift in perspective.

Closing Remarks

The Market Profile® is undeniably a high-level trading approach and clearly a challenge to master. At first glance, one might even call its detailed distributions overwhelming. Perhaps this is why many traders pass it by when they first encounter it. Perhaps this is also the reason that the majority of individuals and companies presently using trading logic—independent futures traders, brokers, money managers, money-center banks, and other financial institutions—are also traders who view futures trading as a business, not a hobby.

This book profiles some of the most successful trading systems in history. What we have tried to accomplish in this short chapter is to introduce you to the real forces behind the market: in a sense, the logic of the market. We have demonstrated that, while even the most basic trading system can make money some of the time, the results can be dramatically enhanced through an understanding of the market. Any trader equipped with a sound understanding of trading logic can extract results from any market—whether he or she uses market logic in tandem with a mechanical system or chooses to go it alone.

■ MARKET PROFILE® GLOSSARY ■

Auction process—In the market's attempt to facilitate trade with both the buyer and the seller, the market rotates price down to find buyers and rotates price up to find sellers. For example, when a market finds buyers, buying pressure naturally forces price up. Eventually, price moves high enough to attract sellers. New-found selling pressure in turn rotates price downward, eventually to a level that attracts buyers once again—and the auction cycle continues.

Balance region—A relatively well-defined trading range characterized by overlapping value. The market is in balance.

Bracket—Brackets are trading ranges established by the interaction of different time frame participants in the marketplace. To identify potential brackets, look for recurring value area tops and bottoms at the extremes of trading ranges. Once a potential bracket is isolated, it is critical to evaluate closely the type of activity occurring around those regions marking bracket highs and lows. Such regions are generally characterized by responsive activity from the opposing timeframe participant.

Buying composite day—A day characterized by an open in the lower 25 percent of the range. In other words, the market spent the majority of the day attempting to auction higher.

Double distribution trend day—A trend day so strong that two distributions form that are separated by single period TPO prints.

Initial balance—Activity identified with the initial floor auction process. The initial balance designates the market's attempt to establish a range that will allow two-sided trade to take place. In most markets, the initial balance consists of the first two half-hour time periods.

Initiating activity—Initiating activity is the strongest form of activity present in a market. As the title suggests, when activity is initiating, a participant has actively assumed control and is moving price under his own initiative. Any activity occurring within the previous day's value area is considered initiating activity for both the other time frame buyer and seller. Initiating buying activity is defined as any buying activity occurring within or above the previous day's value area. Initiating selling is any selling activity within or below the previous day's value area.

249

Non-trend day—A day offering no discernible information. Characterized by a "fat" distribution, a very narrow range and no range extension.

Normal day—A day where the initial balance dominates the range and is not upset throughout the day. There is no range extension.

Normal variation of a normal day—A day where range extension occurs beyond one extreme of the initial balance, and indicates that either the other time frame buyer or seller (whichever is applicable) is present and moving price.

Neutral day—A day characterized by range extension on both sides of the initial balance, indicating that both the other time frame buyer and seller are active. Indicates a market in balance.

Opening range—Important reference point for day time frame trades. Often the conviction present at the market open will set the range development for the entire day.

One-time-frame market—High conviction. A market characterized by the dominance of one time frame, either the other time frame buyer or seller. Price movement is usually one-directional, with little or no rotation. Trend days are one-time frame markets.

Other time frame participant— Longer time frame. All other time frames except for the day time frame.

Price trend—Price movement occurring in only one half-hour time period.

Range extension—Activity extending beyond the initial balance. Range extension occurs when the other time frame buyer or seller enters the market and moves price beyond the range established during the initial balance period.

Responsive activity—Activity characterizing a participant who is responding to an advantageous price (relative to value). Responsive buying is any buy-ing occurring below the previous day's value area. Responsive sell-ing is any selling activity occurring above the previous day's value area.

Selling composite day—A day characterized by an open in the upper 25 percent of the range. In other words, the market spent the majority of the day attempting to auction lower.

Spike—A late-in-the-day price or value trend away from the day's established value area.

Tail—A price range consisting of single TPO prints on a Market Profile® extreme. Tails are created when, in the day time frame, price is perceived to be sufficiently far enough away from value that an aggressive buyer or seller enters the market and quickly moves price.

Time frame—Trading horizon. Day time frame, two- to three-day time frame, one week, etc.

TPO (Time Price Opportunity)—TPOs are the basic unit used to measure market activity, and represent trade occurring during one half-hour segment.

Trade Facilitation—The purpose of the market. The involvement of all time frames in the daily auction process.

Trend Day—A day characterized by a small initial balance and range extension to one side occurring in multiple half-hour time periods. The resulting formation is a long narrow distribution.

Two-Time-frame Market—A market in which both the long term buyer and seller are present and active. Trade is being facilitated on both sides of the market, as is evidenced by the healthy rotation of price up and down.

Value Area—Where 70 percent of the day's business (volume) was conducted. The market identifies a fair value area for the day time frame only.

Value Area Trend—Price movement occurring in three or more time periods.

Value Trend—Price movement occurring in two time periods.

Volume—The truest and best indication of how well a market is facilitating trade.

Endnotes

[1] Steidlmayer and Koy, *Markets and Market Logic*, The Porcupine Press, 1986.

[2] Jones, D. L., "Estimating The Market Profile® Value Area For Intraday Trading," *Technical Analysis of Stocks and Commodities*, 1987.

MARKET
PERSONALITY PROFILE

BILL M. WILLIAMS, Ph.D., C.T.A

■

■

BILL M. WILLIAMS, Ph.D., C.T.A.

Dr. Williams has actively traded for thirty years. Trained both as an Engineer and a Psychologist, he is a registered Commodity Trading Advisor and does consulting with individual and corporate traders. He is a member of the original World Cup Championship Trading Team. During 1989–90 he held commodity trading workshops in ten different countries on five continents. He has appeared on national television numerous times and has been featured in magazines and newspapers across the country.

Dr. Williams conducts "Private Tutorials," during which he brings individual traders into his trading office and works on their trading techniques and psychological implementation for more profitable trading.

He is the first advisor ever to transmit his recommendations directly via satellite pager covering North America, Alaska, Hawaii, England and soon Europe. His instant recommendations will soon be transmitted via satellite to the Pacific Rim countries.

He is the discoverer/developer of the "Fractal" of the Elliott Wave. This "Fractal" has attracted international attention, and traders are coming from all over the world to study with Dr. Williams. He has received front-page recognition in such newspapers as the *Atlanta Journal-Constitution,* as well as other syndicated papers throughout the country.

Dr. Williams may be reached at his office (912) 263-7482 or by writing to him at P.O. Box 838, Quitman, GA, 31643. Fax number (912) 263-4681.

■

■ CHAPTER FIFTEEN ■

I HAVE BEEN TRADING stocks and commodities for over 25 years. The first several years I spent reading, researching and exploring possibilities, and trading anyone's opinion that I could find. This technique, as you might guess, proved fatal to potential profits. Then I learned about automatic systems. Clumsy in those early days, they nevertheless proved to be an alternative to thinking about the markets and trying to understand them. Because of my background and inclinations, I became a dyed-in-the-wool systems person, which I remained until I met Peter Steidlmayer, whose Market Logic/Market Profile® ideas permanently changed the way I perceived the market.

Steidlmayer extracted an enormous amount of information by placing price in a structure and monitoring it over time. From this data, he began to see a logic to the way the market moved. The result was his now well-known Market Profile®. His technique answers such questions as these: Is the market facilitating trade? Who is buying? Who is selling? Who is initiating and who is responding? and probably the most important: What is likely to happen next?

Many traders who begin using market logic concepts experience difficulty, however, because in Steidlmayer's terms, they begin to see both sides of the market for the first time. Consequently, they experience a "paralysis of analysis." In other words, after analyzing a market, they cannot pull the trigger and put on a trade, because they see simultaneously the reasons for both buying and selling. Prior to studying market logic techniques, they would simply take a position and either win or lose.

For the benefit of those traders who would like to use market logic as a trading tool but who have experienced difficulties with it, I will present in this chapter some helpful procedures for establishing a profile of the market's personality—procedures that carry Steidlmayer's work a bit further, and make it more usable.

Personality Profile

In human behavior, knowledge of an individual's personality allows one to predict behavior in certain situations. The same is true with the market. Like people, however, the market has several components to its personality. For example, it sustains varying relationships between the opening price and the closing price of a particular segment of trading. Moreover, it experiences fluctuating degrees of power, and its price values constantly change, which can lead to numerous combinations of factors. The resulting complexity can lead to misunderstandings and misinterpretations unless the observer has a clear, systematic process for observing the separate traits and interpreting them individually and in conjunction with other characteristics. Nevertheless, if a person knows the market's personality, he or she can predict the market's behavior in varying situations and timeframes. With the information contained in this chapter, you will be able to read the various market personalities on any bar chart of any time period, keeping in mind, however, the differences in the interpretation of the different time spans.

To establish a profile of the market's personality, I begin by dividing each bar in the chart into thirds, regardless of the time period represented by the bar: five minutes, 30 minutes, one hour, one day, or longer. Each bar now has a top third, represented numerically by a 1, a middle third, represented by a 2, and a bottom third, represented by a 3.

I now look at the opening price of each bar and assign it a value—1, 2, or 3—depending on its location on the bar. If the opening is in the upper third of the price range, I assign it a value of 1. In the middle range, I assign it a 2, and so on. I then do the same with the closing price: in the top of the range, a 1, in the middle, a 2; in the bottom, a 3.

Thus, a bar with the number 13 means that particular bar opened on or near its high (top third) and closed on or near its low (bottom third). On the chart, it looks like this:

A number 12 would indicate that a bar opened on or near its high and closed at or near the middle of the bar. On the chart, it looks like this:

This system provides only nine possible combinations of opening-closing values: 11, 12, 13, 21, 22, 23, 31, 32, and 33. Displayed as a group, they look like this:

These nine identifying numbers can be helpful in interpreting a market, when we understand the significance of the various combinations. For example, most changes in short term trends are signaled by an 11 or a 33 bar appearing one to five bars in advance of the change. On the other hand, a 22 bar most often predicts a continuation of the present short-term trend. Our research indicates that this holds true about 80 per cent of the time. Identifying numbers in which the second number is one digit smaller than the first (32, or 21) indicate a "climber," and the three identifying numbers in which the second number is one digit greater than the first (12, or 23) indicate a "drifter." Trend periods are represented by a 13 or a 31 and are *not* good continuation patterns, unless accompanied by increased volume.

This much knowledge about market personality already provides us with greater insight into market behavior than we had previously. Before risking money, however, we need to add three more market dimensions to the Market Personality Profile®: volume, value area change, and price change.

Volume

An important dimension of each bar, once its identifying number has been determined, is how much power it has. Power here is represented by volume. However, because no real-time intraday volume figures are currently available, we use the next best thing: tic volume. We note the number of tics on each consecutive bar. If the tic volume of one bar is greater than that of the bar immediately preceding it, we put a + after its descriptive number. Therefore, a 13 with greater tic volume than the preceding bar is represented by 13 +. A bar with approximately the same volume becomes 13 0, while one with less volume becomes 13 -.

Now, along with the open–close price relationship of a particular segment of the market, we can also identify the strength or power that the market has given to each bar within that segment. The next step is to determine the value area relationships among the bars within the market segment we are studying.

Change in Value Area

To determine a change in the estimated value area of a single bar in a particular market segment, we simply compare the range price of that bar with the range price of the preceding bar. If the overall range is higher than the preceding price, we put a + before the identifying number of that bar. If the price is unchanged, we put a zero, and if it is lower, we put a -. Therefore, the complete designation for a bar might be -13+, which would indicate that this bar's *estimated value area* is lower than the one preceding it, that it started the period on or near the top, and ended on or near the bottom, with more volume than the preceding period. The most likely direction of price movement, using this example, would be down. If the identification were + 13-, it would mean that the value area is higher than the bar preceding it, that the opening price was near the high and the close was near the low, with less volume than in the preceding bar. This would also predict the next move to be down, because the market is not facilitating trade at this higher level. An identification of - 13 -, indicating a lower value level with lower volume, would predict the next movement to be up.

At this point, we are well on our way toward being able to read a market's personality and to use that understanding to predict profitably the behavior of the market. As with people, however, the market's behavior at times may be ambiguous, leaving us in a position of being less than confident about making predictions. For those times, and at times when we want to confirm other personality profile indicators, another simple calculation can help.

Tic Mileage

After determining the value area, the open–close relationships, and the volume, one other tool is available that can help clarify ambiguous situations that remain. This last clarifying component is a handy little device I call tic mileage. As I use it, tic mileage tells me how many tics were required to move the price of a commodity X points. For example, if the price of bonds goes up 14 points in two bars, generating a tic volume of 213 in 30 minutes, and the next period the price goes down six points while generating a tic volume of 232, the market is telling me that it is easier—because it requires fewer tics—for the price to go up than down. With such a conclusion, a trader might look for a good location to establish a long position. Other factors always come into play, however. For example, if the increase in price was due to short covering, that would negate the buy signal. Nevertheless, tic mileage is an excellent market indicator to use in conjunction with the market personality profile.

As I promised at the beginning of this chapter, you should now be able to establish a complete personality profile for any market, using a bar chart and the simple procedures I have shown. Moreover, you can make some interpretations and predictions using the personality profile you have generated. In the next two sections, I will use only *two* aspects of the personality profile, volume and value area, to illustrate how the market behaves in rather predictable ways. Once you have an understanding of these market behavior patterns, you will be able to develop valid interpretations and predictions of your own that will improve your trading performance.

Remember, however, that charts of differing periods (i.e., 30-minute charts versus weekly charts) will be interpreted differently.

Natural Cycles of Market Movement

The following example will use a one-day bar chart and the volume/value area components of the personality profile to illustrate how a completely free market would operate. (A free market is defined as a market where no outside information, such as reports, rumors, government announcements, and the like, affects price behavior.) The natural cycle that results would look like this:

Figure 15-4

```
              (+  -)     (0 0)    (0 +)
                G          H        I
              (+  0)                      (- 0)
                F                           J
          (+ +)                          (- +)
            E                              K
       (+ 0)                                   (- 0)
         D                                       L
     (- -)    (0 0)    (0 +)        (- -)    (0 0)    (0 +)
      A         B        C           M         N        O
```

In a free market, we would usually see a bottom at point A(- -), where the value area is lower than the preceding bar and so is the volume. The situation is not facilitating trade at this lower level, so we would predict a higher movement, looking for facilitation. Point B (0 0) gives us little or no information, except in comparison with recent market behavior. The market has been going down, but both the movement and power are drying up, indicating a probable change in the direction unless outside information starts affecting the market. At point C (0 +), the value is overlapping and the volume is increasing, which generally means the beginning of a move. The price at Point D (+ 0) has moved up, but there is little or no increase in volume, so not much power is available at this point.

At point E (+ +), the value area has risen with rising volume, which gives direction and power. This is the time for *initiating trading*, getting on board promptly, and probably buying on the close for the next day's trade location. The value area at Point F (+ 0) is still increasing, but with the same volume (I usually consider a tic volume within 10 percent of the previous bar's volume as unchanged). The value area at G (+ -) is still rising, but with less power (volume), which normally would alert us to trade as a *responsive seller*. As at point B, point H (0 0) gives us little or no information except in comparison with recent market behavior. The market has been going up, but both the movement and power are drying up, indicating a probable change in direction unless outside information starts affecting the market. At point I (0 +), the volume is beginning to build again, but the buyers are not in control; otherwise, the value area would also move up. When the buyers are losing in their attempt at an up auction, we need to watch the sellers' performance closely.

The value area gives way at point J (- 0), but the movement hasn't yet attracted a significant number of sellers. At Point K (- +), however, the value area begins to move down with power. At this point, a new seller would be chasing the markets and should review trading to determine why this opportunity was not noticed sooner. The value area at point L (- 0) is still moving down because of the recent increase in selling pressure. It is not attracting new sellers, however, and gives us early warning to monitor the market more closely. The market at point M (- -) is telling us that the selling pressure is dying and that we should *watch closely with the idea of becoming responsive buyers*. At point N (0 0), the market is again in neutral, with no movement and no apparent change in buyers and sellers, but it is telling us to be alert for signs of either continuation or reversal. From here, the cycle begins to repeat itself, moving again through an increasing value area with fluctuating volume and back through a period of decreasing value area with similarly fluctuating volume.

Trading Signals

Using this idealized cycle of market movement, we can see that there are certain points where the various value area/volume combinations might aid in establishing winning trades. In particular, there are four strong signals:

(+ +) = An initiating buy signal (buy the close today for tomorrow's trading.)

(- +) = An initiating sell signal (sell the close today for tomorrow's trading.)

(+ -) = A responsive sell signal (sell the higher opening tomorrow.)

(- -) = A responsive buy signal (buy the lower opening tomorrow.)

In addition to these four indicators, other combinations can provide helpful information

(+ 0), (- 0), (0 +) These three combinations of value area and volume normally indicate a *continuation pattern* and, therefore, are probably not good points at which to initiate a trade. Rather than to trade here, it's better to wait for one of the four signals above.

(0 -) This is not the best signal to trade, but should alert you to look for a change in the recent trend.

(0 0) This signals you to do nothing. It is the most ambiguous signal, since it indicates no real change in either movement or volume.

Conclusion

In this chapter, I have introduced some new techniques for understanding market personality drawn from Steidlmayer's ideas about market logic and the market profile. I have used these techniques with considerable success in my trading and in my hotline recommendations. The personality profile works particularly well for me because it has allowed me to respond to the reality of the market at the moment rather than responding to rigid rules about the market: rules which work sometimes and sometimes don't, and provide no real-time information about the market. The personality profile has worked well in both choppy and trending markets, giving specific signals about when to trade and when to do nothing. As presented in this chapter, the market personality profile provides a method for reading the market and understanding its personality during continuing up and down cycles which can benefit the trader who has wanted a better grasp of market behavior.

If you would like to be kept abreast of our on-going research in the area of market logic concepts and their application to trading, you may request to be put on our research mailing list. We already have an informal group who are sharing their experience and knowledge about trading the market more profitably. Through this sharing we all hope to become better and more business-like traders.

■ CHAPTER SIXTEEN* ■

HOW TO FIND TRADES WITH 10/1 ODDS

LARRY R. WILLIAMS

■

*From Larry Williams, *How I Made One Million Dollars. . .Last Year. . .Trading Commodities* (Brightwaters, NY: Windsor Books, 1979) 41-62, by permission of the author. Copryright 1979 by Larry R. Williams

■

LARRY R. WILLIAMS

Larry R. Williams is perhaps the most enduring commodity personality of the 60s, 70s and 80s. From his early beginning successfully trading stocks in the 60s to his all time best selling book *How I Made One Million Dollars. . .Last Year. . .Trading Commodities* in the 70s to his winning the World Cup Championship of Futures Trading by turning $10,000 into $1,200,000 in 1987, Larry Williams has proven he is an experienced professional.

Mr. Williams has been a publisher, a registered investment advisor and perhaps the most widely read author of commodity works, including his newest release, *The Definitive Guide to Futures Trading*.

In recent years he has specialized in short term trading. Along with Jake Bernstein, he pioneered in the concept of teaching people to trade at real time seminars.

Larry is a graduate of the University of Oregon, class of 1964, with a degree in journalism.

■

▪ CHAPTER SIXTEEN ▪

ANY SILLY FOOL can buy and sell commodities whenever he chooses. It is the brilliant trader's task to wait until odds are 10 to 1 in his favor before making a commitment to the market. By doing this the astute trader avoids an immense number of headaches and even greater frustrations.

Whenever I think about the thousands of trades made each day, as well as the public's fervor for day trading and short term (4-5 day) trades, I'm reminded of the words from one of the oldest pros on Wall Street. This gentleman (you'd recognize his name in an instant) told me that in his forty years of market experience he knew only one commodity winner. Only one!

According to this man, the reason that person was a winner was that he had enough sense to put most of his profits in an irrevocable trust. Thus, when he started to lose, he still had a fixed income from the trusts. Had the trust not been in effect, this pro would have lost all that money as well!

Let this be a lesson to you. Don't be eager to rush into any trades. After all, "fools rush in where wise men fear to trade." I hope, in this chapter, I can show you how to select the very best possible trades. It's up to you to maintain the discipline required for working the lead-pipe-cinch deals. Discipline, I cannot give you.

Spotting the Best Trades

Let me begin by telling you of my system for isolating trades with odds 10 to 1 in my favor. Those are million dollar odds. Unfortunately, I still haven't developed a method for calling all the big moves all the time. What I have done is develop a set of criteria that, when they coincide, will tell you the odds are heavily in favor of either an up or down move.

This method seldom speaks, but when it does, you have as close to a sure thing as you'll ever get. As you will see, this method will not call all the swings, but that's not its purpose. Its function is to segregate the super trades from trades that are questionable.

Trading in this manner is much easier because it allows you to take a longer-term view of the market. I have found there is no need to monitor the market on a trade-by-trade basis, or, at times, even a daily basis. The signals are so strong that you don't need to concern yourself with a microscopic view.

I use two major tools for selecting "bankable trades." They are: 1) premium relationships, and 2) open interest. When these two click, the odds are 75 percent in your favor. To further substantiate the 75 percent probability, I also check contrary opinion, the market's reaction to news, trend direction, and a few chart formations.

The First Indication of a Million Dollar Trade

I cannot stress the significance of premium too strongly. The existence or lack of premium will be one of your first keys to a sure thing trade. Premiums (the difference between the nearby price of a commodity and the distant contracts,) give signals in two ways.

The usual bull market signal is given when the nearby contracts sell for a higher price than the distants. Such a spread, in favor of the nearbys, is a bullish premium indicating the commercials want the product now and are willing to bid the market to a premium. (See Figure 16-1.)

Invariably, sustainable bull markets start with prices going to a premium. If you are looking to go long a commodity, this will be your first check point. Is there a bullish premium? If not, the odds of a sharp advance are not good.

Please notice in the charts, the spread between November and January orange juice and the July-October cotton spread.

As you can see, the orange juice spread (Figure 16-2) went from a premium to a discount. That is, the nearbys sold for less than the distants starting in February 1973. About this same time, many analysts forecast a bull market for orange juice, but, as you can see, it could not sustain any up trend. While commodities in general had the largest bull market in history, Orange Juice stayed flat to down.

This was a superb example of the lack of a premium signal telling the traders it's too early to start thinking about higher juice prices.

How about cotton? (Figure 16-1) This is an entirely different matter. Notice how prices went to a premium in November 1972 while prices were still low. In fact, most services thought this was a major bear market.

We knew better. If cotton was in a bear market, why would the commercials be willing to pay a premium price for the nearby products? Why not wait until prices went lower in the future? Shortly after this premium developed, cotton staged the largest bull market it has ever known. Had you bought one contract of December 1973 cotton the day the premium

Figure 16-1

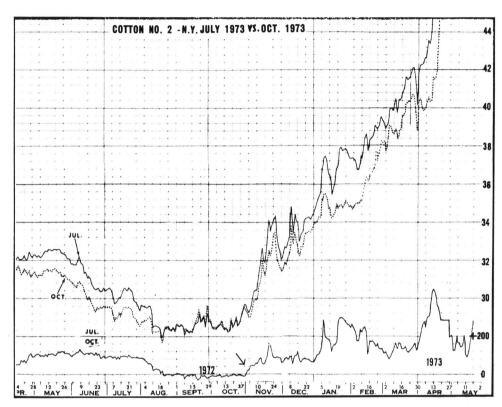

developed (for $1,000) your profit would have soared to $27,500 in less than 12 months!

Still doubt the significance of the premium spread? Then study the cocoa spread chart (Figure 16-3,) paying close attention to the March 1973 time period. This is when a premium developed in the cocoa market. Sharp shooters will scoff at this method, saying it did not call the absolute low in cocoa. And they're right. It didn't. But it did give a strong signal in March, telling us that a substantial and sustainable bull move was under way, and that's what we are looking for.

I'll let someone else call the tops and bottoms. What I want is to trade in sure deals. To my knowledge there is absolutely nothing that calls all the tops and bottoms.

In the cocoa deal, prices began moving up three weeks after the premium developed, giving the trader ample time to prepare for the move. Incidentally, in the case of March 1973 cocoa, had a trader purchased it

Figure 16-2

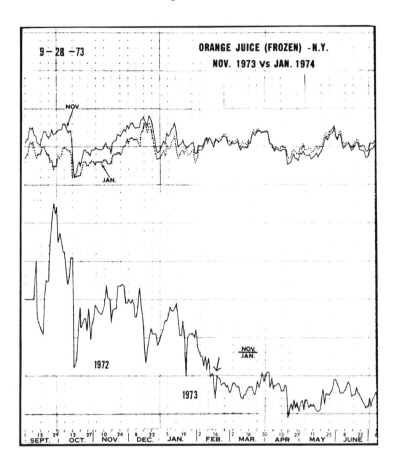

when the premium developed in March 1973 (at $ .37,) he could have sold it for $ .71—a profit of $10,200—a few months later!

Imagine, the person who bought ten contracts (for $10,000) would have made over $100,000 in less than eight months.

Before you mortgage your home and rush out to start buying the premium markets, let me give a word of caution. You still need to know more about the markets to avoid getting tripped up.

Premiums point the way, but they are not an absolute tool; nor are they a timing tool. Finally, I ask you to remember that not all bull markets will exhibit premiums. We have other tools with which to isolate the strong, non-premium bull markets. The 1971 bearish cocoa market was also called quite well by the spread, as you can see.

Figure 16-3

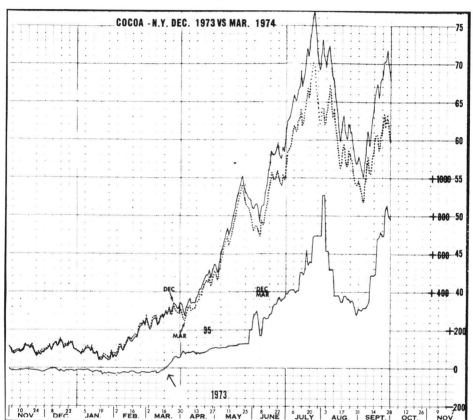

COCOA - N.Y. DEC. 1973 VS MAR. 1974

Your Second Lesson on Premiums

There are many ways to analyze premiums. Rather than confuse you with the various methods I use (I follow the spread in several different fashions), I think it will be best to show you the second most valuable way of using premium spreads.

As the spread between the nearby month and the distant goes to a premium, you have your first indication of a bull market. Now, as this spread increases or decreases we are given additional market information. Essentially, as a premium spread narrows, the market will undergo selling pressures. A rally should start after it begins to widen.

Perhaps this is an overstatement. Let's see.

Figure 16-4

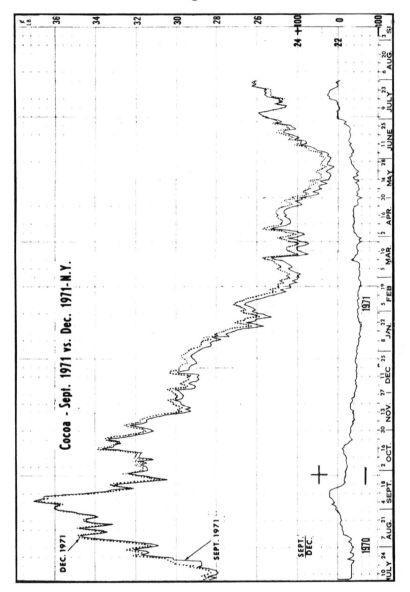

In September 1971, the wheat market went into a tailspin (Figure 16-5). However, the bullish premium was maintained. Then, at the end of September and early October, the spread between May and July started to gain, telling us that the nearby was under commercial buying and a rally should develop. Look at what happened. A $ .15 rally began which, in those days, was a pretty nice swing!

Figure 16-5

The 1973 cotton market also gives us a good indication of the powerful premium signal. Notice the sell-off that started at the end of March. Prices broke sharply, then rallied back to the old highs. What would happen? Was it all over?

Anyone looking at the spread would have seen a sudden increase in the premium of July over October telling us it was still a tight bull market and higher prices were in order. Away went cotton.

Please don't get the impression I'm a perpetual bull just because I've discussed little else but bull signals to this point. Most commodity traders were wiped out in August of 1973 as the red hot bull market went sour. Traders caught long in that market suffered severe financial and emotional set backs.

This would not have happened had they been following market premiums. Soybeans are a good example. Notice how the bean spread began narrowing as prices were in their final upthrust stages, telling us weakness was due. . . that commercials no longer wanted the nearby product.

Now turn your attention to the cattle market (Figure 16-6). The same thing occurred. As these important tops were made the premiums fell apart, giving ample warning of weakness ahead. That's when it was time to fasten seatbelts. I have shown additional examples for your own study, which is what it takes to understand the premium play.

The Second Indication of a Million Dollar Trade

It is important to keep in mind that open interest is an accurate reflection of commercial doings. After all, they are the single largest factor in the market. Equally important is the fact the commercials tend to be the largest short sellers because they are hedging their risks. When commercials are not selling short, or hedging, it is because they believe prices are going higher—much higher.

What we look for here is an indication of a lack of short selling among the market's largest professionals. When such a condition develops, especially in a premium market, you have a bankable trade with odds 10 to 1 in your favor.

By the same token, a market without a premium that suddenly sees a large increase in professional short selling gives you 10 to 1 odds for selling short.

It is my belief that daily open interest statistics will correctly tell you if the commercials are selling or covering short positions. The significance of open interest cannot be overestimated. Time after time I have made substantial money, and by that I mean $30,000 to $100,000 per day, thanks to closely following the open interest picture.

Open interest is one of the most widely followed tools. Thankfully, however, it is the most incorrectly interpreted tool. It is the backbone to my success in the commodity market.

Before showing the actual buy and sell signals from open interest, I'd like to review open interest with you. As you know, it is the total commitment of longs and shorts in the market. Since there is a long for every short, the open interest figure is the combination of longs and shorts, divided by two. Only one thing can make open interest go up, and that's an increase in short selling and an increase in buying. Only one thing can make open interest decline. That's a decrease in buying and a decrease in short selling.

Figure 16-6

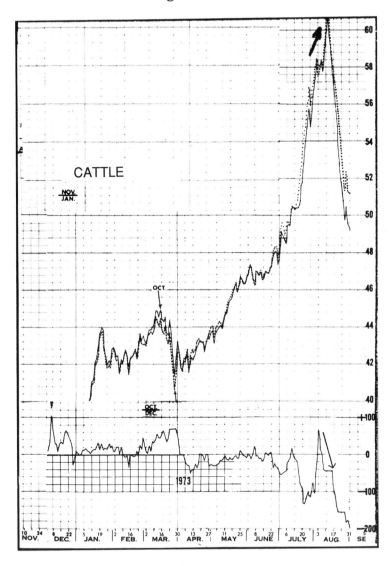

CATTLE

Figure 16-7

Figure 16-8

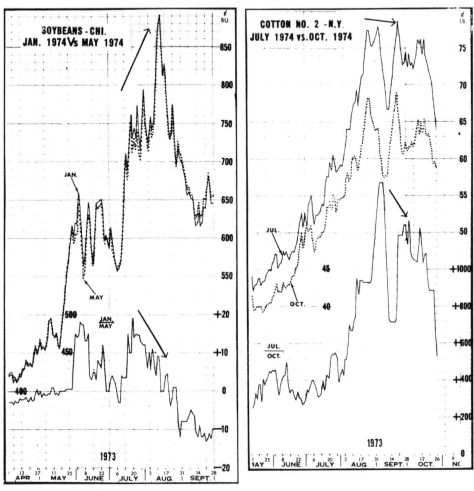

Figure 16-9

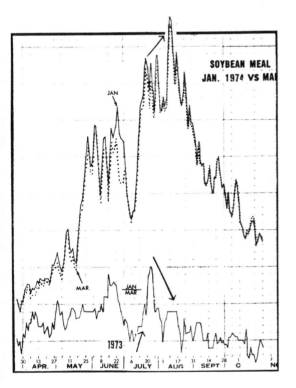

SOYBEAN MEAL
JAN. 1974 VS MAR

JAN

MAR.

JAN
MAR

1973

30 | 13 27 | 11 25 | 8 22 | 6 20 | 1 17 31 | 14 28 | 2
APR. | MAY | JUNE | JULY | AUG | SEPT | O | NC

Figure 16-10

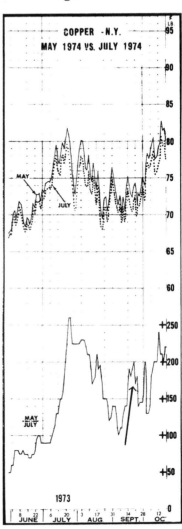

COPPER -N.Y.
MAY 1974 VS. JULY 1974

LB.
95

90

85

80

75

70

65

60

MAY

JULY

+250

+200

+150

+100

+50

MAY
JULY

1973

0

8 22 | 6 20 | 3 17 31 | 14 28 | 12
JUNE | JULY | AUG | SEPT. | OC

Figure 16-11

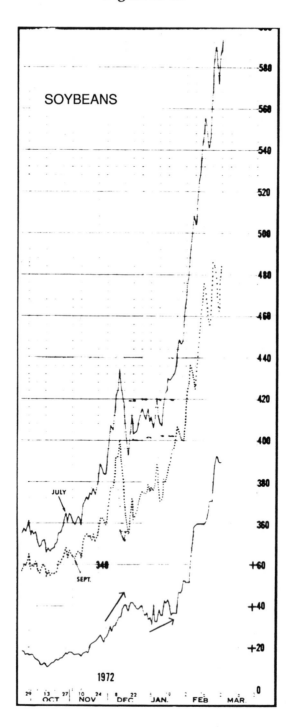

Figure 16-12

Since the commercials are the dominant force in the market, especially in short selling, an increase in open interest would most likely mean they are shorting the market.

A decrease in open interest would probably tell us the commercials are covering their short positions, expecting higher prices.

Those two observations have made hundreds of thousands of dollars for me. If there is one page in this book to which you must pay close attention, this is it.

Figure 16-13 shows the basic buy and sell indications given from the open interest figures. It is imperative that you understand the relationship of price versus the open interest. As you can see in Figure 16-13 the bullish pattern shows prices in a trading range while open interest is decreasing. Hence, the commercials have covered their shorts.

Figure 16-13

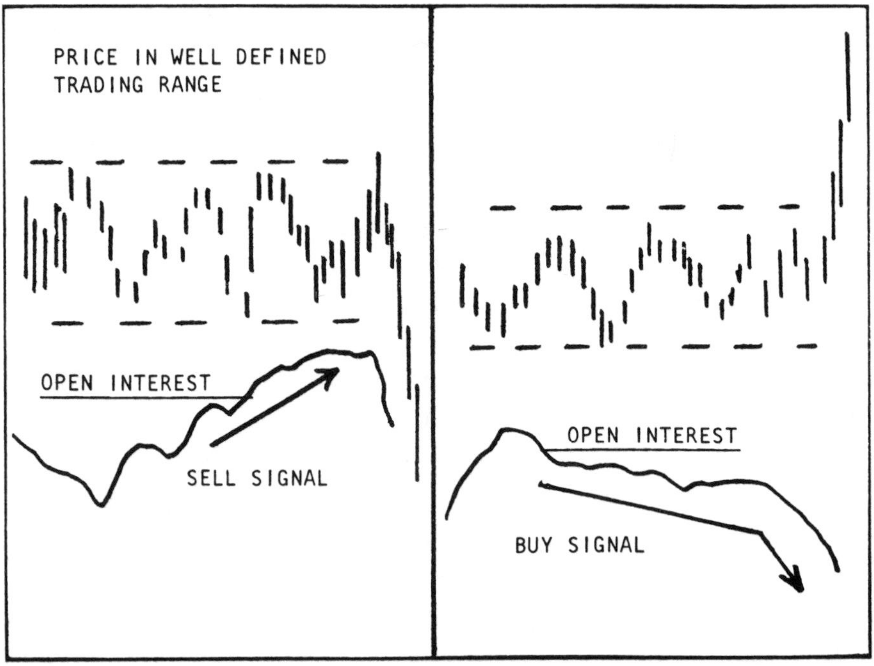

The bearish pattern also sees prices in a trading range while open interest increases. Ideally, for short selling, the trading range will be part of a large down move or will occur at a time when the nearby contracts are strong and the more distant months weak. This sets up a "sure" trade.

If you were to close the book at this point and begin using open interest you could probably smoke out some pretty fair trades. However, you might also fall into some extraordinarily bad deals. I have not yet fully emphasized the importance of the trading range.

A simple increase or decrease in open interest—without prices being in a trading range—is of little significance. You must compare the open interest picture with the price action. In a moment, I'll give you some actual examples.

The few people to whom I have shown the open interest signals have been amazed at its accuracy in selecting long term trades. However, they always try to apply open interest to all commodities, all the time. It just doesn't work that way. After all, we are trying to select the cream of the crop trades where there is little, if any risk. We are not attempting to call every market wiggle and waggle. This means we must adhere to our game plan and that plan calls for finding optimum trades.

There is one other open interest pattern for which you should be alert. This occurs amidst a major bull or bear market. In a major bull market, i.e., strong uptrend, prices will suddenly react against the maintrend; falling sharply. If, at this time, open interest diminishes, a buy point is being set up.

Figure 16-14

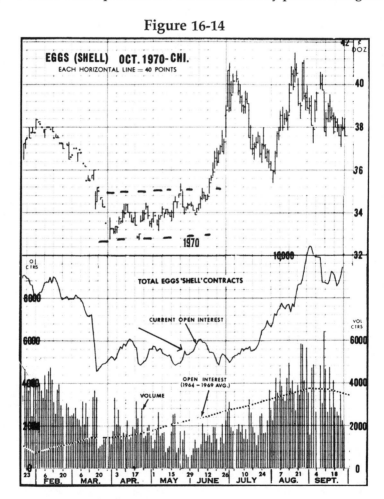

In a strong bear market, a rally against the trend (accompanied by an increase—especially a large increase in open interest) is very bearish, setting up a shorting point.

Incidentally, when I talk about increase in open interest, I should point out that a 25 percent increase or decrease is enough to greatly excite me. Anything less than 25 percent may be due to the market's idiosyncrasies rather than commercial action.

If you'll take the time to study any chart service that plots open interest, you'll quickly see major buy and sell indications. As an example, in April and May of 1970, open interest declined while the price of eggs stayed in a tight trading range, thereby foretelling higher prices. As you can see in Figure 16-14 this is exactly what did ensue.

A good selling indication for plywood was given in September 1970 (see Figure 16-15). For some six months prices oscillated in a large trading range. Chartists saw this as a base for a major advance. However, *you* would have known better because open interest just kept climbing. Finally, as we expected, the market broke down.

Figure 16-15

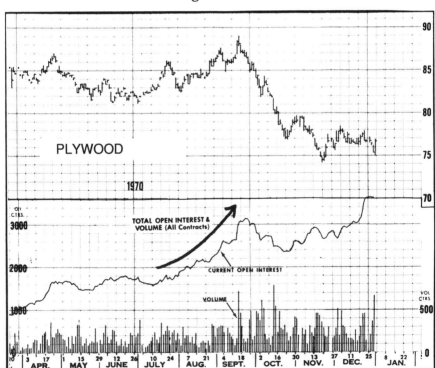

Look at silver in June and July of 1970. Here is a perfect example of the open interest buy indication. For two months prices were in a trading range, yet, the open interest plummeted, giving us clear-cut evidence that a rally was coming. And come it did.

Figure 16-16

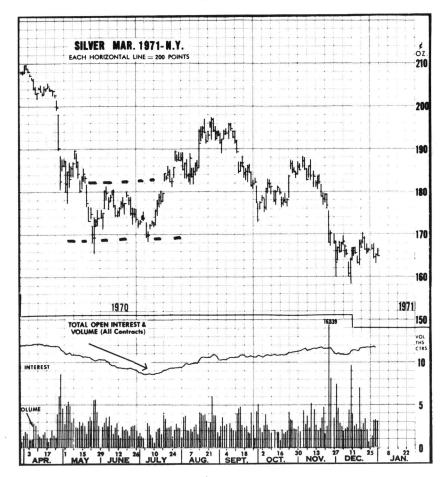

In July, August and September 1970, soybean oil was in a flat to slightly higher trading range. Some of the most astute bean oil analysts were forcasting lower prices and a crash in the market. That never happened. Instead, a sizeable rally began.

What triggered or started the rally? Our trusty open interest figures. See how the line broke sharply, telling us the commercials were covering their shorts as fast as they could. Obviously, they knew the true fundamental picture was about to become more bullish.

Copper (Figure 16-17) works nicely with the open interest data. In January of 1971, copper prices probed for a bottom in a trading range market. At that time, open interest had a drastic peel off, telling us higher prices were most likely in order. Indeed they were, because prices sailed from $ .44 to $ .59 in three months!

An excellent short selling indication was given in the cotton market in 1972 (Figure 16-18). During April and May, prices entered a trading range and open interest steadily increased, thereby warning of an imminent market collapse. And collapse it surely did!

Silver began a sensational bull market in 1972 (Figure 16-20). That's history; but, at the time, the silver bulls had just been flushed out of the market by an October slide. Search as you might, you could not find a silver bull on the street. However, a few of us were able to position this market on the long side. Why? Because prices had entered a large trading range (as defined on the chart) while open interest steadily declined.

The handwriting was on the charts for all to see. Commercials had covered their shorts and the market was ready to explode. And did it ever!

Why These Million Dollar Tools Work

It's pleasant to sip fine cognac late at night and discuss the market's ups, downs, do's and don'ts. My learned college professor friends say the market is entirely unpredictable. I must agree. Much of the market's action defies forecasting, and certainly price action, by itself, is not terribly predictive.

However, when we turn our attention away from price action to indications of the professional's doings, our system will usually work. Certainly, professionals occasionally get caught on the wrong side of the market. However, over any given length of time, the pros still come out winners. That's why the tools mentioned will make money for you. They deal with professional opinion, not price movements.

I'll continue to argue with college professors about just how random or non-random price action is, but let's keep in mind that it's my 45-year-old cognac we're drinking!

Additional Tools to "Clinch" Your Trades

Contrary Opinion

If, at the time my million dollar tools are giving buy indications, most advisory services are going against my indications, your chances for a good

Figure 16-17

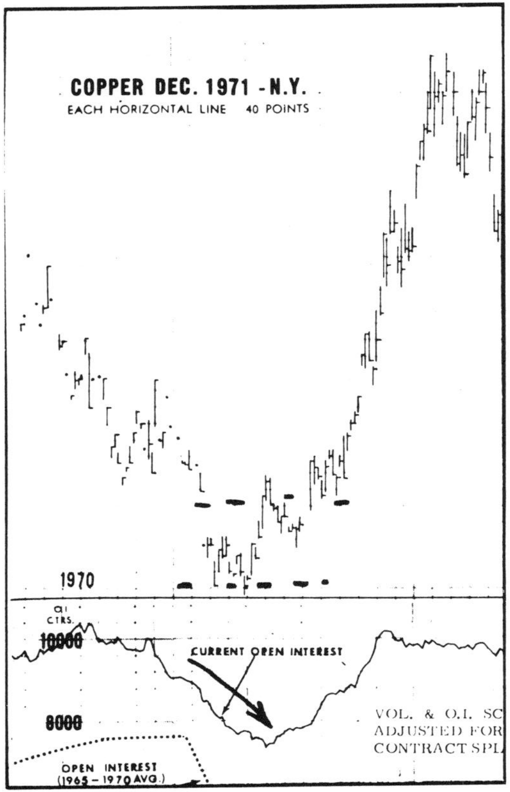

COPPER DEC. 1971 - N.Y.
EACH HORIZONTAL LINE   40 POINTS

CURRENT OPEN INTEREST

VOL. & O.I. SC
ADJUSTED FOR
CONTRACT SPL

1970

OI
CTRS.
10000

8000

OPEN INTEREST
(1965 - 1970 AVG.)

Figure 16-18

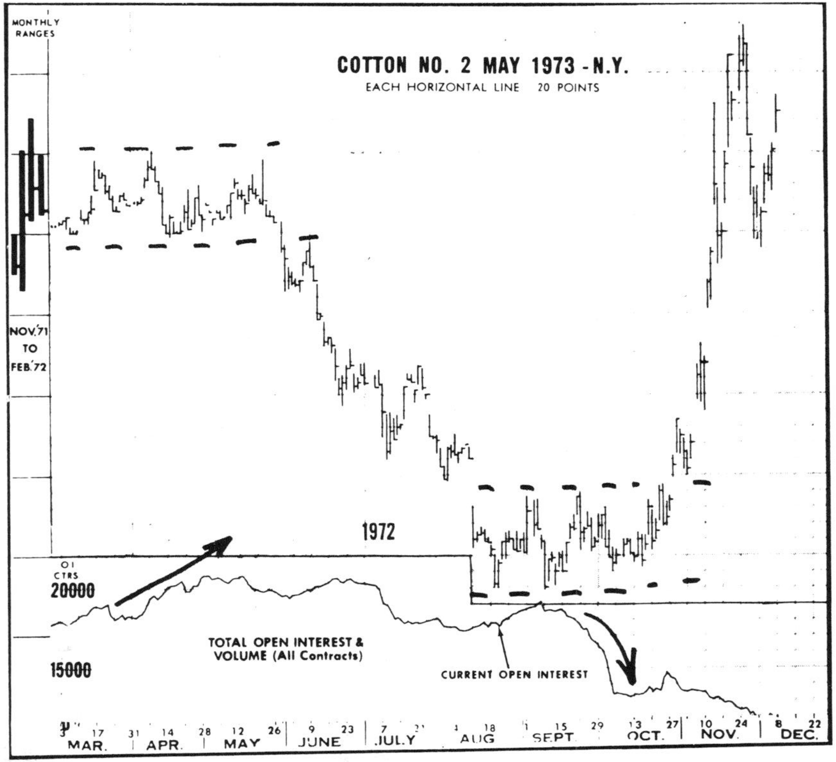

COTTON NO. 2 MAY 1973 - N.Y.
EACH HORIZONTAL LINE   20 POINTS

MONTHLY
RANGES

NOV'71
TO
FEB.'72

1972

CURRENT OPEN INTEREST

TOTAL OPEN INTEREST &
VOLUME (All Contracts)

OI
CTRS.
20000

15000

MAR. 17   31   APR. 14   28   MAY 12   26   JUNE 9   23   JULY 7   21   AUG 4   18   SEPT 1   15   29   OCT 13   27   NOV 10   24   DEC. 8   22

Figure 16-19

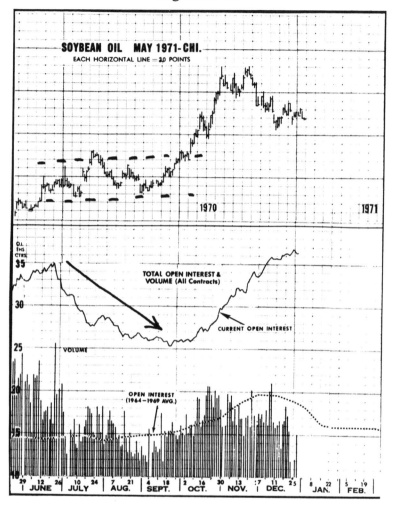

trade are further increased! I mean this sincerely. As with the stock market, when too many people believe something will happen, it never does.

You can objectively measure contrary opinion by subscribing to Market Vane (431 East Green Street, Pasadena, California, 91101, 1-818-441-3457), or by ordering *The Bullish Concensus* from Hadady Corporation (1111 S. Arroyo Parkway, Suite 410, Pasadena, California, 91109-0490, 818-441-3457), a weekly brokerage letter. Both sources will give you the percent of services that are bullish or bearish in the commodity field. Invariably, as the services become 100 percent bullish, trend following, the market sells off. Fifteen percent to 30 percent bullish readings usually evidence a sizeable up move.

Figure 16-20

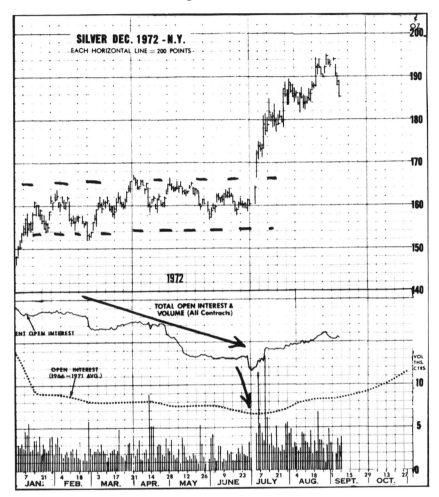

However, it is important that you use bullish readings that are under 30 percent only in markets that are in strong up trends. Sell signals (50 percent to 100 percent bullish readings) are good in bear markets, but only so-so in bull markets.

Newsaction

If, at the same time my million dollar tools are saying "buy," a very bearish piece of news is released that has little effect on the market, you can rest assured that the tools are correct and a large up move will begin.

The 1973 copper bull market was signaled in this fashion. Open interest saw a sharp decline and the premium picture was improving. It was then announced that a large quantity of copper was to be placed for sale on the market. This should have caused a limit down move—that's what was expected. Instead, prices sold off for two hours, then rallied, telling us this market was in very strong hands.

How Charts Forecast

When prices begin gapping on your charts (see Figure 16-21) this is an indication of intensified buying and selling. Gaps are usually found at the beginning of up moves. Gaps occurring after prices have been in a trading range usually indicate which way prices will break out of the trading range. Study the examples given here and you'll see what I mean.

Figure 16-21

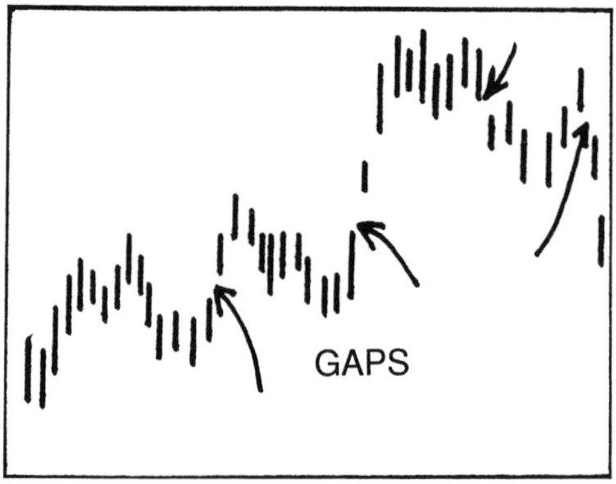

GAPS

Commitment of Large Traders

When you see a commodity in which the large traders are overwhelmingly short or long, you are assured that, at some time in the future, prices should move in their favor. An ideal bullish situation is where the large traders are long five contracts for every one they are short. For selling, they should be short five contracts for every one they are long.

As helpful as the large trader's report may be, it does have some drawbacks about which you should be informed. Much of the large trader activity reflects hedging or spreading, and is due to seasonal crop tendencies. It can be misleading. Nonetheless, it is nice to back up an opinion derived from other data. Perhaps the report's greatest drawback is that it is issued only for the grains and meats.

How to Identify Trend Direction

You've heard the old sayings "You can't fight City Hall," "Don't spit into the wind." Well, they mean the same thing. That's fine, but how are we to tell what the true underlying trend is?

I have no absolute answers. I've tried many systems, but I keep coming back to one very simple index: ten week moving average.

To construct it, you add the Friday close for the last ten weeks and divide by 10. Then, plot this on your chart. As long as the average is slanting upward, the underlying price trend is still up and we can buy without bucking the market.

Figure 16 -22

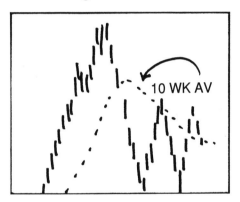

Should the ten week moving average line be trending down, I assume prices are headed lower. This means I sell short only if the 10 week moving average is down. I buy long only if it is up. It's a dandy tool to keep you out of bad trades and will help to further identify the 10 to 1 odds we've been striving for.

Identify the premium spreads and look for open interest increases or decreases during trading ranges. This is your main method for identifying where the next big bull or bear market will commence. Then, substantiate this by checking contrary opinion, news action, large trader reports, gaps, and the trend direction.

Once you find a deal, with an increasing premium and decreasing open interest during a trading range, you are ready to select your point of entry. The tools discussed above are not for timing your buy or sell. They are tools for selecting the commodities on which you should concentrate your energies. Don't expect these tools to do more than that or you'll be headed for big trouble.

Figure 16-23

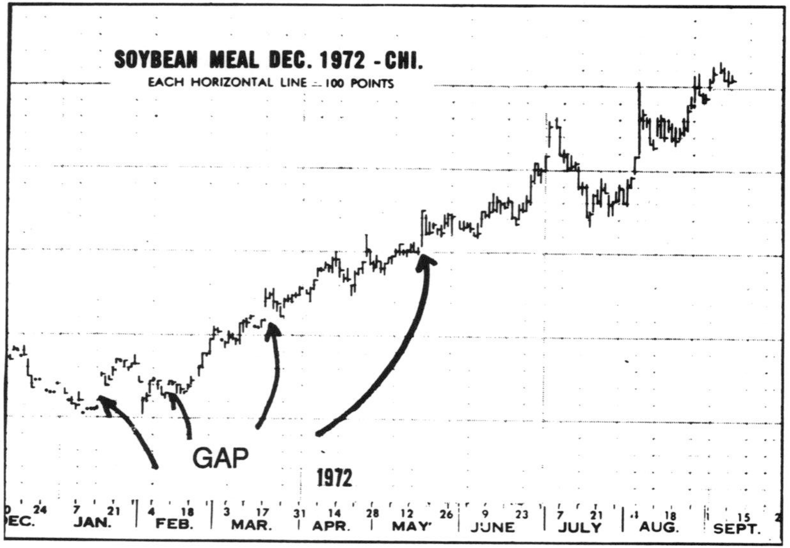

SOYBEAN MEAL DEC. 1972 - CHI.
EACH HORIZONTAL LINE = 100 POINTS

GAP

1972

DEC. 24 | 7 21 JAN. | 4 18 FEB. | 3 17 MAR. | 31 14 APR. | 28 12 MAY | 26 9 23 JUNE | 7 21 JULY | 4 18 AUG. | 1 15 SEPT. 2

Figure 16-24

SUGAR NO. 11 MAR. 1973 - N.Y.
EACH HORIZONTAL LINE = 10 POINTS

MAJOR
GAP

1972

TOTAL OPEN INTEREST &
OPEN INTEREST

8,715
6,502
8,422

31 14 APR. | 28 12 MAY | 26 9 23 JUNE | 7 21 JULY | 4 18 AUG. | 15 SEPT. 29

8.5
8.0
7.5
7.0
6.5
6.0
5.5
5.0
0

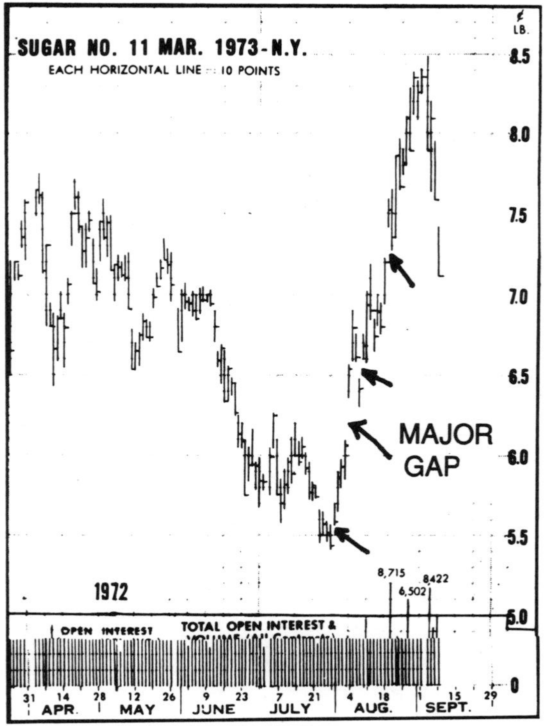

A NEW LOOK AT
MARKET SENTIMENT

MARK LIVELY

■

■

MARK LIVELY

Mr. Lively is a professional trader and futures market technician. Publisher and co-developer of the *Daily Sentiment Index* and monthly newsletter *DSI Futures Sentiment Guide*, as well as advisor for *Trade Line*, an advisory service for active futures traders, his expertise lies in cycle and trend analysis combined with the DSI to reduce trading risks and maximize trading performance.

■

■ CHAPTER SEVENTEEN ■

VETERAN STOCK AND FUTURES TRADERS are well acquainted with the concept of market sentiment as it has been used in its various forms throughout the years. In the stock market such indicators as odd lot short sales and bullish sentiment have been followed by astute traders and investors for many years. In the futures markets the "bullish consensus" was introduced by R. Earle Hadady in an effort to quantify the application of market sentiment to the more speculatively and shorter-term oriented futures markets. In spite of the fact that these ideas are well-known in the futures industry, however, there are still many traders who are either unclear about, unfamiliar with, or misguided about the theory and application of contrary opinion in its various and sundry forms. This is unfortunate inasmuch as it has frequently been true that major market turns occur during periods of time which are accompanied by strong bullish or bearish sentiment. It is my intention to help clarify the nature of market sentiment and to add to the font of knowledge about this vital topic by sharing the results of my recent research. First, however, a few working definitions are in order.

A Closer Look at the Theory of Market Sentiment

The old saying "a million Frenchmen can't be wrong" would send a chill through the blood of those dedicated to the use of market sentiment indicators. Proponents of market sentiment would argue that if, indeed, the day arrives when a million Frenchmen are in agreement about any one thing, it is more likely they will be wrong than right. Why? Because market sentiment theories take the view that strong agreement by a majority of individuals about a given situation or topic is likely to mean that the situation is, in fact, the opposite of what it is perceived to be. In other words, the general theory of market sentiment is severalfold:

1. The majority is usually wrong.
2. The stronger the agreement of the majority, the more likely it is that the majority is wrong.
3. The more emotional the issue, the more likely the majority is to be wrong.

4. The most logical course of action is, therefore, to move contrary to
    the crowd.

When someone yells "fire" in a crowded theatre you are likely to be better off if you head for an exit opposite from the one being taken by the mob.
In other words, when the overwhelming majority sees a given situation the
same way, it is likely that they are caught up in the emotion of the moment,
unable to think clearly and, therefore, most likely to be incorrect.

The futures markets are, in many respects, similar to life itself. The
drama of futures trading as it is enacted in the brokerage houses, trading
pits, and offices of traders is a microscopic view of the struggles of
humankind against nature. Although we like to think that good sense, intel-
lectualism, and skill prevail in the marketplace, the fact remains that emotion
reigns supreme in the markets, particularly at important turning points. It is,
therefore, emotion that limits intellectual and disciplined response. And it is
emotion that causes the majority to be wrong at critically important market
turns. Emotion clouds perception; misperception fosters the growth of strong
sentiment.

How Market Sentiment Has Been Measured

Earlier I mentioned odd lot short sales as a measure of market sentiment in
stock trading. This is one of the most obvious and earliest applications of
sentiment. It is based upon the theory that the small trader (i.e. the trader
with limited funds) is more apt to be wrong than is the well-capitalized
trader. Furthermore, it is a known fact that smaller traders, or novice traders,
are less likely to sell stocks short than are professional traders. A good way
to isolate the activities of the poorly capitalized or inexperienced trader is to
determine his collective short selling activity. This is done by examining the
odd lot short sales figures released by the various stock exchanges. The term
odd lot refers to a block of stock of less than one hundred shares. Odd lots
are generally purchased or sold by smaller traders. Hence, the odd lot short
sales figures tell us what the smaller trader is doing as a group. When the
odd lotters are selling short in large numbers, then it is likely that stocks are
bottoming and about to turn higher. When odd lotters pull back significantly
on their short selling, as a group, then it is likely that stocks are topping and
near a downturn.

Another measure of market sentiment is the bullish consensus as
developed by R. Earle Hadady. In his classic book, *Contrary Opinion*, Hadady
illustrated his ideas graphically, showing how strong bullish consensus correlated with market tops and how weak, i.e., low, bullish consensus—or high
bearish consensus—correlated with market bottoms. Hadady's work was
based on a weekly determination of the bullish sentiment as determined by

his tally of bullish or bearish market opinions expressed by leading futures newsletters.

A less objective but equally interesting aspect of bullish consensus has been mentioned by Zweig and Davis. They conducted an informal survey of headline stories about the stock market in various newspapers and business publications and found that the media was most apt to be bearish near lows and bullish near highs in the stock market.

Certainly, the data and informal studies of market sentiment suggest that there is indeed something out there—that by somehow monitoring the degree of public sentiment we can spot potential market turns fairly close to their occurrence. But the ultimate question is, how can we achieve this end in a reasonably objective and pragmatic fashion? Certainly R. Earle Hadady has established what appears to be a good procedure. In fact, the rules of applying Hadady's bullish consensus to the futures markets are much more detailed than given herein. The reader is referred to *Contrary Opinion* for a more complete understanding and to the *Bullish Consensus* newsletter, now published by Peter Hackstedde, who has taken over Hadady's work.

But a Million Frenchmen Aren't Always Wrong Immediately

A good part of the market sentiment quantification problem is clearly that the majority is not always wrong, nor are they wrong immediately upon the development of their strong collective sentiment. In other words, the market sentiment theory is, like all other indicators and market theories, not always right. It is precisely this aspect of market sentiment that points out the need for additional filters or timing indicators, which are likely to weed out false signals from the various market sentiment indicators.

There are many timing indicators available to today's futures trader; thus, it would appear to be a reasonable procedure to combine market sentiment with timing. The following general approach could be used to filter out false signals from market sentiment:

1. When market sentiment is very bullish, use technical trading indicators to spot sell signals, expecting a downturn due to high bullish sentiment.

2. When market sentiment is very bearish, use technical trading indicators to spot buy signals due to the high bearish sentiment (i.e., low bullish sentiment).

While the above may sound reasonable and logical in theory, it is not necessarily as simple to implement as it seems.

Making a Few Changes

In thinking about market sentiment and in observing its performance, even when technical timing indicators are used, I concluded that the procedures used to assess market sentiment might not be as sensitive or accurate as they could be. I felt that there must be other, better ways in which sentiment could be determined. After considerable study and thought, I arrived at the following conclusions which led to the development of the daily sentiment index (DSI).

1. If the public is more likely to be bearish at major market turns, then why not assess public opinion as opposed to professional opinion?

2. If the public is more emotional than professionals are, then why not survey public opinion as opposed to professional opinion?

3. In the event that professional traders are just as likely to be wrong at important or emotional turning points as is the average trader, then why not evaluate both public and professional opinion?

4. Why wait an entire week before taking the opinion "pulse?" Why not take it daily? It seemed to me that opinions are very fickle, changeable, and sensitive. By evaluating or polling opinions daily, I might arrive at a more sensitive and timely indication of market sentiment.

5. Why not combine daily market sentiment with intraday timing in order to spot potential turns in the various markets?

Here Are Some of My Findings

1. DSI can often signal market extremes. When readings become excessively high or excessively low this is an indication that prices may have moved too far in one direction.

2. DSI does not, in and of itself, signal that a top or bottom has been reached. Two things are necessary: First, DSI must become very high or very low. Second, market timing must confirm a change in market trend. Don't be fooled into thinking that high or low DSI readings automatically signal an imminent or immediate change in trend. High or low DSI readings can continue for many days. Yet, when DSI and timing work together, the combination can be a powerful one indeed.

3. DSI can be averaged over several days to produce a longer-term reading. The daily figures can be averaged into a weekly reading

which may then be used to ascertain the longer-term sentiment picture for each market.

4. DSI can be expressed as a moving average in order to filter out some of its sharp swings. I have found a three- or five-day moving average of the daily readings to be a helpful indicator that is less volatile and, perhaps, more useful for position trading.

5. Some traders may wish to develop DSI readings into a trading system by combining the readings with timing. If you do so, be certain to adhere to good principles of risk management.

6. Whether you use DSI for precise market entry or exit with timing, or as a guide to evaluating current positions or potential positions, remember that daily readings can change dramatically as a function of news, fundamentals, market conditions, reports, etc. As currently employed, the DSI is more of a short term indicator than a long-term indicator. A high DSI reading for one or more days does not necessarily indicate a long-term top, nor does a low DSI reading for one or several days indicate a long-term bottom.

Take Your Own Survey

There are many ways in which daily sentiment can be expressed. You could subscribe to the DSI service*, or you could easily conduct your own daily opinion poll. Simply develop a base of individuals whose opinions you assess daily, preferably shortly before or after market closings. A base of 50 respondents or more is desirable; however, 15 to 25 will usually suffice, provided that these individuals are not in close communication with one another. All you need do is tally their opinions as either bullish, bearish, or neutral. Then arrive at your percent bullish reading by simple arithmetic. That's all there is to it! At DSI we do all of this for you, however, lest you get the impression that this article is designed to serve as a sales tool for our service, bear in mind that you can easily perform this survey yourself. There are no secrets, special formulae, or tricks. At DSI we provide the readings as a service to those who have neither the time, inclination, or base of respondents to calculate the figures daily.

Sample Charts

Note the charts which follow. I have marked the DSI percent readings as well as prices so that you may see how prices have related to high, low, and neutral DSI readings. What conclusions can you reach from these charts?

Daily Sentiment Index, 2905 Newton Dr., Lago Vista, TX 78645, (512)267-3259.

Figure 17-1   Hourly December Coffee 1988

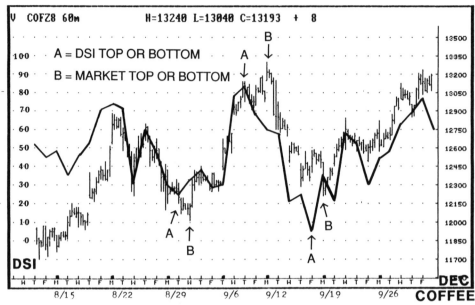

Source: Commodity Communications Corp., Inc. FutureSource Technical Machine, 420 Eisenhower Lane N., Lombard, IL 60148

Figure 17-2   Hourly December Cotton 1988

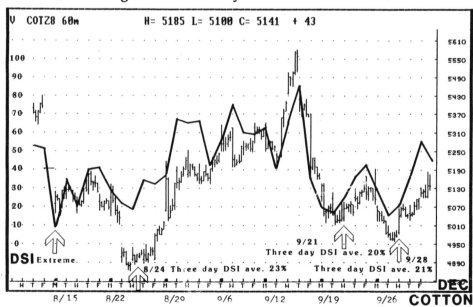

Source: Commodity Communications Corp., Inc. FutureSource Technical Machine, 420 Eisenhower Lane N., Lombard, IL 60148

Figure 17-3 Hourly February Bellies 1989

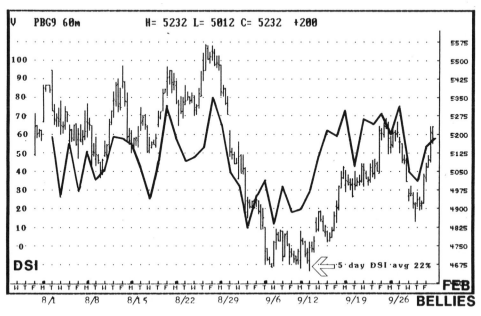

Source: Commodity Communications Corp., Inc. FutureSource Technical Machine, 420
Eisenhower Lane N., Lombard, IL 60148

WEATHER
AND TIMING

HOW TO TURN DROUGHTS, FLOODS, AND HURRICANES INTO SUCCESSFUL SPECULATIVE OPPORTUNITIES

JAMES ROEMER

■

■

JIM ROEMER

A colorful speaker, James Roemer began his love affair with the weather at the tender age of four, after watching lightning bolts strike his neighbor's yard. This early interest led him to Lyndon State College, the breeding ground for some of the nation's premier meteorologists. After receiving his B.S. in meteorology, Mr. Roemer began to develop and nurture his skills as an agricultural weather forecaster.

While working for the respected commodity weather forecasting firm of Freese-Notis Weather in Des Moines, Iowa, he developed an interest in studying and trading the commodities market. After realizing his talent in trading markets based on weather, he began managing several accounts. Mr. Roemer currently supplies brokerage houses, traders, and farmers with weather and/or trading information. During the past four U.S. growing seasons, he has been able to double or triple 90% of his managed accounts.

Recently, Mr. Roemer formed a new company, with Freese-Notis Weather as partner, called Weather Trades Inc., responsible for publishing a weekly all weather-trading newsletter. Weather Trades, Inc. has transcended the boundaries that stereotype the typical meteorologist by rendering *trading advice* in addition to weather forecasts and crop conditions.

■

■ CHAPTER EIGHTEEN ■

A S LONG AS I CAN REMEMBER, weather has held a special fascination for me. I remember sitting, as a five-year-old, in the basement of my parents' New Jersey home playing with water colors in a coloring book. Although I had no artistic prowess at this tender age, what I was painting then, nevertheless, was a vision that I would pursue and study for the rest of my life. These early images of clouds, sun, and storms were only the beginning of my intense interest in nature and particularly the weather, that would follow me into adulthood.

As a child during the spring and summer months, I remember my mother frequently yelling at me for sitting on the front lawn during thunderstorms. She certainly had valid reasons for being angry and concerned. What kind of nut would risk being struck by lightning or just plain drenched by rain? But I was so captivated by these marvelous spectacles of nature that I repeatedly risked her wrath rather than deny myself these awe-inspiring moments. Oh, I was a normal child in all the important ways. I played tennis competitively by the time I was twelve and had dozens of friends, but people thought I was a little strange calling the telephone weather recording ten times a day. Even during special family gatherings, I spent more time gazing at the sky and stars than sitting quietly at home with my grandparents.

In high school I began hanging around local TV stations and dreamed that someday I would be forecasting the weather on national TV. In fact, I attended a Vermont college that specialized in meteorology and TV broadcasting, but many people thought I had little real broadcasting talent. Undaunted, I only intensified my efforts every time a teacher or prospective employer would say, "Jim, you are an excellent forecaster; you're aggressive and you love your work; but you have too much of an Eastern accent. You talk too fast."

I heard this story time and time again after graduating from college. When I was notified by a Connecticut TV station that the news director had turned me down for an important job, however, that particular rejection turned out to be fortuitous. Although I was heartbroken at the time, that experience proved to be the beginning of a new career when the director of that station, who took a personal interest in me, sent a clipping from a 1981 *Wall Street Journal* article. This article talked about the commodities market and the need for accurate weather forecasters in that business. It was from this point that I began developing an interest and talent not only in weather and agriculture, but also in trading the commodities market.

Weather and the Commodities Market

To many Americans, knowing the weather report is an important part of preparing for the day. The average evening TV weather forecaster, however, in an attempt to add entertainment value to an otherwise relatively dull topic, has often trivialized the role of the weather forecaster as part of the news team. Rather than being seen as a highly trained and sophisticated professional, the TV weatherperson's job is often seen as a license to wear funny hats, clown with the audience, and make predictions that often seem to be wrong.

In the 1950s and 1960s, farmers, commodity brokerage houses and food companies had little assistance in determining where rain would fall or how a crop such as sugar or corn was faring. Weather data was sparse, and firms had to trust the TV broadcaster with his crazy hats and zany tricks. Over the years, the development of the National Weather Service and the World Meteorological Organization (WMO), as well as the birth of private sector meteorological services, have helped to alleviate the lack of weather data for commodity traders and producers. Today, several reputable private weather forecasting firms tailor specific forecasts to meet clients' needs. As a result, the private-sector meteorology industry has become a multimillion dollar-per-year business.

Having access to accurate weather information for, let's say, the winter wheat belt from Kansas to Illinois and the Brazilian soybean and coffee growing areas is worth millions of dollars per year. Through the use of satellite imagery, radar and jetstream analysis, the meteorologist can judge short-term weather developments all over the world. These short-term variations in weather have a direct effect on crop development and commodity price action.

Each different crop experiences critical growth stages during which weather is the most critical factor in determining later crop yield. A soybean plant, for example, enters its important blooming and pod setting period during the months of July and August. In the Southern hemisphere, where the seasons are reversed, soybeans are, therefore, planted in November and December and bloom and pod in January and February. Corn, sugar, cocoa, oranges, wheat and cotton all have critical life cycle periods. The amount of rain and warmth these crops receive during those critical stages ultimately determines the volume of crop that is produced.

Of course, the weather in countries that are major producers of a crop is watched more closely by food companies and commodity traders than weather in other parts of the world. Florida citrus growers, for example, have no interest in the orange crop in southern Europe. However, since Brazil accounts for more than 50 percent of the world's total orange juice production, Florida orange growers and processors need to estimate Brazilian production as accurately as possible. Traders and orange companies therefore will sometimes take market positions in the frozen concentrated orange juice (FCOJ) market based not only on domestic weather and crop conditions, but also on those conditions in Brazil.

How to Trade a Freeze Market

The great thing about trading the weather is that a drought, flood or freeze almost guarantees some reaction in the agricultural markets. Of course, an early October freeze in the heart of the Iowa and Illinois corn belt will do little, if any, damage to the corn crop. A trader cannot hope that a positive market reaction will develop. But if the freeze occurs during the critical maturing stage of corn (late August or early September), damage to the crop may occur. If crop damage occurs, traders theorize that lower production means tighter supplies and, hence, higher prices.

The concept is simple. Watch a particular crop—sugar or soybeans or something else—that is entering an important development stage. If the crop is hurt badly, prices for that commodity will trend higher. Help the crop with timely rains, and more ample supplies mean lower prices. Let's look at one example. One of the worst September cold waves in the United States struck large portions of the corn and soybean crop during 1974. The subsequent price move was one of the largest on record for a fall freeze (see Figure 18-1).

How would I trade this market? First, I would determine the percentage of the U.S. corn or soybean crop that could be adversely affected by temperatures below 28 to 30 degrees Fahrenheit for more than four hours. Since the market in this example has already been in a technical uptrend for most of the preceding summer, any additional decrease in crop production would likely keep the price uptrend intact. Market sentiment is extremely important in trading such a market. If the trade has begun talking about a possible freeze such that a slight change in a temperature forecast can alter short-term price action, we've got ourselves a weather market. In this kind of market, judging the relative strength index, using a short term technical indicator or watching bullish consensus figures may be misleading.

After studying the possible affects of a freeze, I would enter a long position in the soybean market one to three days before the freeze itself. Protective stops are not necessary in this type of market, since the rumor of cold weather will keep prices firm. If, however, there is a sudden change in the forecasted air temperature for the corn belt, let's say to 32 to 35 degrees, I would immediately react to the weather maps by exiting my long position.

Figure 18-1 Soybean Weekly Futures

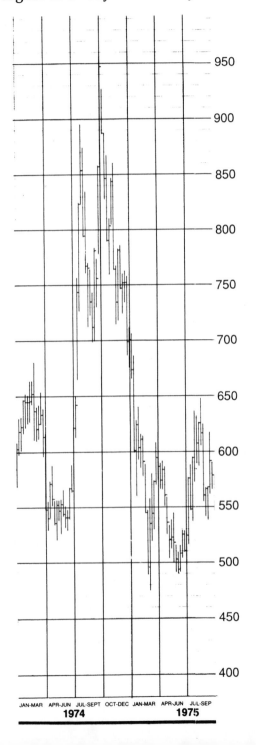

In a weather market, you cannot hope that it will be cold enough to freeze the crop. It has to happen. Anything warmer than that which the trade is already anticipating will spill the market into a down-trend. There can be no hoping; it either freezes or it doesn't!

In this particular situation, two late September freezes created a huge market reaction in the corn and soybean complex. The smart trader may have taken significant profits the first day soybeans traded off the limit. Otherwise, placing stop orders below the previous day's low could (in this situation) have yielded some $10,000 per contract in soybeans.

Other exciting and profitable freeze events were the Brazilian coffee freezes of 1978 and 1981 and the Florida citrus freezes of 1963, 1977, 1980, 1981, and 1983. In all of these cases, successive limit up moves could have propelled trading equity to incredible heights. The freeze move is quick and profitable, but leaves no second chance to enter the market. Either it freezes or it doesn't. By estimating Florida or Brazilian temperatures three to five days in advance, the weather trader can throw away all the technical chart work and jump into the market before the freeze hits.

Types of Freeze Trades

The most obvious freeze trade is a play I call the FRR (freeze-rumor-result). This trade can occur when the price of an agricultural commodity being threatened by cold weather is anticipated by a freeze rumor. The consensus of several weather forecasting companies that a freeze is imminent creates a psychological price reaction, as the market anticipates the freeze. Anything less devastating that than which the market is looking for may result in a big wash-out to the down side after the fact.

An example of this is illustrated in Figure 18-2. In this case, minimum temperatures in central Florida's citrus growing area reached the critical 24 to 29 degree temperature range for a duration of two to four hours. This forecast, a day earlier, resulted in a limit bid in the FCOJ market on the last Monday in December. The previous Friday, cold air building southward from central Canada helped us recommend buying January FCOJ around the $1.60 per pound area. By executing a buy order on Friday prior to the unanimity by other weather forecasters on Monday, a trader could have positioned himself or herself long for the rumor and subsequent limit up move. However, with Florida citrus trees more resilient to cold weather following four previous freezes in five years, the two to four hour cold wave was not devastating enough to create subsequent limit up moves. In fact, prices for FCOJ proceeded to plummet the following two to three days after the cold wave. In this example, the smart trader could have exited positions limit up on Monday, on the consensus rumor of a freeze by other forecasters and taken profits of $750 per contract.

Figure 18-2   Frozen Orange Juice Concentrate—1985

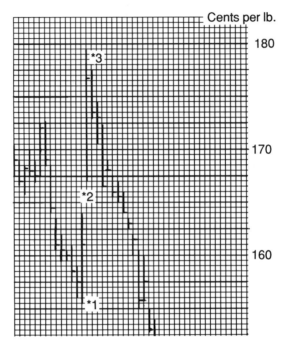

*1 Friday forecast in late December 1985 for a possible freeze the following week.

*2 The following Monday other weather forecasters saw what we saw a few days earlier. This forecst pushed the market up the limit.

*3 Temperatures of 24-29 degrees in Florida's citrus groves were not cold enough to sustain significant damage.

In some cases, the actual freeze yields much greater profit potential than the freeze rumor-result. In the previous example the rumor alone created a trading opportunity. The Florida citrus freeze of 1983 was one such case (Figure 3). Here, a more severe cold wave destroyed numerous Florida Citrus groves and resulted in several limit up price moves following the effects of the freeze. An earlier weather forecast resulted in a small price move on the initial rumor, then the big move followed the freeze. Here, the best strategy would have been to stay for four to five days after the freeze.

The novice trader may make the mistake of either (A) using a technical sell signal and not listening to the pending weather developments or (B) trying to jump into the long side of the market once the market starts trading off limit. The key is to get in early on the rumor of the cold wave and to hold a long position only if you think crop damage will be extensive enough to cut into world supplies. In over two previous examples, the freeze of 1983 was severe enough to stay in while the freeze of 1985 was not.

Figure 18-3

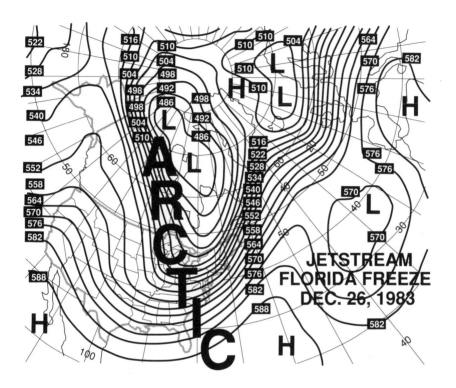

Trading orange juice futures on Florida weather forecasts are more difficult today then they were in the 1960s, 1970s and early 1980s,
because of the sudden expansion of citrus trees in Brazil's Sao Paulo
province. Since 1983, Brazil has captured more than 60 percent of the orange
juice market. Political and economic activities in that country may or may
not have a direct influence on this market, but along with the weather in
Brazil and Florida one must be aware of these developments, as well as the
fluctuating value of the dollar, to catch most moves in the orange juice
market.

Another exciting but sometimes very difficult market to trade is coffee.
Few commodities in the Southern hemisphere are more weather sensitive
than coffee. Man's love affair with this popular breakfast eye-opener may be
best exemplified by the infamous Brazilian freeze of the 1950s, which sent
shock waves through the coffee industry as prices more than tripled in a
matter of weeks. Thousands upon thousands of Americans were so nervous
about soaring prices and a potential lack of supply of coffee that they stood
in line for hours at their favorite grocery store, waiting for some of the last
shipments of fresh coffee to come in before prices soared.

The Brazilian coffee freezes of 1978 and 1981 are two fine examples of the get-rich-quick possibilities in weather trading. Because Brazil produces some 60 percent of the world's coffee crop, an immediate price impact is practically guaranteed upon any crop loss. These two past freezes could each have yielded $40,000 per contract if you had listened to the weatherperson beforehand.

Taking the Opposite Side of the Market

There are times when more money can be made by using contrary opinion and *selling* into a weather market than by buying. One prime example occurred recently in the coffee market. Figure 18-4 represents December 1988 coffee futures. The dramatic 2,000 point dive in prices would have yielded the experienced weather trader about $7,500 per contract in the week between July 27 and August 2, 1988. This is equivalent to ten limit up moves in the orange juice market. In this example, the entire trade was caught up in the seasonal bias of the coffee market. Mid-June through early August typically is an upward period for coffee futures, due in part to the seasonality of the southern hemisphere winter season and the associated threat of a freeze. However, as Figure 18-5 indicates, a high jetstream in South America kept all of the cold air away from the main coffee belt in Brazil. Hence, with the freeze season rapidly winding down, little time was left for damage to occur to the present year's production and prices fell accordingly. It is simple supply and demand. No freeze means a large crop and, hence, lower prices. Not only that, but the International Coffee Organization was unable to arrive at an agreement on a coffee quota, forcing prices even lower. Bingo! Big profits from the short side.

Trading the Grains: The Ultimate Weather Market

Weather conditions in the United States constitute the *supply-side fundamentals* for the grain markets. With more than 50 percent of the world's corn and soybean crops grown in the United States, it's no wonder that drought, freeze or floods create some enormous price moves in those commodities. Droughts are most certainly the evil of all evils for the American farmer, reducing crop yield in some cases to nearly zero. As a consequence, the Chicago Board of Trade often erupts at just the hint of any such disaster.

The dust bowl days of the 1930s featured several devastating droughts in the nation's heartland. John Steinbeck's award winning *Grapes of Wrath* sadly depicts the plight of nomadic farmers and their struggle for survival during that time. Having observed first-hand the devastating consequences that can be imposed on a farmer by adverse weather conditions, one of my personal goals is to help as many American farmers as possible fight the terror of drought through successful trading and hedging strategies.

Figure 18-4

Source: Commodity Quote-Graphics TQ–20/20

Circumstances in foreign countries, such as Russian and Brazilian crop conditions, constitute the *demand-side fundamentals* for the grain markets. In demand driven markets, the weather often plays an important role in determining how much grain a country buys from another. The 1987 drought in India, for example, was the first of a series of occurrences that relieved America's grain glut woes of the early 1980s.

At that time, the grain farmer in America was buried in a huge mound of surplus grain, and prices were at levels not witnessed since the Great Depression. But then *El Niño* (Christ Child) hit in 1987 and eastern Asia experienced severe droughts, floods, and resultant economic hardship. El Niño is a meteorological phenomenon consisting of unusually warm ocean currents off the coasts of Peru and Ecuador, some occurrences of which are believed to be caused by volcanic activity in the Southern Hemisphere. In the case of the 1987 El Niño, the eruption of the volcano Nevada del Ruiz in Columbia during 1985 may have been the spark that set in motion a set of circumstances around the globe, shrinking world stocks of grains and increasing the United States' exports of grain abroad.

Figure 18-5

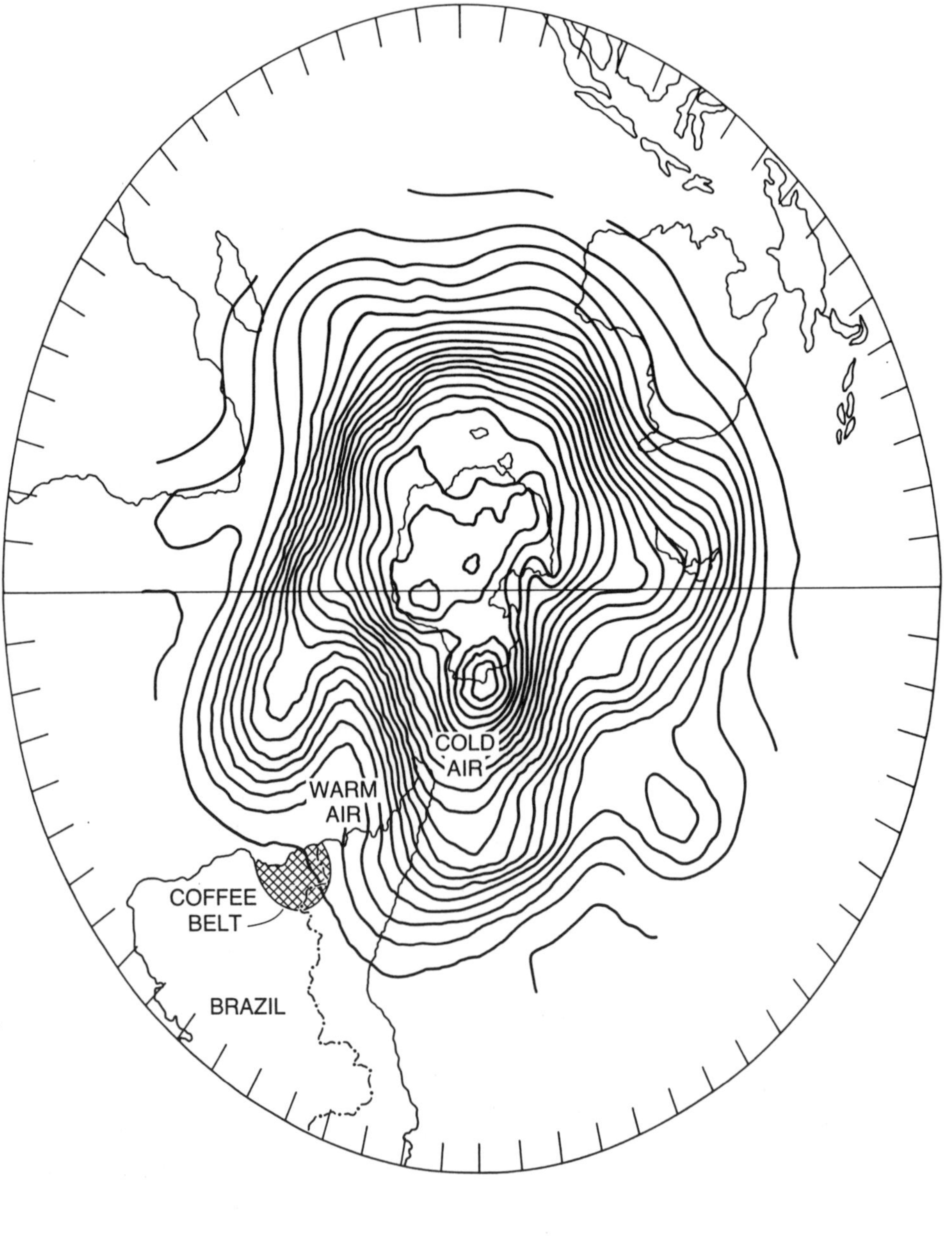

Figure 18-6, drawn in the spring of 1987, represents areas where crop production problems were likely to occur as a result of El Niño. The solid lines represent areas that might tend toward drier than normal weather patterns, while the broken lines portend wetter periods.

Figure 18-6   El Nino & Associated Weather Conditions

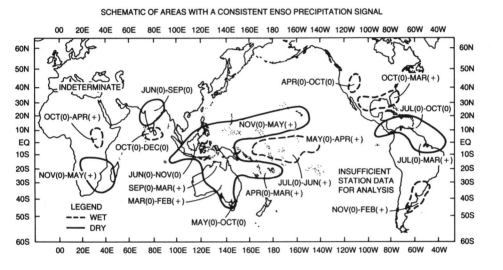

Source: Ropelewski, C.F., Monthly Weather, December 1986, Vol. 11.

The solid line drawn around India accurately predicted the severe 1987 drought in that country. The resulting shortage of wheat in India and the purchase of millions of bushels of surplus wheat from the United States helped lower the excess level of wheat in the United States and drove prices higher. Armed with this chart of expected weather conditions related to El Niño, and knowing India's consumption of wheat, a longer-term weather trader would have entered a long position in July 1988 CBOT wheat futures in the spring of 1987. Holding this longer-term long wheat position typifies a classic demand-related weather trade.

During the spring of 1988, parched soil in the United States and Canada threatened domestic crops and further eroded the grain surplus. India's drought ignited the *demand* fundamentals while the drought in the United States furnished the *supply-side* fireworks. One year after taking a long position in wheat, the weather trader could have exited the position with a profit of nearly $7,000 per contract. When the drought in India became news, the strategy would have been to place a stop loss under $2.50 and then ride the price all the way up (Figure 18-7).

Figure 18-7

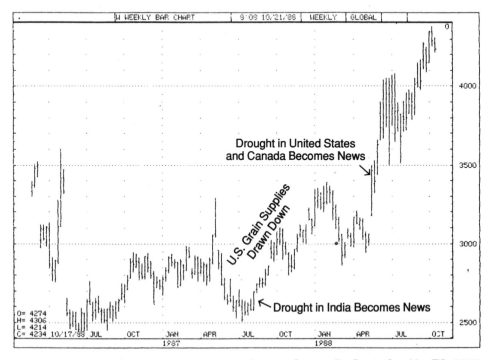

Source: Commodity Quote-Graphics TQ–20/20

In weather markets, the weather creates the technicals. Take a look, for example, at the November 1988 soybean chart (Figure 18-8). Almost every price move from the period May through August was generated by some weather-related event. United States soybean production is greatly influenced by rainfall and temperature patterns during the summer. Figure 18-9 illustrates the importance of July and August precipitation patterns to average soybean yields. For example, notice that there is a reduction of two to three bushels per acre when rainfall averages six to eight centimeters (.25 to .33 inches) below normal The droughts of 1983 and 1988 were quite a bit worse than that.

Figure 18-8

Source: Commodity Quote-Graphics TQ–20/20

Figure 18-9

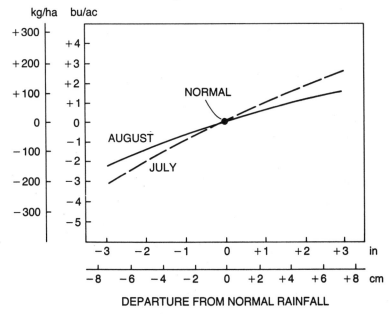

DEPARTURE FROM NORMAL RAINFALL

Source: Dr. Louis Thompson, Iowa State University

The sharp up-trend line in November soybeans is a chartist's dream. But these bullish indicators were generated by a drought that threatened soybean plants before they were even in the ground. An experienced weather trader could have ridden the ups and downs in this market by using accurate weather information. Points A, B, D and E on the chart represent several of the limit up days in the soybean market during the hot, dry periods of 1988. The psychology of these kinds of markets is as tenuous as walking a tightrope: everything can come tumbling down quickly. If it rains, or if there are any rumors of rain and the trade figures the crop supply may be getting larger, prices will fall rapidly.

Note that the limit up moves occurred primarily after weekends, when traders walked into the CBOT on Monday morning sweating in the heat. The trick would have been to anticipate with a long position on Friday what the trade would know the first thing Monday morning, then take profits limit up when everyone else was buying.

Looking at the downside, point C depicts just one of many short-term psychological washouts when bullish consensus and relative strength indicators were soaring and rain suddenly entered the weather forecast. In this kind of market, all it takes is one or two well-known meteorologists reporting a wetter-than-expected forecast, at a point when most speculators are already long the market. When that occurs, there is bound to be a wave of fear and profit taking. The smart traders might decide to sell short November soybeans around this $8.90 area, risking a stop above the recent high of $9.19 and take profits (should any rain actually fall) around the $8.60 to $8.70 area.

Because soybeans are planted in June and need ample rainfall through mid-August, most of the short-term fluctuations reflected by Figure 18-8 are weather-related. As we have seen, each move up or down offers an excellent opportunity to the trader who has access to accurate and early weather information and who is nimble in jumping in and out of the market. Likewise, major worldwide weather patterns like El Niño provide opportunities for longer-term position traders with the foresight to read the weather charts and predict the long-term consequences.

Year after year these kinds of fortuitous market conditions make it possible for the smart weather trader to pull attractive profits from the markets, but never more dramatically than during the summer of 1988. Referring again to Figure 18-8, an early summer drought of proportions unseen since the early 1930s forced soybean prices nearly to $10.00 by the middle of June. Then, without warning, one of the largest soybean crashes in history occurred during the last two weeks of July (point F on the chart), when prices plummeted some $2.00 a bushel. Why did this occur at a time when the drought was still very much a reality?

On Friday, June 17, most forecasters were calling for the drought in the United States to continue unabated, and technical traders figured the trend looked bullish. But the Friday close of $9.72 was not to be seen again that summer. Why? There was so much crop damage already built into the market that anything less than completely hot, dry conditions the following week would pressure prices. However, Freese-Notis Weather and I were calling for more rain than other forecasters.

Most traders were fooled as anywhere from one half-inch to two-inch rains fell over a good majority of the corn and soybean belt and halted, at least for the moment, any further price escalation. The experienced short-term trader would have been out of this market, recognizing the risk and greed already built into the prices.

Hurricanes, Floods and Other Disasters

Hurricanes, with all their sound and fury, are often less traumatizing in the reality than is the fear generated by the sound and fury of the news media, as they predict the apocalyptic destruction that may be wrought by these weather monsters. Without minimizing the true suffering often caused by hurricanes, the actual effect on crops is usually far less than that predicted by the overreactions of newspersons, creating a classic trading opportunity for the weather trader.

Hurricanes have created some exciting short-term market reactions. One of the most notable was Hurricane Allen in 1980. Though it caused millions of dollars in property damage to the Texas coastal areas, the accompanying rains further inland saved the Texas cotton crop from a total disaster. The ten-cent-per-pound move in August of 1980 (Figure 18-10) was one of the largest moves ever made by cotton as a result of a hurricane. For those weather traders who kept abreast of Hurricane Allen, the profit potential was outstanding.

The most recent active year for hurricanes was 1985, in which there were 11 tropical cyclones, six of which were named hurricanes (sustained winds over 75 mph). When Hurricane Elena hit Cuba in 1985, Fidel Castro claimed "disaster to the sugar-cane crop." This hurricane, following the drought problems in Brazil and Cuba, helped sugar prices climb toward six cents per pound, bringing speculators back into the market.

Hurricane Gilbert in 1988 produced a classic case of overreaction, as many commodities rallied prior to September 16 in the face of news media hype. "It will wipe out bauxite production in Jamaica, destroy oil rigs in the Gulf, make rice paddies and soybeans die in the Delta, and blow away cotton crops." When these calamities failed to materialize, those same commodities fell flat on their faces. As with all weather markets, there was opportunity to buy on the early rumor of a hurricane and take profits on the run-up when the rumor became news. Alternatively, a weather trader would sell short near the top of the run-up, then take profits when the worst predictions proved inaccurate and the market fell back.

Figure 18-10

Contract size:	50,000 lbs.
Trading hours:	9:30-2:00*
1 pt. =	$5.00
Limit move:	200 pts.
*Central Time	(subject to change)

DEC. 80 COTTON
Each Horizontal Line = 100 points

Source: Commodity Price Charts 219 Parkade, Cedar Falls, IA 50613

Floods and other natural disasters can cause market reactions very similar to those caused by hurricanes. The effects can come from the supply side, when domestic crops are either hurt or helped by the disaster, or from the demand side, when foreign nations find themselves in a position of needing to increase or decrease imports of grain or other commodities.

Trading and the Weather

Weather markets can vary from the subtlest of snowstorms affecting cattle in the high plains of Texas to biting cold that sends heating oil futures soaring for several weeks, as happened from late December to early January 1983–84. Whether it's orange juice, soybeans, cotton, or sugar, there are literally dozens, sometimes hundreds of short-term to long-term weather plays each year. This, to me, seems a lot safer than trying to figure whether the dollar will weaken or interest rates will climb and whether all of this will lead to a specific reaction in the stock market.

It seems to me that most fundamental traders who have been unsuccessful have been so because what is known of the weather by the public is already old news. By obtaining earlier and more accurate weather forecasts, a trader is peering more clearly into the future and that, after all, is what "futures" are all about.

Following the crowd in a weather market can have grave consequences. The key is to be a step ahead of the crowd with a meteorologist you can trust and who understands the psychological nuances of the market. For this purpose, Freese-Notis Weather of Des Moines, Iowa is one of several excellent private weather forecasting services available.

TRADING
WITH OPTIONS

■

■ SECTION THREE ■

OPTIONS HAVE BEEN THE PECK'S BAD BOY of the futures industry for decades. Banned in the 1860's by the newly formed Chicago Board of Trade, they have been alternately prohibited and permitted ever since. Options were approved for trading on all U.S. exchanges in 1982 by the CFTC, but only on an experimental basis and under very stringent regulations. Having proven themselves to be a viable part of futures trading and a potentially valuable element of hedging strategies, options are presently available on most futures contracts, and more are being established each month. This section presents two options trading strategies: a straightforward approach that attempts to take advantage of large market moves and a more complex strategy that borrows heavily from futures trading strategies. Any trader wishing to trade in options will find both of these plans quite helpful.

Joe Krutsinger offers a strategy that combines options buying with a search for major market moves. Included are 25 rules for trading options.

Michael Chisholm first presents a rationale for trading options rather than the underlying futures, then outlines an options trading strategy that includes 7 key elements as well as specific rules for trading.

MAJOR OPTION MOVES:

A Strategy and Rules for Using Futures Options to Profit from Major Market Moves

JOE KRUTSINGER

■

JOE KRUTSINGER

Joe Krutsinger is the Vice-President of Research for Futures Discount Group.

In addition to co-authoring the commodity futures textbook, *The Commodity Cookbook: Recipes for Success*, and the audio tape, *Winning with Futures Options*, Mr. Krutsinger has developed his own Guided Account Program. He received the Outstanding Senior Award in Food Systems, Economics and Management at Michigan State University in 1973, and was recognized as "Entrepreneur of the Month" by *Entrepreneur Magazine* in 1981 for his work in the field of business consultation. MBH Management Corporation recognized Mr. Krutsinger as one of only six approved brokers in the nation for their managed account programs.

Most of Mr. Krutsinger's activity is focused on interest rate futures. Mr. Krutsinger is considered by many to be one of the leading authorities in the nation on the Commodity Quote Graphics Trading Computer. A technical trader, he has developed various trading programs to help clients achieve their objectives.

■ CHAPTER NINETEEN ■

O
PTIONS TRADING can position a trader to catch major price moves in a way that futures trading can't. Several reasons for that exist, but a major factor is that with options, even a small trader with $5,000 to $10,000 can have a base multiple position in four or five different diversified markets, while futures trading, with its higher margin requirements, limits the number of markets in which positions can be maintained. When the big move comes, the options trader is there, while the futures trader can easily be left on the sidelines.

The best way to understand options is to think of them as a term insurance policy on a particular price movement. If a trader feels that sugar is going higher, but he or she has only a limited amount of capital, the strategy might be to buy a $.09 sugar call with 150 days of time value for $500. This $500 is the insurance premium. If sugar goes to $.11 within the next 150 days, the option will be worth at least $2,240—$.02 per pound times 112,000 pounds in a contract—minus the original cost of $500 and commissions. If sugar doesn't make that move, the option can expire worthless.

Real leverage has always involved risking other people's money. Buying futures options lets a trader profit from all of the favorable movement of a particular future (minus the premium and commission) while only risking the total of the original premium plus commissions. In the sugar example, a $500 call resulted in $2,240 in profits, minus commission. In this case, the option would have allowed a trader to leverage $500 into a profit of over 150 percent, but the total risk was limited to the $500 plus commission.

Many books have been written about options trading, outlining sophisticated strategies that combine puts with calls, selling options with buying options, and options with futures. Each of these strategies is probably an excellent plan. In these few pages, however, I'm not going to get into complex strategies, options writing, calendar spreads and the like. I am going to explain, as simply as I can, why a strategy of buying puts and calls can be preferable to trading futures contracts and how to search for the major moves in the markets. Following that, I will present my 25 rules for options trading.

Recent Major Market Moves

Figure 19-1 lists some of the recent big moves in a few familiar commodities: cotton, Japanese yen, crude oil, S&P 500, copper, soybeans, and hogs. This is not a scientific look at a track record—simply a look back at some of the major moves over the last 29 months and the profit potential using a one contract buy-or-sell-and-hold basis.

Looking at this table of only seven commodities over the past two and a half years, it is easy to see how a simple options strategy might have worked. For example, in 1986 cotton moved from $.30 per pound to $.60 per pound—a $15,000 gain on one futures contract.

Four simple strategies exist for identifying markets that are likely to move soon and are, therefore, candidates for a long-term options trade:

1. Look for a market that has been moving a long time in one direction and has started to break trendlines on shorter term charts against that direction (Figure 19-2).

2. Look for a market that is due for a major cycle low or high on a weekly chart (Figure 19-3). MBH Commodity Advisors is a good source for cycle length tables.

3. An easy way to determine which markets will move is to look at today's price versus the price 20 days ago. If today's price is at least three percent higher or lower than the price 20 days ago, it probably indicates a moving market.

4. Seasonals are also a great help in identifying many future trends. The harvest lows in grains, the summer rally in stocks, the winter run-up in orange juice—all are good starting points for buying futures options.

The skeptical trader, of course, will say, "If it's that easy, why mess with an option? Why not just buy a futures contract and hold it?" And he or she would be right. If a trader's market research is correct, a futures contract will *always* be better than an option. There are two reasons for that:

1. Open trade profit can usually be used as a margin for more contracts.

2. A futures contract has a delta (efficiency) of one. That is, every time the market moves up $.01 per pound, a futures contract will also move up $.01 per pound.

So why should a trader bother with options? Why not just buy futures contracts and pyramid them into a fortune? But how many traders are able to do that? From 1986 to 1988 cotton moved from $.30 to $.60 to $.80 and back down to $.60. Trading only one contract, not counting commissions and slippage, a $45,000 gain might have been possible. But how many traders took that to the bank?

Figure 19-1

Some Recent "Big Moves" of the Last Two Years

Cotton	1986	30¢ to 60¢= $15,000
	1987	60¢ to 80¢= $10,000
	1987	80¢ to 60¢= $10,000
		Total "Big Move" $35,000
Japanese Yen	1986	50 to 62= $15,000
	1987	62 to 82= $25,000
		Total "Big Move" $40,000
Crude Oil	1986	$26 to $10= $16,000
	1986	$10 to $19= $9,000
	1987	$21 to $15= $6,000
		Total "Big Move" $31,000
S&P 500	1986	205 to 275= $35,000
	1987	250 to 325= $37,500
	1987	325 to 200= $62,500
	1987	200 to 260= $30,000
		Total "Big Move" $165,000
Copper	1987	60¢ to 120¢= $15,000
	1988	120¢ to 90¢= $7,500
		Total "Big Move" $22,500
Soybeans	1987	$5.00 to $6.00= $5,000
	1988	$6.00 to $8.00= $10,000
		Total "Big Move" $15,000
Hogs	1986	38¢ to 60¢= $6,600
	1987	60¢ to 40¢= $6,000
	1988	41¢ to 54¢= $3,900
		Total "Big Move" $16,500

Figure 19-2

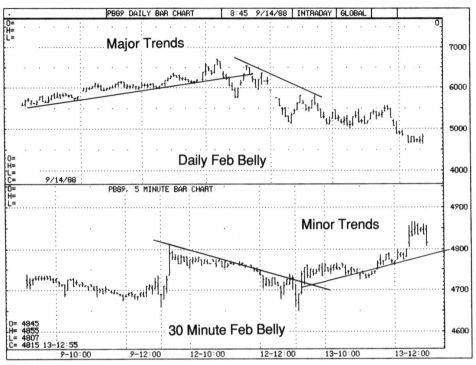

Source: Commodity Quote-Graphics TQ–20/20

Figure 19-3

Source: Commodity Quote-Graphics TQ–20/20

There are three possible reasons why most futures traders don't trade with the big moves in the market:

1. *They can't see the forest for the trees.* As more and more traders have home quotation equipment and discount brokerage accounts, they become much less attuned to the big moves. They develop the "If I can make $200 per day I'll be happy" attitude. They usually can't and they usually aren't.

2. *Big moves are boring.* First, it's boring waiting for them to develop. (Sugar took two and a half years to get ready before it finally made its move in 1988). Second, it's boring once you are in. Watching a market move up $2,000 in four months is boring at best. Every day a trader is likely to say, "What am I doing in this boring trade?"

3. *Most traders want action more than they want performance.* It's somewhat like a pinball machine. Most people would rather play a machine with six balls for $.25 than one with three balls for $.25, even if the game with the fewer balls is easier to win.

In a simple options strategy designed to catch major market moves, however, the options trader is focused on just one thing: watching for a big move and being in a position to catch it. But why use options? Why are options better than futures for the big move? Known risk! No other vehicle allows the speculator to know his or her total risk up front. By buying time, an option buyer can actually stand in front of the freight train of a runaway market.

Long-term options trading does have certain disadvantages, however. If the market doesn't move far enough or fast enough, the options premium will simply decay and eventually disappear. Moreover, options commissions are usually higher than futures commissions, and options are harder to track, because options prices are not as readily available as futures prices. Nevertheless, with an account of $10,000, a trader can maintain a multicontract options position in four or five markets with capital left over to add to the winning trades.

Once an individual has decided to try options trading to catch the big moves in the market, there are rules that, if followed, will make the strategy more likely to succeed. Will this strategy always win? Of course not. Will there be losses? Certainly. But the potential for profits coupled with limited risk make a long-term options strategy worthy of consideration.

25 Simple Rules for Trading Options

Rule 1: Get some good basic trading literature. All of the commodity exchanges have free or low cost literature available. Get all of it. Learn the terms and basic strategy rules. Traders who do this will be miles ahead of most of the competition who "don't have the time."

Rule 2: Start small. Unlike futures trading, where there is fear of margin calls, futures option buyers know that their premium investment plus commission is the maximum risk they will take. Beginning option buyers should, therefore, start with a small amount of capital—$5,000 to $20,000—and simply quit if it is depleted. If there are profits, however, it's a good suggestion to restart the account fresh and withdraw all funds except the original starting balance each year. (In effect, the clearing company keeps an accurate track record using this method).

Rule 3: Diversify the portfolio. For almost every commodity futures contract, there is a corresponding futures option. Most experienced traders buy a mix of grain, livestock, metal, food/fiber, currency, interest rates, and indexes. A portfolio with only copper, gold, and/or silver is not diversified. A $10,000 account buying options of about $750 each can have multiple positions in six markets.

Rule 4: Don't load the boat. A favorite trading method of inexperienced option buyers is to put all of their risk capital into one futures option at one strike price at one time. For example, they might buy $10,000 worth of March 700 silver calls in a $10,000 account. This strategy is sometimes called the *Babe Ruth*, because if it wins it's a real home run, and very profitable. But remember two things: (A) Babe Ruth struck out more than any player in history. (B) If all of the trading capital is lost on the first trade, there is no second trade. Don't put more than 25 percent of available trading capital into any one major move.

Rule 5: Plan to spend more than $350 and less than $800 for each option, not including commissions.

Rule 6: A good futures options broker can be worth his or her weight in gold (even if he or she's a pretty hefty dude). For a trader with experience a full service broker may not be necessary, but new traders will often make mistakes like erroneously trying to sell a put when they mean to buy one. It doesn't take too many of these "caught mistakes" to justify a higher commission rate. Also, as a rule, option buyers don't go in and out of the market with the same frequency as futures traders, so commissions may not be as important.

Rule 7: Cycles are one of the best tools to help analyze which futures options are the best to buy. At cycle *lows*, a futures contract has usually been in a long downtrend. At that point, futures option premiums on calls have contracted and there is little public interest in buying the particular commodity. It is usually the ideal time to buy futures call options. When buying puts, look for commodities that are in the proper timeframe for cycle highs. Puts will be fairly priced at these times.

Rule 8: Only look at closes to determine futures option strategies. Often, in real time trading, prices for futures options that are out of the money are merely a string of bids and offers, not actual trades. When an actual trade does appear, the price might be two hours old! When trading for the long term in futures options, the only "quotes" that are really needed are in the daily paper.

Rule 9: Buy options with at least 60 days of time value not more than three strikes from today's price. For example, when buying a cotton call option and today's price is $.66 per pound, don't buy any farther out than a $.69 call.

Rule 10: Enter using a price order "give up." Rather than buying a position in futures options at the market, obtain a current quote and use a price order. For example, if a bond call option last traded at 30, place the order to buy at 33 or better. Although this procedure gives up about $50, it offers a much better chance of entering the market than waiting for a setback to 30 and, in all probability, a much better fill than entering "at the market."

Rule 11: After entering the market establish a liquidation target and place it in the market as an open order. Lots of people like to watch how the market acts. In futures option buying this can be deadly. Once an option is bought, it is a wasting asset—something that *must* be sold or exercised before expiration. Otherwise, the entire investment will be lost. Many times, an experienced trader will buy two futures options and place an open order to sell one of them at double the entry price. In effect the second option is then free (except for commissions) and the trader is able to play with the remaining option.

Rule 12: When trading $7500 or more, usually buy two futures options at a time: one to sell at double the entry premium and one to keep for the pull.

Rule 13: Buy futures options when volatility is lower than 25 percent and sell out futures options (liquidate all positions) when volatility exceeds 65 percent.

Rule 14: The watched kettle never boils. Although it certainly is not a good idea to go on a six-week cruise to the Fiji Islands with a portfolio of expiring futures options and no liquidation instructions, options should not be watched too closely. The first day after putting on an options portfolio there may be a loss, since in futures option buying commissions are normally charged on entry. But the total risk is known upfront, and once liquidation with profit orders have been placed for at least half of the position, relax. The time remaining on the options before they expire is known.

Rule 15: When an option has 30 days left on it, get rid of it (the "30-day eviction notice"). This is the most conservative strategy. With 30 days of time value left, the option will repay at least part of the original premium. If the commodity still looks attractive for the big move, go back to the beginning and start over. If that market doesn't look good, look at another one.

Rule 16: Handling a loser (or a string of them) is never fun, but unless a trader is clairvoyant, losers will occur. If a trader has chosen to ignore the 30-day-eviction-notice rule and pursue a more aggressive strategy, he or she may find an expiration date fast approaching with the option still out of the money. One mechanical way to handle a loser that has been held longer than the 30-day eviction notice is to exit three days prior to expiration. An alternative strategy is to reevaluate the market and, if the side that was chosen still looks good for the big move, buy a new futures option with more time, while simultaneously selling the expiring option. For example, a March 330 wheat put that was bought for $.10 40 days ago may now be worth $.06 and has only 3 days to go. A May 320 wheat put is selling for $.08. You can pay $.02 more (and a new commission) and switch from the March 330 to the May 320.

Rule 17: Don't be afraid to let them expire. If rules 15 and 16 have been ignored because a big move is anticipated, don't be afraid to let an option expire worthless. The beauty of futures option buying is that mistakes do go away. But one of the experienced futures option buyer's biggest nightmares is not having an option expire worthless. It is, rather, recovering 30 to 50 percent of the premium by liquidating, only to have the futures option explode to the upside without having a position.

Rule 18: Follow the trend. Trend following is one of the major keys to success in the market. Over the years, large managed account portfolios have required increasingly larger amounts of margin commitments. Buying futures call options when a trend following buy signal is flashed and selling out the calls and buying puts when the sell signal is flashed is a very efficient way to speculate in the futures option markets for the long term.

Rule 19: Once a new trend has been established, use setbacks to buy options in harmony with the new trend.

Rule 20: Keep accurate records. Experienced traders keep three sheets: an *equity tracker*, which is the daily total equity in the account; a *position sheet*, which lists the current open trades; and the *closed trades to date*.

Equity tracker. There's no better way for a trader to know where he or she stands than simply to look at the bottom line. Remember, commissions are usually deducted when a trade is initiated in futures options (as opposed to being deducted at the end of a trade with futures contracts).

Position sheet. By knowing his or her current positions, a trader can be ready to add to the winners and kick the losers without digging through pounds of paper.

Closed trades to date. This helps a trader recall how much money was made on each option and analyze which markets have been traded most successfully. We all have more time than money. Keep good records!

Rule 21: Handle news and reports by buying a combination of puts and calls. For example, if a cattle report is due out this afternoon, one might buy both a call and a put close to the market (today's price). On tomorrow's close, when the outcome of the report is known and the market has accepted the news, the option that is not in harmony with the new market direction can be exited. If the report is neutral, both options should be exited.

Rule 22: Trade with your head, not your heart. An options portfolio should be perused every Friday. Trades that are older than 30 days and are not profitable should probably be eliminated, and trades whose premiums are lower than 50 percent of initial purchase price should probably be eliminated. Remember, recovered premium is found money that can be reinvested in better opportunities.

Every Monday, look for *one* new opportunity that meets the right criteria and place an order to buy. Remember, on Monday, futures options have just moved two unproductive days toward expiration, so as a rule they are worth *less* than they were on Friday.

Rule 23: Add more positions only to winning trades. Add to calls when today's futures price is higher than 20 days ago; add to puts when today's futures price is lower than 20 days ago.

Rule 24: Don't write futures options. Futures option writers are limited in profits to the total premium received, and are exposing themselves to unlimited liability. Even if a writer is right and makes small profits on nine out of ten trades, one big loser can literally wipe him or her out of the market.

Rule 25: As trades move in a favorable direction, options become more and more efficient, acting more and more like a "real" futures contract. As trades move in an unfavorable direction an option becomes less and less like a futures contract.

Summary

Options are often preferable to futures contracts when a trader wishes to be in a position to profit from major market moves. Options combine high leverage with known and limited risk. They allow a trader to be in a position in four or five different diversified markets with an account of under $10,000. They don't require a lot of watching, and they protect against margin calls, which provide staying power when a market moves against them.

A parting rule of thumb, when deciding whether to buy a futures contract or a call option, is to consider, "What would happen if this market moved three limit days for me? Three limit days against me?" In the move for me, the option could soon be almost like a futures contract for reward. In the move against me, the option can only lose my premium and commissions. Thus, the higher the risk of the futures position, the better candidate the trade is for an option buying strategy.

Figure 19-4

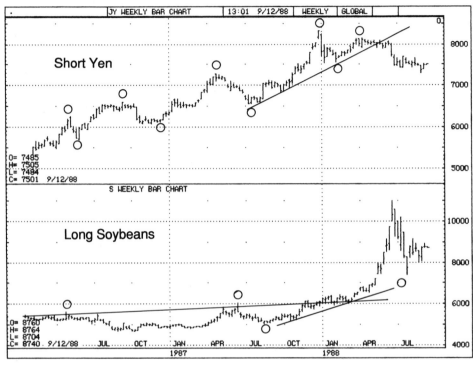

Source: Commodity Quote-Graphics TQ–20/20

Figure 19-5

Source: Commodity Quote-Graphics TQ–20/20

Figure 19-6

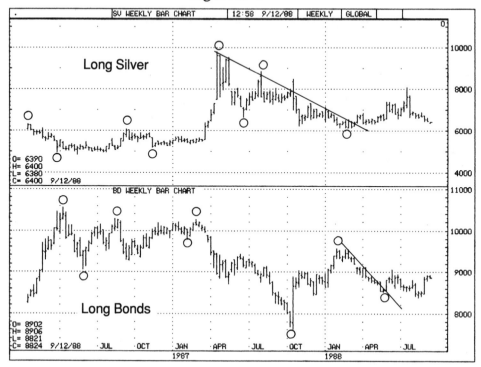

Source: Commodity Quote-Graphics TQ–20/20

Figure 19-7

USING A MOVING AVERAGE SYSTEM TO TRADE COMMODITY OPTIONS

MICHAEL CHISHOLM

■

■

MICHAEL CHISHOLM

Michael Chisholm is editor and publisher of the *Taurus Newsletter*, which has been published continuously since early 1976. In an independent poll of its readers taken by *Commodities Magazine* in December 1981, the *Taurus Newsletter* was voted "the best" and "number one." Mr. Chisholm also is the author of numerous books, including *Games Investors Play* and *The Taurus Method*. He has produced a 12-volume set of audiocassettes on commodity investing entitled *The Master Keys to Riches in Commodity Trading*. In addition, he has produced a 16-hour, eight-volume series of videocassettes on commodity trading called *The Market Master Seminar*. Besides being a frequent speaker at seminars and symposiums around the world, he has been active as a practicing psycho-therapist. His current areas of specialization include systems development for commodity futures and commodity options trading and research into the psychological facets of commodity and other forms of investing.

■

■ CHAPTER TWENTY ■

THERE ARE MANY SPECIFIC INSTANCES in which the risk/reward ratio seems more favorable for a futures position than an options position based upon perceived initial risk. In a great majority of potential trading situations, however, unless the option premiums are grossly overpriced, trading commodity options instead of their corresponding futures contracts offers a number of advantages and presents only one significant disadvantage.

The Advantage of Trading Options Versus Futures

For me, the most important advantage in trading commodity options is the absence of the need to use initial protective stops as they are commonly used in the futures market. Even though a well-constructed commodity options trading system will have rules for initial protective stops (i.e., there will be a predetermined point at which, if the option premium has decreased to a certain amount or by a certain percentage, the position will be liquidated), the possibility of being stopped out of a position because of volatile intraday market action is far less with options than it is with futures. Moreover, by being in an option position, the possibility of being hit by gap openings is also greatly minimized.

Another major advantage of trading commodity options as opposed to commodity futures is the absence of margin calls. In options trading the amount of money you pay initially for your option premium—assuming that you are an option purchaser and not an option seller—is all you will be required to pay regardless of which way the market moves. Therefore, your risk in an option position is clearly fixed and limited to the initial premium you pay, as long as you are buying and not selling options.

The major disadvantage to trading commodity options—at least when buying and not selling them—is the time decay factor, in which the trader pays a premium for the time value left in the option itself. By having a system that takes that factor into account as much as possible and by trading relatively nearby contract months, in which the time value of the premium is not as great, this disadvantage can be greatly minimized.

For all of these reasons, I am sold on commodity options trading—not for every trading occasion, of course, but certainly for the vast majority of potential commodity trades.

Why a System?

Because it can virtually eliminate the psychological element from the process, trading with a system—assuming it is a valid system to begin with—is the only way to win in the commodity futures or commodity options markets. Adopting a systems approach and following that system religiously makes it much less likely that the trader's underlying psychological nature will interfere with his trading.

More traders have gone bankrupt in the marketplace from the effects of their own psyches than from all other causes combined. Although a systems approach can virtually eliminate the trader's psyche from influencing his market success, a trader can still sabotage an otherwise sound systems trading approach by relying upon his own judgment or intuition to select which system trades to take and which ones to stay out of.

The techniques outlined in this chapter are basically sound when followed as described; I know of many traders who have made huge sums of money—as much as $500,000 in 10 days in a single market—by following just this methodology, or slight variations of it.

Key Elements

While it is true that many traders attempting to develop a system to trade commodity futures contracts or commodity options are well aware that they need a set of concrete rules in order to develop their system, it is also true that they frequently overlook one or more of the key elements of an effective trading system. I believe that the following seven key areas must be included in the construction of any trading system, for it to be successful:

1. Trend determination
2. Filtering techniques
3. Entering positions
4. Initial protective stop placement
5. Trailing protective stops
6. Liquidating positions
7. Re-entry or reversal methodology

Of the seven key areas, trend determination should be the most basic element of any systems approach to the marketplace. Simply put, trend determination involves some rule or set of rules that has predictive validity in determining whether prices are likely to move up, down or sideways. Depending upon the nature of the system being developed, this trend determination may be approached on any scale from an intraday basis to a very long-term, multiyear basis. For most commodity futures and commodity options systems, however, an intermediate-term approach is the one most frequently pursued by systems developers. For our purposes, we define an intermediate-term approach as one that results in trades which typically last from three to six weeks.

System rules for entering positions, whether for futures or options trading, should involve precise, mathematical, non-judgmental instructions, that determine exactly when a position should be initiated either from the perspective of time of entry or price level of entry. As with all of the key elements in systems trading, these entry rules should be tailored to the specific type of trading—short-term, intermediate-term, or long-range. The other five key elements of systems trading—filtering techniques, initial stops, trading stops, liquidating, and reversals—should also involve precise mathematical rules for each step of the system's process so that no possibility exists for judgment to interfere with the system's rules.

In addition to the seven key elements I have listed, other specific rules may be required in such areas of the trading process as contract month selection, pyramiding, reversals, and (in the case of commodity options trading) the determination of strike price and the amount of premium to be paid.

The Nuts and Bolts

Keeping in mind the above seven key elements of systems trading, what follows is a step-by-step presentation of a specific set of rules for trading the commodity options markets. As space permits, I will provide some personal observations on these rules. Although this system as presented has proven to be very successful, I nevertheless encourage you to remember that, as with all systems, it can be greatly improved upon either by altering some of the rules or by adding supplementary rules. Regardless of the individual modifications you might wish to make to the system, however, do not forget to follow the seven key system elements to make sure that no crucial component is overlooked. Modifications or back-checking on this sytem or an altered version of it can be quickly and easily accomplished with any good quote screen system or computer program of past historical data, many of which are available on the market.

Trend Determination

As mentioned earlier, trend determination is the single most important and basic element of any systems approach to the marketplace or, for that matter, any approach to the marketplace. While literally an infinite number of indicators can be used as trend determinants, ranging from the phases of the moon to complex logarithmic formulae, one of the most basic and most reliable trend determinants is still the use of moving averages and moving average crossovers. Obviously, the use of moving averages is neither a new nor an original concept. But it is a tried and proven approach to attacking the marketplace and one that is excellent for determining future market trends.

The length of the moving averages chosen for use in any system will be partially determined by whether the system designer is developing a short-term, intermediate-term or long-term approach to the markets. Ideally, moving average lengths could be optimized for each particular commodity or complex of commodities to reflect their individual personalities. I have found, however, that optimized moving averages vary for each commodity overtime. Furthermore, there probably is no such thing as a different optimized moving average for each commodity that would be valid over any extended period of time. In other words, such optimization would have to be carried on continually to reflect the changing volatility of the commodity involved. This is not practical for most traders.

For trading commodity options, my research has indicated that a 10-day and an 18-day simple moving average, based upon closing market prices, constitutes the best universal set of moving averages. While the 10-day and 18-day moving average combination does not work for all commodities all of the time, I have found that, over extended periods of time, it works as well as or better than any other moving average for most commodities. As can be seen in Figure 20-1, for example, when the 10-day and 18-day moving averages cross, there is a high probability that this crossover reflects at least an upcoming six-week- into-the-future change in trend for the Japanese yen.

A very simplified plan for trading commodity options could involve buying calls when the 10-day moving average crosses over the 18-day moving average to the up-side and buying puts when the 10-day moving average cuts through the 18-day moving average to the down-side. This approach by itself would work a high precentage of the time without any additional rules. By adding the other key elements of systems development, however, this rudimentary system can be greatly improved upon.

Filtering Techniques

The second key element in a systems approach is a filtering technique designed to reduce the number of false signals from the trend determination rule and/or to confirm the validity of the signals generated by that rule. Any number of filters can be used for this purpose, just as many different ways exist to establish the basic trend itself. Five of the most popular filters in use are the relative strength index, bullish consensus, volume, open interest, and stochastics.

Figure 20-1

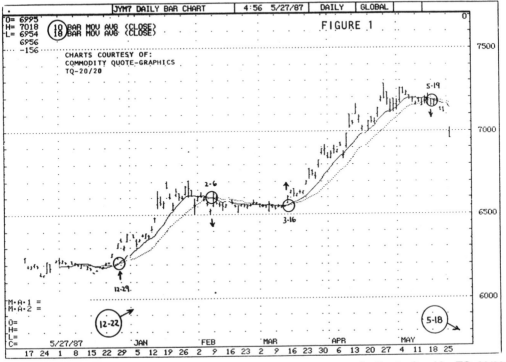

Source: Commodity Quote-Graphics TQ–20/20

The more sophisticated the system being developed, the more filters will be used to discriminate among basic signals developed from the trend determination rule. Of course, the more often you insert filtering rules into a particular system, the fewer trades you will make. In fact, it is not umcommon to see a system so overburdened with filters that it generates very few, if any, actual trades.

For my system development I have found that the simplest but best filter to use in conjunction with the 10-day and 18-day moving average crossover is a 14-bar slow smooth weekly stochastic. Looking at Figure 20-1, notice the two dates in circles at the bottom—12/22 and 5/18—with arrows pointing up for the first date and down for the second date. These dates and the directional arrows indicate changes in the direction of the 14-bar weekly stochastic. Also, you will notice that there are four moving average crossovers, which are circled and dated, with an arrow indicating the direction of the crossover. Note, too, that of these four crossovers, three are valid from the standpoint of offering good profit potential when trading either futures or options. The crossover dated 2/6, however, where the 10-day moving average moved down through the 18-day moving average, provided little if any potential for making profits from either a short futures position or, more important, the purchase of a put. The purpose of a filter, whether for this system or for one you may develop yourself, is to try to eliminate a false signal such as the one generated on 2/6. That is precisely where the weekly stochastic filter comes into play.

Figure 20-2 shows a weekly bar chart for the Japanese yen, giving not only the weekly 14-bar slow stochastic at the bottom of the chart but also, above that, the 10-week and 18-week moving average crossover points. Note that these weekly moving average crossovers occurred too late to be of much practical use as a trend determinant or as a filter, since prices generally had already moved substantially by the time the crossovers occurred.

Figure 20-2

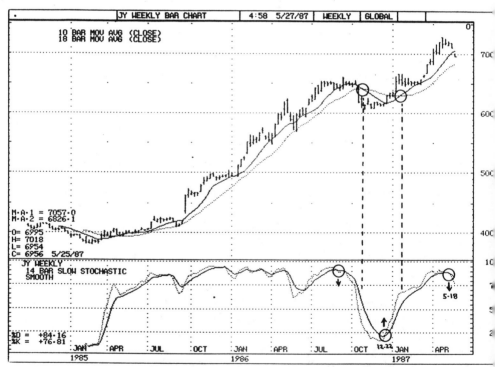

Source: Commodity Quote-Graphics TQ–20/2

At the bottom of the chart, however, where the stochastic crossovers are circled, you can see that the changes in the weekly stochastic—the %K and %D crossovers up or down—were in fact excellent predictors of upcoming changes in trend. Of course, this weekly stochastic indicator—like all others—is not infallible, as you can see from the several false signals it generated during the first quarter of 1986. This occurs sometimes in strongly moving bear or bull markets. The weekly stochastic crossover, however, is sufficiently reliable to make it a valuable tool as a filter or even as a trend determinant by itself. In this particular system, I have opted in favor of the moving average crossover on the daily charts for the trend determinant and the weekly stochastic crossover on the weekly charts for the filter. An alternative system could just as readily be devised, with somewhat different parameters, by reversing this procedure. With access to quote screen service, using a weekly stochastic indicator in either fashion is relatively easy.

Entering Positions

Positions are entered when both the trend determinant (moving average crossover) and the filter (weekly stochastic indicator) point in the same direction. In actual practice, entry is made the day after the moving average crossover occurs in the direction of the weekly stochastic. Generally, the weekly stochastic already will have turned before the crossover occurs. If the crossover occurs in opposition to the weekly stochastic, however, followed by the weekly stochastic turning in the direction of the crossover, positions are initiated the day after the weekly stochastic crosses over.

In Figure 20-3 (cotton) the weekly stochastic crossed over on 1/5. The 10-day and 18-day moving averages were still pointing up, but then proceeded to cross over on 1/16. The next day—1/17— put positions should have been purchased.

On the next moving average crossover—3/12—the 10-day moving average crossed to the up-side, but the weekly stochastic was still pointing down. According to our system rules, we would purchase neither a call nor a put at this crossover, because the moving averages were pointing in one direction and the weekly stochastic was pointing in the other.

On 4/6 the weekly stochastic turned to the up-side and, at that point, the moving averages were pointing up. Hence, a call would have been purchased. On 4/9, however, the moving averages turned back down. Depending upon how the system rules were structured, either the call would be liquidated or, since the moving average crossover was so minimal, it might have been held. In either case, the moving averages turned back up on 4/11. If the previous calls purchased on 4/6 had not been held, new calls would be purchased on 4/11. It is easy to see from Figure 20-3 that the ensuing nearly $ .20 rise in prices would have unqualifiedly been a good position, with a potential profit of as much as $10,000 per contract depending upon where the trader liquidated his calls.

The rule for entering positions is that positions are established the day after the moving average crossover occurs, if this crossover is in the direction of the weekly stochastic. Alternately, puts or calls may be purchased the day

Figure 20-3

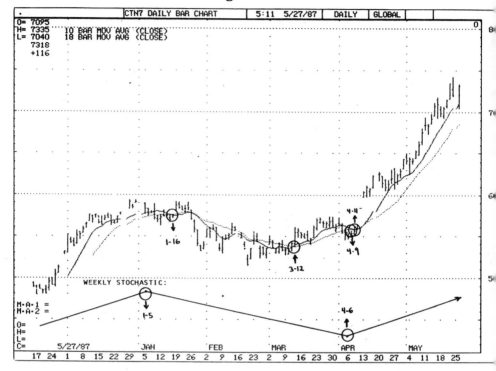

Source: Commodity Quote-Graphics TQ–20

after the weekly stochastic crosses over, if that crossover is in the same direction as the 10-day and 18-day moving averages.

Stop Placement

I mentioned in reference to Figure 20-3 that the calls purchased on 4/6 (when the weekly stochastic indicator turned up) may have been liquidated on 4/9 when the moving averages turned back down, depending upon the rules of the system. This next rule clearly determines whether a position would be liquidated under such circumstances. In effect, what we will do is to establish a protective stop. This stop-loss will be established at 50 percent of the premium paid for the option. If on 4/6 (when the cotton call was purchased) the option premium was 2.00, for example, and that premium had decreased in value by 50 percent—in this case to 1.00—we would immediately liquidate the position, albeit at a loss. An alternative approach would be to disregard this 50-percent reduction-in-premium rule and instead liquidate upon the moving average crossing back over. My research so far indicates, however, that the 50-percent reduction-in-premium rule works better statistically over a long period of time.

The rationale behind this 50-percent reduction-in-premium rule (an individual trader, depending upon his degree of conservatism or aggressiveness, may change the reduction to 30 percent, or 70 percent, or some other figure) is to prevent the entire loss of premium. Options trading particularly lends itself to holding onto positions until they become worthless, because in the minds of most traders, the amount paid as premium can be lost completely without adversely affecting their trading program. This is a fallacious belief. If part of the premium cost can be saved on each losing position, the trader's over-all profit picture will be enhanced.

Liquidating Positions

Regarding the liquidation (or exiting) of positions, I offer three alternative rules, the choice of which depends upon the individual trader's philosophy of approaching the markets: a short-term aggressive approach, an intermediate-range moderate approach, or a long-term conservative approach. All three approaches work and they work well. But since I believe that it is important to have a system tailored to one's own trading philosophy, I offer three different liquidation rules. The short-term aggressive rule calls for liquidating positions the day after a close through a 10-day moving average in the opposite direction. In other words, if you are holding a call and futures prices for that particular contract month close below the 10-day moving average you would liquidate your call position the next day.

With the intermediate-term moderate approach, the rule calls for liquidating positions the day after a close through the 18-day moving average. Thus, if you are holding calls, and futures prices for that contract month close below the 18-day moving average, you liquidate your calls the next day.

The long-term conservative approach calls for liquidating positions the day after the moving averages cross over in the direction opposite to that of the position you are holding (or when the weekly stochastic turns in the direction opposite to the position that you are holding). Thus, if you are holding call positions and the weekly stochastic continues to point up, you liquidate your calls the day after the 10-day moving average crosses through and below the 18-day moving average.

Re-enty or Reversal Methodology

Re-entering an option position is discretionary using this system, since the percentage return and the percentage success rate is lower than for the establishment of the original position itself. Re-entering positions, of course, would apply only to the short-term and intermediate-term approaches, because with the long-term strategy, market re-entry is synonomous with the basic rule for establishing original positions.

The re-entry approach that I have found to work best with both short-term or intermediate-term liquidation rules is the purchase of a new position on a close back through the 10-day moving average, in the direction of the original position. In other words, if the weekly stochastic is pointing up and the 10-day and 18-day moving averages are pointing up, and you have liquidated your call positions because prices have closed either below the 10-day moving average (short-term liquidation rule) or through the 18-day moving average (intermediate-term liquidation rule), new calls should be established if futures prices close back up through the 10-day moving average.

Looking at Figure 20-4, our short-term liquidation rule would have demanded liquidation of calls on 4/21, the day after prices closed below the

Figure 20-4

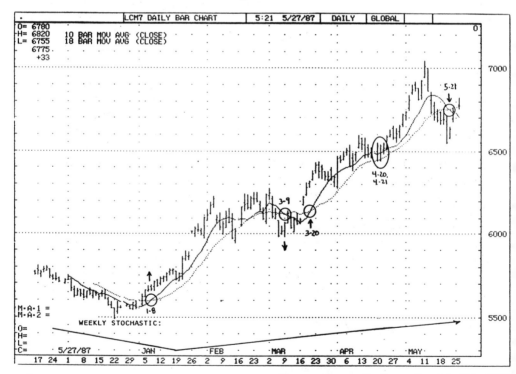

Source: Commodity Quote-Graphics TQ–20/20

10-day moving average (prices did not close below the 18-day moving average). Since on 4/21 prices closed back above the 10-day moving average, however, and since the weekly stochastic was still pointing up, new calls would have been purchased immediately. Had the price action on 4/20 caused a close below the 18-day moving average (which it did not), then intermediate-term positions also would have been liquidated on 4/21. In both cases—whether trading short-term or intermediate-term—new calls would have been purchased on 4/22.

Pyramiding with Options

Pyramiding involves adding more contracts as a move progresses prior to liquidation of the original contract. From the rules just presented, I have found that pyramiding works best only when using the long-term liquidation rule: liquidating only on a moving average or weekly stochastic crossover in the direction opposite to the position held.

For pyramiding, this rule is limited to adding another position on a close through the 10-day moving average in the direction opposite to the position held. In other words, if you are holding a call position and prices close below the 10-day moving average (if they also close below the 18-day moving average, the rule is the same), you add another call position immediately after prices close back up through the 10-day moving average. In Figure 20-5, two such examples are circled in ovals. In early April, prices closed below the 18-day moving average and the next day closed above both the 18-day and the 10-day moving average. Our pyramiding rule would suggest adding another call the day following the close back up through the 10-day moving average. Also, on 5/11 prices closed below the 10-day moving average and remained there for two more days before closing back up through the 10-day moving average on 5/14. Using our pyramiding rule we would add another call the day after—on 5/15. In Figure 20-5, liquidation of all of these positions would occur on 5/18 when the weekly stochastic (shown at the bottom of Figure 20-5) turned back down, thus preserving more profits than would waiting for the moving average crossover to take place, which occurred later on 5/26.

Contract Month Selection

Because of the time decay of option premiums, I have found that generally it is better not to use distant contract months for trading by these system rules. Therefore, if you are using the short-term and intermediate-term approach,

Figure 20-5

Source: Commodity Quote-Graphics TQ–20/2

the rule for contract month selection is to enter a position in the contract
month that is closest to having at least 45 days left before expiration. When
trading the long-term liquidation rule, use the contract month that is closest
to having at least 90 days left until expiration.

A word of caution about expiration dates: since they are frequently different from futures contract dates, check with your broker and/or the exchange to make certain that you have the correct expiration date listed for
the option you are holding.

Strike Price Determination

In addition to having the correct contract month in which to trade, it is also
important to have the optimum strike price. While there are many sophisticated methods of determining strike price/premium valuations to detect undervalued and overvalued premiums, a simple rule of thumb that seems to
work as well as the more complicated methodologies is to purchase the
strike price that is just out-of-the-money.

Looking back at Figure 20-5, on 2/19 when the moving averages turned up (and the weekly stochastic was already pointing up), prices closed above 152.50 and below 155.00. The next strike price—the one just out-of-the-money—would be 155.00. Hence, the trader would purchase a June 155.00 call on 2/20, assuming that the June contract month met the contract month selection rule requirements.

The opposite procedure applies when purchasing a put: the strike price is determined by the next available strike price below the closing price on the day the signal is given.

Conclusion

This chapter has provided the basic elements, in a very simplified fashion, for constructing a commodity options (or futures) trading system. An actual example of such a system was presented using moving averages as a trend determinant, stochastics as a filter, and other rules to complete the system. While the system as presented may appear overly simple, I would like to emphasize that frequently the simplest approaches to the marketplace are the ones that work the best.

PARTICIPATING IN THE MARKETS WITH THE MASTERS

■

■ SECTION FOUR ■

PROFESSIONALLY MANAGED FUTURES ACCOUNTS comprise a fast-growing segment of the futures industry—and one that contributes heavily to the steady increase in trading volume on futures exchanges worldwide. A managed account can provide an excellent alternative to trading one's own account, or an avenue to diversification for the active trader. Jim Schlifke provides guidelines for choosing an account manager, and offers some cautionary advice for investing funds and pools.

An additional alternative to developing a sophisticated trading system is to subscribe to a professional advisory service. With so many available, however, it becomes difficult to choose just the right one. Bruce Babcock explains just how to do it, and how best to use an advisory once one has been selected.

361

ADVISORY SERVICES: HOW TO USE THEM, HOW TO CHOOSE THEM

BRUCE BABCOCK

■

BRUCE BABCOCK

Bruce Babcock grew up in New York State and attended Yale University and the University of California at Berkeley. He received his bachelor's degree in business administration as well as a law degree. His career as a federal prosecutor included the successful prosecution of Manson family member Sandra Good in connection with the conspiracy to assassinate President Ford. Mr. Babcock was also a part-time law professor for thirteen years.

In 1979, he left his law office to concentrate on commodity trading. He has written six commodity trading books. The most recent were *The Dow Jones-Irwin Guide to Trading Systems* and *Trendiness in the Futures Markets*. He is a co-author of *Trading Strategies* and has had numerous articles published in *Futures* magazine and *Technical Analysis of Stocks and Commodities*.

In April 1983, he started publishing *Commodity Traders Consumer Report*. This bimonthly newsletter tracks the performance of the top commodity advisory services and has made a significant impact on the industry. Each issue is a complete reference guide to commodity trading information. He also publishes *Major Moves*, a long-term, special-situation advisory letter.

Mr. Babcock has also designed numerous computer software programs for traders, including twenty-two different optimizable trading system programs, three unique trading tools and a data management program for using continuous contracts.

Mr. Babcock's work has been written about in *The Wall Street Journal, Barron's, Forbes* and *Money* magazine, among others. He has appeared many times on the Financial News Network. He is an occasional seminar sponsor and speaker.

An active commodity trader since 1975, Mr. Babcock continues to trade the markets for his own account. You can request a catalog or write to him in care of Commodity Traders Consumer Report, 1731 Howe Avenue, Suite 149, Sacramento, CA 95825. (800) 999-CTCR.

■ CHAPTER TWENTY-ONE ■

O
NE OF THE BIGGEST IMPEDIMENTS TO SUCCESS in commodity trading comes from a most unlikely source—expert opinion. Almost everyone who tries commodity trading has achieved some measure of success in another field. That's where they accumulated the capital they want to increase. People learn quickly to use experts as a shortcut to knowledge.

In Napoleon Hill's classic book, *Think and Grow Rich*, Hill emphasizes the importance of acquiring specialized knowledge: "The accumulation of great fortunes calls for power, and power is specialized knowledge, but that knowledge does not necessarily have to be in the possession of the man who accumulates the fortune." The novice becomes obsessed with predicting future market action, and what more reasonable way is there to decide which way the markets are going than to consult a market expert? There is no shortage of them.

It is no wonder commodity traders become advisory service junkies. They subscribe to numerous services—as many as they can afford. If one expert opinion is valuable, then ten or twelve should be that much more valuable. For most people this kind of advisory glut is counterproductive. The truth is that commodity experts don't know where the markets are going any more than you do. When they make predictions, they are only guessing. (But please don't tell any of them I said so.) They do it because people like to read predictions, and the more unlikely the better.

Using Advisory Services

This is not to say that you should not subscribe to any advisory services. Depending on your style of trading, advisory services may be very helpful. The key is knowing how to use them. There are at least three distinct ways to use advisory services correctly: (1) like a managed account, (2) for information, or (3) for opinions.

For a beginning trader or one with no confidence in his or her own trading ability, there is nothing wrong with using one or more advisory services like a managed account. In fact, even for an experienced trader, it may be one of the most reliable ways to achieve consistent profits. This approach has some definite advantages over a traditional managed account. You will not need as large an account. It is an unusual commodity trading advisor who will accept even $25,000 these days. Most have a minimum of $50,000 and up. With your own account, you stay closer to the action and can learn more from what happens. You can choose your own broker. The overhead costs of using an advisory service will be lower. The subscription price will be far less than the usual management fee, and there is no incentive fee to chew into profits. Finally, the profit potential of using an advisory service is considerably higher, although the risk may be higher as well. It depends on what service you choose to follow and how well you follow it.

To use an advisory service like a managed account, find one with a trading style you like and that is appropriate for your account size. Then take every trading signal or every trading signal for a specific portfolio of commodities. Your performance should match the advisor's. If you have chosen the service well, you should make money in the long run.

You may be wondering why, if I say that commodity advisors are only guessing when they make market predictions, I still advise following their recommendations. The answer is that their real expertise is not in predicting the markets but in trading the markets. There is a big difference. Predicting only involves knowing where the market will go in the future. Trading involves a complete plan for choosing trades and entering and exiting the positions. It is the complete implementation of the so-well-known, but so-poorly adhered-to, trade-with-the-trend, cut-losses-short and let-profits-run philosophy. Trading success on any one position or in the short-term is mostly luck. Skill comes to the fore in the long-term profitability of an overall trading plan. Therefore, when the "Know-It-All Precious Metals Market Letter" says to buy gold because it is going to move up strongly in the next two weeks, they are only making an educated guess that may or may not work out. However, if they are gold trading experts with a proven track record, you have a good chance of making money by following all their specific gold recommendations for the next year.

May I humbly suggest that the best possible source for information on the trading style and performance of advisory services is my own *Commodity Traders Consumer Report*, which follows the trading recommendations of 26 of the top commodity futures advisory services. Over the last six years, *CTCR* has proven that commodity advisory services are far more effective than most people think. When *CTCR* first started publishing, a subscriber wrote in to predict that not a single service would be able to show a profit over a one-year period. Boy, was he wrong! While a majority have had net losses, between eight and 14 services out of the 26 that *CTCR* tracks have been profitable every year, even after deducting $100 per trade for slippage and commissions. The top performers have made returns of well over 100 percent on the required margin to follow their trades. There has also been consistency of performance from year to year. For example, all but two of 1986's top ten services in profit per trade were in the top 15 in 1987. (I am not including one top-five service that ceased publishing after 1986.) Thus, even a successful trader may want to diversify a part of his portfolio by incorporating the recommendations of one or more successful advisory services.

Here is an example of using an advisory service like a managed account. If, in 1987, you had traded hypothetically all the recommendations of 1986's top-rated service in net equity increase as reported by *Commodity Traders Consumer Report*, your equity would have increased by approximately $77,000 on 200 trades (after deducting $100 from all trades for slippage and commissions). The service, by the way, was the *DeMark Futures Forecast*, published by Tom DeMark.

Inexperienced traders want to follow an advisory service and take only the best recommendations. They want the advisor to rate his recommendations by their probability of success. Some advisors accede to this subscriber request and try to classify recommendations. The reality is, however, that good traders never know in advance which of their trades will work out. They admit that most often the trades that they like the best usually turn into losses, while the ones in which they have the least confidence became the biggest winners. If the advisor himself does not know which of his recommendations are most likely to succeed, you, the subscriber, are certainly not in a position to cherry-pick the best.

You may even get very sophisticated by following a different advisor for each market you trade. The key is not to substitute your judgment for a mechanical method of deciding which recommendations to follow. Once you begin doing that, you are not following the expert's advice, you are using the expert to confirm your own opinions. For most people, that is suicidal. For example, your research might tell you that Advisory Service A is excellent on stock indexes, Advisory Service B is exceptional on T-bonds, and Advisory Service C is the best on gold. Your plan might be to take all of A's recommendations in stock indexes, B's on T-bonds, and C's in gold, while ignoring all other recommendations made by the three services.

If you are going to use an advisory service like a managed account and not second-guess the recommendations, it is probably a good idea to have a broker call the hotline and place the trades for you. This will save you some work and prevent any possibility of your screening the trades. You can read the letters and understand the reasons for the trades, but you will not be in a position to second-guess the advisor. That way, your performance should be identical to the advisor's. If your account is large enough, you may decide to follow several advisors at once for diversification.

Most advisory service subscribers make the natural mistake of waiting for the advisor to have a good winning period before starting to follow his trades. That is the worst time to start. Since everyone has winning and losing streaks, it is better to start following an effective advisor after several losing months. This is difficult psychologically but worth the effort. You may even want to consider suspending trading with an advisor after an especially profitable run. I did some extensive research on mechanical ways to start and stop trading in an effort to smooth the bumps in the equity curve. The results and recommendations are available in a publication called *Equity Curve Conqueror.*

Just as one who enters a trade must have a preset point to exit and cut losses, one who starts following the recommendations of an advisory service should have a set point where he will cease trading with that advisor. Since every successful advisor has periods of ineffectiveness that may last for months, you must be prepared to live with some adversity. It is impossible to know in advance when a normal drawdown marks instead the beginning of an extended losing period. You can examine the advisor's historical record to see just how awful his bad periods have been. On the basis of those figures and your own threshold of pain, you should set a cut-off point. If your losses reach that point, stop trading with that advisor, at least until he has demonstrated that he is once again trading profitably. Be sure to set a realistic cut-off point. Otherwise, you will be constantly bouncing from one advisor to another. In addition, you will probably be abandoning an advisor just before his next winning period begins.

The second correct way to use advisory services is to extract information they provide. You must distinguish carefully between facts and opinions. Advisory services can be an excellent source of all kinds of technical and fundamental information that you can use to execute your trading plan.

A good example is Jake Bernstein's *MBH Weekly Letter.* It has very complete information on cycles and seasonal patterns. Jack has been researching the markets for over 15 years. He arrives at his office every morning at 4:00 A.M. to begin his analytic routine. He conducts extensive historical research with a very expensive computer. If you are going to include cycles and seasonal patterns in your trading plan, why not use the benefit of Jake's work for yourself by getting the figures from his letter. That way you can get up at a reasonable hour. If you want to follow the Elliott Wave Theory in analyzing market structure, why not take advantage of the world's most respected authority on the subject by subscribing to Robert Prechter's *The Elliott Wave Theorist.* Although Prechter is not always right about the market, it is unlikely that your Elliott Wave analysis will be better.

Almost all newsletters have some kind of specialized information that you may be able to use in your trading plan. This does not mean you should subscribe to 20 letters and take a little bit out of each one. That kind of plan would be too complicated. There is a limit to how much analysis can contribute. The trader who looks at 100 indicators will not necessarily do better than one who looks at only a few. Create a simple plan, and then take advantage of those newsletters that can provide information to help you execute it.

You can also employ advisory services to find general ideas that will be the starting point of your own research and analysis. This is the third way to use advisory services—as a source of opinions about future market moves. Since advisors' individual opinions are probably not much better than your own, it is important that you do not act solely on the basis of someone else's opinion. Opinions supported by facts can be useful, however, as a starting point for your own research. You should have a specific and written plan before you do any trading at all. You should know precisely and in advance the conditions required for entering and exiting a trade. You can read advisory services for thoughts about which markets may be appropriate to watch for implementation of your plan. Or you may get an idea of a market that has extra-special profit potential. You could then create a plan for trading that market based on indicators or methods your research has found to be successful in previous trading situations. When you are picking only a few of an advisor's recommendations, do not expect the performance of those few to match the advisor's overall performance.

I have given you three distinct approaches for using advisory services as an adjunct to a successful trading plan. Most people, however, do none of these things. They use advisory services to confirm and support their own ideas. They get a trading idea and immediately start looking for all the support they can find from "the experts." The more the merrier. What invariably happens is that they take the trades that have the most expert support. Those end up mostly losers. They pass the trades where the experts have the opposite opinion. Those are the winners. Most of the time there are experts on both sides. The trader then rationalizes why the ones who agree with him are probably right. He still loses.

The reason the trades with so much expert support fail is that the theory of contrary opinion is at work. When too many people are bullish, most traders have already bought and the market is due for a correction. When too many people are bearish, most traders have already sold, and the market will probably soon react upward. To be successful, a trader must become comfortable going against the crowd. This means going against the opinions of popular experts just as much as going against what you perceive to be the majority opinion of the crowd.

Choosing an Advisory Service

If you are going to use an advisory service's recommendations, you should investigate its track record. While the popular view would be that you should go back for many years, I'm not sure more than a few years are necessarily relevant unless the record is consistent with recent performance. Consider this example:

Two advisors' five-year records are excellent. Advisor X made very good money for the first three years and has lost money for the last two. Advisor Y made losses for the first three years but has done very well for the last two. Which would you prefer? Suppose Advisor Y's overall five-year record was far inferior to Advisor X's. Wouldn't you still prefer Advisor Y because of his outstanding performance during the last two years? He may have changed his trading approach two years ago.

Like beauty, good trading performance is in the eye of the beholder. Reasonable traders looking at the same evidence may not always agree on who the best performer is. Even more important than finding the service with the best track record is finding an effective one that matches your trading style and your account size. The most effective service may trade a large, diversified account, use large stops, and trade markets with large margins. If you have a small account, like to use small stops, and are afraid to trade coffee and the S&P, how are you going to be able to simulate that advisor's superior performance in your account? Remember Tom DeMark, the top-rated 1986 advisor who made $77,000 in 1987? You would probably have needed about $75,000 in your account to trade comfortably all his recommendations in the portfolio followed by *CTCR*. If you had a smaller account, it is not likely you would have duplicated the overall return by selecting fewer recommendations. The neophyte assumes he will just pick the small-market recommendations that he feels comfortable trading and still get the same return on his small account. It seldom works out that way. That is why a majority of subscribers to a profitable advisory service are probably still losing money. One way to extend the diversification in a small account and follow a more active advisor is to trade the smaller-sized contracts available on the Mid-America Exchange.

Total profits are meaningless if the advisor's trading is inconsistent with your trading style. You must feel comfortable with the recommendations if you are going to follow them consistently. In addition to overall profits, you should also consider an advisory service's frequency of trading, the average size of its stops, percentage accuracy if that is important to you, trading method—technical or fundamental, and explanation of trades (is it sufficiently detailed to satisfy you?). Examine whether the service is making profits in the markets you will be trading. You should not try to follow an advisor who made most of his money in silver and feeder cattle if you would never trade those markets.

If you are going to use a service for specific trading recommendations, be sure the advice is unhedged. Being told to "buy dips" or "buy one contract in the 80.00-82.00 area" is worthless unless you are doing your own thinking anyway. Be suspicious of a track record for a service with this kind of hedged advice. Require that any track record be based on fair executions that a subscriber could actually expect to achieve.

Track records published by the services themselves are frequently deficient in these areas.

Evaluating Advisory Service Performance

In order to use an advisory service to its fullest advantage, you must understand yourself and your trading methods. You must also decide what you want from an advisory service. The best way to see what any service can add to your trading arsenal is to take a trail subscription or obtain a sample issue. Most newsletters have an inexpensive trial subscription or will send a free sample. Remember, you are looking for an effective service that matches your trading style and account size rather than the very best performer. You are more likely to simulate the performance of a compatible service.

In order to help its subscribers evaluate trading effectiveness, *Commodity Traders Consumer Report* monitors 26 of the top advisory services. It is a diversified group representing different account sizes and many different trading styles and approaches. The composition changes periodically as new services are added and old ones dropped. The *CTCR* staff reads the letters, calls the hotlines and then paper trades the recommendations using prices published in the Wall Street Journal and according to the rules described in each *CTCR* issue. They try to come as close as possible to the results a trader could expect to achieve if he were actually following the recommendations. For instance, in executing orders, they take account of gaps on the opening and lock-limit moves.

CTCR reports on overall performance in fifteen different statistical categories and three distinct time periods in each issue. The time periods are the last two months, the last six months, and the last twelve months. It also identifies in each issue the top five performers for the current year and the previous year in "the Big Three"—stock indexes, interest-rate futures, and gold. This coverage helps subscribers make specific choices in those areas. *CTCR* also has periodic extended coverage of performance in other individual markets. Back issues to April 1983 are available to subscribers who wish to make a longer-term evaluation. Each January issue covers the entire previous year. Subscribers may also obtain detailed compilations of all the individual trades of a particular advisor or time period for closer examination and analysis.

If you are going to use an advisory service for purposes other than following its specific recommendations, previous trading results may not be important. However, if past trading effectiveness is important to you, *CTCR* provides a wealth of information in the centerfold (17 x 11 inches) performance table that appears in each issue. Here are some of the statistical performance categories with comments about how you may use them to evaluate trading effectiveness.

Number of Closed Trades. This is useful to determine how active the advisor is. Some people are compulsive traders who like lots of action. They may even be more interested in action than profits. Others feel better trading once a week or even less. You should be able to find an effective service to accommodate your preference.

Percentage of Profitable Trades. A high winning percentage may be important to your ego, but it is not necessary for profitable trading. Even the best performers are usually right less than 50 percent of the time. Some have had excellent success with less than 40 percent winners. However, since most traders do feel uncomfortable taking losses, a high winning percentage may help you stay with your plan.

Average Profit on Profitable Trades/Average Loss on Losing Trades. The average profitable trade can give you insight into an advisor's trading philosophy. Does he take quick profits or shoot for bigger moves? The average losing trade shows you how quickly the advisor cuts his losses. Average profit should be substantially greater than average loss unless an advisor's winning percentage is far above 50 percent.

Best and Worst Trades. Sometimes results may be skewed by one especially good or bad trade. Compare these numbers with overall profit. The best trade shows how far the advisor is willing to let profits run. The worst trade gives an indication of your individual-trade risk in following the advisor.

Largest Drawdown in Monthly Net Gain. This important number gives an indication of the advisor's negative equity swings. Most of the time for profitable services the drawdown is roughly proportional to the total profit. By that I mean that to achieve larger profits, a trader must be willing to endure larger drawdowns. However, all other things being equal, it is obviously better to have lower drawdowns. All effective commodity trading methods undergo drawdowns equal to at least 25 percent of the account sooner or later. These negative periods are an unfortunate fact of futures trading life. If you can't accept them, you should not trade in the first place.

Net Profit or Loss on Closed Trades. You must evaluate profitability in conjunction with the number of trades involved and the margin used. Net profit per trade is a better yardstick to compare trading effectiveness between one advisor and another. The more trades recorded and the longer the time period covered, the greater is the statistical validity of the results. That means they are more likely to repeat in the future.

Minimum Margin Necessary for All Trades. This is the total minimum exchange margin required to initiate the largest trade portfolio in effect at any one time during the period. It is intended to give only a rough idea of how large an account would be necessary to follow the recommendations of a particular service. In reality, a trader should have considerably more in his account to cushion any string of losses. Also, margins vary from broker to broker. If you plan to take all trades a service recommends, I recommend having an account at least twice as large as the necessary minimum margin.

Return on Reasonable Margin. This is the change in equity (net gain or loss) for the past twelve months divided by twice the maximum initial margin required. *CTCR* assumes a trader should have about twice the margin of the advisor's largest portfolio in his account to allow for drawdowns.

While no one of these statistics standing alone can fairly evaluate an advisor's trading record, in combination they give a revealing picture of trading style and effectiveness. Careful analysis of these numbers will result in the proper choice of the best services for you. If you choose and use your advisory services wisely, they can be of great assistance in your pursuit of commodity trading profits. Good luck!

COMMODITY POOLS, SELF-DIRECTED ACCOUNTS AND MANAGED ACCOUNTS

JAMES S. SCHLIFKE

■

JAMES SCHLIFKE

James Schlifke graduated from the University of Illinois (Urbana) in 1970 with a degree in General Engineering and in 1973 with a Law Degree. He is licensed as a patent attorney with the U.S. Patent Office. A former member of the IMM and IOM divisions of the Chicago Mercantile Exchange, as well as a member of the Chicago Board Options Exchange, Mr. Schlifke has been engaged in the practice of commodities and securities law since 1977. Registered with both the NASD and NFA, he has passed series 3 (commodity representative), 4 (securities registered options principal), 5 (securities debt options principal), 7 (securities general sales representative) and 24 (general securities principal). Mr. Schlifke has served on two panels for the Chicago-Kent Commodity Law Institute, and has been employed as general counsel and in executive positions at several brokerage firms. At the present time he is general counsel and Senior Vice President of Robbins Trading Company.

▪ CHAPTER TWENTY-TWO ▪

COMMODITY SPECULATORS are faced with a myriad of choices for their investment dollars. Many will choose a self-directed speculative account, a professionally managed account, or participation in a commodity pool. All provide the investor with unique advantages and disadvantages. The selection of a commodity investment will, hopefully, be profitable for the investor—at least from an experiential standpoint if not financially. By paying attention to a few details and making an educated decision, you can improve the likelihood that a venture into commodity speculation will be fruitful.

Self-Directed Accounts

The self-directed account provides sophisticated and experienced investors, as well as commodity professionals, with the opportunity to call their own shots. Such accounts may be obtained at either a full-service or discount firm. The self-directed account allows the investor to make his or her own trading decisions, while a managed account or pool arrangement does not provide for input by the investor. In opening a self-directed account, an investor has the choice of selecting a discount or full-service firm.

The discount firm should be your choice for a self-directed account only if you can meet several rather important criteria. You must subscribe to a data service that can provide you with commmodity and, preferably, news quotations throughout the hours of trading. Without such services, a trader would be trading blind. Discount houses do not want to spend the time providing callers with information about the markets. They want to get your order and get you off the phone. In addition, you should be a very experienced trader before you elect this route. The phone clerks at the discount house will not be willing to provide you with advice about timing or the types of orders that may be available. The person answering the phone may not even be qualified to provide you with such information.

Full-service firms, on the other hand, will provide varying levels of market information and trading advice. Their information, of course, is only as good as the broker who handles your account. Ideally, the broker will play devil's advocate from time to time to counteract the trade impulse that affects some traders all too frequently. If the full-service broker claims each time you call him that he has found the trade that is "just right for you," avoid him like the plague. Trading opportunities do not appear every trading day except under very unusual circumstances. I am not suggesting that those managers with sophisticated trading systems may not get daily or possibly even hourly signals, but I would proceed very cautiously with any registered representative (RR or rep) who finds trades to recommend on a daily basis (whether suggested by his or her own research and trading system, or the firm's) yet has not offered to show you a track record that meets Commodity Futures Trading Commission (CFTC) requirements.

Look for an account executive who is willing to spend some time with you and is able to keep you abreast of what is occurring on the trading floor and what is coming across the wire-service news tapes as well. If you favor agriculturals, find a registered representative who is knowledgeable about crop reports and weather. If you are interested in the financials, then he or she should be knowledgeable about the money supply, the yield curve, and when the next GNP number is about to be released (just to name a few).

You should also realize that your broker will be willing to spend more or less time with you depending upon the amount of money in your account. It is obvious that a broker will want to spend more time with his $100,000 accounts than with his $5,000 accounts. The ideal rep for a trader is one who provides a counterpoint to his trading ideas. Since a rep's compensation is usually tied to the commissions generated by the customer's trading, over-trading or "churning" becomes a very real possibility. If you are a gambler, look for a broker who is inclined to put on the brakes. If you are conservative, seek a rep who will make occasional trading suggestions. Don't be afraid to ask for references of other traders the broker has handled.

All traders should seek brokers who are responsive and carefully follow instructions. Never trust a broker who says he put on a trade for you without asking in advance (for a nonmanaged account) because he "didn't want to miss it." Also note that there is rarely a good excuse for failing to follow your specific instructions. If he does fail to follow them, it is your right to reject the trade. You simply tell him to remove the trade from your account and to replace any lost funds. If he refuses, demand to speak to his supervisor and don't take no for an answer. If the unauthorized trade isn't deleted from your account in a matter of several days call the CFTC in Washington, D.C. (1-202-254-3067) or the NFA in Chicago (1-312-781-1300). Tell the CFTC you want to file a reparations complaint or tell the NFA you want to file an arbitration against the broker.

The exchanges on which the trades occurred also provide arbitration forums, although I would recommend staying with the NFA or CFTC. These proceedings cost a few dollars to file. Reparations is $100 or less if your claim is $10,000 or less and $200 if it exceeds $10,000. NFA arbitration has a similar fee schedule, except that the maximum fee is $200 plus one percent of the amount claimed in excess of $15,000. You may be entitled to an oral hearing depending on the amount of your claim and where you file. You need not be represented by counsel in either forum, and these two proceedings both tend to give the customer an excellent opportunity to obtain a return of money wrongfully taken.

Managed Accounts

Managed commodity accounts are ordinarily offered by commodity trading advisors (CTAs) and registered representatives at brokerage firms. There are a few "exempt CTA's" and others who handle managed accounts. I would recommend only the ones that submit themselves to regulatory scrutiny— the CTAs and RRs. Some of the others are no doubt good, but it is difficult to justify putting your hard-earned money in the hands of someone who is not willing to obtain industry licensing, regardless of how good his or her sales pitch is.

I would also recommend a CTA over an RR for several reasons. CTAs are required to provide a disclosure document to each customer whose account they will manage. The disclosure document provides quite a bit of useful information about the trader, including his or her performance for the previous five years and information about any civil, administrative, or criminal actions that have been brought against the registrant. RRs are not required to provide the same kind of documentation.

CTAs do not ordinarily receive a portion of the commission from your trading, although there are exceptions. Look at the fee section of his or her disclosure document to see if the CTA receives a portion of the commissions. RRs always receive a percentage of the commission, thus there is an inherent incentive for them to overtrade. Not all of them do so intentionally, but the temptation is always there. An RR may even subconsciously liquidate a position too soon, since the RR knows he or she can always re-enter the position and increase personal income at the same time!

Most CTAs charge a management fee and an incentive fee. These fees vary considerably. Both are usually stated as a percentage and are calculated using the liquidating value of your account on the appropriate evaluation date. Management fees are charged against the value of your account, regardless of whether or not your account is profitable. Six percent per year is fairly standard, but don't pay more than that. Incentive fees are only charged to the account if the account is profitable. Thus, your account should only be charged an incentive fee if the advisor's trading takes the liquidating value above the level of your initial deposit. Subsequent incentive fees should be charged only when more "new profits" are obtained.

Managed accounts usually require a higher opening deposit than self-directed accounts. The better CTAs will require deposits of $15,000 or more. Some programs may require a starting balance of as much as $50,000.

It is important to review carefully the past performance of a CTA prior to investing. If he or she has none, think twice before investing. Look for the largest period increase and decrease (drawdown). These numbers will give you an estimate of what you might expect in the future, but the past does not necessarily have any bearing on the future. Look at the overall return for the long term of the statistics. Is there a large difference between the best and worst period? Does the advisor appear to run several successive months of gains or losses? The answers to these questions will assist you in determining whether the risk taken by this advisor is appropriate to your investment goals and whether or not the timing of your investment might be important. Don't forget to ask the advisor how his or her performance has been since the date of the document. If the document is dated more than six months prior to the date you receive it, it is out of date and is required by law to be replaced.

Look for the maximum loss that the CTA will permit. A good one will not want to lose your entire investment. If you can't find it in the disclosure document, ask the CTA.

Commodity Pools

Commodity-pool investors obtain many of the advantages of managed accounts and receive other advantages as well. A pool is by definition a "pool" of investors' money that is traded as one account. Ordinarily, a CTA or a group of CTAs will guide the investment of the pool's assets. Occasionally, the commodity-pool operator (CPO) will guide the pool's trading, although I wouldn't recommend investing in such a pool unless there is a long and excellent track record. There are also exempt pools that are run by nonregistered operators. These are only as good as the operator. If you know and trust him or her, then you might consider it; otherwise just say no.

The fees are much the same as for CTA-managed accounts. The usual arrangement is that the CPO keeps the commission while the CTA keeps the management and incentive fees. Look for a pool with commissions no greater than $50 (per round turn), management fees not to exceed six percent annually, and incentive fees not to exceed 20 percent.

There are several advantages unique to pools. Since they are usually established as limited partnerships in which the CPO is the general partner and the investors are the limited partners, the investors usually cannot lose more than their initial investment. There is also usually a limit on the amount of loss that will be permitted, after which trading will cease. This puts a theoretical percentage loss limit on your investment. I use the term theoretical, since, just as a stop-loss order does not guarantee that your loss will be limited, the loss limit is an estimate and is often subject to adjustment.

Recently some pools have been created where the investors are guaranteed to get back their entire initial investment after five (or more or less) years. These pools are really quite simple. A fixed percentage of the initial investments is used to purchase "strips." These are usually U.S. T-notes from which the interest component has been "stripped." A great enough percentage has been set aside to provide a sum at the end of the period that equals the initial investment. What is left of the initial deposits is used for a foray into the commodity markets. This appears to be a no-cost way to invest in the commodity markets. However, there is no free lunch. You end up losing the interest on your money in return for the commodity investment, and usually your gain potential is reduced because, ordinarily, such funds do not invest more than 25 percent of the initial deposits in futures.

Other advantages of pools are that the investors' deposits usually earn interest. Most pools have a much lower investment minimum than managed accounts. They are also very often IRA qualified. Perhaps the greatest advantage to pool participants is the great diversification offered to the individual investor. Think of a $5000 account for a managed account versus a pool investor. The managed account might take a position in two or perhaps three commodities with that investment. The pool, on the other hand, adds the funds of all investors into one fund, and thus the individual investor might have the benefit of positions in 20 or more commodities at one time for his $5000 investment.

There is also another type of diversification available to the pool investor, when the pool has two or more CTAs guiding separate portions of the fund assets. If the advisors trade different markets, then it is less likely that an unexpected move in one segment of the market will adversely affect the pool.

There are a couple of ways that you can check on all commodity professionals. The National Futures Association at 1-312-781-1300 keeps records of disciplinary action taken against them by that agency and the Commodity Futures Trading Commission. They will not tell you about customer complaints, however. The CFTC in Washington, 1-202-254-3067 will inform you if any customers have filed reparations cases against them. They will send you copies of documents only if you make a written request under the Freedom of Information Act.

In conclusion, pluses and minuses exist in all commodity investments, self-directed and managed accounts, and pools. Since there is usually a rather large amount of money involved, it is worth your while to spend the time to learn a little. Asking a few questions and carefully reading the documents provided will help you make an informed decision regarding your investment.

DEVELOPING YOUR OWN MASTER TRADING SYSTEMS

■

■ SECTION FIVE ■

ONE NEED NOT LOOK FAR to encounter a multitude of hardware, software, computer trading systems, and miracle electronic accessories for the would-be futures trader. Lacking a consumer's guide to such products, an individual can easily feel lost and overwhelmed. To ease the difficulty, an to help avoid the expense of buying systems that may later prove to be inadequate or inappropriate, or just plain no good, Bill Taylor shares the results of his personal evaluation of several systems that are presently available. His hardware and software shopping guidelines, moreover, will help in analyzing systems that are not specifically covered in this chapter.

The trader who wants to design a personal trading system needs to know how to recognize and avoid specific pitfalls that can cause otherwise well-designed systems to malfunction in real-time trading. As a pioneer in the development of computer trading systems, Lou Mendelsohn is well qualified to point out the mistakes that can be made as systems are built and tested. He cautions the reader not to over-optimize, to avoid selecting a "profit island" that will not perform well real-time, and to keep the system as simple as possible. By following Lou's rules, you can design a trading system that will fit well with your own trading style.

■ CHAPTER TWENTY-THREE* ■

WHAT TO LOOK FOR IN COMPUTER HARDWARE AND INVESTMENT SOFTWARE

WILLIAM T. TAYLOR

■

*From William T. Taylor *The Trader's & Investor's Guide to Commodity Trading Systems, Software and Databases* (Chicago, IL: Probus, 1986) 85-96, by permission of the author and publisher. Copyright 1986 by William T. Taylor.

WILLIAM T. TAYLOR

William T. Taylor is Manager of Technology Planning at the Chicago Mercantile Exchange. In this capacity he is responsible for setting technological direction for systems related to the trading floor. His most recent projects include the co-development of the Automated Data Input Terminal (AUDIT) system with the Chicago Board of Trade. This is the "Electronic Trading Card" of the future. Mr. Taylor also has extensive experience in developing software for the testing of trading and hedging strategies. He has been a speaker at the CompuTrac Forums and a contributor to such journals as *Intermarket, Technical Analysis of Stocks and Commodities* and *Wall Street Computer Review.*

■ CHAPTER TWENTY-THREE ■

W HETHER YOU ARE READY to take the plunge now or are just looking, there are a few things to keep in mind when considering computer hardware and software. First, decide which functions you wish the computer to perform: technical analysis, fundamental analysis, accounting, and so on. Keep in mind the possible multiple uses of the computer. Some of these other uses, in my opinion, demand just as much thought and attention as the primary purpose for which you purchased the computer in the first place: *profits*. Second, keep in mind the nature of computer technology and how it is changing. This latter task is not an easy one, but this chapter will help you through some of the tough spots. Additionally, a casual glance at many of the major computer magazines as well as the specialized computer/investment magazines can add to your knowledge of the nature of this ever-changing industry.

Evaluate Your Needs

In the evaluation of your particular needs for the computer, try not only to outline your current needs, but also to anticipate future needs. One major mistake that many investors make is purchasing a computer with a single need in mind, for example, a particular technical trading system to generate buy and sell signals. After a relatively short period of time if you have really spent some time learning about the computer, you find that you want it to do more jobs, such as word processing, electronic spreadsheets or other types of computerized investment analysis. Because the choice of computer was made on the basis of very narrow criteria, it may not be appropriate to the other functions.

Before buying a computer to run a particular trading system, STOP. Actually *write down* other uses that you think you may want in the future. These future needs should include features such as expandability in memory and disk capacity, large existing software base, other types of programs for the home or office like word processing, spreadsheets and even games. If you have more than one purpose for purchasing your microcomputer the task of deciding becomes much more complex than if you are going to use it for investment analysis alone.

In this case the first task is to decide which is the most important task to accomplish. This in itself is not always easy! When the primary goal is determined, then narrow down the available software packages. After that, choose the software for the ancillary functions based on the hardware needed for the primary function. In most cases where the investment analysis function tops the list, there will be software for word processing and spreadsheets available for that hardware configuration.

I use something similar to the following table to examine computer software and hardware combinations in order to evaluate needs and balance them with the appropriate hardware and software.

	Computer 1	Computer 2	Computer 3
Need 1	Yes	No	Yes
Need 2	No	Yes	No
Need 3	Yes	No	Yes
Need 4	No	Yes	No
Need 5	No	Yes	Yes

Each need can be evaluated to see whether it will be satisfied by each particular computer hardware configuration. Costs can also be factored into the decision to find the combination that gives you the most "bang for the buck."

Many investment magazines such as *Futures, Intermarket* and *Technical Analysis of Stocks and Commodities* have computer-oriented columns containing tips and evaluations of the software that is currently available. They also contain advertisements for newsletters and other publications relating to investment software such as *Wall Street Computer Review*. Write for sample copies of these and other publications before you subscribe. Stick with the major investment-oriented computer newsletters. Ask the editor how long the publication has been in existence and how many paid subscribers it has. I have had at least two newsletters to which I subscribed go belly up in the middle of my subscription, leaving me high and dry. Generally speaking, the longer the newsletter has been around, the more likely it will continue.

Another source of information is talking to others who have used investment software for some time, the theory being that you can benefit from the experience (i.e., mistakes) of others; and the information that is shared by experienced users may prove helpful to your own decisions on investment software. However, you may also be led down the same road of mistakes that they followed. Ask questions about how easy the software is to learn and use, whether it delivers what the vendor promises, or whether it actually helps in the investment decisions. While it may not be the most reliable source of information, "talking computers" is, for the most part, a very enlightening experience. Look for advertisements for users groups of invest-ment software. Larger cities should have several.

Microcomputer Technology

In the business-oriented microcomputer industry there is a dominant force: IBM. It is doing for this industry what Kodak did for the photographic in-dustry, that is, setting the standard for others to follow. Knowing that IBM has such a strong marketing position, the software producers will follow along just to remain competitive in this market. Other hardware manufac-turers wishing to jump on the IBM bandwagon will make their computers IBM-compatible, just to tap the growing base of useful software available for the IBM computers.

Just what is "IBM-compatible"? If you ask half a dozen people in the computer industry, you'll probably get six slightly different answers. Basically, it is the ability to run programs that were written for the IBM Per-sonal Computer. But compatibility is only a relative term. Because of certain copyrights that IBM holds, the so-called compatibles can only come so close to being perfectly compatible without infringement. Some computers are more compatible than others. You can even find variation between the same models of the IBM computers that were made at different times. The point is, most of the software for the IBM has been written so that it runs on most of the compatibles. This is not always true for investment software, particularly in packages that involve graphics. Check the literature that the software ven-dor provides to see if it will run on the compatibles and which ones. If in doubt call the vendor. The purchase of an inappropriate computer or software package can be very expensive indeed.

It is very tempting for the person new to the computer world to want to buy the newest and the most famous hardware first and then seek the desired software. The reality hits when one finds out that the investment software (or in many cases any software) that was most important to him or her is not compatible with his or her new computer. A classic case is the Apple MacIntosh. It is a superb machine from a technological standpoint. This is definitely the direction microcomputing will be going in the future. It is extremely easy to use and the graphics are great. However, as of this writ-ing, the software base is only just beginning to grow. The "Mac" has the potential to become a growing force in the computer industry. As far as in-vestment-oriented software is concerned, there are a meager few. Check out Comtrax from Marketsoft, Inc., Suite 200N, 8600 W. Bryn Mawr Avenue, Chicago, IL 60614. (312) 787-7482. They have a one hour video demonstra-tion for $10.00.

A qualified consultant can help you with the problem of compatibility of hardware and software. If you insist on buying your computer though a retail outlet or mail order, be sure you know the hardware requirements of the particular software you plan to use. This information will be available in the literature of the established software vendors.

Most of the investment software available today is supported on a limited number of combinations of hardware. That is, they require specific printers and/or monitors, or other special hardware features like minimum RAM memory, special graphics adapters or minimum disk capacity. If you are not sure, take the time to find out. Bring the literature to a computer store if you have trouble understanding the terminology. It will save you a lot of frustration and possibly wasted money later. After all, isn't that why you're buying the computer: to stop wasting money on bad investments? Some software vendors offer a demonstration package. These are programs that show off the features of the package but do not have all of the features of the full priced version. If you are unsure about a software package, the purchase of the demo can let you get your feet wet without incurring much cost. If you do not have a computer yet, the demonstration package makes it possible to test out the various computers at your local computer store.

Troubles with Computer Stores

If you are purchasing your hardware/software from a retail computer store, don't expect the staff to be as knowledgeable about trading systems and investment software as you are. By now you have spent months or even years reading about and studying the markets and technical trading systems. Perhaps you have attended an investment conference or two. You may be using a calculator now but going over some trading system, you suddenly realize how the computer can assist you in this tedious task. Chances are, the salesperson in the computer store will know little or nothing about it. Why should they? Their job is to push the high-volume general or business applications software with the computers that they sell.

Some packages have been mass marketed by large firms. Most notable of these are several different software programs marketed by Dow Jones & Company. I have nothing against them, you understand. They are fine products for analysis of stocks. The commodity trader, however, will find them of little use. If your interest is stocks, then by all means check these products out. They are well-done and well-documented. I wish all software were produced as professionally. There is one word of caution, however. Even though these packages are sold through the retail stores, the sales staff may not know how they work.

In summary, if your interest lies in the technical analysis of commodities, then be prepared to be met with a blank stare from the salesperson at the computer store. Remember, these computer stores make money by moving their stock, and moving it quickly. They cannot keep their people trained in every commercial software package that comes along, much less the investment software. The limited market for sophisticated investment software, particularly involving technical trading systems, makes selling these types of software packages not worth the effort on the part of the sales staff in terms of having to learn how to use them or the computer store owner in terms of the space and inventory costs.

Here's where a qualified consultant can assist you in the selection of the appropriate hardware and software. They will spend the time talking to you, assessing your needs for both the trading and non-trading activities you feel that you need. They may also suggest possible future needs that you may not have considered. Based on the experience of knowing what is available and, more importantly, which software packages are well designed, easy to use, well-documented and supported by the vendor, you can be assured that you will be receiving the proper hardware and software combination for your needs and budget.

You may be able to get the components for less through a mail order house or a retail store, but you will not get the advice that could make the difference between an intelligent choice and a disaster. I cannot emphasize this point enough! Check advertisements in trading magazines. Be sure to ask for references. Another source of information is referrals from the vendors themselves. While this source of information may not be totally unbiased, it may give you an opportunity to see the software in action.

The Market for Investment Software

When choosing software, do not buy blindly based on the advertising claims. There are many companies and products on the market. Not unlike the software industry as a whole, businesses can be literally run from the basement of the house. Not that this is necessarily bad, mind you. That's how this microcomputer revolution happened in the first place! The point is, it is difficult to ascertain the continuity of a particular business. Vendors come and go. The entry and exit from this business is very brisk, partly because it is very easy to start up a company. All you need is a basement and a computer. Because this market is very competitive, only those that really produce what they promise survive. Even this is not a guarantee. As objective as technical analysis is, presumably along with its followers, traders are very fickle. They jump from one software package to another in search of the "Holy Grail" of computer software.

Compare the recent issues of almost any investment-oriented magazine to the issues one or two years ago. A quick look will show you which ones are still in business. This is one of the best indicators of a reliable vendor and a quality product.

There are some exceptional products out on the market and others are real duds. Some may not even really exist! The nature of this industry is such that the demand for new products is so great that the need to "get your name out" as a software company exceeds the ability to produce the product. These products are called "vaporware" by industry observers.

Price is not always a clue to quality. A more expensive program may not perform any better than, or even as well as, one much cheaper. Do not go by the advertisement claims. If possible, try to ascertain the reputation of the software company. Again, the assistance of a qualified consultant can prove invaluable here.

If possible, attend one of the many conferences on investments. More and more, you'll see computer-related topics discussed, demonstrations of various software packages and, most importantly, there will be people there to answer any questions you may have. Granted, some of these conferences are expensive, but so is the computer system in which you are likely to invest. It can save you the cost of the incorrect choice in computer hardware and software.

Some of the Major Software Packages

In order to give you a flavor of what is available, I have chosen several packages to feature in this section of the book. This selection does not necessarily represent the best packages, but rather a representative sample of the variety of different types that are available. Investment software can be classified into several categories.

Trading-System Software

The first is the traditional trading system type. This software generates the buy and sell signals that the trader will hopefully follow. I say hopefully because this is the purpose of getting the software in the first place: a disciplined trading approach rather than one that is "seat-of-the-pants."

The trader can feed in the data, either from an on-line data base accessed over the telephone lines, or by manually typing in the day's data. If you follow very many stocks or commodity contracts, or use several trading systems, the former method is preferable. There is a direct cost of the data plus telecommunications charges, but these must be balanced against the time and effort required to use the manual method.

Depending on the software involved, the manual method may require separate entry of the same data into each trading system. That is not very cost-effective! Also, with the manual method, there is more of a chance for errors caused by typing mistakes. The cost of a typing error, in terms of a bad trading signal, can cause a loss much greater than that of the cost of the on-line service.

Analytical-System Software

The second type of investment software package I classify as analytical system type software. This type of package is not used to generate the buy and sell signals. Rather, it is used to look at the data and provide insight in how the market is behaving. Many of the packages that fall into this category provide a graphical analysis of the data that is fed into them.

In essence, these packages replace the traditional charting services by allowing the trader to draw trend lines, support and resistance levels, and other annotations to the graph. Unlike the paper graphs, if the trader wishes to change a line, it only takes a few keystrokes to start over. But these packages go beyond that.

Many of the popular technical indicators are calculated under a variety of parameters and can be displayed in various combinations. In addition, a hard copy can be printed out on the printer or plotter attached to the computer. Each graph is fresh and free of erased pencil marks.

Other packages that fall into this category are the options pricing software. These types of programs calculate the fair value of an option using the traditional analysis such as Black-Scholes methods. The ultimate decision to buy or sell a put or call rests with the trader.

Combined Trading and Analytical Software

The third type of investment software packages embody the function of both the trading and analytical software packages. That is to say, they perform the analytical function, allowing the trader to look at the market prices in light of the historical data, and also generate the buy and sell signals necessary to trade in the current market. The vast majority of software falls into this category.

Another distinction in software revolves around the ability of the trader to vary the parameters or decision rules of the particular trading system that is in use. An example of a parameter is the length of the moving average. In a software package that uses the moving average and price to generate a buy or sell signal, it is desirable to vary the length of the moving average to suit the conditions of the current market. In the packages that do both analysis and trading, the trader can simulate the trading rules over historical data for a variety of parameter values and then use those parameters that provide the best performance. This process is called optimization. Some of the more sophisticated software automatically steps through ranges of parameter values and keeps track of the outcome for later analysis.

There are some trading software programs in which the trader has no control over how the decision rules are made. I call these "black-box" type software packages. All the trader has to do is feed the data, which can contain high, low, open, close, volume, and open interest in some combination and the computer does the rest. The trader does not have to know how the system works. He just puts a great deal of faith (and sometimes a lot of money) into the system and hopes for the best.

I must admit, I am a bit skeptical about these types of systems. While these black-box type systems are probably well-researched, my research experience has led me to believe that as conditions change over time, many trading systems fail to remain profitable and must be reevaluated periodically. I really don't believe that a single fixed set of decision rules can work day-in and day-out for a long period of time or for a wide variety of commodities. Much of the excitement over the ultimate trading system feeds on the technical trader's need to find the Holy Grail.

Computerized investment software packages can also be classified as to the ease of use. You all have heard the term *user friendly*. For many traders with little or no computer experience, this aspect can mean a great deal. It can even determine whether or not the trader will use the software.

Most of the trading software can be broken down into those that are menu driven or command driven. The menu-driven system provides the trader with, literally, a menu outlining the various tasks the system can do. The trader just picks the menu item and the computer goes on its way to accomplish the task. If, after one selection on the menu, more information is required, the system will prompt the trader with another menu, and so on, until all of the information that the computer needs is provided. This process, however, can take some time, depending on the amount of information that the trading system requires.

The command-driven system, by contrast, does nothing until the trader gives it the proper command. This requires the trader to either memorize all the commands or keep a list of these commands handy, which ends up being a manual menu system. If there are only a few commands and they are easy enough to learn quickly, the command-driven type software package can be much quicker to run, since you don't have to wait for each of the menus to come up on the screen and make each choice.

Most of the investment software available today is of the menu-driven variety. This is primarily due to the fact that most traders are inexperienced in the use of computers and have too much on their minds to take the extra time necessary to master a set of commands so they can use the computer.

Sometimes it is desirable to have both features in a software package. This allows the beginner to go through the menus and see what data or parameter values to supply in order to run a particular trading system. The more advanced user can avoid the relative slowness of the menus by providing direct commands or even multiple commands that will provide the system with the required information.

A feature of some of the software packages available today is the ability to program all of the steps that it takes to run a particular study. This can include calling up the on-line data service, loading today's prices, running several types of analysis, and the printing of the graphs all at the push of a few keys! If you follow several stocks or commodities with several trading systems, this feature alone can save you a tremendous amount of time.

Some of the More Popular Software Packages

Computrac

P.O. Box 15951
New Orleans, LA 70175-5951
(504) 895-1474

One of the more popular software packages for technical analysis of stock or commodity data is the Computrac system. This product is put out by The Technical Analysis Group in New Orleans, Louisiana under the direction of Tim Slater, the group's coordinator. The software is obtained by becoming a member of the Technical Analysis Group. This requires a one-time initial fee and yearly maintenance charges. Currently, the fee is between $1,100 and $1,900, depending on the type of computer you want to use. Computrac supports the IBM PC/XT/AT and its compatibles as well as Apple II+ and IIe. The Apple version is more expensive than the IBM due to the fact that there are currently more features and studies available for it. Computrac was originally developed for the Apple and they are committed to continuing the support for the Apple version.

The fee for maintenance runs about $300 for the IBM and $200 for the Apple.

There are additional one-time charges for the Apple user: $99 for a special integrated circuit chip called the "Superchip" and $75 for the security control card, a device that is required for the operation of the software. This security card, also used on the IBM version but included in the initial fee, allows the trader to make backup copies of the program diskettes for safekeeping. Unauthorized use is prohibited because the system requires both the software and the hardware key.

The Technical Analysis Group was formed in 1979 by four traders. These traders realized that the microcomputer had untapped potential to assist them in following technical trading systems, charting prices and other indicators and, in general, helping them with their trading decisions. Assisted by Dr. Jim Schmit, Professor of Computer Science at Loyola University in New Orleans, they developed a collection of technical analysis programs for the microcomputer. At the time, this was about the only such extensive software package in existence.

Their software gained the attention of more and more traders, initially by word of mouth. The group became more formally organized with 30 members. Members contributed ideas and expertise to provide ways of continually improving the Computrac software package.

Today, there are in excess of 2,000 members world wide. The basic tenets of the original group, that is, to assist each other in the technical analysis of the stock and commodity markets, still hold. Many of the recent additions to the collection of programs were submitted from the membership and refined by the programming staff at Computrac.

The Computrac software package is much more than the set of programs and technical studies. There is a hot line where, between 8 A.M. and 5 P.M. CST, members can receive assistance with the software or hardware. The staff can walk you through any problems you might have. Members may also access the group's computer bulletin board via phone lines and post or view timely notices, helpful hints and even advertisements for swapping data.

The Computrac package has an extensive collection of different trading systems, analytical tools, and technical indicators as well as the necessary utility programs to maintain the data base that you build up from either manual or telephone input.

The package should appeal to both the stock and commodity trader. The trading systems, called "studies" in Computrac jargon, are some of the most popular in use today. Some of these studies are as follows:

Bar Charts. These include open, high, low, close on a daily, weekly or monthly basis. A single line may also be displayed by requesting the close only.

Point and Figure. The size of the box to indicate a reversal may be specified by the user.

Demand Index. Jim Sibbett's demand index is one of the more popular of the studies available in Computrac. It is derived from a combination of price and volume data.

Welles Wilder. The major studies of J. Welles Wilder, such as relative strength index, directional movement indicator, swing index, commodity selection index, and the parabolic price/time systems. These were featured in his book *New Concepts in Technical Trading Systems.*

Cyclical Detrend. Walt Bressert's technique for determining underlying cycles in the market.

Momentum Index I. Another of Bressert's techniques that is keyed to cyclical movement.

Momentum Index II. This is the classical momentum study that defines momentum as the continuous difference between prices at a fixed interval. It is also called the "rate of change" in price. It can also be smoothed by a moving average.

On Balance Volume. This was made famous by Joseph Granville. This program will chart the OBV as well as provide a numerical table of the values.

Percent Retracement. This study automatically calculates the retracement from the high price of the day to the low price of the day to the last price or, alternatively, low to high to last retracement. It is particularly valuable to the trader in the placement of stops.

Oscillator. This study indicates the difference between two moving averages. It plots the results as a histogram around a zero line.

Overbought/Oversold. This index, known as the %R, was developed by Larry Williams. It has been modified by Walt Bressert to account for underlying operative cycles.

RSI. This version of Wilder's Relative Strength Index allows for changing the number of days in the moving average. It also calculates the number of days in the moving average as well as the price necessary to achieve tomorrow's RSI objective.

Stochastic. Pioneered by George Lane, this study shows how, in a rising market, daily closes tend to accumulate near the top of the trading range and, in falling markets, closes tend to accumulate near the bottom of the trading range. Opportunities are signaled by the crossing of two oscillators.

Regression Analysis. This statistical technique is handy to determine trend in a price series and for forecasting price movement.

Gann Squares. Computrac has two Gann studies: Cardinal Squares and Price and Time Squares.

Spreads. Computrac will calculate the spread between two commodities and display it graphically.

CCI. The Commodity Channel Index is a timing tool that works best with markets that exhibit seasonal or cyclical characteristics.

Fourier Analysis. This is a sophisticated statistical technique that decomposes a time series of data into its cyclical components and measures the relative strength of those cyclical components.

Demand Aggregrate. The demand aggregate is a study that combines price, volume, and open interest movements. It is considered a cousin of the demand index.

Ratio. The ratio study is used to track the ratio of two related but distinct commodities such as gold and silver or hogs and corn to show a divergence in the behavior of the two to similar market factors.

%R. This a modified version of Larry Williams' %R trading system.

Herrick Payoff Index. The index is a commodity trading tool that is useful in the early identification of changes in the direction of price trend.

Moving Averages. There are a series of related programs that calculate different moving average types such as linear, exponential, weighted, etc. with varying length or smoothing factors. Besides prices, they can be used to smooth other data like oscillators or indices.

Harulan Index. This study uses the advance/decline statistics of a stock exchange to calculate the technical conditions.

McLellan Oscillator. Similar to the Haurlan Index, this study is based on the advance and decline statistics.

Arms Index. This study, also known as the short-term trading index or as TRIN, measures the relative strength of volume entering advancing stocks against the relative strength of volume entering the declining stocks.

Volume Accumulator. This study provides a more sensitive intraday measure of volume/price action. Sometimes used as an alternative to Joseph Granville's On Balance Volume technique.

Computrac has an extensive graphics capability in both the IBM and Apple versions. For the studies mentioned above, there is a corresponding graphical display. The trader can get the data in tabular form, as well. Figure 23-1 shows the basic open, high, low, close bar graph from the Apple version. This particular graph is presented in the five-day format. That is, only the five trading days are shown and there are no gaps for the weekends. Notice the top line shows the values for the open, high, low and close. These values correspond to the date on which the cursor, the little x in the middle of the graph, just below the bars, is positioned. This feature allows the trader

Figure 23-1

O:71.99 H:72.05 L:70.82 C:70.95

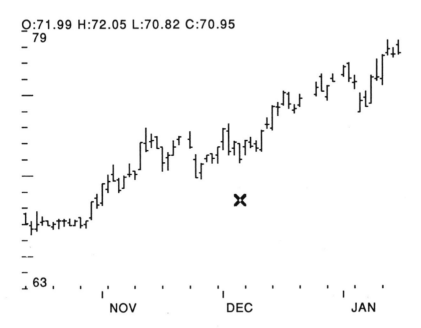

to obtain the actual values of significant data for that date rather than estimating them from the graph itself.

One of the better features of Computrac is to present more than one
study on a single graph. It does this with the use of what is called the split
screen. Figure 23-2 demonstrates this capability by plotting the high, low and
close of the DJIA along with Welles Wilder's Relative Strength Index.

Data other than in daily format can also be represented graphically as
shown in Figure 23-3. In this case, Comex Gold is displayed on a monthly
basis. Up to eight years of data can be displayed in this manner.

Due to the IBM's greater screen resolution, graphs are much clearer than
those displayed on the Apple monitor. Figure 23-4 illustrates this with a
graph of IMM Gold open, high, low and close. Also superimposed on this is
the cycle finder. The trader can vary the distance between the vertical lines to
determine whether there is some underlying cycle in the data.

The next chart, Figure 23-5, shows this same gold price bar chart with
contract volume plotted below it and the closing price overlaid on top of the
volume. Notice that the actual data corresponding to the date that the cursor
is lined up with is displayed below the graph.

Figure 23-2

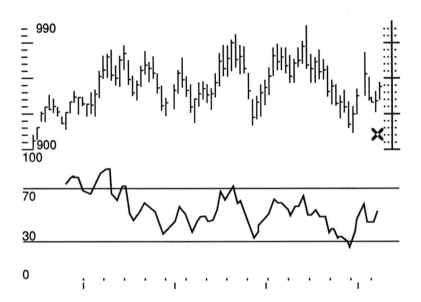

Figure 23-3

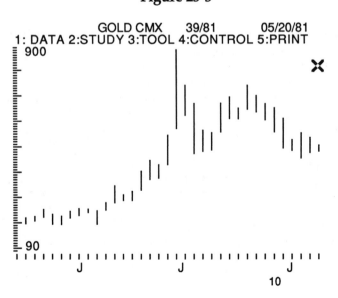

Figure 23-4

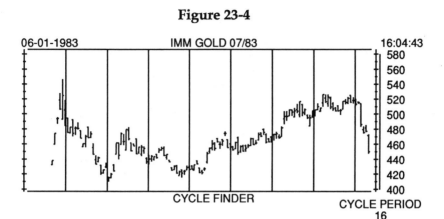

Figure 23-5

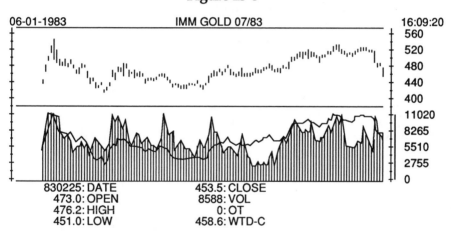

The Computrac system also provides the facility to draw in trend lines and compute the next five day's prices that would fall along that trend line. This feature is most useful for identifying support and resistance levels. Figure 23-6 illustrates this useful feature.

Hard copy of graphics is also possible with the use of the dot-matrix printer. Figure 23-7 illustrates this feature. This type of graph is called the "high-precision chart" and is accurate to 1/84th of an inch.

For testing various parameter combinations of the studies available in the Computrac system, there is a special feature called the "Profit Matrix." This allows the performance of each parameter combination to be stored and later analyzed together in a consistent format. This is a form of optimization of trading systems. One must be careful, however, in the use of optimization.

Figure 23-6

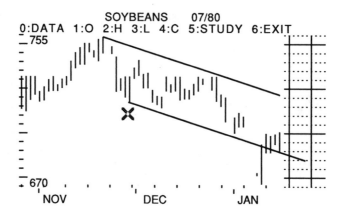

Figure 23-7

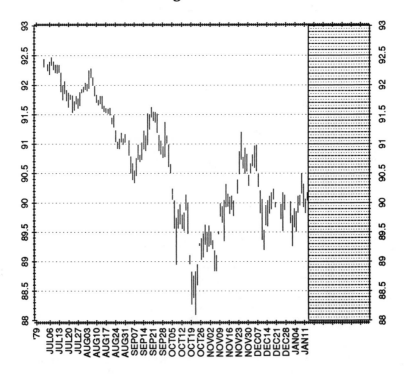

The highest profits in one time period do not guarantee high profits (or even positive profits) in the future.

In order to simplify the task of running the desired studies, Computrac has an auto-run facility. This allows the trader to set up the steps required to complete each study without further manual intervention. If you follow a lot of commodities, this feature is really desirable. You can let the machine run while you do something else, either further study or other book work. You can even spend more time with your friends or family!

Computrac also provides a programming subsystem that allows the trader to design his own trading system within the Computrac system. This allows the trader to take advantage of all of the graphic routines, data manipulation and utility programs available. Several of the studies that are now in the Computrac system were originally developed in this programming subsystem. Use of this feature, however, does require some knowledge of the BASIC language.

To keep track of your positions, the Computrac provides "Equity," a total accounting package for managing commodity accounts. This is particularly important for account executives or brokers to keep track of a client's positions. Within each account, the program can open or close a trade, categorize the position as regular, hedge, spread or spot. It can follow the margin, maintenance and equity requirements. It automatically posts open profit/loss whenever the last data has been added to the system. The results of Equity are displayed on two screens, one containing the account information and the other containing the commodity portfolio information.

The 200+ page manual is in notebook style for easy updating and documentation as the system is modified. There are examples and tutorials for most of the features within the Computrac system, which makes learning much easier. In a system as extensive and complex as this one, this feature allows the learning of the portions that are of most interest, such as particular studies. It is well-organized and relatively easy to follow, taking you from the basics through the advanced features.

As with most computerized systems, it helps to have a basic familiarity with the computer's operating system utility programs such as those that format a disk, disk-copy procedures and listing of the diskette directory. The Computrac manual does give you helpful hints on data organization and general good habits for data processing such as data backup for safe keeping.

The Computrac system provides for access to several on-line commodity and stock data bases like Commodity Systems Incorporated and I.P. Sharp, to name a couple. Use of this feature requires that you have the appropriate hardware (i.e. a modem)) to connect to the telephone lines. Data are acquired at additional cost through an agreement with the database vendor.

Use of an on-line data base can be beneficial when the number of commodities or stocks that are followed is large. It saves time because manual entry can be slow and tedious, and money because your time is valuable and the cost of making a bad trade due to a data entry error could be very significant. If you are following only a small number of commodities or stocks, you'll have to balance the convenience of automatic data feeding with the cost of the automatic updates versus the manual data entry and time costs.

All in all, the Computrac system is well designed and produced. It is relatively user friendly and, with a moderate amount of practice and study, the trader can benefit greatly from its cornucopia of features.

It is rather expensive as far as trading software goes, but you must remember: you're not just buying a collection of computer programs. You are becoming a member in a trading system user's group with access to help and advice in using this software as well as additional studies and other features as they are added to the system. If you do not want to take advantage of the periodic updates to the system, you can stop paying the yearly maintenance fees and keep the system as you currently have it.

ProfitTaker

Investment Growth Corporation
50 Meadow Lane
Zephyrhills, FL 34249
(813) 973-0496

Another software package that allows both historical testing and analysis as well as generating the buy and sell signals is ProfitTaker. This package was designed and developed by Louis B. Mendelsohn, president of Investment Growth Corporation, Zephyrhills, Florida. Mr. Mendelsohn is a registered commodity advisor and widely respected authority in the area of futures software do's and don'ts. I particularly like this package for a number of reasons. First, it is definitely not of the black-box type of software package that I mentioned earlier in this chapter. It allows the variation in parameters that are used to calculate a variety of technical indicators including several moving averages and oscillators. This ability to vary the decision rules, or parameters, allows the system to be tailored for the behavior of very different commodities.

Second, ProfitTaker provides both the trading system aspect of generating the buy and sell signals and, through its Profit Analyst module, the ability to test historical data to determine optimal parameters using a variety of criteria, thus avoiding some of the major obstacles to the optimization by total net profit alone.

Third, it is specifically designed for the futures market. Whereas many other packages are designed to be general technical trading packages used to trade or study futures, stocks, bonds, options and the like, ProfitTaker takes into account the unique factors found only in the futures markets: lock limit days, high leverage and fast pace of trading.

The cost for the ProfitTaker package is $1,920 for the IBM version and $1,420 for the Apple version, plus a $75 one-time registration fee.

ProfitTaker has several features worth mentioning. It produces a "Trading Position Report," shown in Figure 23-8, which allows the trader to see the actual condition of the existing portfolio. For each commodity contract, it shows the price of a signal, position that you're in, and the price at which you should enter or exit a long or short position in a particular contract.

In the testing and generating of buy and sell signals, ProfitTaker allows the trader to time the execution of the trades.

Figure 23-8

LAST UPDATE: 12/19/84   Page: 1

NO ##	CONTRAC NAME	TRADING POSITION SIGNAL	NO CHANGE	ENTR LONG	RNTR LONG	PROT LONG	LIQD LONG	ENTR SHRT	RNTR SHRT	PROT SHRT	COVR SHRT
1	GC-0285	3111	STAY SHRT	3998	......	......	......	......	......	3422	......
2	SV-0385	6395	STAY SHRT	12023	......	......	......	......	......	7383	......
3	BP-0385	11640	STAY SHRT	17969	......	......	......	......	......	12729	......
4	CD-0385	7553	STAY LONG	......	......	......	......	7538	......	......	......
5	DM-0385	3240	STAY SHRT	3817	......	......	......	......	......	3510	......
6	JY-0385	4057	STAY SHRT	4656	......	......	......	......	......	4247	......
7	SF-0385	3918	STAY SHRT	5126	......	......	......	......	......	4267	......
8	TB-0385	9180	STAY LONG	......	......	......	......	8907	......	......	......
9	TR-0385	7928	STAY LONG	......	......	6987	......	3647	......	......	......
10	BO-0385	ENTR LONG	2548	......	......	2419	......	2416	......	......	......
11	C -0385	26025	STAY SHRT	46401	......	......	......	......	......	29772	......
12	S -0385	60375	STAY SHRT	74655	......	......	......	......	......	65642	......
13	SM-0385	1495	STAY SHRT	2506	......	......	......	......	......	1741	......
14	LC-0285	6580	SIDEWAYS	8125	......	......	......	6504	......	......	......
15	LH-0285	5185	STAY LONG	......	......	......	......	2708	......	......	......
16	CO-0385	2036	STAY SHRT	3504	5013	......	......	......	......	2272	......
17	CC-0385	14009	STAY LONG	......	......	......	......	13570	......	......	......
18	HO-0285	7417	STAY SHRT	10609	......	......	......	......	......	7990	......
19	LB-0385	1604	SIDEWAYS	1868	......	......	......	1557	......	......	......

NEW SIGNAL
BUY MARCH BEAN OIL
ON OPENING

Continued on Page: 2

EXIT FEB HOGS
ON CLOSE BELOW 5013

STAY OUT OF MARCH LUMBER
UNLESS CLOSE AT 186.80 (BUY)
OR CLOSE AT 155.70 (SELL)

Most software sends its trading signals based on the close of the day and executes trades on the opening price of the next day. This strategy may not always be the optimal. To provide greater flexibility and to overcome this much-overlooked, yet critical factor, ProfitTaker can show the trader the outcome of several strategies relating to when the trade is executed so that the optimal one may be chosen for future trading.

ProfitTaker also allows user defined "sensitivity bands" which control the way the trading system reacts to the market. Narrow band levels make the system more sensitive and wide band levels make the system less sensitive. The optimal band settings can be determined through the use of Profit Analyst as part of the optimization process. The trader can adjust the system to match his trading psyche by accepting more or less risk.

This Profit Analyst module is a very powerful history tester that allows you to extensively test and fine-tune your trading plans and strategy for each commodity futures contract that you follow. Unlike other systems that provide only a few indicators of performance, Profit Taker calculates and displays over 30 such indicators. These include maximum and minimum winning and losing trades as well as the average winning and losing trade, average profit or loss per trade, number of trades, number of winning long and short trades, percent winning and losing trades, to name just a few.

Judicious use of optimal parameter testing is possible by looking at the other indicators produced also. A sample of the Profit Analyst summary appears in Figure 23-9. The Indicators being evaluated and some of the performance criteria are highlighted.

Figure 23-10 gives you a detailed account of each trade and also shows the effect of rolling over into a new contract as the old one expires a little bit of realism that we must face, but that is frequently forgotten in other so-called optimal parameter testing.

Interestingly, ProfitTaker produces no graphical output. Rather, just summaries of trading positions and results of historical testing. Actually graphs are not necessary if your style of analysis goes by the numbers rather than by sight.

Like most major software producers, Investment Growth Corporation has a strong commitment to customer support. In addition to providing continued enhancements to the software itself, Mr. Mendelshohn has created a companion service called ProfitTuner. This service determines, for each commodity, the most recently profitable combinations of technical indicator values for actively traded commodities.

This testing is done on a mainframe computer and so performs more exhaustive analysis than that possible on a microcomputer alone. Literally millions of combinations of parameter values are tested. The base line values of the optimal parameters, the result of testing on a data base up to nine years long, are available to ProfitTaker customers at no charge. A quarterly service

Figure 23-9

HISTORY TEST FOR;: >>>SWISS FR. D12/84 <<< S4,D2,V0 PAGE: 17

ENTR= OPEN EXIT=OPEN RANGES; TF=4 SD=9 LD=46 LS/BND=.03 SS/BND=.05

TRADING PERFORMANCE RESULTS		INDICATORS BEING EVALUATED
TOTAL CLOSED OUT TRADES	17	
LONG WINNING TRADES	3	
SHRT WINNING TRADES	9	
TOTAL WINNING TRADES	12	
LONG LOSING TRADES	3	
SHRT LOSING TRADES	2	
TOTAL LOSING TRADES	5	
TOTAL BREAKEVEN TRADES	0	
% WINNING TRADES	.705	
% LOSING TRADES	.294	
% BREAKEVEN TRADES	0	
TOTAL REALIZED PROFITS	25596	
TOTAL REALIZED LOSSES	-7801	
CUMULATIVE PROFIT OR LOSS	17795	
RATIO CUMULATIVE PROFIT TO TOTAL REALIZED LOSSES	2.281	
MAXIMUM WINNING TRADE	9987	
MAXIMUM LOSING TRADE	-2538	← LARGEST LOSS
AVERAGE WINNING TRADE	2133	
AVERAGE LOSING TRADE	-1560.200	
RATIO AVERAGE WINNING TO LOSING TRADE	1.367	
AVERAGE PROFIT OR LOSS PER TRADE	1046	
MAXIMUM NUMBER CONSECUTIVE LOSING TRADE	1	
MAXIMUM DOLLARS CONSECUTIVE LOSS	-2538	
MAXIMUM DRAWDOWN -- CLOSED OUT TRADES	2538	← GREATEST DRAWDOWN
PROFIT FACTOR	3.281	
SHARPE RATIO	.024	
TBILL RATE	.090	
LEVERAGE FACTOR	.050	
COMMISSIONS -- CLOSED OUT TRADES	1275	
EXECUTION SLIPPAGE	1875	
CUMULATIVE NET REALIZED PROFIT OR LOSS	14645	← NET RESULTS AFTER COMMISSIONS AND SLIPPAGE
RATIO COMM AND SLIP TO CUM NET REALIZED PROFIT	.215	
TOTAL UNREALIZED PROFITS ON OPEN TRADE	3050	← OPEN PROFITS
TOTAL UNREALIZED LOSSES ON OPEN TRADE	0	
TOTAL TRADING DAYS	638	
TOTAL HOLIDAYS	16	
TOTAL DAYS IN FILES	1515	
TOTAL ROLLOVERS	8	
CONVERSION FACTOR	2	
CONVERTED POINT VALUE	12.500	
CONVERTED DAILY LIMIT	150	

END OF HISTORY TEST FOR RANGE: 1

Figure 23-10

INDICATOR VALUES
BEING TESTED

HISTORY TEST FOR;; >>>SWISS FR. D12/84 <<<   S4,D2,V0
ENTR (OPEN) EXIT (OPEN)   RANGES; TF (4) SD=9 LD (46)   LS/BND .03   SS/BND .05

DATE/IN	ENTR	PRICE	DATE/OUT	EXIT	PRICE	PROFIT	LOSS	LT	MAX $$	CUM/NET
05-12-82	BUY	5561	05-20-82	SELL	5358	0	-2538	1	-2538	-2538
05-20-82	SELL	5358	11-23-82	BUY	4559	9987	0	0	0	7449

ROLLOVER INTO: SWISS FR. D03/83

11-23-82	SELL	4622	12-01-82	BUY	4823	0	-2513	1	-2513	4936
12-01-82	BUY	4823	02-03-83	SELL	4984	2012	0	0	0	6948
02-03-83	SELL	4984	02-23-83	BUY	4905	987	0	0	0	7935

ROLLOVER INTO: SWISS FR. D06/83

02-23-83	SELL	4972	05-12-83	BUY	4942	375	0	0	0	8310
05-12-83	BUY	4942	05-23-83	SELL	4812	0	-1625	1	-1625	6685

ROLLOVER INTO: SWISS FR. D09/83

05-23-83	BUY	4868	05-24-83	SELL	4874	75	0	0	0	6760
05-24-83	SELL	4874	08-23-83	BUY	4714	2000	0	0	0	8760

ROLLOVER INTO: SWISS FR. D12/83

08-23-83	SELL	4780	09-30-83	BUY	4757	287	0	0	0	9047
09-30-83	BUY	4757	11-03-83	SELL	4687	0	-875	1	-875	8172
11-03-83	SELL	4687	11-21-83	BUY	4621	825	0	0	0	8997

ROLLOVER INTO: SWISS FR. D03/84

11-22-83	SELL	4683	02-22-84	BUY	4578	1312	0	0	0	10309

ROLLOVER INTO: SWISS FR. D06/84

02-22-84	SELL	4655	02-23-84	BUY	4675	0	-250	1	-250	10059
02-23-84	BUY	4675	04-11-84	SELL	4690	187	0	0	0	10246
04-11-84	SELL	4690	05-22-84	BUY	4433	3212	0	0	0	13458

ROLLOVER INTO: SWISS FR. D09/84

05-22-84	SELL	4521	08-21-84	BUY	4174	4337	0	0	0	17795

ROLLOVER INTO: SWISS FR. D12/84

08-21-84	SELL	4246	09-28-84	OPEN	4002	3050	0		** UNREALIZED **	

END OF TRADING SIGNALS

OPEN PROFIT

CUMULATIVE PROFITS
(COMPLETED TRADES)
5/12/82 - 8/21/84

AUTOMATIC ROLLOVERS FOR CONSISTENT TESTING

----- ENTER -----   ----- EXIT -----   ----- PERFORMANCE -----

representing the most recent results for each commodity desired is available at extra charge.

Summary. The ProfitTaker system is a well-produced and documented futures trading system. Completely menu driven, it is extremely easy to use. It operates on both the IBM PC/XT with 128K RAM minimum or the Apple II+ or IIe with 48K RAM minimum. It also requires an ASCII Printer.

With all the features, particularly the extensive historical testing, the ProfitTaker system is, in my opinion, one of the best packages available for those traders who don't require graphic representation of a variety of technical indicators, but rather go by the numbers.

Trader

Investment Growth Corporation
50 Meadow Lane
Zephyrhills, Fl 34249
(813) 973-0496

IGC has just released another trading tool called Trader. This software is designed to look at fundamental/economic information from the technician's perspective. Trader is a "pop-up" program. That is, it can be called up while running another program much in the same manner as Sidekick and others. It is therefore literally at your finger-tips.

Trader tracks over 50 major indicators and tells you what will happen to prices in various markets. It shows the direction of influence each indicator will have relative to the others. The trader can even place customized reminders to him/herself as needed for trading. It can be used as a stand alone tool for day traders or in conjunction with other technical trading systems. It is an extremely useful adjunct to any trading system.

Trader sells for $295 ($169 for existing ProfitTaker customers.)
ProfitTaker sells for $995.

Micro Futures

P.O. Box 2765
Livonia, MI 48154
(313) 422-0914

Micro Futures of Livonia, Michigan has been providing software and data services for commodity futures traders since 1978. They have expanded since then to include service to stock, options, and mutual fund traders as well.

Services include "Data on Disk," "Trade Systems," data management and telephone data retrieval software.

The purpose here is to focus on the Trade Systems software packages. This package represents the lower end of the cost spectrum, yet the programs here are relatively sophisticated. There are eight different modules available in Trade Systems. Each may be purchased separately for $75 or all eight for $250. They are available for IBM PC/XT/AT, Apple II, II+, IIe and IIc under DOS 3.3 and TRS-80's model 1, 3, 4, 2, 12 and 16. They will also work on any IBM, Apple or TRS-80 compatible system. Trade Systems will provide both daily trading signals and historical simulations.

The eight modules represent some of the old standards in terms of trading systems. I'm sure you will recognize these.

Maband. A moving average with a percentage band. This is a trend-following system using a single moving average plus and minus a percentage (the band). When prices exceed the limits of the band a signal is generated. If prices retreat and cross the moving average, the trade is liquidated. The parameters that the trader may vary are the length of the moving average and the percentage band value.

Macross. Two moving average with arithmetic or exponential moving averages. This is also a trend-following technique utilizing a two moving average crossover. When the faster MA (i.e., shorter in length) is above the slower MA a buy signal is given. Short positions are liquidated and a new long position is taken. Conversely, if the faster MA is below the slower MA, a sell signal is generated. Long positions are liquidated and a new short position is taken. The parameters that the trader can vary are the length of the moving averages (for the arithmetic MA) or the percent factors (for the exponential MA).

OS. Momentum index using one moving average. An index based on the change in a single moving average on two separate days. If the change exceeds an entry level a signal is generated. If the value of the change reverses signs, the trade is liquidated. Parameters that the trader can vary are the length of the moving average, the lag between days, and the entry levels.

MO. Momentum index using two moving averages. An index using the difference between two moving averages on the same day. When the difference exceeds the entry level, a signal is generated. If the value of the difference changes signs, the trade is liquidated. Parameters are the lengths of the moving averages and the entry levels.

RSI. Welles Wilder's Relative Strength Indicator. The RSI is a type of oscillator/countertrend system. If the market is overbought, a sell signal is generated; if it is oversold, a buy signal is generated. The RSI is based on the ratio of up closes to down closes and the value of RSI is from 0 to 100. A trailing stop-loss point is also provided. Parameters are entry levels for over-bought and oversold and the trailing stop-loss value.

DRF. Overbought/oversold index based on daily prices. Also a counter-trend system, the DRF value is based on daily prices in relation to the daily range. It may be exponentially smoothed to generate fewer signals and mini-mize whipsawing. When the DRF value is over the entry level, the market is overbought and a sell signal is generated. Conversely, when the DRF value is below the entry level, the market is oversold and a buy signal is generated. A trailing stop is included to minimize down-side risk. Parameters are the stop-loss point, entry levels, and the smoothing factor.

CHANL. High/low channel breakout with stop loss. Price channel break-out system based on the high and low price over a given time period. If the clos-ing price breaks out of this channel a signal is generated. The program has a nonretreating stop-loss level. Parameters are the channel length and the dol-lar stop-loss value.

LSO. Lagged, high/low channel breakout with stop loss. This system is similar to the one above except that there can be a lag between the end of the channel and the current trading day. New signals are generated when the price breaks out of the channel. The stop-loss level is based on the midpoint of the channel. Parameters are the channel length, the lag between the end of the channel, and the current date.

Because futures contracts involve limited life, that is, they expire, Trade Systems modules test for the end of the contract. This is done by liquidating the trading position in the month prior to the month of expiration. This prior-month feature checks for an exit signal, based on the appropriate rules of the trading system in use. If no exit signal occurs, the program liquidates the position in this old contract and rolls over into a new contract. This new position is based solely on the price history of the new contract with no regard for the last trade in the old contract. Trading then proceeds on this new contract until it too is near expiration.

When using Trade Systems to follow stocks, mutual funds, perpetual, or non-expiring futures contracts, a full-contract feature is available. These data files can be tested from beginning to end without the need for rollover into new contracts.

Other simulator features include slippage factors or "skids," testing over selected time spans, trades not executed during lock-limit days, and automatic tests of up to 100 data files.

The Trade Systems software relies on the data being in the standard Micro Futures format. This means that you will have to buy the data from Micro Futures, buy their data access software and contract with a data supplier or enter it by hand. If you also have trading software that uses the Computrac or CSI format, then your CSI or Computrac data will be useless for the Trade Systems. If, on the other hand, you have only the Trade Systems software, then there is really no problem, since you would have to buy or otherwise hand enter the data. Just keep in mind, not all data are compatible with all software.

The software packages allow additions and revisions to the data as you add daily prices. The software will allow the data to span more than one disk. This feature is handy when you are looking at a long time period and the data will not fit on one disk. This problem is more likely to surface when using an Apple or TRS-80 because the diskette capacity is smaller than on the IBM.

The historical simulator can be used to optimize the parameters of a given trading system and a given commodity. It can automatically test a series of commodities or stock data over a wide range of possible parameter values. A trade report shows the summary of each trade in a particular futures contract or stock, a summary of each contract or stock and a summary of all of the contracts or stocks held in a portfolio.

Each of these summaries tracks 14 measures of performance of the simulation including total net profit, maximum drawdown, percentage of profitable trades, and average gain. Optimization of a computerized trading system can be tricky business. Don't feel that once you have optimized, there is no need to optimize again. This is a process that must be continually monitored and updated as necessary. You must be the judge as to the benefits of optimization to your trading performance versus the cost of optimization in terms of the time it takes to run the programs and interpret the results.

Summary. Micro Futures' Trade Systems is a general purpose, relatively easy-to-use set of trading system modules. It represents the low end of the cost spectrum, but not necessarily low end as far as quality goes.

Trade Systems allows the trader to get his or her feet wet in steps by purchasing only one or a few of the trading systems. The entire set of modules is available together at substantial savings over the per module cost and really is not that expensive.

Trade Systems runs on a wide variety of computers including IBM, Apple, and TRS-80. It will require that you own the appropriate BASIC language interpreter. This is often included with other software that is "bundled" or included with the computer. Because the programs are written in BASIC, you can make modifications to the systems to customize them to your needs; a familiarity with the BASIC language is necessary for this, however.

If your needs are simple and your budget limited, Trade Systems is a viable alternative to the fancier packages like Computrac. One drawback, however, is the data format incompatibility with many other trading system packages. Micro Futures does have the necessary software to get the data over the phone from a variety of vendors, or you can enter the data manually. (I do not recommend this process for use with any software package. There's too much room for error.) You can also purchase the historical data on diskettes directly from Micro Futures. This is definitely a package worth looking into.

Futures Optionmaster

Com-Tech Software
141 West Jackson Boulevard
Suite 1531-A
Chicago, IL 60604
(312) 341-7557

With more and more traders using options on futures contracts as a means for speculation or hedging, the demand for special options software is becoming greater each day. One package used to analyze the fair market value of an option is the Futures OptionMaster by Com-Tech Software in Chicago, Illinois.

Futures OptionMaster was developed by Chicago Board of Trade floor traders with bond option and grain trading experience. It is used in CBOT training seminars and is currently used by over 100 CBOT floor traders and commercial houses.

The package is currently available for the Apple with 80 column screen option and for the IBM PC. The price for either version is $295. Parameters are preset for Treasury bonds, soybeans, Deutsche Mark, S&P 500 and gold. These parameters can be changed and more options can be added.

Futures OptionMaster gives the trader access to several powerful and useful tools with which to analyze options. They are as follows:

- Fair market value for puts and calls
- Delta (hedge ratio)
- Vega (premium-volatility relationship)
- Common spreads
- Time decay
- Implied volatility solver
- Position manager lets you see the cash risk and Delta change as futures prices move.

This software allows the trader to answer the "what if" questions based on prices, interest rate, exercise prices and volatility. Each factor can be independently changed to see the effect on key values and decision variables.

The printouts are a little confusing to read at first. However, with a bit of practice, the organization and layout of the tables begins to make sense and becomes rather easy. It is definitely for the serious professional interested in trading options.

Stock Option Analysis Program (SOAP)

H & H Scientific
13507 Pendelton Street
Fort Washington, MD 20744
(301) 292-2958

For the futures traders who also dabble in stock options, the Stock Option Analysis Program or SOAP can be useful to calculate the fair price of stock options. SOAP is produced and marketed by H & H Scientific of Fort Washington, Maryland. It uses the Black-Scholes model for calculations based on the price of the underlying stock, dividends paid, volatility, current interest rates and the time remaining on the option. Calendar (horizontal) spreads, vertical spreads, straddles, butterfly spreads, covered options and single positions can be analyzed as either current positions or future holdings.

SOAP begins by calculating the standard deviation from the volatility. The market-assigned volatility as well as the historical volatility of the stock are calculated and the user may use either measure. The prices of the stock are then calculated for three standard deviations above and below the mean value. Within this range, 51 values of price are calculated and examined. The fair price for each of these values is then calculated and the proceeds from closing that transaction, including commission costs, are calculated. The net gain or loss from that investment is determined assuming the stock were to close at that price. Of the 51 prices, only 11 are displayed. SOAP will calculate the probability of the occurrence for each of the particular stock prices and derive an expected return by multiplying this probability times the net gain or loss. The program plots the distribution of profits of the option transaction versus the price of the underlying stock.

SOAP features several commission schedules in its "Commission File" on diskette, which allows the trader to evaluate the expected return under a variety of commission levels. In addition, the user can specify a discount on commissions (for high-volume traders) as well.

A "Volatility File" contains basic information on selected stocks including dividends, ex-dividend dates, option expiration cycles and historical volatilities. This data can be automatically updated from the Dow Jones data service. Volatility changes of over 20 percent are flagged for the user.

A "Download File" contains the names of the stocks (ticker symbols) and the strike prices of the options to be downloaded from Dow Jones. The "Daily File" contains the downloaded stock and options prices from Dow Jones. If the user wishes, the data can be entered manually, but if a large number of options are to be evaluated, the automatic data gathering feature is recommended.

Telecommunications is supported at 300 and 1,200 baud through Tymnet, Telenet and Uninet services. Hayes Smartmodem commands protocols are predefined for automatic logon; however, any modem can be used for manual logon.

In order to use the Dow Jones data service, the user must notify H & H Scientific and return the original diskette so that it can be installed as part of the program. This allows automatic logon. Since the diskette is not copy protected, the user can use a backup copy of the program disk in the manual mode of operation. There is no charge for the installation of the Dow Jones password.

For the serious options trader, a companion package called the "Stock Options Scanner," or SOS, can scan a very large number of stock options and identify those single options, spreads, straddles and neutral hedges that are expected to be most attractive for further study through SOAP.

SOS can scan a list of up to 3,000 stock options, automatically downloaded from Dow Jones via its built-in communications software, or entered manually. It rank orders the top 50 and bottom 50 options (or option positions) according to the statistically expected rate of return for a number of user specified criteria.

Summary. H & H Scientific's Stock Option Analysis Program (SOAP) represents a special application software package that I mentioned in the beginning of this chapter. SOAP is extremely easy to use and highly intuitive. There is extensive prompting and error trapping. The 60+ page manual contains instructions for the program as well as a listing of the important equations, references, and an index.

When using the automatic data collection feature, the trader can gather and evaluate a variety of options and option strategies for different situations such as various commission schedules and volatility of the stock prices. This feature is very beneficial to the serious trader wishing to evaluate a large number of options.

Data can be entered manually or, more desirably, through the Dow Jones on-line data service. A modem is required for this feature. Arrangements for an account and password must be made directly with Dow Jones & Company. Instructions and help in this matter is provided in the manual.

The SOAP package is available for both Apple II and II+ under DOS 3.3. The price is $250. The IBM version requires PC-DOS version 1.1, 2.0 or 2.1

and 128K RAM. Its price is $350. The SOS package is $350 for the Apple version and $400 for the IBM.

The Technical Investor

Savant Corporation
P.O. Box 440278
Houston, TX 77244-0278
(713) 556-8363

The Technical Investor from the Savant corporation in Houston, Texas is a charting package with many of the desirable features that I spoke of earlier in this chapter. Part of the Savant Investor Series, it is designed to stand alone or work with its companion modules Fundamental Investor and The Investor's Portfolio.

Technical Investor runs on the IBM PC/XT/AT series of computers. It requires 256K RAM, dual disk drives, and an IBM compatible color graphics card. In addition, a modem and a graphics capable dot-matrix printer such as the Epson FX-80 or equivalent are strongly recommended.

This software is primarily a charting package, although it has many advanced features that can prove indispensable. It allows up to four mini-screens to appear on the monitor at one time. The user can switch size and number of graphs on the screen without losing the other graphs.

The package is menu and/or command driven. This allows the novice to be prompted and otherwise guided throughout the necessary steps to produce a graph. The expert, on the other hand, can zip on quickly by providing easy-to-learn and -remember two-digit commands without being interrupted by the menu changes. By typing "??" the menu will return. This allows the intermediate level user to use the commands he remembers and to be helped on those aspects of the package's operation that he is still unfamiliar with.

The commands that it uses are fairly intuitive. For example, "EA" indicates that the user wants to calculate an exponential moving average. The system will respond and ask you what length moving average you want. As more experience is gained, commands can be "chained." That is if you want to calculate a 12-day exponential moving average, you would type: "EA;12." If you are looking at a significant number of charts using several other options of the package, any short cuts that you take will add up to significant time savings. After all, that's what you got the computer for in the first place!

There are a variety of charts that you can produce using Technical Investor. You can do the conventional bar charts of open, high, low, and close; volume charts; and simple, weighted, and exponential moving averages of either price or volume. You can plot trading bands around the price using any of these averages. Point and figure charts with varying box sizes are also possible. Support and resistance lines are also automatically positioned, but you can override this feature and place them anywhere you want. A special feature called the "drawing mode" allows you to draw lines by using the cursor control keys. The system will also provide the values of the data plotted by aligning the cursor on a particular day's data. The values will appear at the bottom of the screen.

Often-used command sequences, such as those necessary to call up and modify a particular graph of interest, can be programmed. This feature can also save you time when looking at a large number of graphs or stocks.

Technical Investor has a built-in communications option that allows the trader to access the Dow Jones or Warner Computer Systems data bases. The program will dial the phone, log on to the data base, retrieve the quotes and store them on your diskettes, then log off the data base and hang up, all automatically. If you miss a few days because you were on vacation, the system will automatically detect that you have not received that back data and will update from the last day you have on your diskette.

There are extensive editing features for the data in the technical data base. You can make corrections or additions manually. You can set flags for high and low prices that will trigger a message to you when these points are reached or exceeded. This enables you to set stops or buy and sell signals. A summary report of the current data will also tell you when a price flag is reached.

The Technical Investor is extremely easy to use. Most information can be entered in plain English, not computerese. Numbers and dates can be entered in a variety of ways. For example, numbers can be entered as fractions or decimals; dates can be entered in month, day, year or day, month, year or MM/DD/YY. In short, Technical Investor makes it EASY. It even interprets many misspellings of some commands.

Another feature that is available as an option is the Databridge utility module. This allows data to be transported from The Technical Investor or Fundamental Investor to and from many of the popular spreadsheets such as 1-2-3 by Lotus and VisiCalc. If you're a do-it-yourselfer, this feature will allow complex data manipulations on the spreadsheets and the return of the data for the charting capabilities of the Technical Investor.

Summary. The Technical Investor is a full-featured charting package for stocks. It is as flexible as it is powerful. Commands can be entered directly or through the use of menus. The manual is well-written and easy to understand by both novice and expert. Data may be entered manually or through the built-in telecommunications software and either the Dow Jones News/Retrieval service or Warner Computer Systems service.

The package is professionally produced and packaged. It is sold through retail computer stores at $395. A demonstration can be arranged with a dealer in your area.

If chart analysis of stock data is your bag, this package offers quite a lot for the money. A technical staff is available for consultation about problems with the software.

Additional modules such as the Fundamental Investor and the Investor's Portfolio that integrate with this package can be added later for a total investment analysis package. The utility module Databridge allows transport of data to and from spreadsheet programs for additional complex manipulation.

The Technical Investor by Savant has been called the "Cadillac of Investment Programs." I think that it really lives up to its reputation. I highly recommend it for stock traders wishing to perform chart analysis on the computer.

CSI & Financial Micro-Data, Inc.

CSI-Stop, CSI-Trend, PDI, and Quickstudy
200 West Palmetto Park Road
Boca Raton, FL 33432-3788
(305) 392-8663

CSI has long been known as the leading data service to the trading community. They also produce a fine line of professionally developed software for traders. The Quickstudy software gives the trader a collection of traditional technical analysis tools such as moving averages, oscillators, stochastics, and so on. Over the past couple of years, they have introduced a new series of proprietary software studies.

These studies have been developed based on experience in digital signal processing, adaptive analysis, and statistical theory. CSI-Stop is used to determine where the optimal stop should be placed, and adjusts this point based on the data. CSI-Trend measures the randomness of the market for trade screening. PDI is the Probable Direction Index and predicts future direction of the market.

One of the advantages of the CSI product line is that it is integrated with the CSI data service and associated data management software. One of the most difficult aspects of dealing with large amounts of data is how to manage it without losing it. CSI's software makes that task relatively easy.

All of the CSI products are well designed and produced. The company is very stable and has been in the business from the days when microcomputers were only in their infancy. These products are well worth looking into.

Market Research Language

Futures Software Associates, Inc.
P.O. Box 263
Lima, PA 19037
(215) 872-4512

Trading system software has been in the process of evolution. As microcomputers have become more and more powerful, so has the trading software. One of the manifestations of the new forms of trading software has been generalized systems with which the trader can not only test the "traditional" trading systems (moving averages, oscillators, etc.) but develop and test his own.

One such system is *Market Research Language* (MRL). This system gives the trader data management functions such as adding new data and correcting or combining data on various commodities. It also provides statistical and mathematical functions which the trader can use in various combinations to create the necessary calculations for customized trading systems.

Market Research Language is truly what its name implies, a language with which to study the markets. Its functionality reminds me of some of the sophisticated statistical packages available, until recently, only on mainframe computers.

MRL offers the ability to graphically depict the data in a variety of formats. The familiar high-low-open-close chart, line graph and bar chart are easily chosen for the data at hand. Three different layouts allow the trader to view data as a full screen, split screen of equal sizes, and 2/3 – 1/3 split screen. Trend lines can be superimposed on the graphs. A cursor function allows the trader to point to a specific day and see the values of each of the data variables that are graphed.

The manual supplied with MRL is very thin relative to the power of this system. It describes the commands used and how they can be combined to create custom indicators for just about any type of system. Being small is not a hindrance to learning the system. The descriptions are clear and there are several examples of how each command is used. Several of the more popular systems have been pre-programmed and can be examined to see how MRL puts them together.

Data is brought into the system in ASCII format. Most data services, such as CSI, I.P. Sharp, etc., have the ability to format data in this fashion. MRL takes this data and converts it into its own format that it recognizes. The user has to have some knowledge of MS-DOS in order to manage the data, but I don't feel this is a significant drawback.

MRL may seem confusing to the beginner. It does require some learning, but the trader can grow into this system and still get useful research done. Obviously those with more experience will be able to utilize the more advanced features sooner than the novice.

I think the MRL is a must for the serious researcher/trader. It is extremely powerful, yet with commands easily understandable by the user. At $695 it is a bargain. A demonstration disk and audio tape is available at nominal cost. I would recommend this in order to get a feel for the system. It also provides a good tutorial for basic as well as some advanced features of this package.

Futures Software Associates has been around for some time. They have developed as a "quiet" company, not aggressively marketed, but producing some of the highest quality products in the business. I highly recommend this package.

Closing Comments Regarding Investment Software

It would be impossible to evaluate every computerized investment package that comes along. I have discussed only a few representative packages that perform a variety of tasks and have a variety of features: daily trading signals, historical testing and optimization, menu versus command driven, evaluation type software (i.e., options fair-value calculation). I liked all of the packages that I evaluated, but they may not suit all investor's needs.

If you are serious about your investing, also be serious about choosing an investment package. Consider your needs, budget, and hardware configuration (if you already own a computer). Demonstration packages are available on many of the major packages or separate modules can be purchased and added later. This allows you to evaluate the software and how it fits your needs without a large dollar outlay.

If there are investment software consultants in your area (most likely in the big cities), please contact them. You may pay more for a computer or software through them, but a bad mistake in choosing software or computer hardware also costs.

Try to keep additional uses of the computer in mind when evaluating investment packages.

DESIGNING AND TESTING TRADING SYSTEMS:

How to Avoid Costly Mistakes

LOUIS B. MENDELSOHN

■

LOUIS B. MENDELSOHN

Louis B. Mendelsohn is a well-known developer of technical analysis software. He created the concept of historical testing of trading strategies/models in investment software for personal computers. This innovation lets futures traders design, test, and apply unique models for each market to get consistent daily trading signals. Building on this innovative concept, he developed ProfitTaker futures trading software, long recognized as one of the leading software programs for trading futures.

Before becoming a technical analyst and investment software developer, Mr. Mendelsohn was an avid stock, options, and commodities trader while employed as a hospital administrator. In 1980 he left hospital administration to become President of Mendelsohn Enterprises, Inc.

He has been the focus of numerous articles in *Futures, Investor's Daily, Forbes, Barron's, Stocks & Commodities*, and *Wall Street Computer Review*, as well as in several recent textbooks on technical analysis. Mr. Mendelsohn has authored over a dozen articles on investment analysis during the past seven years, and is best known for his research on the pitfalls to avoid when doing historical testing. He has been a seminar leader at various investment workshops and symposia in the United States, as well as a guest on Financial News Network.

Mr. Mendelsohn, a Rhode Island native, has lived in Florida for the past twelve years. He holds a Bachelor's degree in Administration and Management Science from Carnegie Mellon University, and a M.B.A. with Honors from Boston University.

■ CHAPTER TWENTY-FOUR ■

W ITH THE ADVENT OF MICROCOMPUTERS A DECADE AGO, the window of opportunity opened for individual futures traders to design and test technical trading systems. Initially, only those traders who were also proficient programmers could do so, since the early trading software was neither very elegant nor user-friendly. At first, two basic approaches were available to traders: "tool box" and "black box."

Early Approaches Lack Testing Capability

The tool-box approach was limited to charting prices and calculating individual technical indicators. The main drawback was that traders still had to analyze subjectively all of the information to decide what action to take. Since this approach did not generate actual trading signals, it cannot be considered a trading system.

By comparison, the black box approach did generate signals. However, they were based on secret indicators that had fixed, preset values. There was no way to verify whether a system's logic was even based on sound technical analysis principles. Therefore, all traders using a particular black box system, regardless of their differences in risk propensity, trading style, and financial goals, received the identical signal at the same time and were expected to act on it on blind faith.

Neither approach had a history tester. Traders could not design and test their own trading models on real price data to find the best model to use for each market.

Introduction to Historical Modeling

ProfitTaker, which I developed, was the first full-blown futures trading system with disclosed trading rules. It enabled traders to design and test customized trading models using actual contracts with rollovers under simulated real-time trading conditions. With its innovative modeling concept, ProfitTaker ushered in a new generation of software.

But historical modeling did not become practical until the replacement of the Apple computer (with its limited memory and disk capacity) by the much more powerful IBM and low-cost compatibles as the computer of choice among traders. Before long, a plethora of trading systems followed suit, adopting ProfitTaker's modeling concept. Then, as satellite technology became more cost effective and daily prices more volatile, traders turned increasingly to day-trading. Now, even traders with limited trading capital can analyze realtime tick-by-tick prices on their computers. Quotation services, which previously provided only price quotes and news information, now offer built-in technical analysis and system modeling software.

Costly Mistakes Must Be Avoided

Today's traders easily develop and test customized trading models, which can be retested and adjusted as market conditions change. All that traders have to do is pick the price data to be tested and specify the indicator values to use. Depending on the number of models involved and the computer's speed, this procedure may need to be performed in a two-step process: coarse testing followed by fine testing. First the increment size between values is set relatively large for each indicator. Once a narrow range of profitable models is found, the increment size is reduced. These models are then tested within this more limited range, until the best model is isolated.

This process, by which traders design trading models, test their profitability and search for the best model to use, is widely known as "historical optimization." Too often, however, after models founded on historical data are applied to current prices in real-time trading, the expected profits are not realized. With so many traders now using computers to design and test trading systems, it is important to examine the intricacies of the modeling process itself and to identify commonly made mistakes that could be costly to your bottom line.

Full Disclosure

First, you should avoid using trading systems that intentionally keep some or all of their trading rules secret. These unwarranted restrictions prevent you from understanding the rationale behind the signals and undermine the discipline and confidence needed for implementing a sound trading strategy.

Testing is the Means to the End

Another mistake occurs if you become so involved looking for profitable models on historical data that you completely lose sight of the forest for the sake of the trees. Testing is only a means to an end, not an end in itself. You should not try to find the most profitable trading model on historical prices. Otherwise, you risk selecting an isolated model that is surrounded on both sides by poorly performing ones. I call this type of model a "profit island."

The goal of historical modeling is to find models that have a high likelihood of producing profits and remaining stable in the ensuing period when you are actually trading in real time. To do this, you should look for a broad band of profitable models with the best performing one located near the middle. To either side of the best model are other profitable models, with their performance dropping off gradually the further they are from the best one. A model chosen from this profit cluster is more likely to remain stable even with subsequent changes in price characteristics.

Keep it Simple

As you make an arithmetic increase in either the number of indicators in a system or the range over which each of the indicators can vary, the number of models to be tested increases geometrically. Table 24-1 illustrates the effect that the number of indicators has on the number of models to be tested.

You can see that a system with three indicators, each of which can have a range of 25 values, results in a universe of over 15,000 models. When a fourth indicator is added, the number of models increases to nearly 400,000. Adding a fifth indicator raises the number of models to nearly 10 million. Increasing the range of values over which the indicators vary also causes the number of models to increase, but less dramatically. For instance, a system with five indicators, which can each have twenty values, creates a total of over three million models. Keeping the number of indicators constant at five, but increasing their range of values from 20 to 25, increases the number of models to nearly 10 million.

The amount of time it takes to test a system varies in direct proportion to the number of models tested. Therefore, it would be impractical on a microcomputer to test a system on even one market using more than four or five indicators. The coarse testing/fine testing method would be required, and even then the increment sizes might need to be so large that only a small percentage of possible models could actually be tested. Under these circumstances, there is a tendency, after you pick a model to use in real time, to feel compelled to change to other models or to switch indicators each time you incur a string of back-to-back losing trades. This syndrome, known as paralysis of analysis, can become immobilizing.

Still, many traders believe that the more indicators a model comprises, the better the system's profitability. This may be true up to a point, but then diminishing returns set in. If you use a limited number of indicators in the modeling process, you will discern a general pattern to a market that object-

Table 24-1
Effect of Number of Indicators on Number of Models to be Tested

Range of Values Each Indicator has:	Number of Indicators				
	1	2	3	4	5
5	5	25	125	625	3,125
10	10	100	1,000	10,000	100,000
15	15	225	3,375	50,625	759,375
20	20	400	8,000	160,000	3,200,000
25	25	625	15,625	390,625	9,765,625

ively exists. By contrast, when you employ too many indicators, you merely superimpose a pattern, which actually does not exist, onto the historical data. This is particularly true of indicators that are highly correlated with one another. Then you risk using seemingly profitable models in real time trading. They look good on paper, but conform so closely to the historical data that they have little, if any, predictiveness. This serious pitfall is commonly known as "curve-fitting." Such models tend to be unstable, decay rapidly, and will therefore subject you to unnecessary losses.

Some software programs now give traders considerable flexibility to write their own trading rules. While this much flexibility may be useful to certain traders who have the time and resources to engage in extensive trading system design, most traders find this much flexibility to be a hindrance to their success as traders. Such software encourages traders to build complex systems with numerous indicators, in the search for the "Holy Grail." By doing so, traders risk picking "curve-fitted" models, or becoming immobilized by the paralysis -of-analysis syndrome. Most off-the-shelf systems already offer more than enough user flexibility. Unless you have considerable spare time to spend, or are a full-time professional technical analyst, it really isn't cost-effective to recreate the wheel by designing your own system from scratch. You're better off leaving that to professional trading system developers.

Know When to Re-Optimize

Each market should be re-optimized routinely, on a preemptive basis. Many software programs can screen models to find those that meet your financial performance objectives, saving this information on a disk file. Then you can view the information on your monitor. With fast computers, such as those based on the 80286 or 80386 microprocessor, testing can be done on a rotational basis, one market each night, and several on a weekend. This way, even with a large diversified portfolio, you can easily re-optimize every market that you trade at least once a month.

To make this process virtually a turn-key operation for my clients, I provide a monthly report to them, called *ProfitTuner*, which tests eighteen actively traded markets on a mainframe computer. In some the models may change from one month to the next, while in other markets the models are quite stable. Since the object is to find models that are not curve-fitted, Profit-Tuner lists the 50 best-performing models for each market, rather than the one model that produces the maximum profit.

Whenever a fundamental event takes place, affecting specific markets in a way that could not have been anticipated by the modeling process, you should retest. For instance, a weekend meeting of the G–7 trading partners, with an unexpected announcement of a revised trading range for the U.S.

dollar, should immediately raise a red flag for you to perform retesting on those markets.

Check Your Models for Curve-fitting

Perform blind-simulation testing to see whether your models are curve-fitted. To do this, test your models on a defined time period of historical prices, which I call a testing window. The best model selected is then applied to a trading window composed of entirely different historical prices that were not included in the original test. In this way, real-time trading conditions are simulated, with the performance of the model assessed for its stability, predictiveness and profitability prior to actually risking capital.

Blind-simulation testing should actually be performed as part of your routine testing. Different size testing and trading windows for each market could be explored, since the window sizes affect the test results and choice of models. Finding the optimal window sizes for each market could substantially improve real-time trading performance.

Make Realistic Assumptions

You should also set realistic assumptions about overhead costs, particularly the amount of slippage. If your chosen model isn't derived under realistic conditions, its performance in real time may be both disappointing and costly. Table 24-2 illustrates the effects that various overhead costs have on a model's performance.

As you can see in this example, Model A has $10,000 total profit,25 trades, and $2,000 maximum drawdown. Model B has $12,000 profit, 45 trades, and also $2,000 drawdown. At first glance, when overhead is excluded, Model B appears to be superior to Model A. The risk/reward ratio of profit to drawdown is higher for Model B.

Then, when a $100 overhead for slippage and commissions is included, both models produce identical net profit and risk/reward ratio. The inclusion of $100 overhead costs is more damaging to Model B because of its higher frequency of trading. This pattern is further exacerbated as overhead costs are increased. At $250 per round turn, Model B's ratio of profit to drawdown is less than 1.00. At $300, it has a net loss of $1,500.

In effect, the impact of overhead is magnified on models that generate a substantial number of trades. Models that look good when overhead costs are not taken into consideration may prove to be big losers when realistic costs are factored in. Overhead assumptions regarding slippage should reflect differences in each market's price volatility.

Table 24-2
Comparison of Two Trading Models with Various Overhead Assumptions

Overhead Assumption	Model A						Model B					
	Number of Trades	Total Profit/ Loss	Total Overhead Cost	Net Profit/ Loss	Maximum Drawdown	Ratio Net Profit to Maximum Drawdown	Number of Trades	Total Profit/ Loss	Total Overhead Cost	Net Profit/ Loss	Maximum Drawdown	Ratio Net Profit to Maximum Drawdown
Test Excludes Overhead	25	10,000	0	10,000	2,000	5.00	45	12,000	0	12,000	2,000	6.00
Test includes $100 Overhead per Roundturn	25	10,000	2,500	7,500	2,000	3.75	45	12,000	4,500	7,500	2,000	3.75
Test includes $250 Overhead per Roundturn	25	10,000	6,250	3,750	2,000	1.875	45	12,000	11,250	750	2,000	.375
Test includes $300 Overhead per Roundturn	25	10,000	7,500	2,500	2,000	1.25	45	12,000	13,500	-1,500	2,000	-.75

You also need to set realistic values for the limit move in each market. Otherwise, your modeling results will not be based on realistic execution prices. It is incorrect to record the execution of a trade as occurring at the time that the signal is generated when that market is lock-limit. Limit conditions must be accounted for and executions deferred until feasible.The big move in the silver market in 1979–1980 is a classic case where hypothetical track records of trading systems overstate profits due to unrealistic locklimit assumptions.

A major improvement in this area could be made if data suppliers were to report each market's daily limit value and the 90-day T-bill rate on a daily basis along with prices, volume, and open interest. Then modeling software could be programmed to check precisely for normal and expanded daily limits during testing to avoid unrealistic price executions, and compare a system's daily rate of return to the risk-free return.

Test the Right Contracts

The type of contract tested also affects the results and model selected. You can choose between actual contract months with rollovers, single contracts, or artificially derived continuous contracts. My suggestion is to use actual contracts with rollovers because this minimizes unnecessary distortions. Results are less valid when you test single contracts over periods of low volume and open interest. Distortions also occur when you test continuous contracts that don't realistically handle the price spread between two contract months, at a time when the model has a position on in the expiring contract.

Test the Right Data

It is better to err on the side of more rather than less data. Statistical validity is increased when the testing window size is larger. It would be unwise to select a model based on just a few trades that occurred in the past couple of months. Such a model would not work very well under different market conditions that you might be faced with in the immediate future. Also, you should know about the model's distribution of profits. If you discover a highly profitable-looking model, but most of its profits were made over a year ago on one or two good trades and it has lost money since, that's not a worthy model. One quick way to look at the distribution of profits over the test period is to calculate for each model its ratio of profits in the last half of the test period to total profits over the entire test period. Any model with a ratio of less than 50 percent should be rejected, regardless of how well it does on other performance measures.

Of course, you should also verify the accuracy of your data. If it is not clean, your test results will be distorted. Automatic daily updating using a modem will eliminate typo errors that would otherwise be introduced when prices are updated manually from daily newspapers. The cliché garbage-in, garbage-out must be respected when doing historical testing.

Know Your Own Risk Propensity

Experiment with a trading system before actually trading it in real-time. You should be comfortable with it, both in terms of its operation and the indicators that it employs to generate buy/sell signals. Table 23-3 lists a number of performance measures that you can look at when comparing models to one another.

Table 24-3   Performance Measures to Use When Evaluating a Trading Model

- Total number of closed out trades
- Percentage of winning trades
- Percentage of long winning trades
- Percentage of short winning trades
- Gross cumulative profit or loss
- Net cumulative profit (Gross profit less overhead)
- Maximum drawdown
- Ratio of net cumulative profit to drawdown
- Maximum winning trade
- Maximum losing trade
- Average winning trade
- Average losing trade
- Average profit or loss per trade
- Number of consecutive losing trades
- Unrealized profit or loss in open position
- Distribution of profits over time

Check the ratio of cumulative net profit to maximum drawdown. Examine the drawdown. Drawdown should not be calculated as the dollar value of back-to-back losing trades. It's the maximum equity drop from a high point in equity to the subsequent low point in equity until the high point in equity is breached to the upside.

This ratio gives you a good indication of your risk/reward payoff. Essentially, it tells you the number of dollars you can expect to win for every dollar you put at risk. You should know your own risk propensity. Some traders are willing to risk a dollar to make a dollar. Others need more payoff for each dollar put at risk. Ask yourself how many dollars you would need to make on a given trade to motivate you to risk a dollar by taking that trade. That's the minimum ratio of profit to drawdown that you should accept.

Make sure that the system's characteristics and performance are compatible with your temperament, style of trading, and the depth of your pockets. If you can't handle emotionally or financially the frequency of back-to-back losing trades or the short term drawdowns that a particular system incurs, what good is it if it's a big money maker in the long run?

Other Modeling Ideas to Explore

Instead of developing models based on recent price data, you might want to test data from previous time periods that closely resemble today's market conditions. For instance, if you want to find a model that works well during a current drought affecting the soybean market, you might go back and test prior data in which beans were bullish because of earlier drought conditions. The grain markets, in particular, lend themselves to this type of seasonal testing.

Another interesting approach is to incorporate economic or fundamental indicators into your trading strategy. For instance, you might use one or more fundamental indicators to identify a bias for each market as either bullish, bearish, or sideways. Then, for instance, you would only act on your technical system's buy signals if, at the same time, that market's fundamental "bias" is bullish. In effect, you are applying a fundamental filter to confirm the technical signal generated by your trading system. This approach can eliminate false signals and alert you to impending turning points in the markets. Recently, I developed a software program called Trader that lets the user do just this by correlating the effects of 50 economic indicators on the price direction in each market.

Conclusion

With system design and testing still more of an art than a science, you are not guaranteed a free lunch from the futures markets. Common sense and businesslike decision making are needed for sound money management and proper portfolio diversification. Costly mistakes in designing and testing trading systems must be avoided. The computer is only a tool. It can help improve your trading if you are already knowledgeable about market dynamics, technical analysis methods, and modeling pitfalls to avoid. But it can't turn a trader who has not done his homework into an instant winner.

■ SECTION SIX ■

CONCLUSION

■

COMMON THREADS OF THE MASTER STRATEGIES (AND STRATEGISTS)

SUSAN ABBOTT

■

■

SUSAN M. ABBOTT

Susan Abbott has devoted her career to understanding and writing about all aspects of the commodity and financial markets. Ms. Abbott joined *Futures* Magazine in 1978 as Assistant Editor, later being named Associate Editor, where she covered a number of agricultural and financial futures markets. She joined the magazine's Chicago bureau in 1981 and was named Senior Editor in 1983.

At *Futures*, Ms. Abbott focused on articles concerning trading techniques, industry news and profiles of leading industry figures.

She joined the Chicago Board Options Exchange in 1987 and currently is the staff writer in its marketing department.

Ms. Abbott attended the University of Illinois in Champaign-Urbana, where she earned a Bachelor's degree in Agricultural Communications. During her academic career, she filled a summer internship as a reporter covering the corn market at the Chicago Board of Trade for Commodity News Services (now Knight-Ridder Financial News). She was raised on a Northwestern Illinois corn and beef farm.

■

▪ CHAPTER TWENTY-FIVE ▪

NOW THAT YOU'VE READ THIS BOOK, you should have no doubt that the common goal of trading approaches is *profit*. There is no other reason for analyzing and trading the futures markets. Each trader, in his or her own way, tries to decipher and make sense of a relatively small amount of information in order to make trades that will produce profit.

Some people, however, say they trade futures for profit, but they really don't mean it. The people trading futures on a "not for profit" basis are those who really are more interested in excitement, action, and cocktail party conversation.

But for any of the master strategies to work, you must be devoted to profits and nothing else. And, if you are, it will be hard work. Anything less and you might as well take your money to Las Vegas and try your luck.

Luck Plays No Part

Futures trading is *not*—I repeat, is not—gambling. In Las Vegas, *luck* is the primary determinant of success. The odds are constant. In futures, you can significantly improve your odds of success with knowledge, money management, and a commitment to profits.

The most fascinating thing about futures trading is that there are so many ways to look at the limited amount of data available. Price is the most obvious, with its highs, lows, opens, and closes. Although that may not seem like much, consider that traders analyze those four aspects of price in every imaginable time frame—yearly (or, even, decades) down to minutes and seconds.

Analyzing price in terms of time is common, and many master strategies consider time in its own right with the discovery of certain rhythms, or cycles, in the market's behavior. Minutes, hours, days, weeks, months, and years go by. Planets revolve around the sun. Time is the one true constant in the markets.

Volume and open interest are derivatives of the market itself, but many master strategists find useful clues to the market's strength and participants by studying these two factors. Remember, these strategists are trying to glean as much insight as possible into the market's behavior, so they can put on trades that result in profit.

But, will knowing when and where prices will go and with who in charge automatically result in profits? Maybe and maybe not. You can study and make accurate predictions about where prices might go, but unless you know how to *trade,* you might find yourself getting in late, putting up too much money, and afraid to cut losses short (or let profits run). In the end, your knowledge about prices will be for naught—your money is gone.

That's why all the master strategies require *discipline,* which mainly involves intense lessons in understanding yourself and your emotions. This aspect of achieving profits is more than half the battle, according to the traders represented in this book.

The Real Factors of Success

Knowledge

Does the thought of somebody keeping a secret from you make you work all the harder to discover it? If so, you're in the company of the master strategists. Bill Eng puts it most succinctly in chapter 14: "I couldn't allow the market to hide this ultimate secret from me. I had to learn to anticipate when and how the markets reversed."

The market, with its many diverse forces and participants, is a constantly changing and evolving story—a mystery novel with twists and turns you sometimes don't recognize until after the fact, with chapter endings that sometimes are obvious, sometimes elusive.

The market is itself. It will do what it wants when it wants, with total disregard for any individual's hopes, wishes, or expectations. It is bigger than any of us, yet represents our collective opinions. It is the ultimate mind game.

But, it is a game that accepts challengers from all fronts. These challengers, motivated by profits, know that to win, they must learn to recognize the changes in the market's trend. Whether you trade for long-term profits or daily profits, what you're trying to do is find the *trend* for your time frame and go with it.

Price analysis is based on the theory that history repeats itself. Master strategists study historical price patterns, trends, and actions in order to recognize similar events as current markets unfold.

What they see is what gives the various methods their names. For example, a consolidation area that an Edwards and McGee chartist might call a *flag* could be a *fourth wave* to one who follows Elliott Waves, or a *value area* in Market Profile® parlance. What Market Profile® calls a *bracket* is similar to *support* and *resistance* areas to others—and it's likely the numbers involved will be familiar to followers of Gann or Fibonacci techniques.

It's not that any of these approaches is necessarily better than the next—except that the method you choose must be suitable for you and your style of trading. Obviously, many, many ways exist to look at the market in an effort to discover its secrets, and the few mentioned above are only a partial list.

Whatever the approach, the master strategies have another common thread. Each starts with the big picture and works down toward a microscopic view. That brings us back to *trends*. The master strategists want to know the major trends so they primarily take trades in the direction of the larger trend. You never know when that one small trade could turn into what Joe Krutsinger describes as the big one "to hang over the mantel like a moose head."

Monthly charts are the place to start; then, weeklies; then dailies. To perfect order entry as much as possible, many master strategists then turn to their microscopes—trusty quote machines with bar charts of intraday action.

Time is another common thread among the master strategies—to the point that it *is* the master strategy for many traders. To the master strategists, time can be as celestial as the premise that the planets and their revolutions define time, as intellectual as the thought that the amount of time price spends at a certain level equates to value, and as observant as discovering a market's rhythmic cycle.

The purpose behind deciphering the market's timing also relates to profits. Who cares what the price level is as long as you know what's going to be a turning point in time?

The next step beyond time in its literal sense is a couple of notions that include price. To Gann, price should equal time as the markets move in a natural, harmonic progression. To Pete Steidlmayer, originator of the Market Profile®, Price × Time = Value. Another method applies Fibonacci retracements to both price and time.

Emotions

There are two kinds of emotions the master strategists all learn to deal with—the market's and their own.

The market's emotions are similar to our own because they are created by human traders whose eagerness to enter or leave a trade is reflected in the way prices move.

The Elliott Wave Theory, for example, is entirely based on the idea that these emotions—evident via price action—take the same pattern at all levels of price movements, be it minutes or years.

The master strategies also seek to recognize areas of extreme disinterest and excitability. For example, the bullish consensus figures and other overbought/oversold indicators are primary tools in the master strategist's tool-box. With the advent of options on futures, a new tool in the emotional area is coming into play—options volatility.

The second, and no doubt more difficult, area of emotions in the market is learning to deal with your own emotions. People have figured out how to measure the market's emotions, but no one yet has mastered an over-bought/oversold indicator for a trader's emotions.

Every one of the master strategists, I'm sure, would tell you that the system you eventually trade with is the easiest part of trading. Learning how to deal with your emotions while you are trading is the far more difficult task. There is no room for hoping in trading. There is only room for logical, clear-cut, disciplined action. But, that's easier said than done. Maybe that complete concentration is why most traders I've met tend to be loners. They know that to be successful, they must rely on no one's opinion but their own. On the other hand, most of the traders I've met have no problem with believing their own opinion. They have to, or they'd never have enough nerve to make a trade when they should. As Bruce Babcock wrote in chapter 21: "One of the biggest impediments to success in commodity trading comes from a most unlikely source—expert opinion."

You, too, must do what each of the master strategists has done—discover the time frame in which you feel most comfortable trading and develop your own unique approach to the market.

You must decide for yourself if long-term trading or day-trading appeals to you, fits your schedule and lifestyle, and is the way you want to approach the markets. You also will develop your own unique trading system by taking bits and pieces of analysis methods that appeal to you and your sense of how the market works and that complement one another.

Simplicity

Despite what you might think, the master strategists ultimately find that simplicity is a key in trading. The system should be simple, and the number of markets traded should be manageable. Like the old saying that too many cooks spoil the broth, they've found that too many analytical tools spoil the trading system. And they've come to realize that everything needn't have an answer. As Jake Bernstein wrote in chapter 11: "Ours is not to reason why, ours is but to sell or buy."

Discipline

This is the ultimate common thread. Without discipline in following what you know will work well for you in the markets, you've lost any chance you might have had in your pursuit of profits.

The markets demand the discipline and devotion that you may be familiar with in a successful career. You must do your homework. You have to learn from your mistakes.

"Losses are tuition," writes Jake Bernstein in chapter 2. "Learn from each loss and do your very best to avoid taking the same loss twice or more for the same reason."

Common Threads

The master strategies and master strategists have common threads: profits, trends, simplicity, and discipline.

The strategists want to find market trends in a simple way. They must possess the discipline to carry out their plans without the baggage of emotions.

In short, they seek *profits* from the markets with the tools of the master strategies. Many traders have achieved this goal, and you can, too—if you heed their lessons.

RESOURCES

■ RESOURCES ■

Bibliography

Angell, George. *Computer-Proven Commodity Spreads*. Brightwaters, NY : Windsor, 1981.

Baratz, Morton S. *The Investor's Guide to Futures Money Management*. Columbia, MD : Futures Publishing Group, 1984

Barnes Robert M. *Megaprofit Commodity Methods: Ten New Technical Trading Methods*. Brightwaters, NY : Windsor, 1983.

Barnes, Robert M. *Taming the Pits: A Technical Approach to Commodity Trading*. New York: John Wiley & Sons, 1979.

Bernstein, Jacob. *Short-Term Trading in Futures: A Manual of Systems, Strategies and Techniques*. Chicago, IL : Probus Publishing Co., 1988.

Bernstein, Jacob. *Jake Bernstein's Facts on Futures: Insights and Strategies for Winning in the Futures Markets*. Chicago, IL : Probus Publishing Co., 1987.

Bernstein, Jacob. *The Handbook of Commodity Cycles: A Window on Time*. New York: John Wiley & Sons, 1982.

Bernstein, Jacob. *The Investor's Quotient*. New York: John Wiley & Sons, 1981.

Bernstein, Jacob. *MBH Seasonal Futures Charts: A Study of Weekly Seasonal Tendencies in Commodity Futures Markets*. Winnetka, IL : MBH Commodity, 1979.

Blumenthal, Earl. *Chart for Profit: Point and FigureTrading*. Larchmont, NY : Investors Intelligence, 1975.

Bolton, A. Hamilton. *The Elliott Wave Principle: A Critical Appraisal*. Hamilton, Bermuda: Monetary Research, 1960.

Bookstaber, Richard M. *Option Pricing & Investment Strategies*, Rev. ed. Chicago, IL : Probus Publishing Co., 1987.

Chisholm, Michael. *The Taurus Method*. Brightwaters, N Y : Windsor, 1985.

Chisholm, Michael. *The Mega-Trade Method*. Brightwaters, N Y : Windsor, 1984

447

Chicago Board of Trade, *Commodity Trading Manual.* Chicago Board of Trade, Chicago, IL: 1985

Dahl, Dale C. and Jerome W. Hammond. *Market and Price Analysis, The Agricultural Industries.* New York: McGraw-Hill, 1977.

Elliott, R.N.. *The Wave Principle.* New York: Elliott, 1938.

Eng, William F. *The Technical Analysis of Stocks, Options & Futures: Advanced Trading Systems and Techniques.* Chicago, IL: Probus Publishing Co. 1988.

Gann, William D. *How to Make Profits in Commodities,* Rev. ed. Pomeroy, WA: Lambert-Gann, 1951.

Goldberg, Harold. *Advanced Commodity Spread Trading.* Brightwaters, NY: Windsor, 1985.

Hamon, J.D. *Breakthroughs in Commodity Technical Analysis.* Brightwaters, NY: Windsor, 1985

Hamon, J.D. *Advanced Commodity Trading Techniques.* Brightwaters, NY: Windsor, 1981

Hieronymous, Thomas. *Economics of Futures Trading for Commercial and Personal Profit,* 2nd ed. New York: Commodity Research Bureau, 1977.

Hill, John R. *Scientific Interpretation of Bar Charts.* Hendersonville, NC: Commodity Research Institute, 1979.

Hill, John R. *Stock and Commodity Market Trend Trading by Advanced Technical Analysis.* Hendersonville, NC: Commodity Research Institute, 1977

Jiler, Harry, ed. *Forecasting Commodity Prices: How the Experts Analyze the Market.* New York: Commodity Research Bureau, 1975.

Kaufman, Perry J. *Technical Analysis in Commodities.* New York: John Wiley & Sons, 1980.

Kaufman, Perry J. *Commodity Trading Systems and Methods.* New York: John Wiley & Sons, 1978

Leslie, Conrad. *Conrad Leslie's Guide for Successful Speculating.* Chicago, IL: Dartnell Press, 1970.

Longstreet, Roy W. *Viewpoints of a Commodity Trader,* New York: Frederick Fell Publications, 1967

Oster, Merrill J. *Professional Hedging Handbook: A Guide to Hedging Crops and Livestock.* Cedar Falls, IA: Investor Publications, 1979.

Weiss Research. *Timing the Market, How to Profit in Bull and Bear Markets with Technical Analysis.* Chicago, IL: Probus Publishing Co., 1986.

Teweles, Richard J. and Frank J. Jones. *The Futures Game, Who Wins, Who Loses, Why.* New York.: McGraw-Hill, 1987.

Taylor, William. *The Trader's & Investor's Guide to Commodity Trading Systems, Software and Databases.* Chicago, IL: Probus Publishing Co., 1986.

Weintraub, Neal T. *The Weintraub Day-Trader, Self Teaching Day Trading Technical System for Predicting Tommorow's Prices and Profits.* Brightwaters, NY: Windsor, 1986.

Williams, Larry R. *The Definitive Guide to Commodity Trading, Volumes I and II,* Brightwaters, NY: Windsor, 1988

Williams, Larry R. *How I Made One Million Dollars Last Year Trading Commodities.* Brightwaters, NY: Windsor, 1979.

Williams, Larry R. and Michelle Noseworthy. *Sure Thing Commodity Trading, How Seasonal Factors Influence Commodity Prices.* Brightwaters, NY: Windsor, 1977.

Zeig, Kermit C., Jr. and William N. Nix. *The Commodity Options Market: Dynamic Trading Strategies for Speculation and Hedging.* Homewood, IL: Dow Jones-Irwin, 1978.

Newsletters, Magazines and Advisory Services

The Bullish Concensus Newsletter. Includes hotline updated weekly
Hadady Corporation.
1111 S. Arroyo Parkway, Suite 410
Pasadena, CA 91109-0490
818/ 441-3457

The Cambridge Financial Manager. Includes hotline updated nightly.
Cambridge Financial Management
One Broadway, 11th Floor
Cambridge, MA 02142
617/ 661-6600

Chartcraft Weekly Commodity Service
Chartcraft Inc.
30 Church Street
New Rochelle, NY 10801
914/ 632-0422

Chartcraft Weekly Options Service
  Chartcraft Inc.
  30 Church Street
  New Rochelle, NY 10801
  914/632-0422

Commodity Closeup & Pro Farmer. Includes hotline updated three times daily.
  Oster Communications, Inc.
  219 Parkade
  Cedar Falls, IA 50613
  319/277-1271

Commodity Perspective. Chart service and technical analysis.
  Commodity Perspective
  30 S. Wacker Dr., Suite 1820
  Chicago, IL 60606
  312/454-1801

Commodity Research Bureau Futures Chart Service
  Commodity Research Bureau,
  30 S. Wacker Dr., Suite 1820
  Chicago, IL 60606
  312/454-1801

Commodity Traders Consumer Report
  Advanced Trading Seminars
  1731 Howe Avenue, Suite 149
  Sacramento, CA 95825
  916/677-7562

CRB Commodity Index Report
  Knight-Ridder Commodity Research Bureau
  100 Church St., Suite 1850
  New York, NY 10007
  212/406-4545

The Elliott Wave Commodity Forecast
  New Classics Library
  P.O. Box 1618
  Gainesville, GA 30503
  404/536-0309

Futures Market Alert. Trading strategies and futures industry news.
  Robbins Trading Company
  222 Riverside Plaza
  Chicago, IL 60606
  312/454-5000

Futures Factors—The Futures Portfolio Advisor. Includes hotline updated nightly.

Wasendorf & Associates, Inc.
802 Main St.
Cedar Falls, IA 50613
319/268-0441

Futures, The Magazine of Commodities & Options   312.977.0999
Oster Communications, Inc.
219 Parkade   FAX ?
Cedar Falls, IA 50613
319/277-6241 (319-277-6341) 3,268.9499

Futures Truth Market Newsletter—Computerized Performance Summary of Publically Offered Trading Systems.
The Futures Truth Co.
815 Hillside
Hendersonville, NC 28739
704/697-0273

Managed Account Reports. In-depth reports of commodity trading advisors
LCR Communications, Inc.
5513 Twin Knolls Road, Suite 213
Columbia, MD 21045
301/730-5365

MBH Weekly Commodity Letter. Includes Day Trader hotline updated nightly. S&P Traders hotline also available.
MBH Commodity Advisors, Inc.
P.O. Box 353
Winnetka, IL 60093
312/291-1870

Norwood Index Report. Monitors the performance of managed commodity futures accounts.
Stark Research, Inc.
P.O. Box 591
Palatine, IL 60067
312/359-4508

Opportunities in Options
Opportunities in Options
P.O. Box 2126
Malibu, CA 90265
213/457-3199

The Profile Report. Includes hotline and on-line information updated twice daily.
Dalton Capital Management, Inc.
372 W. Ontario, Suite 301
Chicago, IL 60610
312/988-9688

Taurus & Optimum Trades. Includes hotline updated nightly.
The Taurus Corporation
P.O. Box 767
Winchester, VA 22601
703/667-4827

Trade Winds Newsletter. Weather-related recommendations. Includes hotline updated twice daily
Freese-Notis/Weather Trades
1453 N.E. 66th Avenue
Des Moines, IA 50313
515/289-247

North American Commodity Futures Exchanges

Chicago Board of Trade
Attention: Education and Marketing Division
141 West Jackson Street, Suite 2280
Chicago, IL 60604
312/435-7217

Chicago Mercantile Exchange
Attention: Educational Department
10 South Wacker, North Tower
Chicago, IL 60606
312/930-3330

Coffee, Sugar & Cocoa Exchange
Attention: Education Department
4 World Trade Center, 8th Floor
New York, NY 10048
212/938-2800

Kansas City Board of Trade
    Attention: Vice President of Public Affairs
    4800 Main Street, Suite 303
    Kansas City, MO 64112
    816/221-1312
MidAmerican Commodity Exchange
    Attention: Education and Marketing Division
    141 West Jackson, Suite 2210
    Chicago, IL 60604
    312/ 435-7217

Minneapolis Grain Exchange
    Attention: Marketing Department
    400 South 4th Street
    Grain Exchange Building, Room 130
    Minneapolis MN 55415
    612/ 338-6212

New York Cotton Exchange
    Attention: Education Department
    4 World Trade Center, 8th Floor
    New York, NY 10048
    212/938-2650

New York Futures Exchange
    Attention: Publication Department
    20 Broad Street, 10th Floor
    New York, NY 10005
    212/656-6247

New York Mercantile Exchange
    Attention: Research Department
    4 World Trade Center
    New York, NY 10048
    212/938-8041

Winnipeg Commodity Exchange
    Attntion: Library
    500 360 Main Street
    Winnepeg, Canada R3C 2 ZED
    204/949-0495

Computer Software

See chapter 23, "What to Look for in Computer Hardware and Investment Software" for detailed descriptions of functions and capabilities.

Computrac
    P.O. Box 15951
    New Orleans, LA 70175-5951
    504/895-1474

CSI-Stop, CSI-Trend, PDI and Quickstudy
    CSI & Financial Micro-Data, Inc.
    200 West Palmetto Park Road
    Boca Raton, FL 33432-3788
    305/392-8663

Futures Optionmaster
    Com-Tech Software
    141 West Jackson Boulevard, Suite 1531-A
    Chicago, IL 60604
    312/341-7557

Market Research Language
    Futures Software Associates, Inc.
    P.O. Box 263
    Lima, PA 19037
    215/872-4512

Microfutures
    P.O. Box 2765
    Livonia, MI 48154
    313/422-0914

ProfitTaker
    Investment Growth Corporation
    50 Meadow Lane
    Zephyrhills, FL 34249
    813/973-0496

Stock Option Analysis Program (S.O.A.P.)
    H & H Scientific
    13507 Pendelton Street
    Fort Washington, MD
    301/292-2958

The Technical Investor
    Savant Corporation
    P.O. Box 440278
    Houston, TX 77244-0278
    713/556-8363

Trader
    Investment Growth Corporation
    50 Meadow Lane
    Zephyrhills, FL 34249
    813/973-0496